Creative Advertising
Theory and Practice
Second Edition

Sandra E. Moriarty
University of Colorado

Prentice Hall, Englewood Cliffs, New Jersey 07632

Library of Congress Cataloging-in-Publication Data

Moriarty, Sandra E. (Sandra Ernst)
    Creative advertising : theory and practice / Sandra E. Moriarty. -
- 2nd ed.
        p.   cm.
    Includes bibliographical references.
    ISBN 0-13-189911-2
    1. Advertising   I. Title.
HF5821.M62   1991
659. 1—dc20   89-71107
                                                        CIP

Project Supervision and Interior Design: The Total Book
Cover Design: Marianne Frasco
Photography: George Mattei
Manufacturing buyers: Trudy Pisciotti / Bob Anderson

 ©1991, 1986 by Prentice-Hall, Inc.
A Simon & Schuster Company
Englewood Cliffs, New Jersey 07632

Printed in the United States of America
10 9 8 7 6 5 4 3 2

ISBN 0-13-189911-2

Prentice-Hall International (UK) Limited, *London*
Prentice-Hall of Australia Pty. Limited, *Sydney*
Prentice-Hall Canada Inc., *Toronto*
Prentice-Hall Hispanoamericana, S.A., *Mexico*
Prentice-Hall of India Private Limited, *New Delhi*
Prentice-Hall of Japan, Inc., *Tokyo*
Simon & Schuster Asia Pte. Ltd., *Singapore*
Editora Prentice-Hall do Brasil, Ltda., *Rio de Janeiro*

CONTENTS

Part II: Media Specifics

Part III: Situations and Decisions

PREFACE

This book is intended to be an introduction to the creative side of advertising—both foundation theories and practical applications. In advertising it is not enough to know *how*; you also need to know *why*. Most advertising books that discuss the creative side focus on practice. They teach you how to do it, but not necessarily why you do it—or why not. This book would like to challenge you to think about the whys and why nots, as well as the how tos.

Advertising is an evolving field. It continually confronts new situations and changing conditions. In order to be able to cope with a field of change, you need an understanding of basic principles, as well as basic practices.

One source for insights into the whys, as well as the hows, is the professional advertising community. This book uses stories, anecdotes, quotes, and other types of explanations compiled from the experiences of working professionals. Another source of insight is theory and research from academia. Research is developed as the field develops, but it is difficult to find and compile because it is buried in such diverse areas as psychology, sociology, aesthetics, education, public opinion, and consumer behavior. One of the goals of this book is to introduce research and theories that are relevant to the creative side and glean information from these studies and articles that might explain the hows and whys of advertising.

One problem with a book like this is the breadth of the creative side of advertising. It includes the two professional areas of copywriting and art direction. Those areas are distinct enough that many textbook writers align with one or the other, depending upon their own personal backgrounds. This book will attempt to cover both writing and design, in addition to the analytical area of creative strategy.

An important topic for a book of this type is creative thinking, and that topic is also covered here and referred to throughout the book. One thing you learn from reading the literature on creativity is that creative thinking is a process—and so, too, is the development of advertising ideas. The first half of the book has been restructured in this edition to focus more clearly on the advertising process.

Another change from the first edition is the emphasis on professionalism and how to think like a professional. The book starts off with a discussion of the difference between student thinking in advertising and professional thinking. You will also be introduced to many of the giants and stars in advertising, the thinkers and practitioners who have made a difference in how advertising has developed. Hopefully this will help you learn to think like a professional and make the transition from being a student to being an expert.

Another focus of this edition is on changing technology and the opportunities it allows for innovative uses of production and media.

It may seem impossible to cover all these topics in one book. However, many of our courses do, in fact, approach the creative side of advertising as a comprehensive topic. Furthermore, there are professionals in advertising who have to figure out objectives, come up with ideas, write copy, design their own layouts, and critique the work of others—they are responsible for it all. What is needed for instruction on the creative side of advertising, then, is a comprehensive book that covers all the relevant topics—copywriting, design, creative thinking, strategy, research, production, and management—as well as all media from print to broadcast and specialized areas such as brochures and Yellow Pages.

The creative side is exciting because it offers so much variety. You never know what you will be working on next. This book tries to maintain that same spirit. It is dedicated to all those people, students and professionals, as well as their teachers, who are well rounded, well read, and excited about the creative side—the whys as well as the hows.

ACKNOWLEDGMENTS

This book has been evolving for many years and during that time a number of students have commented on the material and brought ads to my attention. I would particularly like to thank all the students who have shared their enthusiasm with me in the beginning, advanced, and graduate level creative courses at various universities.

Equally valuable is the advice from professors and colleagues who have taught the creative side and have made suggestions which have been incorporated in this revision. Kathy Frith and Tom Duncan made particularly important contributions.

Thanks also to the various advertising professionals who have shared their thoughts on how the advertising process works and how best to communicate the basics of the creative side to the soon-to-be new professionals. Their work is an inspiration.

I would also like to acknowledge the host of editors, publishers, account executives, advertising managers, and other executives who supplied facts, made available quotes and illustrations, and helped obtain permissions for the many ads that are used to illustrate the theories and practices described in these chapters. Thanks also to Audrey Boltz who handled permissions and Cherita Campbell who helped with research.

Finally I would like to gratefully acknowledge the support, encouragement, and patience of the Prentice Hall team who made this book possible, including marketing editors Whitney Blake and Chris Treiber, editorial assistant Rachel Nelson, and Annette Bodzin of The Total Book.

Creative Advertising
Theory and Practice

THE ADVERTISING PROCESS

1

Fifty-Seven Words and Thirty Seconds

KEY POINTS

- An advertisement is a conversation with a consumer that gets attention, provides information, makes a point, and encourages someone to buy, try, or do something.
- Analyzing the advertising message means looking at both elements and structure.
- The receiver of the message—viewer, reader or listener—may not believe, understand, or care about the message.
- Strategy is the logic behind the "encoding," or the design of the advertising message.
- The first step in learning to do advertising is to learn to think like a professional.
- You don't have to reinvent the wheel; you can build your experience and judgment by learning from professionals.

When Bill Demby was in Vietnam, he dreamed of coming home and playing a little basketball. The dream died when he lost both legs to a Vietcong rocket. Then researchers discovered that a Du Pont plastic could make lifelike artificial limbs. Now Bill is back on the basketball court and starring in a Du Pont commercial. The commercial by the BBDO agency showed Demby playing a game of pickup basketball—his artificial legs visible to the camera—and competing with able-bodied men (see Exhibit 1-1).

Part of the magic of the commercial came near the end when director

Exhibit 1-1: Bill Demby, a double amputee, demonstrated in a commercial for Du Pont that disabilities don't have to be a handicap. (Du Pont Company photo)

Rick Levine wanted something special, something touching. He asked Demby if he would mind if one of the players knocked him down. The players were tired; they had been playing all day. It was quite a question—just imagine asking that of a person with artificial legs.

That sequence—especially the expression in Demby's eyes looking up at the other player after he hits the ground hard—is a moving piece of human drama. And as he gets to his feet, it becomes, in the words of writer Bob Greene,[1] "one of those magical television instants—a second or two of film that gives the audience goose bumps and stays with them for a long time."

After the commercial aired Demby went from being completely anonymous to famous. He spoke to colleges and appeared on ABC's *20/20* program. He was interviewed by newspapers and magazines. Suddenly people saw him as a symbol of bravery and hope. For the first time in his life people were treating him as if he were special.

"I walked into a McDonald's the other day to get something to eat," Demby said. "This guy said hello . . . I thought he was just friendly. But then he said, 'I liked the commercial.'" He is finally accepting the idea that strangers will approach him and tell him how much they admire him. He tries to keep it in perspective. It's amazing, Demby says, "that thirty seconds could completely change a man's life."

While advertising rarely affects other people's lives as it did Bill Demby's, it can still provide a moving experience. It can touch emotions and feelings; it can arouse curiosity; it can tell people something they didn't know; it can remind people of good times and good friends; and it can pull people out of their chairs and into a store. Advertising is communication. If it is successful, it tells stories with drama, humor, and emotion while it presents reasons why people should buy, believe, or do something.

1.1 ADVERTISING AS COMMUNICATION

A Conversation with a Consumer

An advertisement is a conversation with a consumer about a product. It gets attention, it provides information, it tries to make a point, and it encourages you to buy, try, or do something. It tries to create some kind of response or reaction. It speaks to the heart as well as the head.

An advertisement is plain talk, but like other forms of vernacular art, it can also be literature or maybe even poetry. Generally, though, it speaks the same language that we use in order to persuade someone we know about something—using street talk, savvy, and sales expertise.

The legendary David Ogilvy, founder of the advertising agency that bears his name, explained his view of an advertisement: "I always pretend that I'm sitting beside a woman at a dinner party, and she asks me for advice about which product she should buy. So then I write down what I would say to her. I give her the facts, facts, facts. I try to make it interesting, fascinating, if possible, and personal—I don't write to the crowd. I try to write from one human being to another. . . . And I try not to bore the poor woman to death, and I try to make it as real and personal as possible."[2]

Mass Communication

mass communication: public communication, such as radio, newspapers, magazines, and television, that reaches very large audiences

Advertising is also a form of **mass communication**, and that is much more complex—and indirect—than a simple conversation. The process of mass communication has been depicted in a communication model that outlines the important players (see Figure 1-1).[3] It begins with a *source* who *encodes* a *message* that is presented through *channels* of communication, in spite of *noise*, and that is *decoded* by a *receiver* and responded to with *feedback*.

This description of the mass communication process uses a mouthful of communication theory jargon. To make more sense, let's translate the

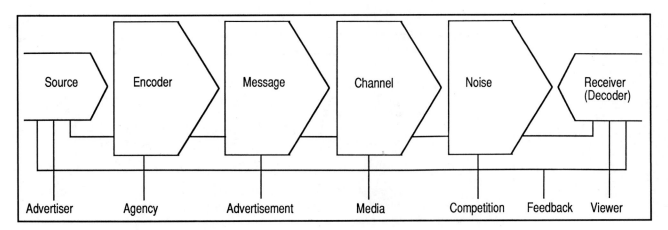

Figure 1-1: Advertising and the communication model.

terms and apply them to advertising. A manufacturer (source) hires an advertising agency to develop (encoding) an advertisement (message) that will be presented through various media (channels). This message must be powerful enough to overcome the clutter of competing messages (noise) so it will be understood (decoded) by the viewer, listener, or reader (receiver). To know if you are successful you have to get back information (feedback), however difficult it may be to obtain, about how that person reacts to your message.

Process. Advertising is a *process*, and in this book we'll discuss the basic steps followed in putting together an advertisement, which is the *product* of this process.

Message. Primarily this book will focus on the message—both *elements* and *structure*—and the way it is encoded, or designed, by professionals in advertising. We'll discuss the advertising message in terms of two things: its elements and its structure. The elements of advertising are the pieces—the words, the pictures, the music, the characters, the setting, the action; the structure is the way they are combined to create an effect or a coherent message.

"Encoding," or designing the message, is not easy. You have to use the right "code" to communicate; you don't speak Dutch to the British or the words of a professor to your buddy on the basketball court. In developing ads, advertising professionals have to use not only the right language, but also the right nuance, the right tone of voice, the right appeal, the right gesture—and all that is expressed in phrases and pictures that work together to create the intended effect. The emphasis on the word *right* means that there are wrong, or at least ineffective, ways to use these elements. Knowing which, and how, and when to use these elements is the role of the professional in advertising, and that is what we mean by *message design.*

Jerry Della Femina, cofounder of Della Femina, Travisano & Partners, criticized advertising for not talking to the consumer in the right voice. He observed, "We still haven't really learned to communicate with the consumer to the point where he can understand us all the time. I know this is going to sound crazy, but I sometimes don't understand why we can't talk in commercials and ads the way we *really* talk."[4]

Clutter. The media environment is loud, busy, and cluttered with competing messages all shouting for attention. The typical American is exposed to approximately 3,000 commercial messages a day—including billboards, newspapers, magazines, radio, and television. On television the number is increasing dramatically with the sudden rise in popularity of the 15-second commercial, which puts two spots in a 30-second time period instead of one. The clutter enormously complicates the already difficult communication process.

Viewer. One of the biggest problem areas in advertising communication lies with the independent, self-directed consumers at whom the message is aimed.* The problem is that advertisers have no control over

---

* For simplicity's sake, throughout the book we'll call these people "viewers" even though we know they may also be described as readers or listeners, depending upon the medium. The term *viewer,* in this book, will refer to the advertisement's audience. We'll also use the term *consumers* to refer to people who are buyers of products and services.

consumers' attention. That's good if you believe in strong-minded and independent consumers, but it certainly makes the advertising task more difficult.

American Express found itself in a communication tangle when it tried to develop a campaign for young business people. For years it has had success with its "Do you know me?" commercials aimed at its traditional market of successful, older businessmen. Then AmEx decided to pursue the large number of younger women entering the work force and launched the first of its "Interesting Lives" series. The commercial showed a young woman taking her husband out to dinner to celebrate the arrival of her card. The commercial scored big—applications from women were up—it won awards and praise for showing a strong, successful woman. Furthermore, it appealed to men as well.

AmEx decided to extend the "Interesting Lives" series to attract young male executives. Over the next three years its ad agency, Ogilvy & Mather, wrote and shot six new ads, but they were pulled one by one as audience reaction arrived. Two never made it past preliminary testing. One showed a woman paying for dinner on a first date, the other a husband accompanying his wife on her business trip. Audience reactions included such words as "abrasive" and "castrating."[5] How could O&M have produced one commercial that was such a winner and then a group of successors with the same message that said all the wrong things?

The problem with the viewer (listener, reader) audience is that you seldom know what is going on in their minds—you don't know if they are attending to your message, if they understand it, or if they care about it. They may hear different meanings in your words and see different things in your pictures. They may misinterpret everything you say. They may not believe you. And, as Ogilvy points out, they may be bored to death.

Response. What makes advertising different from other forms of mass media is that the writer is tremendously concerned with viewer response—reactions such as awareness, understanding, a change of attitude, feelings, or an interest in trying a new product. Since advertising plays to a disinterested audience, or a marginally interested audience at best, in most cases the response is simply disinterest.

The thing to remember, however, is that all advertising has to face the test of a real preson reacting and responding to it. The J. Walter Thompson ads (see Exhibit 1-2) are from the "J. Walter Response" series. They illustrate how important response is to a major agency.

Strategy

As in war games, military metaphors are very important in advertising. Advertisers talk about targets and objectives, about campaigns, and about assaulting positions. While, as some critics point out, this warlike mentality may get in the way of seeing consumers as people,[6] it does provide a *method* for approaching the development of an advertisement. The method is to figure out the decision points and all the options, develop several alternative approaches, and then choose the best one.

Strategy is the thinking, the *logic* behind the encoding of the message. A strategic message is one that works, and by that we mean that *it says the right things to the right people.* Advertising strategy involves making three critical decisions based on an understanding of the total

strategy: the logic behind the advertisement, a plan that distinguishes the best approach from a number of alternatives

J. WALTER CLICKS

Watch out, world
I'm goin' click, click, click
I'm gonna get you
With the Kodak disc

So it begins—a foot-stomping, hard-selling TV and radio campaign created by J. Walter Thompson USA for the Kodak disc camera.

Not many commercials get fan mail. These commercials do. Letters. Phone calls, too. Best of all, this advertising

arrived just in time for the Christmas selling season. So our client Kodak had a very merry one.

It's the kind of response we've been winning for our clients year after year.

We call it J. Walter Response. Write to Burt Manning, J. Walter Thompson USA, 466 Lexington Avenue, New York, New York 10017. You'll find out more about it.

J. WALTER THOMPSON USA · Atlanta · Chicago · Detroit
Los Angeles · New York · San Francisco · Washington

J. WALTER BLUE EYES

"Could you look into those big blue eyes and skimp on her?" the commercial asked.

Most Americans replied "Not anymore." Not after they discovered there are five ounces of milk in a slice of *Kraft* Singles pasteurized process cheese food.

For consumers it was compelling news. News that made them think twice about substituting a less expensive brand with little or no milk.

For Kraft, it was good news, too. Because a 15% jump in advertising

awareness translated into dramatic increases in sales and market share. All in the face of intensified price competition.

It was those big blue eyes that opened America's eyes. That's what we call J. Walter Response. The way we see it, any advertising that doesn't get response like this isn't worth a second glance.

If you want your advertising to open more eyes, write to Burt Manning at J. Walter Thompson USA, 466 Lexington Avenue, New York, New York 10017.

J. WALTER THOMPSON USA · Atlanta · Chicago · Detroit
Los Angeles · New York · San Francisco · Washington

J. WALTER SUNSHINE

This little boy eats mustard sandwiches. Sings "You Are My Sunshine." And sells more mustard than anybody around.

He's one of the kids in the Sunshine Mustard commercials created by J. Walter Thompson USA for French's.

No cast of thousands. No budget-busting cost in either media or production.

Nothing big, except response.

An independent research company, Video Storyboard Tests, surveyed 22,000

consumers to find America's best remembered, best liked TV campaigns.

Right up in the select circle of winners was the Sunshine Mustard campaign.

It also helped win an impressive gain in French's market share.

That's response for you.

J. Walter Response.

Call Burt Manning at (212) 210-7250. He'll tell you more about it.

J. WALTER THOMPSON USA · Atlanta · Chicago · Detroit
Los Angeles · New York · San Francisco · Washington

J. WALTER SLICE

It's blowing the competition out of the water.

After just one year, Lemon-Lime Slice® has captured a 3% share of the category in its markets, putting it ahead of Sprite.® And with the introduction of new flavors, Pepsi-Cola® expects the Slice family to become its second-largest brand.

What does it take to make that kind of splash?

A brilliant marketing concept—a soft drink

with 10% juice. And the kind of advertising that drives it home. Breakthrough product imagery. A preemptive theme —"We Got the Juice®." And a song that never stops selling.

That's the way to bottle success.

Maybe we can do the same for you.

Write to Burt Manning, J. Walter Thompson, 466 Lexington Avenue, New York, N.Y. 10017.

J. WALTER THOMPSON USA · Atlanta · Chicago · Detroit
Los Angeles · New York · San Francisco · Washington

8

Exhibit 1-2: Response is important to advertising, and this series of "house" ads for J. Walter Thompson describe the agency's emphasis on that aspect of advertising.

communication situation: (1) who to talk to, (2) what to say to them, and (3) how to reach them. Reaching them is the role of the media planners and buyers, but the first two critical decisions provide the foundation for all the work done on the creative side. We'll discuss this in much more detail in Chapter 4.

STRATEGY AND COMMUNICATION

1. Who to talk to   (targeting)
2. What to say to them   (message planning)
3. How to reach them   (media planning)

Breakdowns   Keep in mind that advertising is a complex web involving other people and many steps. Like all forms of communication, it can fail. It can fail at any point in the process—because you use the wrong language (encoding), your competitor speaks louder (noise), the television isn't tuned to the right station (channel), the audience isn't listening (receiver), or the audience doesn't understand the point (decoding). Breakdowns are all too common in communication, and they plague advertising messages just as they do speeches, news reporting, and personal conversations. Just because you write a wonderful ad doesn't mean someone will see it, read it, understand it, or care about what you have to say. It's a tough game.

1.2 THE PROFESSIONAL APPROACH

We talked earlier about an advertisement as a message designed by *professionals*. Professionalism is important because it takes experience to develop the judgment needed to know *what to say* and *who to say it to*.

But here you are, a student in a creative advertising course. You know you are not a professional yet and you're probably wondering what you've gotten yourself into. You may not know if you are a good writer or artist, and you're not sure you are "creative," whatever that means. Consider this book your survival kit. Its role is to talk you through the things professionals know by instinct and have learned from experience. It will give you the background you need in order to produce great ads for class and get you started on your **"book,"** a portfolio used by professionals to display the work they've done.

*"**book**":* a portfolio of work that demonstrates your capabilities

Think Professional   To do well in a professional course you must learn to think and act like a professional. That means when you get a copy assignment or a layout assignment, you approach it the same way a professional does, using the same techniques and processes, and the same ways of thinking.

You become a professional by thinking of yourself as professional. Remember what it was like to learn a new sport—something like baseball, basketball, skiing, or ice skating? Do you remember taking the snap or driving for the net and imagining yourself to be Joe Montana or Chris Evert? That's what professionals do. In their minds they see themselves doing the best they are capable of. They don't step up to the net and think, "I'm Martha Mediocre and I never do anything above average." You can think yourself into doing breakthrough work; you can also lock yourself into being average. This is called "visualization," a technique used by high achievers in every field to inspire themselves to do great work. You can use the same technique to learn to be a professional in advertising.

Find a professional you admire and make this person your mentor, your role model. Then try to think like he or she does and approach your class assignments as that person would his or her work assignments. Imagine yourself being someone great in advertising like David Ogilvy, Bill Bernbach, Mary Wells Lawrence, or Hal Riney. You will be introduced to many professionals in this book, and you can learn about others by reading trade magazines such as *Advertising Age* and *Adweek*.

Outgrow student role.   First you have to leave behind the role of student. Students think that the professor is the rule maker, the initiator of the assignment, and the evaluator of the work. Most students spend more time trying to figure out what the professor wants than what the assignment requires. These students also assume that if they didn't get an A on an assignment, it's because the professor didn't tell them enough about how to do the assignment. "I got a C. It's the professor's fault because she didn't tell me what she wanted to see."

Self-initiate and self-evaluate.   The difference between a professional and a student is that a professional *assumes the role* of assignment giver and evaluator. A professional sees something that needs to be done and does it, just because professional judgment tells him or her that it needs to be done. Furthermore, professionals evaluate their own work and decide for themselves if it's good. A professional doesn't think about B's and C's, because everything in a professional's world is pass/fail. It's either great or it gets done over.

Leo Burnett, founder of the agency that bears his name, wrote once about the need for professional judgment, "The creative person's wee small voice . . . your best source of inspiration for ideas, your best copy research, your best test market. . . . The saddest sight of all is the good creative person who loses confidence in his own judgment and intuition—who tunes out that little voice and listens only to the voices of other people."[7]

Study the standards.   The professional remains forever a *student of the field* and has a good sense when a piece of work is great or average or poor. While that kind of judgment comes from experience, you can start developing it now by becoming a *student of your own profession* rather than a student in a class. In the last chapter in this book, we'll also give you some suggestions on how you can evaluate your own work and the work of others.

Focus efforts.   Most students just want to get an assignment done. It's only one more little hassle in a busy college day. Professionals, however, live for their assignments. The assignments keep them going, drive them on, inspire them, and provide the charge that keeps the creative machine finely tuned and productive.

Professionals on the creative side of advertising "get into" an assignment totally. No matter how many accounts or clients they serve, they are able to focus their efforts very efficiently. You do it occasionally, like when you concentrate totally on a test, oblivious to everything else going on around you. That's the kind of focus that professionals bring to an assignment.

Polish and revise. An advertisement goes through many levels of review—from critiques by colleagues down the hall to comments by bosses and clients. Every critique, including continuous self-critiquing, involves a revision. So one thing professionals learn—and you must learn too if you intend to think like a professional—is that your work will be critiqued and other people will make suggestions. Sometimes people won't like your work.

You will be revising and polishing your work continuously and even tossing it out and starting over again from scratch. That's the way advertising operates. Nobody enjoys being critiqued, but professionals work at getting over being thin-skinned. They appreciate how their work improves as they polish and rewrite it. You'll not be a professional until you can take criticism and revise and polish your work. Bert Manning, chair and CEO of J. Walter Thompson, once wrote poetically about not giving up too early. He said, "The essence of great creative work is only extracted by the last agonizing twist of the rose petal."[8]

THINK LIKE A PRO

- Find a role model and visualize yourself as that person.
- Take charge and initiate your own assignments.
- Be your own toughest critic.
- Develop a set of professional standards.
- Focus your efforts and lose yourself in your assignment.
- Care deeply and develop a professional sense of pride.
- Appreciate criticism and don't be thin-skinned.
- Polish and revise until your assignment is perfect.

Bridging Experience

Professionals know a lot about how advertising works. Some of them have studied it in school, but many of them learned advertising on the job. The gut feelings, the ability to read a problem and predict the best way to solve it, come only from confronting these situations over and over again. This book is meant to provide you with a foundation of knowledge, theories, and explanations that will serve you until your experience level develops to that of an experienced professional. It's a bridge, not a bible.

Learning from Professionals

So where should we start? Let's begin with a procession of professionals, the giants who have built and continue to shape the field of advertising. Their collective experience is available to you in their work and their writings. You can move a long way toward professionalism by learning from these masters. Many of them developed a unique approach to advertising and built their agency's reputation on this distinctive philosophy.

Lasker and Kennedy: from news to salesmanship.   Albert Lasker started with the legendary Lord and Thomas agency (now Foote, Cone, & Belding) in Chicago in 1898. By 1905 he was a partner in the firm. Lasker constantly tried to develop theories to explain what works in the field of advertising and what doesn't. Lasker concluded that advertising is basically *news*, news about products and services; he handled most of his advertising as news announcements. In 1905 John E. Kennedy, a young copywriter, sent him a note that said, "I can tell you what advertising is." He said, "Advertising is *salesmanship in print*." Lasker and Kennedy wedded this concept of salesmanship to news to create the philosophy that an effective advertisement should give reasons *why* for buying a product.

Calkens and graphics.   The turn of the century was the golden age of the poster, and one of the advertising professionals who realized the power of graphics was Earnest Elmo Calkens of the Bates agency. During the twentieth century advertising moved from being mostly type, to using an occasional illustration, and finally to being predominantly visual. Calkens realized that poster-design graphics adapt beautifully to the medium of magazines. Calkens's ads not only attracted the viewer's attention but also increased the status and image of the advertiser. His work represented the first venture into image advertising.

Hopkins and research.   Claude Hopkins worked for Lord and Thomas and is generally conceded to be one of the greatest copywriters. Not long before he died in 1932, his salary was the unheard of amount of $185,000. A student of mail-order advertising, Hopkins studied its results to determine a set of basic copy principles. He realized that advertising should be directed to an individual, and not to a group or crowd. His book, *Scientific Advertising*, was published in 1923 and is one of the first systematic analyses of copytesting research.

Caples and headlines.   John Caples, of BBDO, spent 20 years studying all sorts of advertisements and copytesting results, but he was particularly interested in the pulling power of headlines. He summarized his findings in a book, *Tested Advertising Methods*, published in 1932. Caples believed that a headline should promise something. One of Caples's classic headlines is the famous: "They Laughed When I Sat Down at the Piano . . . But When I Started to Play!" This technique was demonstrated in the title of another Caples book, *How to Make Your Advertising Make Money*. Caples believed in hard-hitting, hard-sell advertising. His philosophy was, "What you say is more important than how you say it."

Bedell and selling stratagems.   Clyde Bedell worked in mail-order and retail advertising, where you can see an immediate response to your advertising. He summarized his experiences in the first textbook for the creative side of advertising: *How to Write Advertising That Sells*. It was published in 1940 and included Bedell's famous set of "31 Proved Selling Stratagems." He was particularly interested in identifying a product's "selling points." He also pointed out the important relationship between product attributes and consumer benefits.

Rubicam and originality.   Ray Rubicam, cofounder of Young and Rubicam, called for originality and fresh ideas. "Our job is to resist the usual," was the principle he laid down for his staff, explaining that "The value of an advertising idea is in inverse ratio to the number of times it has been used." Rubicam believed that original ideas make the advertisement more interesting, more convincing, and more effective. One of the greatest advertising slogans of all times was written in 1920 by Rubicam for Steinway: "The instrument of the immortals." A more recent example of Y&R's work includes "Be all that you can be" for the Army.

George Gribbon, who worked for Rubicam, once said, "You were apt to redo an ad after discussing it with Rubicam anywhere from 3, 4, up to 15 or 20 times before he would say it was good enough. . . . You don't get away at Y&R with writing a headline. You sit down and you write 10, 15, 40 headlines."[9]

Cone and personal interest. Fairfax Cone, founder of the Foote, Cone & Belding agency, said that good advertising must immediately make clear what the basic selling premise is and this proposition must be important and presented in personal terms. Under his direction FC&B created such classic ad campaign themes and slogans as, "You'll wonder where the yellow went" for Pepsodent and, "When you care enough to send the very best" for Hallmark.

Reeves and the USP. Rosser Reeves, chair of the Ted Bates agency, created advertising that established a "unique selling proposition," a proposition that is both (1) important to the consumer and that (2) sets the product apart from the competition. Considered the father of the "hard sell," Reeves's contribution to the field, explained in his book, *The Reality of Advertising*, emphasized the logic behind the sales message. Examples of USP-based advertising include: "Cleans your breath while it cleans your teeth" for Colgate, "Melts in your mouth, not in your hand" for M&Ms, and "Strengthens bodies in 12 ways" for Wonder Bread.

Bernbach and artistry. To Bill Bernbach, founder of Doyle, Dane, Bernbach, advertising effectiveness is found in its artistry. Keith Reinhard, chair and CEO of DDB Needham Worldwide, calls Bernbach "the Picasso of advertising."[10] Bernbach never stated an agency philosophy but focused his efforts, and those of his staff, on great ideas beautifully executed. Effective advertising, he believed, is original, dramatic, and startles people into awareness by touching their emotions and feelings. The closest he came to a statement of philosophy is the comment, "Finding out *what* to say is the beginning of the communication process. *How* you say it makes people look and listen and believe."

Examples of his unique approach to advertising include, "Lemon" and "Think small" for Volkswagen, "You don't have to be Jewish to love Levy's" for Levy's Jewish Rye bread, and the Avis "We try harder" campaign.

Bernbach's influence spread through advertising. Jerry Della Femina credits Bernbach as being an inspiration. Della Femina has said, "In the beginning there was Volkswagen. . . . That was the day when the new advertising agency was really born, and it all started with Doyle, Dane, Bernbach. The Lemon ad. . . . It was the first time anyone really took a realistic approach to advertising."[11]

BBDO and consumer problems. Tom Dillon, president of BBDO, wrote that advertising's purpose is "to affect a human decision." BBDO's consumer-focused approach fit perfectly into the new philosophy of the consumer-oriented "marketing concept." More specifically, Dillon and BBDO believe that advertising is effective when it answers a human problem. The BBDO approach to advertising was built on the concept of "problem detection" to find out what really bothers people about a product.

Burnett and inherent drama. The "Chicago School" of advertising is characterized by the work of the Leo Burnett agency, with its emphasis on fundamental Midwestern values and respect for the consumer. Burnett used the phrase "inherent drama" to describe how a strong brand image can be created for a cigarette from the mythology of the American cowboy. He also found drama and a brand image for a fast food restaurant in a fussy old man in a white suit with white hair and a goatee. Inherent drama created magic like the Jolly Green Giant, a genial giant that parents could use to get their kids to eat vegetables.

Leo Burnett described the work of his agency, and at the same time summarized the "Chicago School" of advertising: "We try to be more straightforward without being flatfooted. We try to be warm without being mawkish."

Ogilvy and brand images. The sophisticated and urbane David Ogilvy, founder of Ogilvy & Mather, is a proponent of a type of advertising that seeks to develop "story appeal," which he considered a primary ingredient in a lasting brand image. Ogilvy believed that a creative concept that is interesting, perhaps even provocative, will build attention and memorability. Ogilvy's classic example is the man in the eyepatch used as a continuing figure for Hathaway shirts. There is a touch of mystery, an untold story, about this figure that has made Hathaway advertisements highly effective over many years.

But Ogilvy was also a strong believer in research and he developed lessons and rules about what works and doesn't work in advertising. These are formulated in his books, *Confessions of an Advertising Man*, *How to Advertise*, and, most recently, *Ogilvy on Advertising*. Although Ogilvy had an immense sense of style, he was very much focused on the selling message. He depended on research to tell him what works and what doesn't. He summarized his philosophy (which contrasts with that of Bernbach) as, "What you say is more important than how you say it." Gerry Scorse, a former N. W. Ayer creative director, wrote an article comparing the two philosophies.[12]

Ayer and human contact. The N. W. Ayer agency uses the phrase "human contact" to describe its advertising philosophy, which uses emotion to touch the common chords in humanity. But Ayer's brand of human contact involves more than just emotion. It also mixes emotion with warmth and soft humor to reach out and touch its audiences. Ayer's philosophy is based on some fundamental values: People respond to friendliness and to facts that help them solve a problem. People smile at gentle humor and warm up to the person (or company) that knows how and when to use it. People like pictures and tunes that are pretty. Given a choice between the silly and the sincere, people will choose the sincere.

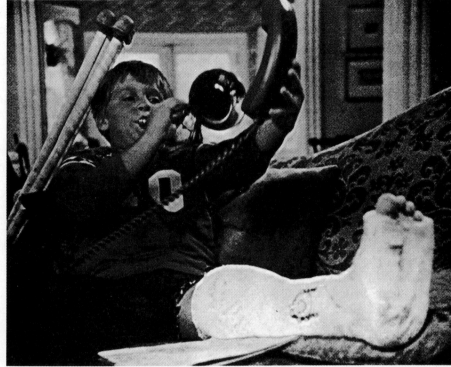

Reach out and touch someone.

In New York, a writer from Iowa thought about home.

"When I made the call," he said, "I got this terrific feeling. And the same from the other end."

That's the beauty of a phone call from far away. Wherever you are, you're never too far to reach out and touch someone you love.

It's also the beauty of the new Long Distance advertising for AT&T.

According to research, it's reaching out. And one of the most important, pleasurable and successful advertising assignments we've ever worked on is working better.

Sooner or later, you've got to make human contact.

A phone call can make it.

So can advertising.

Not only for the new clients just coming to us, but for a client who's been around here for a long time. Like seventy years.

Ayer makes human contact

NW Ayer ABH International. U.S. Offices: New York, Chicago, Los Angeles, San Francisco. Overseas offices throughout the Americas, Europe, Asia.

Exhibit 1-3: The N. W. Ayer agency has developed a "human contact" philosophy to reach out and touch people.

Given a choice between beauty and ugliness, people will choose beauty. These are the fundamental values that guide Ayer and they are best expressed in the classic "Reach out and touch someone" campaign for AT&T (see Exhibit 1-3).

Gossage and the unconventional. Howard Gossage was a San Francisco adman who hated advertising, or so an article in *Ramparts* described him.[13] Unorthodox and original, Gossage constantly challenged the industry with his sophisticated humor and iconoclastic views. He once wrote, "I love the advertising business. I truly do, although it's no business for a grown man. I love it because it's such a lovely Augean stable to clean up."

He questioned the economics of advertising. In one of his more enduring phrases, he described advertising as a "multi-billion dollar sledgehammer driving a 49 cent thumbtack."

A member of the Copywriter's Hall of Fame, Gossage did brilliant work, admittedly unorthodox. One campaign for Rainier Ale sponsored a 79-year-old retired mail carrier who wanted to walk from San Francisco to Seattle to prove that the Post Office was wrong when it retired him. Rainier ran very little advertising due to the extensive press coverage.

Eagle Shirtmakers wanted to develop brand identification. In a *New Yorker* ad, Gossage offered to send free Eagle labels to owners of shirts resembling the one illustrated. Two hundred wrote in for them. Another Eagle ad offered a free sample of shirt material (which Gossage referred to as a "shirt-kerchief," "Shirtkin," or "Napchief") that set an all-time record for responses for a *New Yorker* ad. He did memorable ads for Rover including one extolling the virtues of the car as a getaway (and chase) car. Perhaps his most celebrated promotion was a series of sweatshirts of Bach, Beethoven, and Brahms, printed on behalf of Rainier Ale and advertised on his favorite classical radio station. He called the offer of the sweatshirts, "a brewer's idea of culture."

Iconoclastic to the end, he brought sophisticated humor to the serious, bombastic advertising industry. Gossage has been described, along with Ogilvy and Bernbach, as "responsible for changing the whole concept of American advertising."

A Procession A *procession* is defined as people or things moving forward continuously in a systematic way, and that's what we have presented in this review of the leaders and giants in advertising. You can learn a lot from this procession of innovators, and everything you learn about them can help develop your own professional judgment.

The creative side of advertising has been developing since the late 1800s, and there is now a wealth of literature and published experiences from which to learn. You need to develop your own professional skills, but you don't have to reinvent the wheel. Many people for many years have been studying and analyzing how to do effective advertising. Learn and apply everything you can from their work. You will see references to these advertising leaders throughout this book.

SUMMARY

This chapter covers advertising as a form of communication and professionalism:

1. Advertising is a form of mass communication and involves
   - a source (the advertiser)
   - encoding (the professional in advertising)
   - a message (the advertisement)
   - a channel (the media)
   - noise (clutter, competition, and other communication obstacles)
   - decoding (understanding)
   - the receiver (viewer, reader, listener)
   - feedback (the viewer's response)
2. How to learn to think like a professional
   - visualize yourself doing great work, like your professional role model
   - put aside the passive student role
   - initiate your own assignments
   - be your toughest critic

- be a student of the profession and of its standards
- focus your efforts and concentrate totally
- care deeply and develop a professional pride
- don't be thin-skinned
- polish your work until it's perfect

3. Learn professionalism from the masters
- the foundation of news and the power of sales expertise
- the power of graphics and visual images
- the power of a well-crafted headline or phrase
- the value of research and testing
- the logic of a sales premise
- the aesthetic power of artistry
- the importance of originality
- the use of story appeal to create enduring brand images
- the importance of consumer beliefs and problems
- the use of emotion and the impact of touching human feelings
- the power of the unconventional

NOTES

1. Bob Greene, "Thirty Seconds," *Esquire*, November 1988, pp. 67–69.
2. Denis Higgins, "Conversations with David Ogilvy," in *The Art of Writing Advertising* (Chicago: Advertising Publications, 1965).
3. Wilbur Schramm, *Men, Messages, and Media* (New York: Harper & Row, 1973).
4. Jerry Della Femina, *From Those Wonderful Folks Who Gave You Pearl Harbor* (London: Sir Isaac Pitman and Sons, 1971).
5. Mark N. Vamos, "Behind the Scenes at an American Express Commercial," *Business Week*, May 20, 1985, pp. 84–85.
6. Kim Rotzoll, "Advertising in Its Communications Context," in *Defining the Core of the Discipline*, ed. Charles F. Frazer (Working Paper No. 18. Urbana, Ill.: Department of Advertising, University of Illinois, January 1985).
7. Leo Burnett, "Keep Listening to That Wee, Small Voice," *Readings in Advertising and Promotion Strategy*, eds. Arnold A. Barban and C. H. Sandage (Homewood, Ill.: Irwin, 1968).
8. Carl Hixon, "Leo," *Advertising Age*, February 8, 1982, p. M3.
9. Denis Higgins, "Conversations with George Gribbon," op. cit.
10. Keith L. Reinhard, "Advertising: Yesterday, Today and Tomorrow," speech to American Marketing Association, Montreal, Canada, May 28, 1987.
11. Della Femina, op. cit.
12. Gerry Scorse, "Ogilvy versus Bernbach," *Advertising Age*, October 26, 1987, p. 18.
13. Howard Luck Gossage, *Is There Any Hope for Advertising?*, eds. Kim Rotzoll, Jarlath Graham, and Barrows Mussey (Urbana: University of Illinois Press, 1986); Kim Rotzoll, "Gossage Revisited: Reflections of Advertising's Legendary Iconoclast," *Journal of Advertising*, 9:4 (1980), pp. 6–14; "The Adman Who Plays with Paper Airplanes," *Business Week*, February 11, 1967, pp. 74–80.

2

Getting Started

KEY POINTS

- Advertising is a process, a series of steps generally followed by professionals.
- The key players on the creative side perform a specific set of writing, design, production, and management functions.
- Curiosity, empathy, and intuition are important characteristics of people who work on the creative side.
- "Creatives" need to gather as much information as they can about their assignment by reading, interviewing, listening, watching consumers, using the product, and working in stores.
- The three types of information needed concern the marketplace, company and product, and consumer.

2.1 THE PROCESS OF CREATING AN ADVERTISEMENT

Given the same assignment, chances are that two advertising professionals will produce two entirely different ads. There are commonalities, however, in how they *approach* doing the assignment. Since advertising is a process, there is a fairly standard approach. Not everyone follows exactly the same procedure, but if you survey the collective experience of most professionals on the creative side, you'll find that there is a recognizable set of steps.

A *process* is a particular series of steps or actions directed toward some end, and it is this series of steps that we want to call your attention to as one very important part of the professional way of thinking. We'll present it briefly here for you and it will serve as the outline for the first part of this book.

The Process

1. *The assignment.* Normally you begin with an *assignment;* someone wants an advertisement for something—usually a product or a service. Sometimes the most difficult part of advertising is understanding exactly what the assignment is.

2. *Background research.* Before you begin actually writing the ad, there are three "prewriting" steps to be accomplished. First is *background research,* and by that we mean reading articles and reports, talking to people, and observing consumers. In other words, you must become familiar with the topic, product, or category.

3. *Strategy development.* Advertising is purposive communication—it intends to accomplish something, to have some specified effect on its intended audience. Strategic thinking, then, another step in prewriting, focuses your attention on who you are speaking to and what it is you want to say to them to create the intended persuasive effect.

4. *The creative concept.* The third prewriting step is to start formulating ideas about how to do the advertisement, looking for that strong creative idea, the *creative concept,* that brings the strategy to life in an attention-getting and memorable way.

5. *Doing the ad.* Finally you actually get to the advertisement—writing the copy and designing it. The process of working out the details of the ad's appearance is called the **execution**. The execution outlines what is required to bring the creative concept to life. The words are typed and the execution visuals are present in hand-drawn forms such as roughs, comprehensives, or storyboards.

execution: the form of the complete advertisement; how the ad looks and reads

The execution step was described in a poem by Leo Burnett that describes the loneliness of those who must "get out the ads."[1]

> When the day's last meeting is over
>   and the VPs have left for the train
>
> When account men are at the bar with clients
>   and the space men have switched off the brain
>
> We shall work and, by God, we shall have to
>   get out the pencils and pads
>
> For finally, after the meeting—someone
>   must get out the ads

6. *Production.* The last step in the process is production; what it takes to get the advertisement in print or on the air. This involves such technical activities as typesetting and printing, taping, filming, and distribution of copies to the media.

THE PROCESS OF CREATING AN ADVERTISEMENT

1. Understand the assignment.
2. Begin background research.
3. Develop strategy: what to say.
4. Search for creative concept: how to say it.
5. Figure out the execution details: how it reads and what it looks like.
6. Produce the advertisement.

This *process approach* is the structure behind this book. The first half of the book will focus on this process, which is universal regardless of the type of advertising being created. The second part of the book will look at different types of advertising and the characteristics that make them different.

The Key Players In this introduction to the process of advertising, you also have been introduced to some of the people—and roles—involved in the process. The focus of the book is on the creative side of advertising, on the doing of ads. People who "do ads" are called "creatives." There are two primary roles on the creative side—copywriting and art direction—and they usually work together as a team. The *copywriter* writes the words and phrases used in the ad, and the *art director* (AD) designs the way the ad will look—in both print and commercials. A *producer* is sometimes a member of the creative team for commercials.

In advertising agencies *creative directors* (CDs) manage the creative process; they may come from either a copywriting or an art direction background. In bigger agencies there may also be *copy supervisors* who review the work of a group of writers and help them do the best work they can. The *traffic* department handles all the pieces of the ad as it goes through production to see that everything gets done on schedule.

Account executives (AEs) handle the account management function. They are the liaison between the agency and the client. They handle scheduling, budgets, and the approval process and may sit in on creative team meetings. If they know their client well, AEs should be able to respond as the client would, giving an early reading on the acceptability of the creative approach.

In local media—such as newspapers or broadcast stations—the creative functions may be handled by copywriters and art directors who are specialists, but the creative function may also be handled by the *sales rep* who sells the ad to the local business. The sales rep is the person who presents the creative work to the local business and gets approval for the concept and execution. The production is usually done by the production staff for the newspaper or the radio or television station.

On the client side the advertising process is usually managed by someone called an *advertising director* or *advertising manager* or by the *marketing manager.* In most companies advertising is one of the marketing functions, so the advertising function reports through the marketing department. The ad manager usually works in tandem with the agency's account executive. A company may have its own *in-house agency* and, in those cases, a small agency structure with copywriters, art directors, and a traffic department. The in-house agency reports directly to the ad manager and/or the marketing director.

If you hope to work on the creative side and "do ads," then you have to be either an excellent writer or an excellent designer to get into the business. Writers frequently come from a journalism, communication, or English academic background, although agencies will hire people from any kind of background if they can write. Media will hire people with strong sales skills; these people are also expected to be able to write ads. Art directors usually have a background in graphic design and either a BFA or an MFA degree.

The creative side of advertising is extremely competitive, so you have to be very good to get a job. Prospective creatives put the best samples of their work in their "book" to present in interviews. The work can be real assignments that have been produced for clients or class assignments that are done as an exercise. Frequently creatives will collect advertising they feel is poorly executed and revise the ads for their books.

2.2 BACKGROUND RESEARCH

Ideas just don't come from out of the blue. It's hard work getting ideas, and the work begins with background research. Larry Plapler of Levine, Huntley, Schmidt, Plapler, and Beaver calls the idea process "long term perspiration" rather than "instant inspiration."[2]

You need tons of information to find the elusive fact that ultimately will be the foundation for the advertising strategy or the creative theme. You're looking for something—the little nugget that will turn your strategy or concept to gold. It's a form of "presearch" rather than research.

You're also building a foundation of information and facts. You can't build a brick wall without bricks, and the little bits of information gathered in the backgrounding process are the bricks used to build the content of the ad. Foote, Cone & Belding's Ron Hoff says, "I tell my writers they should never start writing until they have seven times as many facts as they will actually use in an ad."[3]

Shepard Kurnit, chair of DKG Advertising, interviewed a number of his colleagues in advertising on their views of research and reported the comments at an advertising research conference.[4] They have a consistent view. Here are a few of their quotes:

- "Research is absolutely essential to the creative process."
  John O'Toole, president, Foote, Cone & Belding
- "I want to be as knowledgeable as I can. . . . Research can help you break new ground. . . . It can be the springboard to doing something innovative and great."
  Amil Gargano, president and CEO, Ally & Gargano
- "Up-front research is very important because all too often what you think is perfectly clear, is *perfect mud!*"
  Tom Dillon, chair, BBDO

Curiosity People who work on the creative side of advertising are inquisitive. What's the difference between the two brands? Why does it work that way? Why did she choose that style? This curiosity shows up in the fact-finding effort. Creative people are dilettantes; their interests are broad. They float from one topic, one fashion, one fad to another. They sponge up ideas almost unconsciously. Joel Raphaelson, executive creative director at Ogilvy & Mather, says, "The most productive people are always the most curious. They are the ones who have the most ideas, good and bad."

According to research, creative people are better at something the psychologists call "incidental learning," a process by which previously unrelated facts or ideas are associated.[5] The more miscellaneous information you carry around, the more material you have to work with when it comes time to develop new ideas.

Fact-Finding Techniques

Read. Advertising people are known for taking books to bed with them. Late-night reading, as well as reading on the bus or train, reading while waiting in line, reading while eating, reading in the bathtub, and, when there's time, reading at the desk is how creatives get much of their information.

For an assignment you will need to read published research reports, focus-group transcripts, books, trade magazines, general interest articles, scholarly journal articles, traffic studies, annual reports, profit-and-loss statements, interviews, medical reports, technical studies—everything you can get your hands on related in any way to the product or service you have been assigned. Somewhere in all that reading there is the elusive, unrecognized fact that will spark a creative theme or pull the strategy together.

Ask. Interview everyone involved with the product—the designer, the engineer, the home economist, the accountant, the programmer, the systems engineer, the line worker, and, especially, the user. Here again, you're looking for that isolated remark that makes the bells ring.

Bud Robbins of the Kresser & Robbins agency describes his fact-finding for a piano account in a house ad that runs for the agency. He describes how he discovered the Capo d'astro bar and wrote an ad about it that created a six-year wait in orders for the piano company (see Exhibit 2-1).

An interview can take a number of forms. You can go out with a pad and pen, like a reporter, and interview people on the street, in their homes and offices, or in a store. The interview can also be a formal questionnaire designed for gathering large quantities of responses. You can also use open-ended surveys for in-depth probing of motives and reasons. Open-ended surveys don't lend themselves to "number crunching," so with this type of questionnaire you will find yourself talking to a smaller number of people but probing deeper into their reasons and opinions.

Learn to interview, to ask questions, draw people out, follow up on an aside, stimulate an opinion. People like to talk about what interests them; the knack is to get them started. Believe it or not, most people are flattered when you ask them their opinion.

Listen. Learn to listen. William Bernbach said, "The great mistakes are made when we feel we are beyond questioning."[6] Listen to what con-

"Looking for the Capo d'astro bar."

By Bud Robbins

Back in the sixties, I was hired by an ad agency to write copy on the Aeolian Piano Company account. My first assignment was for an ad to be placed in The New York Times for one of their grand pianos. The only background information I received was some previous ads and a few faded close-up shots…and of course, the due date.

The Account Executive was slightly put out by my request for additional information and his response to my suggestion that I sit down with the client was, "Jesus Christ, are you one of *those*? Can't you just create something? We're up against a closing date!"

I acknowledged his perception that I *was* one of those, which got us an immediate audience with the head of our agency.

I volunteered I couldn't even play a piano let alone write about why anyone would spend $5,000 for *this* piano when they could purchase a Baldwin or Steinway for the same amount.

Both allowed the fact they would gladly resign the Aeolian business for either of the others, however, while waiting for that call, suppose we make our deadline.

I persisted and reluctantly, a tour of the Aeolian factory in Upstate New York was arranged. I was assured that "we don't do this with all our clients" and my knowledge as to the value of company time was greatly reinforced.

The tour of the plant lasted two days and although the care and construction appeared meticulous, $5,000 still seemed to be a lot of money.

Just before leaving, I was escorted into the showroom by the National Sales Manager. In an elegant setting sat their piano alongside the comparably priced Steinway and Baldwin.

"They sure do look alike," I commented.

"They sure do. About the only real difference is the shipping weight—ours is heavier."

"Heavier?" I asked. "What makes ours heavier?"

"The Capo d'astro bar."

"What's a Capo d'astro bar?"

"Here, I'll show you. Get down on your knees."

Once under the piano he pointed to a metallic bar fixed across the harp and bearing down on the highest octaves. "It takes 50 years before the harp in the piano warps. That's when the Capo d'astro bar goes to work. It prevents that warping."

I left the National Sales Manager under his piano and dove under the Baldwin to find a Tinkertoy Capo d'astro bar at best. Same with the Steinway.

"You mean the Capo d'astro bar really doesn't go to work for 50 years?" I asked.

"Well, there's got to be some reason why the Met uses it," he casually added.

I froze. "Are you telling me that the Metropolitan Opera House in New York City uses this piano?"

"Sure. And their Capo d'astro bar should be working by now."

Upstate New York looks nothing like the front of the Metropolitan Opera House where I met the legendary Carmen, Risë Stevens. She was now in charge of moving the Metropolitan Opera House to the Lincoln Center.

Ms. Stevens told me, "About the only thing the Met is taking with them is their piano."

That quote was the headline of our first ad.

The result created a six year wait between order and delivery.

My point is this. No matter what the account, I promise you, the Capo d'astro bar is there.

I found it hidden inside Burlington Mills' stay-up sock.

I found it within the rough, tough skin of the Baggies' Alligator.

Equitable's computers stored it and Master Charge built it into their convenience.

It was there in the 1,001 uses of Handi Wipes and saturated amongst the tangles and split ends of Clairol's world.

I found it in people. People like Ernest Gallo who, during my three year stint as Y&R's Creative Director, proved to be as dedicated to perfection in his art as I am in mine.

And most recently, I found it in Bob Kresser.

Bob's total involvement in our clients' marketing is as vital to him as the air he breathes.

Maybe that's how we've managed to attract the finest caliber of talent in the country. People who understand the trust our clients place in us.

In short, no one at Kresser & Robbins is in advertising because it beats heavy lifting.

That's why we practically doubled our billing in the past year alone.

If you put the same care into your product as we put in ours and no one has been gutsy enough to dig it out, call Bud Robbins at (213) 553-8254 and just say, "I'm looking for my Capo d'astro bar."

Kresser & Robbins, Inc.

2049 Century Park East / Los Angeles, California 90067 / Advertising & Public Relations

Home of the Capo d'astro bar.

Exhibit 2-1: "Looking for the Capo d'astro bar" was a house advertisement written by Bud Robbins for Kresser & Robbins, Inc., which demonstrates how important background research is to the agency. (Written by Bud Robbins for Kresser & Robbins, Inc.)

sumers are talking about among themselves. Haunt stores, malls, restaurants, kitchens, video arcades, and other hangouts. Listen to employees on their coffee break. Listen to people as they talk to one another while they shop.

Most of all, listen to your client. Listen between the words. Advertising people sometimes miss the point of the assignment because they have preconceived ideas about the problem. Hal Newsom of Cole and Weber explains, "No one has ever found an advertising solution by talking. But thousands of brilliant solutions are discovered by listening, by hearing what people have to say."[7]

focus group: a group interview that tries to stimulate people to talk candidly about consumer problems, products, or advertising

A more formal way to listen is to use a **focus group**. A focus group is a research method that gets a group of people together to talk in a discussion format about a consumer problem, a product, or advertising. Get a dozen people together, set up a tape recorder, develop a list of topics, and then let the people talk. Focus groups are useful because you can use the synergism of different people's comments to elicit responses beyond anything you might think to ask. People bounce off one another in a group interview—one idea leads to another. Copywriters sit in on these sessions and watch from behind one-way windows. In some situations they can even send follow-up questions to pursue interesting lines of thought.

Watch. Observation is a very important part of fact-finding. Watch consumers like your family and friends. Observe how they use products at home, at work, and in their kitchens, garages, and basements. Advertising professionals often do observation studies, either formal or informal, in grocery store aisles and department stores to watch how consumers make decisions at the point of purchase.

Use. A cardinal sin for creatives is to develop advertising for a product with which they are not personally familiar. Use it, taste it, drive it, touch it, test it. In a tribute to Bernice Fitz-Gibbon, when she was named to the Advertising Hall of Fame, Reva Korda tells a story about the importance of familiarity with the product. Fitz-Gibbon was head of advertising at Gimbels in New York and was a legendary figure in retail advertising. Korda recounts: "I remember Fitz fired a girl because the poor wretch didn't know if the belt on a dress she had written about was a self belt, or a leather belt. It turned out she had actually written about the dress without ever having seen it."[8]

The necessity to know the product also breeds loyalty. Many people at the Campbell-Ewald agency drive Chevys; Chevrolet is their largest client. A story is told about Leo Burnett, who suffered from low blood sugar, which caused him to grow faint. At a marketing meeting, he grew weak and collapsed into a chair whispering "candy bar." One of his staff ran to a vending machine and Burnett called after him: "Geno, make sure it's a Nestlé!"[9]

Work. Foote, Cone & Belding has a program of consumer research involving both the creative and the research departments. Called, "Know the Consumer,"[10] the FCB program puts the creatives out "on the street" to meet the person they must persuade, in person, in groups, in face-to-face dialogue, over the phone, or in any of a dozen other types of encounters.

One copywriter went back to an inner-city neighborhood where he grew up to shoot baskets with the kids. He was working on the Sears gym shoes account. He learned that the hero figures in the youngsters' lives were their big brothers, and this little piece of understanding became the heart of an advertisement that "sold shoes like crazy."

Likewise, N. W. Ayer staff worked behind the counters after winning the Burger King account. DDB Needham Worldwide staff had to go through complete makeovers when they picked up the Maybelline account—including the men. The Goldsmith Jeffrey agency rode the New York subway from 6:30 AM to 7:30 PM after winning the Metropolitan Transportation Authority account. One of the most exciting stories is told by an art director and a copywriter for Bozell, Jacobs, Kenyon & Eckhardt who were given the opportunity to take a "million-dollar ride" aboard T-38 jets to get a feel for the U.S. Air Force account.[11]

FACT-FINDING TECHNIQUES

- Read published reports and articles.
- Interview and ask questions.
- Listen carefully to client and consumer.
- Watch consumers shop and use products.
- Use the product and become familiar with its features and those of the competition.
- Work in the store and meet the consumer face-to-face.

Types of Information

From the preceding discussion you should be able to figure out the three areas of information needed to conduct background research: (1) marketplace, (2) company and product, and (3) consumer. Advertising is a marketing function, and sometimes some of this information is already available for you in the company's marketing plan, although it is usually not available in the depth you need in order to develop a creative strategy.

Marketplace. What's the economic health of the industry—is it growing, declining, maintaining? Is it crowded? Is there room for growth or does growth have to come at some competitor's expense? What can you find out about share of market—who leads, who's moving up, who's declining? No market is static, and information over time lets you flesh out the picture.

You also need to know everything there is to know about the competitive situation. Who are the competitors—both direct and indirect? If you ask people who Hallmark's competition is, they will probably respond with the name of other greeting card companies. The real competitor for Hallmark, however, is the telephone, and Hallmark sees Bell as its chief competitor for the "sentiment" market. Sometimes you have to dig beneath the surface to understand the complexities of the competitive situation.

The importance of research is recognized by clients as well as agencies. John Bergin of McCann-Erickson said, "Of all the companies I've served, I know not one that studies the market, the consumer, its own advertising and its competitors' advertising more deliberately and more exactingly than Coca-Cola."[12]

Also investigate the competition's promotional strategies. What attributes are they featuring, what positions are they taking? What are the various product images—both yours and theirs? Build a file of all advertising by all competitors. You need to know every headline, every copy point, every slogan that's in use or has been used. There's nothing more embarrassing than to propose a great new idea to a client only to find that it was discarded by the competition five years earlier.

Company and product. Start your investigation into your client company with corporate history. Describe the staff and key executives. What are the sales objectives? Investigate the company's pricing and profit picture. What are the advertising expenditures and advertising costs per unit? Is this a profitable line? How is distribution handled and is there a geographical factor? How is the distribution system organized—retailers, distributors, sales reps, franchisees, dealers, drivers? What is the consumers' image of the company? Collect all the client's past advertising.

When you do background research for your product, get excited about it. There is no such thing as a dull product. Someone invented it, and to invent it he or she had to see a need. It was created to solve some problem. In doing your research, you want to reexperience the excitement of creating that product. Develop the initial enthusiasm that the product's inventor must have felt.

Bill Bernbach believed in product research. He said, "You write better when you have something to write about. . . . Know your product inside out before you start working. Your cleverness, your provocativeness and imagination and inventiveness must stem from knowledge of the product."[13]

In order to develop convincing advertisements, you have to be convinced yourself. Your conviction is often a product of your research and reflects how much you know about the product. Investigate the details of construction. Advertising professionals call these the product's **attributes**. The product's **features** are those attributes which will be highlighted in the advertising. You'd be surprised how much there is to know about something as simple as a pencil, a nail, or a paperclip. If a hairpin is complicated, think how much more challenging a tire must be—or a television set.

Shirley Polykoff, the first "living lady" to be elected to the Advertising Hall of Fame, is best known for her work with cosmetics and hair coloring. She legitimized the idea of women coloring their hair. Prior to her famous "Does she, or doesn't she?" campaign, women who colored their hair were thought to be "loose." Polykoff said in an interview that "for me the reality of the product's performance has always been of vital importance." But it goes beyond just performance. Polykoff also believes in her products. "I really do believe in the promise of cosmetics. . . . I believe cosmetics do make me look prettier. What's even more important, they make me feel prettier—and younger."[14]

Consumer. When you do background audience research, you are trying to find out everything you can about the potential **prospects**, the

---

attributes: distinctive details or characteristics of a product

features: those attributes which will be focused on in the advertisement

prospects: consumers who might be in the market for your product

people you feel might be in the market for your product or service. At this point in the process, you are not making any decisions about targeting a specific audience—that comes later in the strategy stage. What you are doing here is spreading your net and sweeping up every little bit of information you can find about consumers in general, and specifically about people who *might* use or buy your product or service.

Who are the *users* of your product and your competitor's—is there any difference between your users and theirs? Who are the *nonusers* and why are they not using your product? If it's a new product, then you'll be looking for people who face the problem, whatever it is, that this product was designed to solve.

Know your consumers intimately. You want to know everything about groups of people who might be prospects for your product, beginning with **demographic** characteristics like age, sex, income, level of education, and marital status. But demographic data are not enough to explain why Tom and Bob buy different cars (or any other product) even though they are on the same age, income, educational, and profession level, and live in similar neighborhoods.

To get a more complete picture of their targeted consumers, creatives use **psychographic** characteristics, which describe personalities, opinions, interests, and lifestyles. Buying behavior is another important category of information. How do consumers go about making a decision on this product? Do they search or do they buy on impulse?

Self-image is an important part of the psychographic profile. It is an important factor in how people make decisions about purchases. People buy products that express how they see themselves or want to be seen by others. Find out who they think they are.

An example of change in self-image comes from the motorcycle market. In the sixties only "bikers" in black leather jackets rode motorcycles. Then Honda advertised, "Nice people ride Hondas." It became okay for people who don't see themselves as "bikers" to ride motorcycles.

Consumer problems are another important area of research. What are the nagging little things that you don't like about your car or your home? John Caples explained the importance of investigating consumer problems: "It is important to discover what problems people have with various products. Don't ask them, 'What do you like about this product?' Instead, ask them, 'Have you had any problems with this product?'"[15]

BBDO uses a research method called "problem detection" to develop a list of potential consumer problems related to a product. The people on the BBDO staff have found that generally they can come up with more than 100 possible problems for virtually any product or service in existence. The "big problem" is determined by having consumers rank the list of little problems.

When BBDO got the Burger King account, the research indicated that one of the consumer problems was that the burgers were too small. BBDO's promotion of the "whopper" turned that problem around. But then all the burger places started advertising size. The continuing research indicated that a new problem being recognized by consumers was that the hamburgers were all prefabricated with the same lettuce, pickles, and ketchup. BBDO spoke to that problem with the campaign, "Have it your way."[16]

demographics: the vital statistics about a group of people, including such things as age, income, gender, where they live, and household size

psychographics: the psychological variables that make people different, including such things as interests, opinions, values, attitudes, personality, and decision processes

Some cultural anthropologists work in advertising agencies, helping to identify new ways to communicate to specific groups of people. Charlotte Cerf, an anthropologist and project director at Lowe Marschalk, explains that the subject is to "hit the right people in the areas anthropologists understand—consumers' psychological and emotional buttons, and their cultural norms."[17]

Empathy and Intuition

Another source of information is your own *intuition*. Most experienced copywriters will warn you against projecting your own needs and views onto the minds of your prospect, but your own intuition is still a good source for "crap detection." You are capable of noticing phony lines, insincere statements, and excuses—in interviews and in advertising.

As you become more skilled at audience analysis, you will be better able to rely on personal intuition to get a reading on consumers. You are a reservoir of personal experiences. While you may not be able to decide the best appeal for a group of people who are quite different from yourself, you do share certain universal needs and face universal problems. In those areas your own intuition is a valuable resource.

Hand in hand with intuition is *empathy*, the ability to project yourself into other peoples' shoes—to experience their lives, thoughts, needs, and problems as your own. Leo Burnett put it bluntly: "If you can't turn yourself into your customer, you probably don't belong in the business."[18] Empathy comes from self-knowledge. Shirley Polykoff explains, "It's only when you know yourself—when you can dig deep into your own motivations and recognize them—that you can understand what it is other people want."[19]

The ability to empathize was one of Leo Burnett's greatest strengths. He was described in an *Advertising Age* article as a small, shy boy from a small town in Michigan. "Perhaps in his shyness he learned to 'imaginate' himself out of himself and into the identities of other people, where he could feel their feelings and understand their wants." The article describes this ability to "imaginate" as an almost mystical sensitivity.[20]

GET THE PICTURE

1. Marketplace information
   a. The industry
   b. The competitive situation
2. The company and product
   a. Company history, pricing, profits, budgets, distribution
   b. Product's reason for being
   c. Product performance, attributes, features
3. The consumer
   a. Demographics, psychographics, and buying behavior
   b. Users (light, heavy), nonusers, and competitor's users—how and why are they different?
   c. Consumer problems

Backgrounding and Creative Thinking

Fact-finding is the necessary first step to creative thinking. As we said earlier, ideas don't come from out of the blue. A scholarly article on creatives in advertising concluded that creative people need research in order to be creative. The authors explained, "The highly creative person has more ability to associate research data into problem-solving communications than has the less creative person."[21] So read those books, talk and watch and listen, and stockpile those facts.

SUMMARY

This chapter outlined the process of creating advertisements and then focused on the beginning steps of background research.

1. The process of creating an advertisement
   - understand the assignment
   - background research
   - strategy: what to say
   - creative concept: how to say it
   - execution: figure out the details
   - production: technical activities needed to get an ad in print or on the air
2. Who does what in the process: copywriters, art directors, producers, creative directors, traffic department, account executives, sales reps, advertising directors
3. Fact-finding techniques: read, ask, listen, watch, use, work
4. Types of information
   - marketplace: industry and competition
   - product: performance, attributes, features
   - consumers: demographics, psychographics, buying behavior, users and nonusers, problems

NOTES

1. Carl Hixon, "Leo," *Advertising Age*, February 8, 1982, p. M25.
2. Larry Plapler, "Perspectives on Creativity," *Advertising Age*, June 4, 1979, p. S20.
3. Ron Hoff, "Ron Hoff Talks Corporate Advertising," *Wall Street Journal,* house ad series.
4. Shepard Kurnit, "The Impact of Creative Research on Creativity," Speech to Advertising Research foundation annual conference, New York, October 1979.
5. Leonard N. Reid and Herbert J. Rotfeld, "Toward an Associative Model of Advertising Creativity," *Journal of Advertising*, 5:4 (1976), pp. 24–29.
6. William Bernbach, "Insight Is Key to Creativity," *Advertising Age*, December 11, 1978, p. 73.
7. Hal Newsom, "Good Newsom," *Wall Street Journal,* house ad series.
8. Reva Korda, "Fond Memories of a Hall of Famer: How Bernice Fitz-Gibbon Trained the Troops," *Advertising Age*, March 29, 1982, p. M11.
9. Hixon, op. cit.
10. Nancy Millman, "Don't Shoot Until You Know the Whys of Their Buys," *Advertising Age*, January 16, 1978, p. 36.

11. Casey Davidson, "Client to New Agency: 'Walk a Mile in My Shoes'," *Adweek*, August 29, 1988, p. 17; Steve Saari, "They Flew Through the Air with the Greatest of G's," *Adweek*, January 30, 1989, p. 37.

12. John Bergin, Address to American Advertising Federation, Atlanta, June 15, 1982.

13. Denis Higgins, "Conversations with William Bernbach," in *The Art of Writing Advertising* (Chicago: Advertising Publications, 1965).

14. Shirley Polykoff, "Will You or Won't You Take a Chance," *Advertising Age*, February 1, 1982, p. 45.

15. John Caples, "A Dozen Ways to Develop Advertising Ideas," *Advertising Age*, November 14, 1983, p. M5.

16. E. E. Norris, "Seek Out the Consumer's Program," *Advertising Age*, March 17, 1975, pp. 43–44.

17. Ron Gales, "Consumer Culture: An Emerging Anthropological Workshop," *Adweek*, March 13, 1989, p. 30.

18. Hixon, op. cit.

19. Polykoff, op. cit.

20. Hixon, op. cit.

21. Leonard N. Reid and Herbert J. Rotfeld, op. cit.

3

How Advertising Works

KEY POINTS

- Effective advertising has stopping power, holding power, and sticking power (it is attention-getting, interesting, and memorable).
- Miscommunication derives from clarity, completeness, and organizational problems.
- Advertising develops both associations and understanding.
- Persuasive advertising is credible, believable, and transforms the product.

A cover story in *Adweek* headlined "What Works? and Why?" explains that "there's a new hunger to understand what advertising does."[1] In order to *do* advertising that works, it is helpful to understand *how* advertising works, and that is what we will look at in this chapter—the psychology of advertising.

Harvey Bailey, a creative director who writes columns for *Advertising Age*, says, "The psychology behind the work you produce is (dare I say it out loud?) even more important than a well turned phrase or a nifty new television optical. . . . That's what it is all about: getting inside people's heads and getting them to act."[2]

Our approach to strategy will begin in this chapter with a discussion of psychology, because you need to know how advertising works before you can write realistic objectives for an advertisement. Throughout this chapter we will also discuss the concept of "branding" and how branding works.

Different ads do different things, so not every ad works the same way. However, most advertising works its way through the same general process. We will refer to the steps in this process as perception, communication, learning, and persuasion. While these are clearly *steps* in a process, they also identify the primary *effects* of an advertisement on a viewer. In other words, certain features of an ad are there to aid in the viewer's perception, communication, learning, and persuasion.

This section may seem a little heavy going because it presents basic psychological principles behind advertising, but stick with it. Terms like *attention, memorability,* and *believability* are used all the time in advertising, and this chapter will help you understand what those terms mean and how important they are in the process of advertising.

3.1 PERCEPTION

In order to understand what happens at that point of impact when the viewer gets the message—or doesn't get it—professionals in advertising need to understand some of the basics of perceptual psychology. One of your biggest problems in doing an ad is simply to get people to *notice* it.

perception: the process by which a viewer gets information, interprets it, and files it away in memory

Perception is the process by which the viewer receives messages through the various senses, interprets the messages, and files them away in memory. The message, in other words, *registers.* There are three concepts that are important in the perception of advertising: (1) attention, (2) interest, and (3) memorability. All three are basic to effective advertising.

Attention

Attention is a mental state indicating some level of awareness, that the mind is engaged, and that it is focused on something—in other words, "tuned in." An ad that is attention-getting fights back with "stopping power." Several examples by Jerry Della Femina are illustrated in Exhibit 3-1.

Advertising that grabs attention is intriguing, novel, unusual, or surprising. Zany ads that use unexpected effects—such as the ones for Irish Spring in which a bar of soap foams in a person's pocket or squirts the person in the face, and the ad for Crest Tartar Control Toothpaste which shows people inside a giant mouth lining huge teeth with tartar—are designed to fight the attention problem.[3] Odd noises, such as droning, panting, buzzing, as well as strange sets and unusual bits of action attempt to grab the viewer's attention.

MAKING AN AD ATTENTION-GETTING

- Make it intriguing, novel, unusual, or surprising.
- Tell your audience something they didn't know.
- Speak to a personal interest.
- Offer something the viewer wants.
- Shout or whisper.
- Do the opposite of what everyone else is doing.

Exhibit 3-1: The ad for Intervisual Communication focuses on the attention-getting work of Jerry Della Femina.

Advertising that gets attention shouts or whispers. It tells people something they didn't know; it arouses their curiosity. It speaks to their personal interests or offers something they want. An ad with stopping power grabs the audience by the ears and/or the eyeballs.

The biggest perceptual problem for advertising is *inattention*. Many advertising messages simply "wash over" viewers without any attention being paid to them at all. Advertising can be like wallpaper, a background rarely noticed. Another problem is *divided attention*, when the audience is doing something else and is only half listening or half watching the ad. Many ads get only half the mind and one eye.

Clutter, which we discussed in Chapter 1, adds to the inattention problem. In one of his newspaper columns George Will said that, "Ordinary advertising is losing its power to get attention." He feels that part of the problem is clutter, particularly on television, when viewers can be bombarded by up to 50 messages in a prime-time hour.[4]

Intrusiveness.   Attention is triggered by something; in other words, something "catches" the viewer's attention. Since advertising operates in an environment of consumer inattention, few people are waiting to hear or read your ad. If the ad doesn't get noticed, then it is very difficult for the message to make any impression. As David Ogilvy has said, "You can't save souls in an empty church."[5]

intrusive: a characteristic that makes a message hard to ignore

Most advertising, therefore, is designed to be **intrusive**. *Intrusive* means someone or something thrusts itself upon you without an invitation. That's what we mean by "catching attention." In advertising an intrusive message is one that is hard to ignore. The most successful advertising, however, is voluntarily attended to even when it is intrusive—what a former advertising professor, Charles Mauldin, used to call the "Hey, Martha" phenomenon. That's when the viewer likes the ad so much that he or she wants to share it—"Hey, Martha, come and see this."

An ad can be intrusive for the wrong reasons. Professional advertisers use the phrase "the gorilla in a jock strap" to describe the technique of using irrelevant attention-getting gimmicks. These "tricks" can create enough viewer resentment that they backfire; the ad might get remembered, but the resentment can be so strong that the consumer resists trying or buying the product.

The amount of intrusiveness needed varies with the medium, the product category, and the interest level of the consumer. For example, an advertisement on television has to be more intrusive than an advertisement in a trade journal, because the level of audience interest is lower in a broad mass medium than it is in a specialized medium like a trade publication.

An ad can be intrusive without being bold and brash. Some recent award-winning ads use a "minimalist" style and speak very quietly. An example is a commercial for La-Z-Boy recliners that shows a young father pacing the floor late at night and humming to his whimpering baby. As he sits down in the rocker and cuddles the child, the announcer says, "Nobody has rocked more babies to sleep than we have." As the name La-Z-Boy flashes on the screen, the father whispers, "Night, night, angel." It's unusual to see a heart-tugging approach used for a category like furniture.[6] It also has a different "look." The beginning scene through the porch door is like a painting, the action is very simple, and the message is quiet. It's attention-getting because it is so different from the loud, hard-sell that dominates so much of television advertising today.

selective perception: the process people use to screen out information that does not interest or agree with them

Selective perception.   Far more messages are presented to people than they are able to concentrate on; therefore they have to sort out the messages some way. **Selective perception** is the term used to describe how we sort those messages, according to what interests us or what we agree with. We filter out the items that don't interest us and that we don't agree with, and we simply don't pay any attention to those messages.

Page through a newspaper or magazine and notice how your own selection process works. What did you notice and what did you ignore? Why did you pay attention to some stories and ads and ignore others? The filter is your own pattern of *personal interest*.

zapping: avoiding a commercial by changing the channel or turning down the sound

zipping: avoiding a commercial on a videotape by fast-forwarding past it

Avoidance.   Consumers are bombarded with commercial messages, and they have become very good at *avoidance*, which is to say they refuse to look at ads that don't appeal to them. They may leave the room or use the remote control to **zap** or **zip** the commercial, by turning off the sound, changing the channel, or fast-forwarding past the commercial. Now the big challenge to the creative side is to make commercials so attention-getting and interesting that they are "zap-proof" (see Exhibit 3-2).

Interest

interest: a state of absorption, or mental concentration, on a message

The next level of perception, **interest,** is defined as a state of absorption in the message. It differs from attention in that there is an element of curiosity, concern, or fascination bonding the viewer to the message. The opposite of interesting is boring. Remember, as David Ogilvy said, "You can't bore people into buying."

relevance: something that "connects," that means something to people

Relevance.   Interest occurs when a message is *relevant* to people; it addresses them with something that they care about. Interest, however, is a momentary thing and it dies easily as attention shifts. R. D. Percy & Co., a company that provides rating services for television commercials, has developed a new measure that will determine the "holding power" of a TV commercial. The Percy system tells how many people watch an entire commercial, how much of that commercial is viewed, and at what point people tune out.[7]

MAKING AN AD INTERESTING

- Be relevant.
- Open with a question.
- Be entertaining.
- Use ambiguity.
- Create suspense.
- Stimulate involvement.
- Use closure.
- Speak to self-interest.

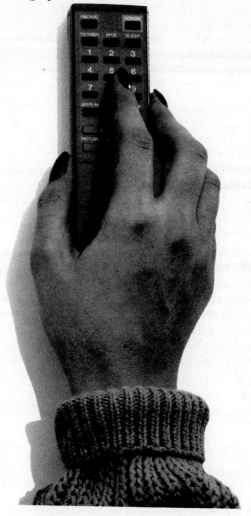

Before a television spot can begin to grab market share, it must first grab someone's attention. It must interrupt and intrigue before it can inform. If your upcoming commercials could use a fresh, provocative approach, call Brian Brinson at 577-8077 for a sample of our work. Or write 8335 Allison Pointe Trail, Suite 310, Indianapolis, Indiana 46250.

Jehs & Wallis
Advertising will never be the same.

Are people giving your commercials the finger?

Exhibit 3-2: This house ad for Jehs & Wallis dramatizes the use of remote control to ''zap'' television commercials that aren't attention-getting. (Reproduced by permission of Jehs & Wallis, Inc. Indianapolis, Indiana)

Types of interest. There are three types of interest that concern advertising professionals: product interest, self-interest, and interest in the message itself. Some products are inherently more interesting than others. Most Americans pay attention to ads for cars; few are interested in ads for hemorrhoid remedies. When a person offers to help others learn to do something or give them a free sample, that person is appealing to self-interest.

A message that is interesting is one that has "holding power" (rather than stopping power). It stimulates curiosity in order to maintain interest and make the viewer want to know more. Interesting ads often open with questions, suspense, entertainment, or ambiguous statements that compel the viewer to attend.

Memory

memorable: that characteristic of information and past experiences that make them easy to retain and recall

It is very important to advertisers not only that their messages are heard, but also that they have "sticking power," the power to lock into the mind. If a person can't remember seeing the ad, then that person might as well have not seen it at all. The editor's column in AAF's *American Advertising* comments that ads are effective when "they get in your head and stay there."[8]

Awareness. When you are aware of something, you know that you have seen it or heard it before. You may not be able to recall much about it, but you are aware of having seen it. Advertising agencies test to see if consumers are aware of certain products, brands, or advertisements. Consumers don't have to be able to say much about the advertisement; they must simply be aware of having seen it. Awareness is particularly important for new products.

The editors at *American Advertising* have this to say about awareness: "It's a laudable goal in the beginning, when no one knows who you are or what you have to offer." But awareness is a rather low-level response, and the editors point out its limited value: "Once it's achieved, which can happen in a relatively short period of time when the advertising is on target, shouldn't it be turned into something else that can build over time?"[9]

Advertising agencies also do *top-of-mind awareness* studies by asking people to name the brands that come to mind when a product category is specified. For example, what brands do you think of when you think of toothpaste, soap, jeans? You have top-of-mind awareness of those brands.

Traces and fragments. The human memory is like a filing cabinet. Advertisements are filed according to some personal pattern of organization using slots, or files, that contain related information. Ad messages are usually compressed and restructured to fit into the individual filing system. Sometimes the message is changed beyond recognition. Bill Bernbach recognized that problem when he said, "Most readers come away from their reading not with a clear, precise, detailed registration of the contents on their minds, but rather with a vague, misty idea. . . ."[10]

cue: a word or visual that acts as a reminder

Most information is filed as fragments or traces. These fragments are pulled back to the "top" of the mind by the use of **cues**, which are certain words or visuals that will elicit previously learned information. Distinctive characters like Betty Crocker, the Keebler elves, and the Snuggle teddy

Exhibit 3-3: The cuddly teddy bear used as a product "spokesperson" for Snuggle fabric softener develops a strong, memorable brand image.

bear (see Exhibit 3-3) are examples of cues that stimulate emotional responses, as well as recall of the brand.

In order to be memorable, the message has to be easy to compress for filing. That's why writers develop *key phrases* like *slogans* and *key visuals* for television. The Snuggle teddy bear photo in Exhibit 3-3 is an example of a key visual from a television commercial. The creators of this ad understand that only the essence of the message will remain in memory, so they provide a prepackaged memory trace.

Organizing is also important. Psychologists know that it is easier to remember things that are grouped together rather than separate elements. This is important for advertising designers, who use the graphic principle of grouping to bring things together physically that belong together, by using placement and space.

Repetition. Repeating an advertisement helps reinforce the message and locks it into the mind. Psychologists suggest that people need to hear something three times before it crosses the threshold of perception and enters into memory. The number of times varies with the type of information. People would rather not hear a joke over and over again, but a *jingle* can repeat a phrase or product name many times without boring the audience.

The bizarre.   Recently consumers have said that the commercials they remember the best are the ones with oddball characters. Video Storyboard Tests, which does a yearly list of the best remembered commercials, found in 1988 that the singing claymation California raisins were remembered more than any other commercials, followed by Bud Light's Spuds MacKenzie. The president of Video Storyboards explained that, "People are just tired of standup announcers and celebrities." Other winners on the list were Bartles & Jaymes, and the ever-lying Joe Isuzu. Even the negative, some say obnoxious, Noid character for Domino's Pizza was number 10 on the list.[11]

Branding and brand equity.   National product advertising has developed as it has because of a contemporary marketing phenomenon: Products are unique because of their advertising rather than because of their features. *Undifferentiated* or *parity* products have little physical differences. Modern technology makes it possible to match the product design and manufacturing standards of almost any product. Therefore, a successful new product is soon followed by scores of imitators. The difference between the brands, then, is not in the products but in the minds of the consumers. And this perceived difference is created over time by the ads.

The memorable branding elements include distinctive brand names, clever phrases and catchwords like **slogans**, riveting visuals like **logos**, and brand characters and symbols, all of which are used to anchor the brand in memory. The visuals and words and characters combine to create a brand image or personality. Over time these elements build **brand equity**, the value of the ownership of the brand concept. Ultimately this builds share of market and sales—the bottom-line results of linking certain values with specific products and services.

At the heart of David Ogilvy's philosophy is the idea that advertising's primary goal is to develop a strong brand. He said, "Every advertisement should be thought of as a contribution to the complex symbol which is the brand name." Ogilvy defines a brand as a distinctive and consistent personality. He sees it as a long-term investment. He wrote, "The manufacturer who dedicates his advertising to building the most sharply defined personality for his brand will get the largest share of the market at the highest profit."[12]

The Pillsbury Doughboy is one of many product characters that represent a tremendous investment in brand-building over time. Other effective product characters are the Campbell Kids, who were introduced in 1904, Betty Crocker, who has been around since the thirties, RCA's fox terrier "Nipper," who first appeared in 1929, the Kool Aid smiling pitcher face, the Hathaway man with his eyepatch (current models include sportscaster Bob Costas and artificial-heart designer Robert Jarvik), and the most universally recognized of all—the Marlboro cowboy.

slogan: a catchy phrase that identifies a brand or provides continuity to a campaign

logo: a distinctive mark that symbolizes a company or brand

brand equity: a long-term investment in the development of a distinctive brand concept

Just a little reminder from Xerox.

XEROX

You may have heard a phrase like, "I Xeroxed my recipe for you" or "Please Xerox this for me." And they may seem harmless enough.

But they're not. Because they overlook the fact that Xerox is a registered trademark of Xerox Corporation. And trademarks should not be used as verbs.

As a brand name, Xerox should be used as an adjective followed by a word or phrase describing the particular product.

Like the Xerox 1075 Copier. The Xerox 640 Memorywriter. Or the Xerox 9700 Electronic Printing System.

Our brand name is very valuable to us. And to you, too. Because the proper use of our name is the best way to ensure you'll always get a Xerox product when you ask for one.

So, please remember that our trademark starts with an "X."

And ends with an "®."

XEROX® is a trademark of XEROX CORPORATION.

Exhibit 3-4: A *logo* is a distinctive way of writing a company's name. It is a *key visual* that helps make the product memorable. This ad for Xerox spells out that the product's brand name is registered and exclusive.

A brand can dominate a category, in spite of competitors. When people think of soup, it's Campbell's, and when people think of cake mix, it's Betty Crocker. However, the brand name has to be used exclusively by the company and protected from becoming a category label. Band-Aid, Kleenex, and Xerox all fight to keep their brand names from becoming "generic" category names (see Exhibit 3-4).

MAKING AN AD MEMORABLE

- Package it as a key visual or key phrase for easy filing.
- Use cues to tie in with previously learned information.
- Repeat it enough times to get past the threshold.
- Use bizarre, oddball characters.
- Use clever phrases and riveting visuals that stick in the mind.
- Build long-term brand equity.

---

recognition: the viewer is aware of having seen the ad before

recall: the viewer can remember specific information from the ad

Recognition and recall. There are two other types of memorability of concern to advertising professionals: recognition and recall. **Recognition** means that the viewer is aware of having seen the ad before. **Recall** is a higher-order level of memory and means that the viewer has the ability to remember specific information. Both recall and recognition are measured by various types of copytesting services.

Impact

impact: the effect an ad has on the viewer's perceptual process—it startles and makes an impression

An ad that gets through the perceptual process effectively is described as having impact; it has collided with the senses and made an impression. **Impact** refers to an advertisement's ability to control the viewer's perceptual process—overcoming audience indifference, grabbing attention, maintaining interest, and anchoring the product firmly in memory.

Half a century ago Raymond Rubicam wrote a famous ad defining impact in advertising. He illustrated it with a stop-motion photograph of a punch in the jaw. His ad is a visual definition of that quality which strikes suddenly against the reader's indifference. The overall effect is to startle.

Impact in advertising is exceptional, even unusual. Most ads have an incredible sameness to them. They are derivative and uninspired; they are safe because they've been done before. With little impact, they make little impression. To survive in the cluttered media environment, ads need to make more impact. Breakthrough advertising has impact; it's startling.

PERCEPTION AND ADVERTISING

- Attention: it has "stopping power"
- Interest: it has "holding power"
- Memory: it has "sticking power"
- Impact: it is startling

3.2 COMMUNICATION

As we explained in the first chapter, an advertisement is a message about a product, service, or an idea that attempts to motivate people in some way. In this section we will discuss three characteristics of communication that works: clarity, completeness, and organization.

Clarity

If advertising is to communicate effectively, it must present its message clearly. In other words, the receivers "get the message" as the source intended. This is harder than you might think because clarity can be compromised both at the sending end and the receiving end.

Clarity is measured by the level of understanding of the viewer. If the viewer can tell you what was in the message and get most of the main points right, then the message was understood. The ad is clear if it is free from impediments and obstacles to communication, such as undefined terms, unfamiliar references, poor organization, and faulty logic. A clarity problem often results from muddy thinking, not really knowing what you want to say.

One way to strengthen the clarity of an advertisement is to make it single-minded. Many ads suffer from a "kitchen sink" strategy, with too many points crammed into too little space. As Bruce Stauderman explained in his *Advertising/Marketing Review* column, "It is virtually imperative that we take just one aspect of the product—the most important one—and *talk only about that.* It's a hard enough job, believe me, getting just that one point into the viewer's head."[13]

Completeness

One of the most difficult problems in communication is to know how much to say and when to quit. If you say too much, you may bore your audience. If you say too little, you oversimplify the topic until it doesn't make sense. The amount of completeness needed varies with the message. A reminder ad, whose function is to create simple brand awareness, doesn't need to provide much information. On the other hand, an advertisement for a major purchase like a refrigerator may need to provide enough information to instruct the consumer about the features of the appliance and how they compare with the features of competing products.

Organization

The way a message is put together, both words and visuals, determines how the viewer proceeds through it. Different parts of an ad do different things. The beginning is used to catch attention, the middle is to elaborate and explain, and the ending is to anchor something in memory. Ineffective communication can result from poor order.

Logic is also a function of organization. When you are trying to establish a reason or explain a point, the logic of the argument must follow clearly from point to point. Big jumps in logic, as well as faulty logic, can cause confusion.

Miscommunication

Studies of television news, general programming, and advertising have found that there is a generally high level of miscommunication across all three types of broadcast information.[14] Communication through the mass media is extremely difficult.

Miscommunication happens in advertising—probably more often than successful communication. The creative team can package a message and not realize that the points are unclear or irrelevant, the logic is faulty, important explanations are missing, or the terms are unknown. But more than that, miscommunication means you may get across a message, but not the one intended. Confusion can be created by poor organization or by mistaking one thing for another. For example, symbols or vernacular language may not mean the same thing to everybody. Problems like these happen all the time and haunt those who try to make advertisements.

In his column in *Advertising/Marketing Review*, Bruce Stauderman described an experience Rosser Reeves had with Kool cigarettes. His agency had produced a TV campaign in which the main visual was a length of chain which snapped when the announcer said, "Break the hot cigarette habit." Sales dropped for the cooling, menthol product until the agency finally did some research and found out that viewers thought the commercial was addressing chain smokers rather than people who were dissatisfied with "hot" cigarettes.[15]

The only way to know if a message is perceived, if it is comprehensible, if it teaches the right things—and is persuasive—is to test it out on someone. Have someone who is totally unfamiliar with the subject read your ad copy and see if he or she thinks it makes sense. Ask that person to replay what the message said. Go over it together sentence by sentence and phrase by phrase to diagnose problems with wording or structure.

MAKING AN AD COMMUNICATE EFFECTIVELY

- Clarity: eliminate obstacles to clarity such as undefined terms and unfamiliar references
- Completeness: know how much to say and when to stop; be single-minded
- Organization: use order and logic to structure the message

3.3 LEARNING

learning: the process by which people become knowledgeable or gain information

To advertising professionals, **learning** means becoming informed or gaining knowledge about the product or service being advertised. Advertising provides information—it teaches people about products and services. Some brand advertising is designed primarily to teach people how to say the name and recognize the package, a simple learning objective of identification and definition. Ads for new products have a more complex problem because they must bridge the gap in people's experience and make viewers feel that they know what the product is and does, as well as how to use it. Explanation is used to bridge this experience gap. Comparative advertising is even more complex, since it must build arguments as well as discrimination.

There are two primary schools of thought in psychology about how society acquires such knowledge. The connectionists believe people learn things by making associations for which they receive rewards; the cognitive theorists believe people learn by acquiring insight, understanding, or comprehension of the whole picture. As far as advertising is concerned, both schools are right. Advertising seeks to develop both associations and understanding.

Association

association: connection or linkage between products and situations, activities, lifestyles, or certain types of people

image transfer: when a product takes on characteristics of valued associations

The process of making connections and linking ideas, called **association**, is particularly important to how advertising works.[16] Advertising frequently tries to link a product or service to a certain situation, activity, lifestyle, or type of person. **Image transfer** occurs when a product takes on characteristics of these associations. Mountain Dew links itself with teenagers having fun outdoors.

The idea is that when people think of these situations, they also think of the product. Some products, like BMWs and Rolex watches, are linked with successful executive lifestyles. Adidas identifies itself with professional sports and athletes. These advertisers hope the consumer will link their products with these types of people and lifestyles and then identify with them.

Understanding

Cognitive learning explains how understanding is developed from pieces of information that serve as cues. It focuses on comprehension and understanding based on *insight*. In other words, people acquire little pieces of information until all of a sudden they see the big picture—the "aha" experience. Advertising uses cognitive understanding to follow the logic of an argument, make discriminations and see differences, compare and contrast features, comprehend reasons, and, in general, make sense of important ideas.

A good example of cognitive learning in advertising is found in Ogilvy's classic advertisement for Rolls-Royce, which begins with the line: "At 60 miles an hour, the loudest noise in this new Rolls-Royce comes from the electric clock." Readers understand that the tiny detail of the clock ticking stands for the entire concept of excellence in automotive engineering.

Brand Loyalty

brand loyalty: repeat purchases that follow a positive experience using a product or service

When something is learned, that means the information or experience has been anchored in memory. Consumers who have tried a product and liked it have learned something positive from the experience. They likely will use it again. That is how **brand loyalty** is built up from a series of satisfactory experiences. Brand loyalty is learned. John Caples recognized

---

MAKING AN AD INSTRUCTIVE

- Identification: a way to recognize product, brand, or package
- Information: the basic facts about the product
- Demonstration: a method for using the product
- Discrimination: a way to differentiate among or compare products
- Associations: concepts that link ideas and/or images, sometimes with a promise of a reward
- Comprehension: insight or understanding of the whole picture
- Definition: an explanation of unfamiliar terms
- Explanation: an answer to questions of how, why, and so what

the importance of brand loyalty when he said, "People who buy once are your best prospects for buying again."[17]

3.4 PERSUASION

persuasion: a conscious intent to influence someone and motivate certain actions

After Lasker and Kennedy coined the phrase, "salesmanship in print," advertising became a persuasive tool focusing on attitude development and change. **Persuasion** is defined as a conscious intent on the part of one person to influence another. In general, persuasive messages motivate people to do or feel something. More specifically, persuasion affects the structure of people's beliefs, opinions, attitudes, convictions, motivations, and emotions; these, in turn, motivate people to act.

Attitudes

An *attitude* is a state of mind that is positive, negative, or neutral. Consumer attitude structure is organized around opinions about products, the purchasing environment (when and where to buy, how much to pay), social environment (what others are buying), and self-concept (how the consumer sees him- or herself). This provides a rich fabric of feelings, all interwoven and interactive, held together by certain basic patterns. To motivate people to buy something, you have to understand and sometimes change their existing belief structure.

Changing an attitude is very difficult. Attitudes are entrenched deep in people's psyches and are interwoven with lots of other related values and opinions. It's like trying to turn around one brick in the middle of a brick wall. It can be done, however. Before World War I men wore pocket watches. Wristwatches were considered bracelets, that is, for women. In battle it was sometimes difficult to free up the hands to get at a pocket watch. In order to get the men over the line at the right time, the troops were made to wear wristwatches. When the war was over, men didn't mind wearing wristwatches.

Clairol had the same problem with hair coloring. In the 1950s coloring hair was a tedious process done only by women whose reputations were questionable. Shirley Polykoff, the legendary Foote, Cone & Belding copywriter, was faced with a monumental task: turn around a public attitude that was, at best, negative and bring respectability to hair coloring. During the next two decades, Shirley Polykoff was responsible for some of the most famous slogans in the annals of advertising as she turned a public attitude around: "Does she . . . or doesn't she? Only her hairdresser knows for sure," "Is it true blondes have more fun?," "If I've only one life . . . let me live it as a blonde," and "The closer he gets . . . the better you look."[18]

Likability. Likability occurs when an advertisement creates positive feelings—about self, about the ad, and, most of all, about the product or brand. Liking is important to advertisers because most advertising messages try to build positive attitudes toward the product.

Product characters are an important part of stimulating positive feelings toward a brand. In an *Advertising Age* "Whom Do You Love?" contest, readers were asked to vote for their favorite commercial character.

The Pillsbury Doughboy came in first, followed by Morris the Cat, Frank Bartles, the Keebler Elves, Ed Jaymes, Mikey, Ronald McDonald, Tony the Tiger, the Snuggle teddy bear, and the California raisins.[19]

Emotions

When people's emotions are touched, they experience a strong personal feeling such as love, joy, sorrow, hate, or some other kind of passion. Ads use *appeals* to the emotions because they are by their very nature interesting—and also very effective motivators. Most people respond positively to pictures of cuddly babies, cute kids, kittens, and puppy dogs. Emotion creates **resonance**, that is, the viewer's response is "in synch" or sympathetic.

resonance: the viewer's response is "in synch," "in tune," or sympathetic

Bill Bernbach talked about empathy and insight, abilities needed to "sense what people respond to." He explained, "If someone has that ability, she or he can do effective work. Because if they touch you at your instinct for survival, or your desire to be admired, or your love for your children, they touch you at the core of your being."[20] For example, the soft, cuddly Snuggle teddy bear (see Exhibit 3-3) is used internationally as a symbol for a fabric softener; the agency, SSC&B Lintas, found through research that the depth of feeling for teddy bears is enormous, and universal.[21]

Believability

Believability, the ad's ability to make the consumer believe in the truth of its message, is a challenge for advertising professionals. Most consumers realize that advertising is trying to sell them something; consequently they are skeptical. The effectiveness of the ad, in many cases, depends upon how well the copywriter can make it "ring true."

Source credibility. One of the things communication theory makes clear is that word-of-mouth communication among peers is more believable than mass communication from an anonymous source. Furthermore, a message is more credible when someone believable delivers it. In advertising, professionals look at three sources of influence: reference groups, opinion leaders, and peers. Advertising uses celebrities (reference group), authority figures such as doctors (opinion leaders), or the "typical user" (a peer) to try to influence viewers. An advertisement that uses an authority figure, like a car mechanic or a dentist, is trying to build credibility and believability.

Preference. Advertising often tries to develop a feeling of preference, the opinion that one product is more desirable than another. **Preference** is relative; it comes to the surface only in a choice situation. It means that the consumer likes one choice better than another. Preference is based on information about product features such as price, construction, style, and past experiences with the product or its competitors.

preference: the opinion that one product is more desirable than another

Conviction. A successful persuasive message builds **conviction**, a strong belief in something. Conviction usually results when proof is provided or an argument is delivered effectively. Advertising is believable when product claims are "proved." Also, when an advertisement provides reasons to buy a product or service, it is meant to develop conviction. If consumers don't believe your ad, then it is hard to convince them to try your product. A study of advertising claims found that the most con-

conviction: a belief based on certainty

vincing ones are based on user surveys and the least convincing are celebrity endorsements.[22]

Involvement

Involvement is an important concept in advertising. Actually, the term is used to refer to several important concepts.

Participation. Involvement, or participation in the development of the ad message, is another persuasive technique. Anything that involves viewers in doing something either physically or mentally is useful. For example, if you start with a question that interests viewers, then they will probably become involved in developing the message by trying to answer the question. The more involved the prospects are in developing the message, the more impact the message has.

Closure is a psychological technique that involves viewers in completing the message. Viewers are less likely to leave or switch if they are immersed in developing the message from their own personal experience (see Exhibit 3-5).

Product interest. Involvement is also used to describe the "interest level" of products and product categories. People are more concerned about some products than they are about others. For example, when a consumer is getting ready to buy a car, he or she tends to spend time reading about cars, visiting dealers, test-driving different models, and talking to friends about their experiences with cars. In other words, this is a "high-involvement" product.

On the other hand, it's not as easy to get excited about buying hand soap or toothpaste, and people probably don't spend a lot of time deliberating about chewing gum or candy before they buy. *Low-involvement products* like these are often bought on *impulse*. *Reminder* messages that build general awareness of a brand are more effective for these types of products. The persuasion is more indirect, and the impact of the message builds slowly over time.

Transformation and Brand Personality

The *personality* of a brand is a composite of attitudes that the consumers hold about the brand. These attitudes, more like "mental pictures," have accumulated from past personal experiences with the product, peer comments, and advertising messages. The brand personality is like a human personality—it can be friendly, honest, frank, tough, cold, or fussy. It can also be negative or positive.

How are these brand or product personalities created? Bill Wells, director of marketing services at DDB Needham Worldwide, has developed a concept he calls **transformation advertising** to explain how brand personalities work.[23] Wells explains that buying jeans is one thing, but buying Levis or Guess or Calvin Klein jeans is an entirely different experience.

transformation advertising: the values associated with the brand image change the experience of buying and using a product

The brand image, which is communicated by the advertisement, *transforms the experience* of buying and using the product. Wells suggests that sending your mother a watch in a box from K-Mart and one in a box from Tiffany's would create entirely different responses. The product, therefore, is transformed by the advertising as it takes on a brand image. This is also called the *added value* of advertising.

Exhibit 3-5: Closure is a psychological technique that involves the reader in completing the message, as in this ad for Volkswagen. It was used when the price of gas increased. (©Volkswagen of America, Inc. Used with express permission)

Behavior and Action The ultimate success of a persuasive message in advertising is to affect behavior, although corporate messages are often designed to affect attitudes only. *Behavior*, or action, is the final test of persuasion. In advertising the behavioral objective is usually stated as "trying the product," "buying the product," or "visiting the store."

Behavior as a result of advertising can take several forms. An ad can result in consumers trying a free product sample. Response cards in magazines are effective at getting people to request more information. *Trial* is an important form of action that is stimulated by the use of coupons. Other types of action include generating inquiries or stimulating traffic in a store or mall. The most complex form of action is the decision to purchase a product after investigation and comparison.

MAKING AN AD PERSUASIVE

- Attitudes: work with consumer's belief structure
- Likability: create positive feelings
- Emotions: touch emotions, create strong personal feelings
- Influence: use credible sources to deliver your message
- Conviction: create beliefs that are strongly fixed
- Transformation: communicate a brand image that adds something to the experience of buying and using a product
- Behavior: create messages that will result in consumer actions

---

Making It Work As we mentioned in the beginning of this chapter, different ads do different things. Now that you understand a little better the psychology behind advertising and the effects you can expect to create with your advertisements, it is time to begin to develop advertising strategy. What you have just read is the background for objectives-setting, the first step in developing a strategy, which is what you will consider in the next chapter.

SUMMARY

This chapter outlined the steps necessary to the process of "doing" an ad. These steps also identify effects that can be created by an advertising message:

1. Perception
- is attention-getting
- is interesting
- is memorable
- has impact

2. Communication
- is clear
- is complete
- is well organized

3. Learning
- uses identification
- provides information
- provides demonstration
- helps with discrimination
- uses association
- builds comprehension
- offers explanation

4. Persuasion
- affects attitudes and beliefs
- creates likability and positive feelings
- touches emotions
- influences
- creates believability
- builds convictions
- transforms brands, adding something special to the brand image
- stimulates behaviors and actions

NOTES

1. Jeffrey L. Seglin, "The New Era of Ad Measurement," *Adweek's Marketing Week*, January 23, 1989, pp. 22–25.
2. Harvey Bailey, "The Copywriter's Biggest Job," *Adweek*, March 15, 1982, p. 15.
3. Eileen Prescott, "An Agency's Turn to Madcap Ads," *New York Times*, June 7, 1987, Section 3, p. 1.
4. George Will, "Getting Our Attention Is Getting Out of Hand," *Muncie Star*, December 23, 1987, p. 12.
5. Gerry Scorse, "Ogilvy versus Bernbach," *Advertising Age*, October 26, 1987, p. 18.
6. Ronald Alsop, "Furniture Marketers Pull at Heartstrings in New Ads," *Wall Street Journal*, January 13, 1989, p. B1.
7. Verne Gay, "TV's 'Holding Power' Tracked," *Advertising Age*, November 16, 1987.
8. "Editor's Galley," *American Advertising*, June 1988, p. 2.
9. Ibid.
10. Bill Bernbach, "A Creative Credo for the Advertising Business," *Advertising Age*, April 30, 1980, p. 206.
11. "If a TV Ad Is Bizarre or It Barks, the Public Probably Will Remember," *Denver Post*, March 13, 1988, p. 6D.
12. David Ogilvy, *Confessions of an Advertising Man* (New York: Dell, 1964).
13. Bruce Stauderman, "Do You Say What You Mean?" *Advertising/Marketing Review*, April 1985, p. 4; Bruce Stauderman, "Singlemindedness," *Advertising/Marketing Review*, August 1986, p. 6.
14. Jacob Jacoby, Wayne D. Hoyer, and David A. Sheluga, "Viewer Miscomprehension of Televised Communication: Selected Findings," *Journal of Marketing*, 46 (Fall 1982), pp. 12–26.
15. Stauderman, op. cit.
16. Ivan Preston, "The Association Model of the Advertising Communication Process," *Journal of Advertising*, 11:2 (1982), pp. 3–15; Leonard N. Reid and Herbert

Rotfield, "Toward an Associative Model of Advertising Creative Thinking," *Journal of Advertising*, 5:4 (1976), pp. 24–29.

17. John Caples, "50 Things I Have Learned in 50 Years in Advertising," *Advertising Age*, September 22, 1975, p. 47.

18. Abbott C. Jones, "Clairol: Quiet Revolution," *Advertising Age*, January 26, 1981, pp. 47–48.

19. Leonore Skenazy, "Soft Spot: Doughboy Heats Readers' Hearts," *Advertising Age*, May 9, 1987, p. 3.

20. "The Quotable Bill Bernbach," *Adweek*, October 11, 1982, p. 26.

21. Roger Neill, "Concepts That Cross Boundaries," *Campaign*, May 1986, pp. 57–58.

22. "They Believe These Claims," *Communication Briefings*, 7:11, p. 3.

23. William Wells, "How Advertising Works," speech to St. Louis AMA, September 17, 1986.

4

Advertising Strategy

KEY POINTS

- Advertising is both art and science—disciplined and creative
- Advertising objectives specify the communication effects on the target audience
- The objective of targeting is to identify the prospects who are most likely to respond
- A problem statement focuses the effort on a problem that can be solved with an advertising message
- A position is the consumer's perception of a product as it exists in the competitive marketplace

Advertising is a disciplined art. The art comes from writing, designing, and producing creative messages. The discipline comes from strategy, from thinking through the logic of the problem and coming up with a message that offers a solution. Effective advertising is advertising that is both artful and disciplined—it is both creative and meets objectives. Advertising that works, works on both levels of art and science.

A *strategy* is a plan of action. As we discussed in Chapter 1, the process of *strategic thinking* involves identifying all possible alternative approaches, weighing their chances of success, and then choosing what you hope will be the most effective approach (see Exhibit 4-1). In advertising there is no *right* way, there are lots of ways. The challenge is to find the *best* way that will stimulate the hoped-for response from the viewer.

Strategy focuses on *what* you will say in the advertisement; the executions, or the actual print ads and commercials, focus on *how* you will

Exhibit 4-1: Young & Rubicam used this "house ad" to dramatize the agency's philosophy about the importance of advertising strategy.

say it. This chapter is about strategy. Executions will be discussed in the chapters that follow.

Harvey Bailey, an executive creative director, explained the importance of strategy to creatives: "Refuse to pick up a pen until you're satisfied with the strategy. . . . You can't start laying tracks until you know where your railroad's going. Who, precisely, are you talking to? What do you want to tell him or her?"[1]

Advertising strategy is broader than *creative strategy* (also called *message strategy*) because it covers the development of all parts of an advertising plan. Creative strategy will be discussed in the following chapter.

Advertising strategy begins with four critical areas of concern that are often addressed as part of the marketing plan. Sometimes, however, the company isn't using a marketing plan, so the advertising people jump in and address these concerns. These four critical areas are objectives, target audience, problem identification, and product position; the decisions concerning these areas provide the foundation for the message strategy.

4.1 OBJECTIVES

Objectives state what you intend to accomplish with your advertisement. They are based upon what you have learned about how advertising works. You will probably find in the marketing plan a set of marketing objectives. Usually these deal with *sales* (by unit or dollar) and *share of market*.

Advertising Objectives Advertising objectives are not the same as marketing objectives. They state the effect of the message on the prospect. They are *communication objectives*, rather than sales objectives, and describe the impact you hope to have with a message.

Formulas A number of formulas exist to help with the task of setting objectives. Probably the most famous is one known as AIDA. It describes four steps in the buying process: *attention, interest, desire,* and *action.* DAGMAR

HEIRARCHY-OF-EFFECTS FORMULAS

AIDA	DAGMAR	Think-feel-do
Attention	Awareness	Cognitive
Interest	Comprehension	Awareness
Desire	Conviction	Knowledge
Action	Action	Affective
		Liking
		Preference
		Conative
		Conviction
		Purchase

(defining *a*dvertising goals for *m*easured *a*dvertising results) proposes a set of steps that include awareness, comprehension, conviction, and action. These terms should be familiar to you from our discussion of the psychology of advertising in the previous chapter.

Think-feel-do model. Another approach, called the "think-feel-do" model, identifies six steps in the buying process: awareness, knowledge, liking, preference, conviction, and purchase. These six levels are grouped into three basic categories of *cognitive* (the intellectual, mental, or rational state), *affective* (the emotional or feeling state), and *conative* (the striving, deciding, or action state).

FCB model. Another view of advertising effects was developed at Foot, Cone & Belding. The FCB model[2] includes elements of the "think-feel-do" model arrayed against a low-involvement–high-involvement dimension. The idea is that there isn't a standard buying process or hierarchy that all people move through. Instead the steps vary with the product category and medium. The resulting matrix can be used to analyze objectives in terms of product categories, media, message strategies, and testing methods.

THE FCB MODEL

	Thinking	Feeling
Hi Involve	**1.** Informative (thinking) Model: think-feel-do Products: car, house Creative: demonstration, specific details	**2.** Affective (feeling) Model: feel-think-do Products: jewelry, cosmetics Creative: execution impact
Lo Involve	**3.** Habit formation (doing) Model: do-think-feel Products: liquor, household items Creative: reminder	**4.** Self-satisfaction (reacting) Model: do-feel-think Products: cigarettes, liquor, candy, gum Creative: attention

---

The ads for Spiegels, Mallards, Hush Puppies, and Ralph Lauren demonstrate how a common product like shoes can be approached in a variety of different ways. Mallards provides information about features of the shoe. The Hush Puppies ad relies on executional impact to develop an affective response. (In the ad the bassett hound's toenails are painted the pastel colors of the sandals.) The Ralph Lauren shoe is strictly a reminder image ad and serves as a "habit formation" example. Spiegel uses lifestyle association to get attention, illustrating the "self-satisfaction category (see Exhibit 4-2).

Exhibit 4-2: The ads for shoes on pages 56–58 illustrate different ways to approach the same product. Hush Puppies uses soft humor to create impact. (The puppy has colored toenails to match the colors in the shoes.) Polo is strictly an image ad and functions as a reminder. Mallard focuses on features, and Spiegel uses a celebrity association to make people feel good.

Exhibit 4-2: continued

Advertising Effects

Objectives can also be built on what is known about the way advertising works. The areas of perception, education, and persuasion provide most of the objectives you will see specified for advertising. (For professionals, effective communication is a *characteristic* of advertising rather than a *goal*.)

The idea behind the following model, based on those three categories, is that advertising affects many different areas of the heart and mind, all simultaneously but to different degrees. When you plan your advertising message, you have to decide which of these effects are the most important to you. The chart below outlines typical objectives that can be constructed by thinking through what you know about how advertising works.

FRAMEWORK FOR ADVERTISING OBJECTIVES

Perception	Education	Persuasion
Attention Create awareness of product, brand, ad **Interest** Create concern, excitement **Memory** Recognize ad, image, slogan, logo, copy points, position Recognize brand, product Recall ad, image, slogan, logo, copy points, position Recall brand	**Learning** Register claim, features, selling premise Associate product with logo, slogan, theme, key visual, jingle, lifestyle, image, mood Establish position Reposition Comprehend selling premise, viewpoint Differentiate features, claims	**Emotion** Register response to appeal **Attitudes** Register positive disposition Evaluate features, claims, views positively Create preference for brand **Argument** Accept claim Reason, promise Correct false impression Challenge position, claim, viewpoint Counter facts **Behavior** Increase traffic Stimulate inquiries, trial, purchases, repurchases

---

Writing Objectives

An *objective* is a statement of goals—what the message is supposed to accomplish. The "to accomplish" phrase is the key. Your ad is supposed to ___ *do* ___ (fill in the blank). Sample phrases you might use to fill in the blank include: induce trial, sustain preference, intensify usage, create an image, increase store traffic, stimulate trial, change habits, build ambience, and build a reputation platform for the brand.

As was mentioned in our discussion of communication in Chapter 3, a good advertisement is *single-minded*; it focuses on one problem and delivers one strong message. For an advertisement it is not unusual to have just one key objective. However, an advertising *campaign*, with its variety of executions, will often have a set of objectives.

4.2 TARGET AUDIENCE

targeting: the process of identifying the most likely prospects for the product and advertising message

The objective of **targeting** is to identify the most profitable *prospects*, people who are in the market for what you have to sell or say. Not all people will use your product or service. There is a large population of *consumers* who buy products, maybe even buy products in the same category, but who are not in the market for your particular product or service.

THERE WAS A TIME WHEN THIS WAS THE ONLY WAY A WOMAN COULD GET MONEY FROM A BANK.

It's hard to believe just how difficult it once was for a woman to get a business loan or a line of credit.

Actually it wasn't difficult. It was nearly impossible.

Until we opened our doors in 1975. And forever changed the history of banking.

Today we are a successful commercial bank and half of our clients are men.

But we still express our special commitment to women through Park Avenue Select Banking, our new private banking service. It offers products, and personal attention few other banks provide. Like house calls, bill paying, and the Concierge Club.

And Swingline, a remarkable way to maximize the in-terest you earn on balances, minimize the interest you pay on loans, yet maintain ultimate flexibility with funds so that you can always respond to investment opportunities.

To find out more about this unique concept call Stacie Weiner, Vice President of Private Banking at 212-644-0670, ext. 668. She'll tell you about all the services we offer. Not only to those with established wealth, but to the dynamic, new wealthmakers. The successful professional, execu-tive, and entrepreneur.

Now you know some of the reasons we more than quadrupled our assets last year.

And why people looking for an example of the right way to do banking always hold us up.

THE FIRST WOMEN'S BANK

Member FDIC   111 East 57th Street at Park Avenue New York, NY 10022 (212) 644-0670   NYCE

Exhibit 4-3: The First Women's Bank ads target professional women who would be in the market for financial services other than just checking and saving accounts.

THERE WAS A TIME WHEN WOMEN GOT THE SAME TREATMENT FROM A BANKER.

That was before 1975, when we opened our doors. It was the first time in history that a financial institution was created by and for women.

Since then the relationship between a woman and her banker has changed forever. No matter where she banks. If she banks with us, however, she continues to benefit from fresh and creative thinking.

For example, our new private banking service, Park Avenue Select Banking, offers ideas, products, and services no other bank provides.

Like Swingline, a unique state-of-the-art cash management system that constantly monitors your account to maximize the interest you earn on balances, and minimize the interest you pay on loans. And our Concierge Club extends extraordinary perquisites to your private life.

We offer this not just to those with established wealth but to the new wealthmakers. The successful professional, executive, and entrepreneur. And we tailor our services for these exceptional, busy individuals precisely to their needs.

It's no wonder that we more than quadrupled our assets last year.

To be that successful, you have to have a good head on your shoulders.

THE FIRST WOMEN'S BANK

Member FDIC   111 East 57th Street at Park Avenue New York, NY 10022 (212) 644-0670

The process of targeting entails sorting out all the different types of consumers in the various markets and identifying people who are logical prospects. A *target market* is a group of people to whom a product is sold. A *target audience* is a group of people to whom an advertising message is directed. Marketers talk about target markets, advertisers talk about target audiences—sometimes they are the same, sometimes they aren't.

Efficiency. The underlying principle of targeting an audience is that not all people use your product or service, and, of those who do use it, not all use it to the same degree. It's a problem of efficiency: you try to reach those people who will most likely respond to your message (see Exhibit 4-3). That doesn't mean others are forbidden to hear the message or buy the product just because they aren't in the target. All you are trying to do is focus your message on your best bets. There's a rule of thumb called the 80:20 rule; it suggests that 80 percent of your products are sold to 20 percent of the market. Targeting tries to draw a circle around that 20 percent.

Demographics and psychographics. Demographics, the vital statistics about a group of people, are used to define the group. Such characteristics as age, income, education, gender, and occupation enable you to draw a circle around the group, identify their most important distinguishing characteristics, and estimate the size of the group.

But demographic information has some limitations. Two executives can work in similar jobs, earn the same salary, live in the same neighborhood, and yet drive entirely different types of cars. Why would one buy a BMW and the other buy a Chevy? To understand those differences, you have to dig into psychographics, the personal variables that combine to shape people's inner selves, such as personality, interests, opinions, values, attitudes, decision processes, and buying behaviors.

Psychographics can give you insight into more complex behavior patterns such as why one mother opts for disposable diapers while another uses cloth diapers. These differences are extremely critical to creatives because most advertising messages attempt to either reinforce or change the attitudes and belief structures of the target.

Profiles. Advertising is most believable when it is written directly to one person—a warm, living, breathing person—preferably someone you know. As John O'Toole, CEO of Foote, Cone & Belding, has said, "The way to move millions is to talk to one single person. . . . And when the chord is struck in one, the vibrations reverberate in millions."[3]

In order to think on that level, creatives take all the demographic and psychographic data and develop a *profile*, a biographic sketch, of the typical prospect. Give this person a name and, if possible, identify him or her with someone you know.

In the profile, focus on the relevant details that truly make a difference in identifying prospects. Use only those characteristics, the critical discriminating variables, that identify the common links between people in the targeted audience, those characteristics that separate them from the rest of the market.

Approaches to targeting. Usage is a common way to target a group; categories such as heavy user, medium user, low user, nonuser, and competition's user can be used to distinguish one target from another. Ge-

profile: a biographical sketch of the typical prospect in the targeted audience

ography is often used for targeting people who live in certain areas such as the Northeast, Southwest, Midwestern rural, major metropolitan areas, mountain areas, and the sun belt. Lifestyle and interests can be used to identify groups such as yuppies, young mothers, nature lovers, music lovers, computer freaks, and international travelers.

Some creatives maintain a photo file of thousands of people in order to make the task of profiling more intimate. They go through the file until they find a picture of the "typical person," then they develop a personality to go with the picture. What moves this person, what appeals to him or her, what does he or she scorn or value, how does this person make decisions, what does he or she understand or not understand? Then they keep that picture above their typewriter when they start to write.

segments: subgroups within a larger market or targeted audience

Segments. Within the targeted group of prospects, there may also be individual **segments**—smaller groups of people with different patterns of needs. Sometimes these groups are identified as the primary or secondary audience—frequent business travelers, for example, would be a segment of the corporate executive market.

For another example of slicing up a market, consider the athletic shoe market. There are different shoes for people who jog, play tennis or basketball, and do aerobics. On top of that different brands target different segments. Reebok is known as the fashion shoe, Adidas ties in with professional athletes, and Avia has used a strange advertising campaign that tells people not to buy its shoes if they drink, smoke, or are otherwise unfit to wear the company's high-tech athletic shoes. Apparently only superjocks are wanted as customers.

Another type of segmentation based on *personality* has been developed by the Stanford Research Institute (SRI) called the Value and Lifestyle System (VALS).[4] The model describes four basic types of consumer groups: the need-driven, the outer-directed, the inner-directed, and the integrateds. There also are subcategories within these categories.

benefit segmentation: a type of segmentation that separates people into groups based on how a product serves their specific needs

Benefit segmentation. Segmentation strategies can also be based on the *benefits* different types of users receive from a product. **Benefit segmentation** identifies groups based on the specific appeals to which they respond.

Toothpaste advertisers, for example, know that different people buy different brands for different reasons. One consumer is interested in antiplaque features, another is looking for fluoride, someone else is concerned with the flavor, while yet another prefers a toothpaste that whitens the teeth or cleans the breath. Different brands of toothpaste are positioned to speak to these different needs (see Exhibit 4-4). Viadent is a relatively new brand that specializes in plaque removal. Gleem's campaign focuses on whitening: "Teeth aren't white until they gleem." Colgate's ad for its new decorator pumps sells toothpaste as a bathroom accessory. Crest has even developed a Crest for Kids.

4.3 PROBLEM IDENTIFICATION

From your preliminary discussions with the client you should have some general idea what problem needs to be solved with the advertising. Advertising is rarely done just because the client has money to throw around.

Exhibit 4-4: Colgate's Tartar Control Formula is an example of a niche created in the highly segmented toothpaste market.

Usually there's a *need* for advertising, and that need should give you a clue to the problem you have to solve with your advertising message. There's no sense throwing darts at the wall if the bull's-eye is invisible.

Advertising Problem

The *problem statement* should focus on an *advertising problem*, something in the marketing situation that you can solve with advertising. There may be a distribution problem, but that is not something you can solve with advertising. On the other hand, if the consumers see your product as high-priced when it really isn't, or if it is high-priced but it is also a great value, then those are problems that can be solved with an advertising message.

You might also want to remember that the focus is on the product's problem, not your own personal problem in doing this assignment. Don't approach the problem statement in terms of what *you* have to do; for example, don't say to yourself, "The problem is to make this ad exciting and attention-getting." That's your challenge as a professional, it's not a problem in the marketplace that your product has to face.

Marketing Situation

Category. The problem might be analyzed by looking at the marketing situation. For example, different types of product categories require different message strategies. Characteristics of the product category can create communication problems; for example, it's very difficult to get consumers to pay attention to unpleasant product categories like feminine hygiene products and corn plasters.

Differentiation. Product differentiation is a typical problem faced by many products in today's competitive marketplace. When products are differentiated—in other words, there are major differences between brands—then advertising's problem is to dramatize the uniqueness and differences. With undifferentiated products, where there are few differences between brands, advertising's problem is to establish a unique and powerful image for the product.

An example of an advertisement that tries to differentiate its product is one for Mrs. Paul's Light and Natural Fish. The headline says: "Presenting fish fillets for people who would rather eat fish than bread crumbs." The body copy explains that Mrs. Paul's fish has more fish and less breading.

Most frozen fish fillets have about 50% fish and 50% breading.

But not Mrs. Paul's Light and Natural Fish Fillets.

We start with a higher quality, more expensive cut of fish that's twice as thick and three times as big as an ordinary fillet.

Then, each piece is prepared with a thin, crunchy bread crumb coating, which gives you 40% less breading, and more fish in every bite.

Life cycle. The product's stage of market development, or life cycle, may create problems. New products have to inform people who may be totally unaware of the need for such a product. A mature market may be highly cluttered with many competitive messages, so the problem is to break through the noise. The consumer can be the source of the problem; for example, computer software has to be handled one way for knowledgeable computer experts and in an entirely different way for new users.

Loyalty. Brand loyalty is another factor that gives clues to the advertising problem. Brand-loyal customers are a brand's most important target. They are, however, under constant bombardment from your competitors, who would like to steal your product's market share by enticing them to switch.

Consumer problems. The most fertile problem area centers around the consumer; consumer problems with the product or category should emerge from your background research. Joel Raphaelson, executive creative director at Ogilvy & Mather, says, "The creative process should concentrate on defining the problem accurately and finding a precise solution."[5]

Dustbuster®, for example, looked at the problems consumers encounter when cleaning. One problem is dragging out the bulky vacuum cleaner—something most people don't want to do any more frequently than they have to. A multipage ad for Dustbuster® began with the curiosity-arousing question: "Why wait a week to pick up on the latest dirt?" On the following double-page spread, the headline read, "What you need is a Dustbuster®. The vacuum for the other 6 days."

BBDO agency uses a technique called "problem detection" to develop a list of potential consumer problems related to a product.[6] The second step is to cull the list down to "the big problem" by asking consumers if the problem is important, whether it occurs frequently, and whether the solution to the problem has been offered by some other product or service.

BBDO staff criticize traditional attribute/benefit studies because they tell you only what consumers have been hearing in other advertising. For example, attribute/benefits studies of the dog food market find that consumers identify "balanced diet," "good nutrition," and "contains vitamins" as the three most wanted attributes. In contrast, BBDO research, using problem detection methods, found that the three biggest consumer problems were: "it smells bad," "it costs too much," and "it doesn't come in different sizes for different dogs." Ads based on solving consumer problems consistently outscore ads that address attributes.

4.4 PRODUCT POSITION

position: the way in which a product is perceived by the consumer in a competitive market situation

How do consumers view the product or service that you are trying to advertise? How do they view your competitors' products? A product's **position** is the consumer's perception of your product as it exists in the competitive marketplace.

Jack Trout and Al Ries, who developed the concept of positioning, point to a classic example of a successful positioning strategy in the Avis "We try harder" campaign. It positioned Avis as "number 2" but made that position a symbol for drive and hard work, the appealing position of the underdog.[7] Another example of positioning warfare is in the cola marketplace. Pepsi is positioned as the cola for young people and young adults—the "Pepsi Generation." The implied position forced upon Coca-Cola, as a result of Pepsi's strategy, is the cola for older people.

SAMPLE PRODUCT POSITIONS

- Crest is positioned as the fluoride toothpaste.
- Pepsi is positioned as the cola for young-minded people.
- BMW is positioned as the car for upscale consumers who appreciate fine automotive engineering.
- Saab is positioned as the thinking person's car.
- Ivory is positioned as the natural soap that is pure and free from irritating additives.
- Lava is positioned as the tough soap that gets rid of tough dirt.
- Oil of Olay is positioned as a medium-priced moisturizer for women who are older or worried about getting older.

Positioning strategies.   Your goal in strategy development is to identify your current position, if you are an existing product, and then decide if it is clearly focused or if it needs to be changed. The biggest problem for most products and services is lack of focus. If the product is new, then you will be *establishing* a position. If it has been around for a while, then you will *focus, reinforce,* or *change* the existing position, a process called *repositioning.* You have to know both where you are and where you want to be in order to develop a positioning strategy.

Much of the success of the new product Softsoap, which also introduced a new category of liquid soap to the consumer market, lies with its position.[8] The president of the company explained that Softsoap was positioned as "eliminating messy bar soap." He says that strategy didn't meet with a lot of enthusiasm because everybody said eliminating messy bar soap wasn't a proprietary position. In other words, everybody who produces liquid soap can use that position. It worked because, while other liquid soaps could claim that position, no one else had. Softsoap got there first and was able to "own" the position. That is called **preemptive advertising**; you stake out the claim first.

A position is a bundle of impressions that include product features and personality as well as comparisons with other products. In order to better understand this complex concept, let's look at some of the pieces.

Product personality.   As part of the development of a position, and also a brand image, products take on distinct personalities (see Exhibit 4-5). For example, Oxy-5 is a no-nonsense acne cleanser, Camay is a delicate complexion soap, and Ivory is a natural and pure product. All these personalities were created by advertising.

The Bloom agency has developed a concept called "personality description model" (PDM) to create consistent, effective brand messages.[9] PDM is a description of the product as if it were a person with a human personality. The following is an example of a PDM created for Southwest Airlines:

> She is probably somewhere between 20 and 25 years old and looks somewhat younger, perhaps 18 to 20. She is charming and goes through life with great flair and exuberance.
> The first thing you notice about her is her exciting smile, her friendly air, her wit. In reality, she is quite efficient, and approaches all her tasks

preemptive advertising: a type of advertising that is first to stake a claim to a common attribute or position that any of the competition could otherwise have used

They've lettered in the Big Ten, and spent Sundays in the NFL. Now they're available for your own personal fitness program.

For many of you, working out is serious business. So before we chose the workout clothing for our catalog, we gave serious thought to what good sweats should be.

They should be heavy enough to hug you with warmth, and hold up for years. They should be comfortable in action not just for the first few months, but for the life of the garment. And, of course, they should be cotton. Not for us the flimsy, fashiony synthetic options.

To make sure our "Serious Sweats" are all these things and more, we go direct to Champion, America's foremost maker of cotton sweats for college and professional teams.

Champion makes our sweats of a heavyweight, 90% cotton fleece that breathes away moisture to keep you cool. And readily survives the rough and tumble of machine washing (even <u>daily</u> machine washing).

Even the best sweats shrink, but...
Our "Serious Sweats" control this errant tendency with an oversized cut, and Champion's unique Reverse Weave* construction that minimizes the vertical shrinkage that plagues conventionally-made cotton sweats. So "Serious Sweats" maintain their generous, comfortable fit for as long as you wear them.

Perhaps that's why the real experts, equipment managers for both pro and college teams, swear by these "Serious Sweats" by Champion. A typical quote from one at a major university: "The best Sweats made in America, period. All our teams here use them."

Is it any wonder we call them the "Serious Sweats" from Lands' End?

We're serious about everything we offer you.
Our catalogs detail for you in living color all the wonderful, useful items we have to offer—every one of them subject to <u>quality</u> standards rigidly maintained. Then subjected to a realistic struggle with <u>price</u>, to make sure the end result is <u>value</u> for the customer. All this, plus relentless attention to service and the industry's most challenging guarantee—our two-word, no-holds-barred assurance:

GUARANTEED. PERIOD.

Send for our free catalog today. Better still, dial our toll-free number (800-356-4444) and find out what it means to talk to a friendly, helpful Lands' End operator—your key to the full Lands' End experience.

The sooner you get in touch, the sooner you can get in shape in just the right size of "Serious Sweats" for you.

The "Serious Sweats" from Lands' End

LANDS' END
DIRECT MERCHANTS

Please send free catalog.
Lands' End   Dept. J-090
Dodgeville, WI 53595

Name _____
Address _____
City _____
State _____ Zip _____

Or call Toll-free:
800-356-4444

Exhibit 4-5: The "Serious Sweats" ad establishes a strong personality for this line of exercise clothes by Lands' End.

with care and attention. However, because of her dynamic personality, her efficiency is not obvious, and is generally taken for granted.

She is friendly and warm. Her hobbies are most likely horseback riding, swimming, and metal sculpture.

features: product attributes that are important enough to be emphasized in the advertising

Feature analysis. Products have attributes, as well as personalities, and some of these attributes are important enough to the consumer to be emphasized in advertising. These are called product **features**. Furthermore some are distinctive features—in other words, the competition doesn't have them. Parity products, of course, have few distinctive features.

Feature analysis is the process of analyzing all the features in terms of which ones are the most important to your target and how distinctive they are to your product. Ernest Dichter, a psychoanalyst and the father of motivation research, tells an interesting story about the product features of coffee: "If you ask people what is the most important thing to them about coffee, they'll tell you it's the aroma or consistency or body. Hardly a single person will say color. So we brewed colorless coffee. Nobody wanted to try it, or if they did, they said it was terrible."[10]

With feature analysis you are analyzing your product in terms of two important decision variables: (1) relevance to target, and (2) distinctiveness in the marketplace. These also are important pieces of the position held in a consumer's mind. Ideally your advertising strategy will emphasize some feature that is both important to the target as well as distinctive to your product. The chart below illustrates how a feature analysis might be set up.

FEATURE ANALYSIS FOR A RAINCOAT

Feature	Importance to target	Distinctiveness
Style	10	7
Price	9	2
Durability	5	2
Construction	6	3
Liner	7	0
Waterproofing	8	9
Colors	7	5

Competitive advantage. The next step in developing a positioning strategy is to analyze the competitive situation. Not all potential competitors are equally important. Some are unassailable, while others are vulnerable. What you are searching for is the area where your product has an advantage over the competition. This is a form of targeting, although you are now targeting the competition rather than the consumer.

To do competitive targeting, do a version of feature analysis, except this time include the competition's products and compare on the basis of *performance* as well as importance and distinctiveness (see Exhibit 4-6). Performance means how well your product does on this dimension compared to the competition—is it tops, in the middle, or at the bottom?

Exhibit 4-6: The J.C. Penney advertisement positions the "fox" against the more expensive "alligator." (J.C. Penney Advertising Department. Copy: Rose Baker. Art director: Toby Aurilia)

COMPETITIVE ADVANTAGE FOR ICE CREAM BAR

Feature	Importance	Your product perform.	Your product distinct.	Competitor A perform.	Competitor A distinct.
Taste	10	8	5	9	6
Size	7	7	4	5	5
Price	6	7	7	4	6
Flavors	8	8	8	4	3
Nutrition	5	5	5	7	8

Contrast your product's distinctive features and performance with the competitor's features and performance, and then compare all sets of features with the wants and needs of your target. From this analysis of features, performance, and needs, you should be able to see, in fact, who is your most direct—and most vulnerable—competitor.

You may find that the direct competition may, in fact, be the strongest marketer in the field. It's very difficult to steal market share from an entrenched leader. Look for signs of vulnerability among your competitors; you may be stronger than your competition on features that are important to the consumer. Build your strategy on the features that emphasize this competitive advantage. The chart above demonstrates how to analyze competitive advantage.

Perceptual mapping. It is not easy to draw a picture of consumer perceptions. Typically a product or service will have a complex image with a variety of strengths and weaknesses. A positioning study is done

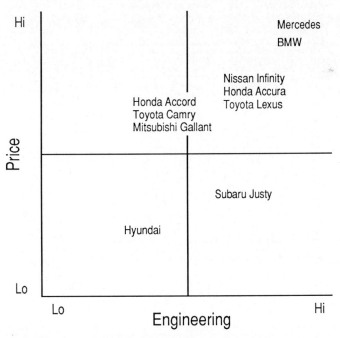

Figure 4-1: A perceptual map of import car positions on the factors of price and quality of engineering. (Reprinted from the *Journal of Advertising Research.* © Copyright 1987, by the Advertising Research Foundation)

by trying to determine what consumers consider to be the most important features or decision factors.[11] In other words, you have to focus in on several key features—probably those of most importance to the consumer. You can evaluate your product and your competition along a single dimension; however, most positioning research uses two factors to get a better picture of the competitive situation.

For example, you might find in the automotive market that price and engineering are the two most important factors. Then you would ask a group of typical prospects to rate all the cars they consider on those two factors. Figure 4-1 shows the results of a hypothetical **perceptual map**, a chart that displays the relative positions, for this market.

perceptual map: a matrix that shows how your product compares with the competition on the basis of several critical variables

There are many ways to do these perceptual tests. You may want to plot your product and its competitors on the basis of some critical variables (see Figure 4-1). You can also map various features in terms of their importance to the target audience (see Figure 4-2). You can also plot various products according to how they are perceived by consumers. Figure 4-3 compares 60 different products on the two dimensions of involvement and think-feel.[12]

Developing a sound and logical positioning strategy for a product is not easy. A successful position is not communicated using a mouthful of marketing jargon. It can't be complex and multifaceted. A position statement is short, usually a phrase, and it is expressed in natural language focusing on critical distinctive features (for example, "the easiest to use," "the biggest or brightest picture," or "the most lifelike sound").

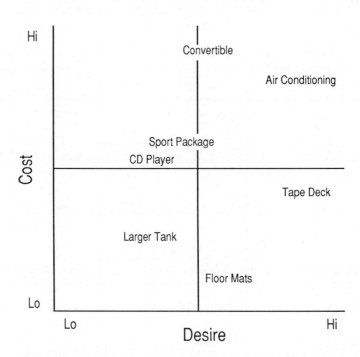

Figure 4-2: A perceptual map of automobile features on the factors of cost and desirability. (Reprinted from the *Journal of Advertising Research.* © Copyright, 1987, by the Advertising Research Foundation)

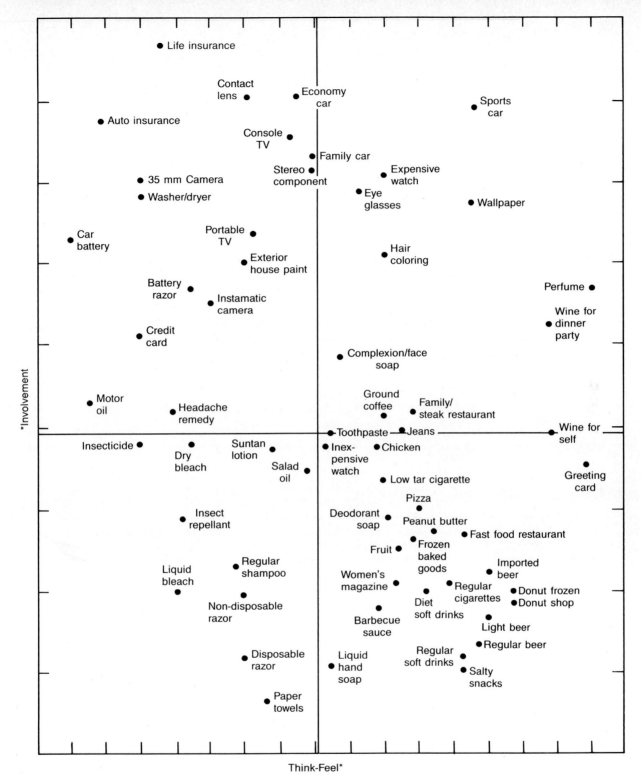

*Involvement

Think-Feel*

*Numbers are scale values × 100.

Figure 4-3: This map of 60 common products locates them on the involvement and think-feel dimensions of the FCB grid. (Reprinted from the *Journal of Advertising Research*. © Copyright 1987, by the Advertising Research Foundation)

The test of a position is to ask your prospects, after the ad is run, how they see the product. You want them to respond with something like the phrase you have developed for the product's position. Will they respond with your phrase? Would they actually say that? It has to be something simple, single-minded, and distinctive.

SUMMARY

This chapter discussed four elements of advertising strategy: targeting, problem statements, objectives, and positioning.

1. Objectives state communication goals—what you hope to accomplish with your advertising message.
2. Targeting uses demographics and psychographics to identify the prospects that will respond the best to the advertising.
3. Segmenting is used to slice the market into smaller, more closely knit groups.
4. The problem can be located in the marketplace, the competitive situation, the product's life cycle, or the minds of the consumers.
5. A product's position is in the mind of the consumer. It is based on the product's personality and image, distinctive features, competitive advantage.
6. Perceptual mapping is used to plot how consumers compare products, features, and positions.

NOTES

1. Harvey Bailey, "The Copywriter's Biggest Job," *Adweek*, March 15, 1982, p. 30.
2. Richard Vaughn, "How Advertising Works: A Planning Model," *Journal of Advertising Research*, 20:5 (October 1980), pp. 27–33.
3. John E. O'Toole, "Are Grace Slick and Tricia Nixon Cox the Same Person?" *Journal of Advertising*, 3:3 (1973), pp. 32–34.
4. Philip H. Dougherty, "New Way to Classify Consumers," *New York Times*, February 25, 1981, p. 16.
5. Joel Raphaelson, "Creatives Take a Look at the Creative Process," *Advertising Age*, June 4, 1979, pp. 5, 19.
6. E. E. Norris, "Seek Out the Consumer's Problem," *Advertising Age*, March 17, 1975, pp. 43–44.
7. Jack Trout and Al Ries, *Positioning: The Battle for Your Mind* (New York: McGraw-Hill, 1981).
8. Rebecca Fannin, "Hard Sell for Soft Soap," *Marketing and Media Decisions*, October 1980, pp. 66–67; Steve Raddock, "Now He Sings in the Shower," *Marketing and Media Decisions*, Spring 1982, pp. 123–131.
9. "Product Personality Will Help Ads," *Advertising Age*, October 11, 1976, p. 89.
10. Katherine Barrett and Richard Greene, "Work Motivates Psychoanalyst," *Advertising Age*, November 1, 1984, pp. 43–48.
11. Hugh J. Devine, Jr., and John Morton, "How Does the Market Really See Your Product? Diagnosing Your Product Position with Perceptual Mapping," *Business Marketing*, July 1984, pp. 70–79.
12. Brian T. Ratchford, "New Insights about the FCB Grid," *Journal of Advertising Research*, August/September 1987, pp. 24–38.

5

Copy Platforms

KEY POINTS

- A copy platform is a document that outlines the strategy behind an advertisement.
- Creative, or message, strategy focuses on *what* you will say to the targeted audience about the product or service.
- Appeals state the human need the advertisement addresses.
- Advertising tends to be divided between rational/informational and emotional/image.
- Five basic creative approaches center on: argument, information, image, emotion, and entertainment.
- Selling premises state the logic of the sales message.

copy platform: the document used to outline the strategy behind an advertisement

The **copy platform** is a document used in most agencies to outline the creative strategy. It is used for preliminary discussion, debate, and compromise. Not all agencies use a document like this, and some that call their planning document by a different name such as a "work plan," or "blueprint." Some develop a brief statement, while others prepare a manuscript complete with discussion and justification. Generally, however, some kind of document is used during the planning stage to make sure everyone agrees on the approach.

The first elements in a copy plan are the basic advertising decisions discussed in the previous chapter—objectives, target audience, problem statement, and product position. This chapter will focus on the decisions involved in developing the advertising message itself, such as the appeal, main message, selling premise, and execution format.

5.1 APPEALS

appeal: something that moves people, speaks to their needs, and excites their interest

Some professionals in advertising like to refer to the appeal of an ad as a way to describe how the ad moves, motivates, attracts, or interests its viewer. An **appeal** is a message about a need that has the power to arouse innate or latent desires.

For example, a business ad for Epson printers speaks to computer users addressing a familiar problem: "It was always so frustrating. Changing from continuous paper to single sheets. Or envelopes. But not anymore. Not since I got my Epson LQ-1050. It changes the paper as fast as I can change my mind." Epson has put its finger on the need of this target for an easy-to-use, convenient paper-changing system. And anyone who has wrestled with changing paper in a computer printer knows exactly what the problem is.

Human Needs

Advertising messages speak to human needs. Those needs usually are depicted in a hierarchy. As described by Abraham Maslow,[1] they start with the most basic survival needs at the bottom and proceed up the ladder to the more individualized and personal needs such as self-expression (see Figure 5-1).

What is important for you to remember is that the lower-level needs must be fulfilled before you can move on to the higher-order ones. There is no sense promoting expensive jogging shoes to a mother with six kids who can barely afford to buy one cheap pair of sneakers per child. Also, the needs at the bottom are the most universal, while the ones at the top are the most individualized. Mass marketing speaks to broad universal needs, while highly specialized and narrowly targeted products tend to use more individualized appeals (see Exhibit 5-1).

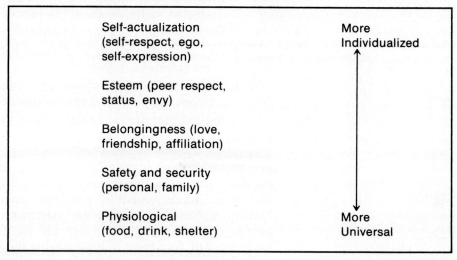

Figure 5-1: Maslow's Hierarchy of Needs.

Common Advertising Appeals

Hundreds of appeals are used in advertising; however, some are more common than others. Professionals often refer to the ad's basic appeal when they are presenting a strategy. They will say something like: "We're

Exhibit 5-1: The Michelin tires ad with its picture of a lovable baby illustrates an appeal to family love and safety. (Used with permission of Michelin Tire Corporation. All rights reserved)

using an economy appeal here" or, "This is an appeal to convenience" or, "We're aiming at appetite appeal."

For example, an ad for Morningstar Farms Scramblers uses a health appeal. The headline says, "Why eat your heart out?," followed by "Lower your dietary cholesterol now with good-tasting Scramblers, the yokeless egg." An ad for Aramis men's products appeals to the longing for eternal youth with this headline for its Anti-Aging Supplement: "It can make a man's skin firmer, smoother, and younger looking in 3 weeks."

The following list contains most of the basic appeals used in advertising. You can see how these appeals are used in advertising if you watch an evening's worth of commercials or page through one issue of a magazine. The emotional appeals, in particular, are what those in the advertising industry refer to as "hot buttons," because they speak to powerful human responses. Watch for such lines as "Bake someone happy" (family affection), "Happiness is a Met Life security blanket" (security), "Your Wind Song stays on my mind" (romance), and "You are never too rich or too thin" (wealth and health).

ADVERTISING'S BASIC APPEALS

- Acquisitiveness: money, possessions, materialism, getting rich
- Aesthetics: pleasing, appreciation of the beautiful
- Appetite: hunger, taste, cravings
- Affiliation: belonging to a group
- Aspiration: achievement, accomplishment, self-fulfillment
- Attractiveness
- Avoidance
- Cleanliness
- Comfort
- Convenience: saving time and effort, ease of use
- Economy: saving time, money
- Efficiency
- Egoism: recognition, approval, pride, status, prestige
- Emotional appeals
    Excitement
    Fear: danger, personal embarrassment
    Family: love, protection
    Guilt
    Love: affection, romance, companionship
    Nostalgia
    Pleasure: humor, happiness, joy, laughter, amusement
    Poignancy
    Pride
    Relief
    Sorrow: grief, suffering
- Health
- Identification: respect, hero worship, role models
- Luxury
- Mental stimulation: curiosity, challenge, involvement
- Patriotism
- Responsibility
- Safety and security
- Sensory pleasure: touch, taste, smell, sound, sight
- Sex
- Thriftiness

5.2 CREATIVE STRATEGY

Advertising strategy is based on such things as target audience, objectives, and positioning. Creative strategy focuses on the message itself—what you will say and how you will say it. We'll review a number of terms used in advertising to describe these decisions. They describe the basic, or most common, approaches used in deciding both the main message and the execution.

Product/Prospect   Does the approach focus on the product and talk about attributes and features? If so, that's considered a product-centered approach. Announcements about new products and product formulations are typical examples of this style of advertising, as are performance claims.

If the approach centers on the prospect and focuses on consumer needs and benefits, then it's a *prospect-centered approach*. Another type of prospect-centered advertising focuses on users and their lifestyles.

Head/Heart   Another way to talk about approaches to creative strategy is to differentiate between ads that are *rational* (factional, informational, logical) and speak to the head and those that are *emotional* (images, feelings) and speak to the heart. This is not the same distinction that we discussed in product/ prospect advertising. A prospect-centered advertisement, for example, can be either rational or emotional.

Rational.   There have always been these two schools of thought— the head and the heart—about advertising strategy. Bruce Stauderman explained the rational school: "One school says, 'give the consumer a logical, convincing argument for the product.'" According to the Rosser Reeves and John Caples school of advertising, an ad should be *informative*. Rational advertising, then, is built on facts and reasons—information and logic.

An example of a straight informational ad is one for Mercury that starts out: "The 68 standard features of new Mercury Tracer." The body copy is a straightforward list of the 68 features, which demonstrates the point that many of the features are standard on this American car, a position previously owned by foreign makes.

Emotional/image.   The other school is that of image advertising, which doesn't barrage the consumer with words, facts, or claims. Stauderman explains that many products are purchased for *emotional* reasons.[2] Rather than marshalling facts, we should create a *feeling* and a strong *brand image* (see Exhibit 5-2). Emotional approaches intend to excite feelings such as love, anger, hate, joy, fear, or sorrow. A classic example of emotional advertising is N. W. Ayer's famous campaign for Bell Telephone long distance, "Reach out and touch someone."

Hal Riney, who is head of his own agency and the creative genius behind the Bartles & Jaymes campaign, observes that most products and services don't really have anything to say that distinguishes them from the competition: "Most of the time the facts haven't done me a lot of good." He continues, "We're asking advertising to depend too much on the rational, and much less, or not at all, on the *effective* element of our business, which is emotion. The rational element is often merely what people use to justify emotional decisions. Knowing when and how to use emotion is the most important part of an advertising person's job."[3]

While emotional advertising can be extremely moving, its biggest problem is that the product or selling message can get lost when the message is too compelling and the product isn't tightly embedded in the emotional release. The product or service shouldn't be an afterthought.

Stauderman concludes that both schools are right in their own way. Beyond that, he says, there is a third school, so far small in size, that

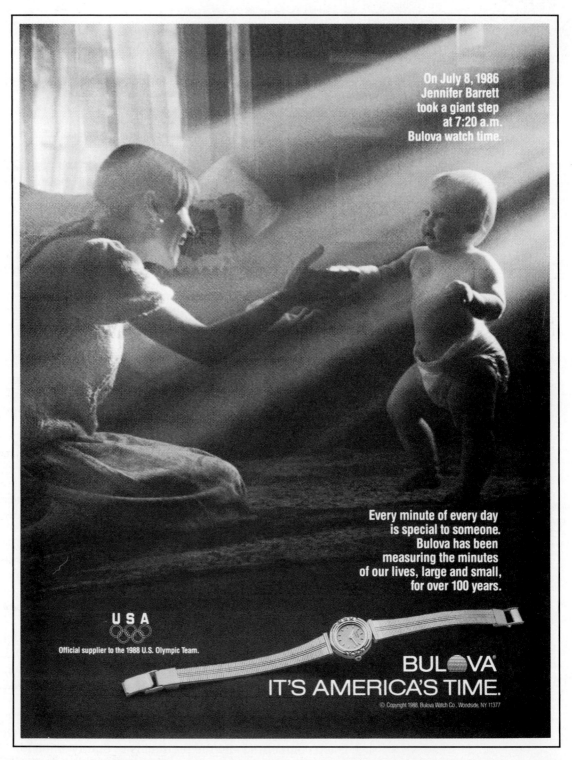

Exhibit 5-2: The "baby's first step" ad for Bulova highlights the brand's unique and emotional importance to America—in support of the brand's position: "Bulova, it's America's time."

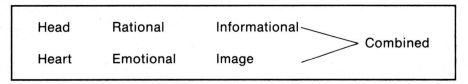

Figure 5-2: Advertising, combining head and heart.

realizes that rational and emotional are not warring competitors but allies that can work together (see Figure 5-2).

Frazer's Strategies

Another author, Charles Frazer of the University of Colorado, developed a more complex set of seven categories to describe the thrust of a creative strategy.[4] This list is particularly useful because the message strategies are categorized in terms of their relevant marketing situations. In other words, you can analyze the situation you are in and from that decide which type of message strategy or approach makes sense.

FRAZER'S CREATIVE STRATEGIES

1. **Generic:** makes no effort at differentiation; claims could be made by any in the market; used in monopolistic situations
2. **Preemptive:** uses a common attribute or benefit but gets there first; forces competition into "me too" positions; used in categories with little differentiation or in new product categories
3. **Unique selling proposition:** uses a distinct differentiation in attributes that creates a meaningful consumer benefit; appropriate in categories with relatively high levels of technological improvement
4. **Brand image:** uses a claim of superiority or distinction based on extrinsic factors such as psychological differences in the minds of consumers; used with homogeneous, low-technology goods with little physical differentiation
5. **Positioning:** establishes a place in the consumer's mind relative to the competition; suited to new entries or small brands that want to challenge the market leaders
6. **Resonance:** uses situations, lifestyles, and emotions that the target audience can identify with; used with highly competitive, nondifferentiated product categories
7. **Anomalous/affective:** uses an emotional, sometimes even ambiguous, message to break through indifference and charge the product's perception; used where competitors are playing it straight

---

Main Message Strategies

Another way to look at these creative strategies is to focus on what has been called the "main message," the central idea behind what is being said by the advertisement. This classification scheme was presented in a *Journal of Advertising* article and tested by professional researchers who used the labels to categorize television commercials. The scheme is split into two categories: informational and transformational. Within both of those are additional categories.[5]

MAIN MESSAGE STRATEGIES

- Informational advertising
  Comparative: competition explicitly mentioned
  Unique selling proposition: explicit claim of uniqueness
  Preemptive: testable claim of superiority based on an attribute or
     benefit
  Hyperbole: untestable claim of superiority
  Generic: focus on product class
- Transformational advertising
  User image: focus on user
  Brand image: focus on brand personality
  Use occasion: focus on usage occasions
  Generic: focus on product class

The AIIEE Strategies   You can use any of the categories discussed above to talk about the basic approach you want to use with your advertising. What you are looking for is a handle, a way to describe the central thrust of your creative strategy.

This author uses a set of five broad approaches to describe the general orientation of most advertisements. From the rational category come the two approaches of *argument* and *information*; the two categories of *image* and *emotion* are treated separately; and a new category that hasn't been discussed yet is *entertainment*. The initials AIIEE can help you remember these five basic approaches.

AIIEE STRATEGIES

- **Argument**: uses logic to develop a selling premise
- **Information**: presents a straightforward statement of fact, an assertion
- **Image**: uses association to establish identification of the brand with a
  lifestyle or type of person
- **Emotion**: attempts to touch feelings
- **Entertainment**: grabs and holds attention by presenting amusing, in-
  teresting messages

Argument.   An argument strategy uses logic to develop a selling premise. This logic-based strategy is for complex messages that demand that the audience "follow through" to reach a conclusion. It is used with major purchases, like cars, and high-involvement products that have distinct differences. It is often used in competitive situations.

If your research identifies a major consumer problem, then it might be appropriate to focus on that and use a *problem-solution* message format, which is a type of argument strategy. With this approach the consumer

Exhibit 5-3: The "heavy traffic" ad for Volvo is a dramatic demonstration of the car's safety, durability, and quality engineering.

is usually stumped by some situation, and the product comes to the rescue and solves the problem. It's a strong approach because the product is tightly woven into the logic of the message—the *product as hero*.

An example of problem-solution advertising is found in an ad by American Express targeted tightly at one segment of the market—the young businesswoman. The headline asks: "How will you pay for your first business lunch?" The copy answers: "With American Express of course—your first business card. Because having the Card says a lot about your understanding of the business world. Even if you're only getting started in it."

Information. Strategies that present straightforward information include news announcements, assertions, claims, and performance tests. This approach is often used to announce new products and improved product features. It is also used in highly competitive categories to announce test findings.

Examples of straightforward, informational headlines include: "Anacin, the ingredients three out of four doctors recommend"; "Excedrin is the extra-strength pain reliever"; and "Chevrolet Caprice, one of the 'Ten Best Cars,' foreign or domestic."

Demonstration is an informational technique used to teach "how-to" information. It is particularly effective when there is curiosity and suspense. Torture tests are dramatic demonstrations. *Before-and-after* or *side-by-side comparisons* are also informative (see Exhibit 5-3).

The DDB Needham agency developed a great demonstration for All-Temperature Cheer to demonstrate its cold water capabilities. The announcer wiped a handkerchief on something dirty, then put it in a martini shaker with some Cheer, water, and ice cubes. After shaking it like a martini, he pulled out a now clean handkerchief.

The Federal Trade Commission, and your competitors, watch demonstrations very closely to make sure they are accurate and relevant. For example, the FTC suggests that dropping a car off a 20-foot cliff to demonstrate durability is not valid. That's just not the same wear incurred by driving a car to work for five years.

Image. Advertising that uses a symbol to wrap up all the pieces of a perception into a tight, simple concept of a brand or a user is called *image advertising.* Image advertising is indirect and long-term.

Branding is the most common type of image advertising. Here a product takes on its own personality and character. This identification builds up over time through use of the brand name, package, product characters, and standardized advertising approach.

The classic example of brand-image advertising is the Marlboro Man, its message links independent thinking to cowboys, who are challenged by their environment but remain very much in control of it. It brings to mind all the old western myths of "good guys in white hats" and "hard work pays off." That's how image advertising works. It symbolizes a bundle of impressions, myths, and cultural values that can be interpreted only from the viewer's experience (see Exhibit 5-4 on pages 85 and 86).

Leo Burnett was a master of brand images. His agency developed such memorable symbols as the Jolly Green Giant, Tony the Tiger, the

Exhibit 5-4: Ralph Lauren's advertising has developed a strong brand image for his classic and timeless fashions.

Exhibit 5-4: continued

Marlboro Man, the Pillsbury Doughboy, Morris the Cat, and Charlie the Tuna. Burnett developed mythical figures that have been described as "big, nonverbal archetypes" of American culture. They are some of the most enduring images in advertising, ideas that may prove to be their owners' single most valuable property. Hal Riney is another important figure in advertising who creates strong brand images (see Exhibit 5-5).

Lifestyle, or user-image, advertising, is another type of image advertising. It focuses on people using the product, and they become models for consumer behavior. These people are usually attractive and represent a lifestyle that many people in the target audience would aspire to. Yuppies, romantic young men and women, happy families, older well-off couples—all can represent an attractive lifestyle. Phil Dusenberry is CEO of

Exhibit 5-5: Frank Bartles and Ed Jaymes are two product characters that have been highly successful establishing a strong brand image and personality for the Bartles & Jaymes wine coolers.

the BBDO agency and its creative director. Well known for his user-image advertising, Dusenberry explains that, "Rather than sanctify the product, we exalt the people who use it."[6]

Emotion. Strategies that touch feelings use emotional advertising. It is often used with parity products and products that elicit a low level of involvement or commitment. Emotion is also used with cosmetics and sentiment-producing products such as greeting cards, phone calls, and photographs.

To build up the emotion, commercials concentrate on "touching moments" and expressions. Bob Gage, art director at Doyle Dane Bernbach (now DDB Needham), says, "You have to hit 'em where their heart is. You can sell far more if you're emotional rather than intellectual. Take Polaroid. They don't sell cameras, they sell love. People take pictures of people they love."[7]

Entertainment. The last approach on our list is *entertainment*. The dictionary defines entertainment as "diverting, amusing, or absorbing." Entertainment techniques, such as dramas, comedies, and little *playlets*, are often used to switch attention from the program to the product and to charm or please the audience, as well as to catch the eye and mind of the viewer.

Production values for this type of advertising are high, particularly for television extravaganzas. Entertainment is often used with low-involvement, parity products that are frequently purchased and low in loyalty. It is a reward for the viewer for paying attention and, if it works, it makes people feel good about the product.

Television, in particular, is a form of show business. Programs are intended to be entertaining, and commercials have to compete with them. High-budget commercials, described in the industry as *spectaculars*, are used to shift audience attention from the programming to the commercial. *Song-and-dance* spectaculars like those used for Dr. Pepper compete with extravaganzas for Coke and Pepsi which use Lionel Ritchie, Michael Jackson, Madonna, and George Michael.

Humor is a technique used by advertising to be amusing. Sometimes advertisements are outrageous and uproarious, but more often the humor in advertising is soft and gentle. Humor can be effective because people like to laugh and be amused. It can create warm feelings that carry over to the product.

The problem with humor is that the idea has to be universally funny, and that's very hard to accomplish. There is another problem with humor—the funny idea may take off and leave the product behind. The audience remembers the joke but forgets the product. That's an example of "vampire creativity."

Special effect ads are a type of message format also considered in the entertainment category. This type of advertising uses some novel production technique to generate attention. In print, you will find scratch-and-sniff, pop-ups, and computer-generated music. Computer graphics, like those used for movies such as *Star Wars*, *2001*, and *Tron*, are also used in television advertising to create new, mesmerizing images.

5.3 EXECUTION FORMATS

We have been discussing general message strategies that identify the main message of an advertisement. At the same time we have also referred to various types of execution approaches—ways to present the message. There are standard *formats* used in advertising, and sometimes we refer to a creative approach in terms of "this format" or "that technique." Below is a list of specific types of commonly used formats.

EXECUTION FORMATS

- News announcement
- Problem solution
- Product as hero
- Demonstration
- Torture tests
- Song-and-dance spectaculars
- Special effects
- Before-and-after and side-by-side comparison
- Competitive comparison
- Announcer
- Dialogue/interview/conversation
- Slice of life
- Spokesperson
- Vignette

Comparative Advertising

Comparative advertising, in which one product compares itself to a competitor, provides information in an intensely competitive situation. Consumer groups and the FTC look upon comparative advertising with favor because it can provide useful price and performance information that helps consumers make rational decisions. Detractors say that comparative advertising is not good strategy because the named competitor benefits as much from the ad as your product does.

According to Stanley Tannenbaum, former chair of Kenyon & Eckhardt, there is only one marketing situation in which it makes sense to use comparative advertising, and that is when there is an established market leader and your company is either number two or up and coming. If you decide to use comparative advertising, Tannenbaum has some suggestions from K&E's experience[8]:

- Use comparison only in significant product attribute areas.
- Use comparison when there is demonstrable superiority.
- Use comparison when the major brand is perceived more positively than your brand.
- Identify but never disparage the brand leader.

- Whatever advantages you might gain by using comparison, you could lose if the brand leader is able to counterargue in a more meaningful attribute area where the leader enjoys superiority.
- Lean over backward to be fair or you may generate sympathy for the competition.
- Consumers must be able to verify the comparison; they must be able to prove it.

The *Wall Street Journal* commented on a new type of comparative advertising used by carmakers. The article described ads by Hyundai comparing itself to BMW, Acura pitting itself against the pricier Mercedes and BMW, inexpensive Subaru Justy comparing itself to the expensive Range Rover. The article called this "aspiration advertising," placing the product next to a more expensive model in hopes that the proximity to "luxe" will polish the product's image, too.[9]

Announcer/Dialogue/Conversation

Various types of spoken approaches can be used to present a message. An *announcer*, for example, can stand before the camera or speak directly to the reader about the product. An *interview* has one person asking another's views—someone who is usually an expert, an authority, or even a "typical user." The witty repartee between two sophisticated people is a conversational technique that can be used effectively. The content can be informational or humorous, or it can even develop the logic behind a sales argument.

Slice of Life

slice of life: a little piece of daily life that focuses on a problem, a doubter who has to be converted, and a product that solves the problem

One of advertising's most criticized formulas is called the **slice-of-life** commercial, in which a doubter is converted to the product. It uses a little problem-solution drama that is presented to viewers as if they are eavesdropping on a conversation. This is a common technique used by package goods manufacturers such as Colgate-Palmolive, General Foods, and Procter & Gamble.

Procter & Gamble, the company most closely associated with slice-of-life advertising, mapped out a set of guidelines for its agencies to use. "All drama is based on two elements," the P&G memo said, "conflict and resolution. Conflict is what 'hooks' the viewer; it is dynamic, out of balance and cries out for something to happen. Resolution is the force that moves the dramatic imbalance to a conclusion." P&G's memo also recommended that the conflict should be visual, such as a dirty shirt, rather than some internal state that can't be pictured.[10]

Testimonials

spokespersons: people who speak on behalf of a product

Spokespersons are used to speak on behalf of a product, usually to give some kind of a testimonial. John Caples believes strongly in the persuasive power of a good testimonial. He advised, "Include testimonials in your ads." He continued, "Some of the most successful mail order ads have been built entirely around testimonials." In addition, "Localized testimonials in local media are especially effective."[11]

There are three types of spokesperson. The product spokesperson can be an *authority figure* (doctor, dentist, Karl Malden, Bruce Jenner), a *celebrity* (George Burns, John Wayne, Catherine Deneuve), or a *satisfied product user*. The testimony itself can be a monologue, a dialogue, or a little playlet.

There are also manufactured authority figures, such as Mr. Goodwrench for car maintenance and Madge the manicurist for hand care. Some authority figures are real but relatively unknown until after their advertising campaigns—such as Lee Iacocca for Chrysler and Frank Perdue for chickens.

The key to using an authority spokesperson is to match the person to the product. If there isn't a natural link, then the authority appeal won't work. The association between Catherine Deneuve and Chanel No. 5 is obvious, and Hank Aaron is a natural for Wheaties. George Burns was not effective when he tried presenting for a catfood, because the audience found it hard to believe that he is a cat lover or that he would be involved in feeding a cat. Michael Landon, on the other hand, presents very well for Kodak because he has that "All-American family man" image that links naturally with the product's message.

Celebrities are used because they are glamorous, and it is hoped that some of the excitement and glamor will transfer to the product. One problem with celebrities is that their images overpower the product. You can remember Susan Anton and Raquel Welch, but can you remember the products they advertise?

Another problem is that celebrity activities may cause negative associations. Pepsi had to cancel a Madonna commercial after the star released a music video in which she used religious symbols in ways that many found objectionable. Bruce Willis's image as a wild party guy made him increasingly less effective as a spokesperson for Seagrams wine coolers. Mike Tyson's very public marital problems knocked him out as a product spokesperson.

The most serious problem, however, is that researchers have found that celebrity advertising is one of the lowest-scoring categories of advertising in terms of persuasiveness and product recall.

Vignette

vignette: a message that builds from a series of fast-paced images

A **vignette** technique uses pictures of different scenes and people edited together in rapid succession. It is used frequently in lifestyle or user-image advertising to illustrate variety and options within the lifestyle and soften the stereotyping. The General Electric "We bring good things to life" theme is usually presented as a series of vignettes involving different GE products in natural settings with lifestyle cues. John Hancock has a series of commercials focusing on the new "reality" of the 1980s anxiety age. It's "Real life, real answers" campaign uses dark vignettes of "real" people speaking "real" dialogue about daily cares and worries intercut with title cards giving their financial histories.[12]

5.4 SELLING PREMISES

selling premise: the logic behind the sales "pitch," the motivation to buy

A **selling premise** is the logic behind the sales "pitch," for those strategies that use a sales argument. A premise is a proposition upon which an argument is based or a conclusion is drawn. It's the content of the message that motivates the target audience to respond in some way. You can see that the term refers to the rational side of creative strategy. There may be selling premises for image or emotional advertising, but the propositions are not stated as directly and the logic that motivates the purchase is not emphasized as much. That's the difference between "hard-sell" and "soft-sell."

There are two primary categories of selling premises used in advertising: **claims**, which are product-centered, and **benefits**, which are prospect-centered. Benefits are the most important and most commonly used premises. We will discuss three types of benefits: promises, reasons-why, and unique selling propositions (USPs).

Claims

claim: an assertion, or statement of fact, about a product feature or product performance

A **claim** is an assertion, a simple statement of fact. It focuses on what the product can do or has done. It's usually a straightforward statement about a strong product feature that motivates a response from the target. An example is "New research shows Gatorade improves athletic performance."

Claim advertising is a logical approach and demands that the consumer have some latent interest in the product or product category. It can get attention, but it may not be very persuasive because it doesn't engage the prospect's needs directly the way benefit advertising does.

An ad for Canon cameras starts off with this headline: "Nobody has been able to make fine photography this simple." The ad announced the introduction of Canon's new automatic 35mm camera. Many people consider the 35mm camera difficult to use, so the statement that Canon makes fine photography simple appeals to those people who like professional-looking photographs but who don't want to mess with focusing and f stops.

The headline is a simple assertion followed by body copy that explains how simple the camera really is to operate. Most copy that is built around a strong claim in the headline is followed up by body copy that amplifies, explains, substantiates, or proves the claim.

Proof is important. An unsubstantiated claim is ineffective advertising because it strains the viewer's credulity. If there is no proof, the claim is likely to be dismissed. John Caples said, "You can do your prospects a favor by giving them evidence that what you say is true."

Benefits

benefit: personal buying motives, what a consumer hopes to gain from using a product

A **benefit** states what a product or its features mean to the consumer. It translates the feature, describing it in terms of how it helps, aids, or rewards the user. To identify a benefit, ask yourself: What can this product do for me? What does this feature mean to me? Benefit advertising is a rational message strategy that focuses on the prospect and speaks to self-interest. It is considered more persuasive than a claim. An example of a benefit is found in a commercial for Dial: The viewer looks into a crowded and uncomfortable commuter train, and the announcer asks, "Aren't you glad you use Dial?" (see Exhibit 5-6).

Benefits are the personal buying motives behind a consumer's decision making. These buying motives may be obvious or implied. For example, some stereo tape recorders have a feature called "Dolby"—but what does Dolby mean *to me* when I listen to a tape? How does Dolby benefit me? Likewise, why should I care about rack-and-pinion steering, disc brakes, or an overhead cam engine? The benefit statement translates those features into advantages or rewards gained by the consumer.

An example from a Texas Boot advertisement illustrates how a product feature is first identified and then interpreted in terms of consumer

Conductor: "We are sorry to announce there's going to be a slight delay..."

Exhibit 5-6: The benefit is obvious in this commercial for Dial soap. (Commercial frame and text reproduced with permission of The Dial Corporation)

needs. "Texas Boots have a unique double pegged shank so my feet will never again suffer from fallen arches." The product feature is the "double pegged shank"; the benefit is never having to worry about fallen arches. The word *so* is the cue to the reader that a benefit is being stated.

The Texas Boot ad continues with another feature and benefit statement: "Texas Boots also have double lined leather inner soles and leather outer soles. This means my feet can breathe—so they stay dry. And that's important, particularly when I'm hunting." The feature is the leather inner and outer soles; the benefit is to stay dry. And, to make sure the reader gets the point, the copywriter anchors the benefit in a realistic situation. That's a double-layered benefit statement.

promise: a prediction about what will happen to a consumer after using the product

Promise.   One specific type of benefit advertising is a **promise**, which makes a prediction about what will happen to the consumer in the future if he or she uses the product. The logic behind a promise is:

"If you buy **(product)**, then **(promise)** will happen."

An example of a promise is found in an ad by Scott for its Plus 2 Turf Builder. The headline says: "We'll get those dandelions out of your lawn and that's a promise." An ad for PAM cooking spray shows a baking tray with the arm and leg of a gingerbread man still stuck on it. The headline promises, "PAM can save you an arm and a leg." An example of another promise-based ad strategy is used by IBM for its Displaywriter Typewriter (see Exhibit 5-7). The headline not only promises what the product delivers (easy corrections), it demonstrates it when it says, "It makes impossibel impossible." The promise statement behind this ad would be: "If you buy IBM Displaywriter, it will correct your spelling errors."

reason-why: a benefit statement that states a reason to buy

Reason-why.   The phrase "reason-why" advertising was coined at the legendary Lord and Thomas advertising agency. Albert Lasker and Claude Hopkins established the concept of reason-why advertising in the early 1900s. **Reason-why** is a type of benefit statement that provides a strong rational motivation—a reason—to buy.

Reason-why is based on a tight logic. The structure behind a reason-why statement is a proposition that states a fact and then follows immediately with a reason in support. It is usually connected with words such as "because," "that means," or "so that." The formula for planning a reason-why statement is:

"The fact is **(claim)** because **(reason-why)**."

An example of reason-why copy is found in an ad by Wilkinson Knives for its "Sword," a type of self-sharpening knife. The headline says, "Finally a kitchen knife that sharpens itself." The subhead continues with, "Introducing a knife that is sharp every time you use it, year after year." The body copy further explains,

> The new Wilkinson Sword Self-Sharpening Knife is actually a knife and sharpener in one. Every time the stainless steel knife is inserted or removed from its storage case, it receives a professional sharpening. So it is sharp time after time, year after year.

The reason-why statement behind this ad would be: "The Wilkinson Sword stays sharp *because* it sharpens itself every time you use it."

Unique selling proposition.   The concept of the unique selling proposition (USP) was developed by Rosser Reeves.[13] The USP interweaves the consumer's perceptions about the product with the competitive situation and a strong claim based on distinctiveness. The key is

It makes impossibel impossible.

The IBM Displaywriter System.

When an error in spelling mars an otherwise perfect piece of work, a strange thing happens:

People remember the spelling error more than they remember the otherwise perfect piece of work.

The IBM Displaywriter helps stop spelling errors like these from happening.

Because it's more than just a text processor. It's a text processor that lets you check the spelling of up to 50,000

words *electronically*. At up to 1,000 words a minute. In 11 different languages.

The Displaywriter also lets you edit, revise, change your format, do math, merge, and file with electronic speed.

All of which goes toward giving you a flawless finished document.

Which is exactly what you want to stick in people's minds.

As opposed to the alternatove.

I am interested in learning more about the IBM Displaywriter System. Please have your representative get in touch with me.

NAME _____ TITLE _____
COMPANY _____
ADDRESS _____
CITY _____ STATE _____ ZIP _____
BUSINESS PHONE _____

IBM.

400 Parson's Pond Drive—Dept. 804
Franklin Lakes, N.J. 07417

2-1-11-82

Call *IBM Direct* 800-631-5582 Ext. 2. In New Jersey 800-352-4960 Ext. 2
In Hawaii/Alaska 800-526-2484 Ext. 2

Exhibit 5-7: The "impossibel" advertisement uses visual communication to demonstrate a product feature. (Courtesy of IBM)

product differentiation. The more distinct the product is in the market-place, the stronger the advertising message will be.

In his book, Reeves outlines the three characteristics of a strong USP:

1. Each advertisement must make a proposition to the consumer. Not just product puffery, not just show-window advertising. Each advertisement must say to each reader: "Buy this product and you will get this specific benefit."

2. The proposition must be one that the competition either cannot or does not offer. It must be either unique in the brand or preemptive in the claim.

3. The proposition must be strong enough to move the mass millions, i.e., pull over new customers to your product.

An example of a USP is found in an ad for the Nissan Pulsar NX which focuses on a unique feature for a car: This car has several types of removable tops. You can use the standard sedan hardtop, take off the "T top" and the rear hatch to make it a convertible, or add the "sportbak" to make it a utility wagon. The USP behind this ad would be: "Nissan Pulsar NX is *the only car* that gives you three types of cars in one, a car that can change its appearance as quickly as you change your clothes."

Another example of a USP is the ad for Xerox announcing that the Xerox 5600 can copy both sides of a page. The headline reads: "Now you can copy both sides of this page without. . . ." The headline was completed on the back side of the page ". . . . turning it over." The USP behind this ad would be: "The Xerox 5600 is the first copy machine that lets you copy both sides of a page without turning it over."

5.5 EXAMPLES OF COPY PLATFORMS

As we mentioned in the introduction, there are lots of ways to organize the strategy behind an advertisement. This book tries to cover most of the commonly used terms. The outline of this discussion can be used as a copy platform.

COPY PLATFORM OUTLINE

- Target audience:
- Advertising problem:
- Advertising objectives:
- Product position:
- Psychological appeal:
- Creative approach:
- Selling premise:

Other long and short copy platforms used in classes follow.

OPTIONAL PLATFORMS

Version #1
- Advertising problem:
- Advertising objectives:
- Distinctive features:
- Target audience:
- Competition:
- Position:
- Message strategy:
- Execution details:
- Supporting copy points:

Version #2
- Objectives:

- Target audience:

- Major selling idea (or key consumer benefit):

- Other usable benefits:

- Creative strategy:

You can see the variety of ways used to structure this effort when you study the following six platforms or work plans that professionals use.

The Bloom Companies

Advertising objective:
Target audience:
Consumer benefit:
Psychological benefit:
Product reasons-why:
Primary point of difference:
Focus of sale:
Mandatories:
Executional guidelines:

Karsh & Hagan

What is the problem/ opportunity?
What net effect do we want from advertising?
Who are we trying to reach?
What is the doubt in the mind of our prospect?
What or who is the competition?
What is our key persuasion?
How do we support the above?
How will we measure effectiveness?
Are there any obligatory elements to consider?

Warwick, Welsh & Miller

Target audience:
Product position:
Primary benefit:
Secondary benefit:
Reason-why:
Advertising personality:

Tracy-Locke

Target audience:
User benefits:
Reason why:
Brand character:
Focus of sale:
Tone:

Campbell-Mithun

Business goals:
Consumer profile:
Current attitudes:
Desired attitudes (objectives):
Desired actions (objectives):
Main selling proposition:
Personality:

Brewer

Key fact about product:
Problem advertising must solve:
Advertising objective:
Creative strategy:
   A. Prospect definition:
   B. Principal competition
   C. Promise
   D. Reason-why

SUMMARY

This chapter outlined the decisions involved in developing a basic creative, or message, strategy and a copy platform.

1. The overall creative, or message, strategy describes the basic thrust of your advertising—*what* you intend to say to your targeted audience about your product.
2. Advertising appeals address the underlying psychology of human needs.
3. There are many ways to describe your basic approach to message strategy, but the most basic distinctions are between product and prospect, rational and emotional.
4. Five of the most common approaches include argument, information, image, emotion, and entertainment.
5. Selling premises state the sales logic behind the advertising message.
6. There are two basic types of selling premises: claims (product-centered) and benefits (prospect-centered).
7. Promises, reasons-why, and unique selling propositions are common types of benefit strategies.

NOTES

1. Frank Goble, *The Third Force* (New York: Simon & Schuster, 1971) (Contains Maslow's 1970 revision).
2. Bruce Stauderman, "Rational vs. Emotional," *Advertising/Marketing Review*, March 1987, pp. 8–9.
3. Joseph Winski, "He Swims Against the Tide," *Advertising Age*, April 26, 1982, pp. M3–4.
4. Charles Frazer, "Creative Strategy: A Management Perspective," *Journal of Advertising*, 12:4 (1983), pp. 36–41.
5. Henry A. Laskey, Ellen Day, and Melvin Crask, "Typology of Main Message Strategies for Television Commercials," *Journal of Advertising* 18:1 (1989), pp. 36–41.
6. Joseph Winski, "Kid from Brooklyn Grows into a Power Hitter: The Book on Phil Dusenberry Is All Major League," *Advertising Age*, March 28, 1983, pp. M4–5, M29–31.
7. "True Gage," *Wall Street Journal*. A house ad that ran in *Advertising Age*.
8. Stanley I. Tannenbaum, "Comparative Advertising: The Advertising Industry's Own Brand of Consumerism," 1976 Annual Meeting of the American Association of Advertising Agencies, White Sulphur Springs, W. Va., May 1976.
9. Joanne Lipman, "Car Makers Polish Products Through Proximity to Luxe," *Advertising Age*, January 31, 1989, p. B6.
10. Harry McMahan and Mack Kile, "Slice Sells with Drama," *Advertising Age*, September 14, 1982, p. 68.
11. John Caples, "50 Things I Have Learned in 50 Years in Advertising," *Advertising Age*, September 22, 1975, p. 47.
12. Barbara Lippert, "John Hancock Elevates Reality to a Loftier Plane," *Adweek*, March 20, 1989, p. 21.
13. Rosser Reeves, *Reality in Advertising* (New York: Knopf, 1963).

6

Creative Concepts

KEY POINTS

- Creative thinking is a universal skill, needed and valued in all areas of business and advertising.
- The "big idea" delivers attention, memorability, and impact to the advertising message.
- An original idea is novel, an idea that hasn't been used before.
- There are a number of ways of thinking, but certain styles of thinking are more likely to produce original ideas.
- Creative thinking is a process, and you can learn how to do it better by understanding and practicing the basic steps.
- People who are creative thinkers have techniques both for working alone and for brainstorming in groups.

In a guest column in *Adweek*, Malcolm MacDougall, president of SSC&B, emphasized the necessity for strategy and creativity to work together. He said that "Advertising people are beginning to realize two simple things: Brilliant creative execution does not move the consumer unless it is built upon a unique and powerful strategic position and, second, a unique and powerful strategic position will not move the consumer unless it is brought to life with a brilliant creative execution. In advertising, strategy and creative thinking must work hand in hand."[1]

The development of an advertising strategy is a very careful and logical process. It is a rational process aimed at arriving at conclusions using either inductive or deductive thinking. A creative idea, however, doesn't evolve the same way strategy does. Getting "big ideas" involves entirely different ways of thinking. This chapter will discuss these ways of thinking, the creative process, and how to develop attention-getting and memorable creative concepts.

Creative thinking is not limited to the "creative side" of advertising. Everyone in advertising and in business who is charged with solving problems (a very practical form of getting ideas) uses creative thinking techniques. In advertising, that includes media, research, traffic and production, even account management. The entire field of advertising is an idea field, so everything that is said here relating to creative thinking can apply to every other side of the business.

And business, too, is serious about creative thinking. Stanford University offers a very popular Creativity in Business course. The professors have written a book about the course called *Creativity in Business*.[2] Even business magazines are running features on creativity, and "the big idea" has become a catchword in industry. Creative thinking experts have developed professional seminars, and business people are flocking to them with the thought that anyone can learn to be more creative. Bill Moyers put together a series of award-winning documentary programs on creativity for public television. "The big idea" is a hot topic.

The Big Idea

creative concept: a central theme, or "big idea," around which an advertising message is built

In effective advertising there is a central idea—a thought, a point of focus, a theme—around which an advertisement is built. This is called a "big idea," or the **creative concept**. This idea, or concept, is what delivers attention, impact, and memorability to the message—it produces the impression. David Ogilvy once said, "Unless your advertising contains a big idea, it will pass like a ship in the night."[3]

An editorial in *Advertising Age* focused on the value of big ideas and asked, "What's a Big Idea Worth?" It answered, "Millions, even billions, of dollars to the fortunate client." It points out that the Marlboro Man idea is "worth more to Philip Morris than all the company's brick and mortar," and "Does she . . . or doesn't she?" built the category of hair coloring as well as the dominance of Clairol. Furthermore the dancing California raisins idea now grosses more money in licensing fees than growers are getting for their raisins.[4]

Fallon, McElligott, the Minneapolis hot shop that has won an avalanche of awards for its work, provides a good example of a simple creative concept it used successfully to promote a restaurant. Murray's Restaurant started serving traditional British afternoon tea to increase business but found that tea time is an unfamiliar concept to Americans. The ad simply ran the word *Afternoon* with the "t" missing: "A f e r n o o n." The copy said, "Afternoon isn't complete without it. Tea Time at Murray's."

Grey Advertising's campaign for the launch of Mitsubishi's new model, the Eclipse, was built on the solar phenomenon that gives the car its name. One commercial shows the Eclipse acceleratinag in front of a spectacular stylized burning sun. The idea is attention-getting and memorable because it is simple and ties in with the car's name.

Another car company has found a strong idea in the character of Joe Isuzu, the lying car salesperson who makes fun of the car salesperson stereotype. As *Adweek's* critic, Barbara Lippert, commented, "That's a lot of powerful metaphor to roll into a single sleazeball." This is a controversial "'big idea" that many professionals in advertising love to hate. But the truth is that Joe Isuzu consistently scores in the top 10 ads as measured by the Video Storyboard research firm. It must be touching a nerve in the viewing public. Lippert points out that it's the same nerve—an ethical one—that Clara Peller touched with her famous question, "Where's the beef?" when she questioned the integrity and quality of fast food stores.[5]

Creative Thinking

Research in psychology and education has found that creative work is the result of "a magical combination of intuition and experience."[6] People who are creative are tuned in to their world—they harbor an incredible mix of experiences, ideas, mental notes, quotes, and personal observations. Dick Karp, executive vice president and director of creative services at Grey Advertising, explains, "In all the years I've been in the business, the successful people are those that are eclectic, interested in life around them."[7] These *experiences* become their "idea bank." *Intuition* involves insight and hunches rather than reasoning. Creative people use their reservoir of experience to fuel the intuitive process.

A group of researchers, the Hovland-Wilcox team, developed a more extensive list of the personal characteristics of creative people. They found that creative people in advertising tend to be: intuitive, risk-taking, enthusiastic, open to personal feelings, motivated, nonconformist, hardworking, goal-directed, imaginative, self-confident, curious, self-demanding, observant, independent, and resourceful. The researchers also found that creative people like the unknown and do not mind being alone. Furthermore they are not afraid of the ideation process—they enjoy toying with ideas and they think ideas are a dime a dozen (see Figure 6-1).[8]

Creative people develop new ideas—that's their mission. But new ideas are always challenging and frequently break with old ways of doing things and thinking about things. That means that an important characteristic of creative people is risk-taking, as noted in the Hovland-Wilcox list. In his column in *Advertising/Marketing Review*, Bruce Stauderman observed, "Creativity requires, first of all, the open mind of the generalist. Instead of being closed, and therefore protected, one has to be open, and therefore vulnerable."[9] That's why Rollo May titled his book on creativity *The Courage to Create.*

John Keil, a former ad executive, wrote in his book *How to Zig in a Zagging World: Unleashing Your Hidden Creativity*, that there are four primary characteristics of creative people. He says they are *independent* and look at things differently because they do not try to conform or please others. Second, creative people are *curious*; they have the curiosity of a child and they wonder about people and things and why they do what they do. Third, they have *flexibility*, which means they can bend and change course and try a concept again from a different approach. Fourth, they are good *problem solvers* and even relish the challenge of dealing with something that is unknown.[10]

Bill Moyers, in doing the research for his documentary on creativity, found that there are some common characteristics among creative people: "Almost all of them are infinitely curious. They never take for granted what they're told. That's why they're sometimes considered 'difficult' because they're so independent in the way they think and act." He continued, "They take risks, take advantage of the unexpected and are not fearful of being wrong."[11]

Analyze yourself on the following characteristics using the 5-point rating scale. This is not a scientific test; it's purpose is simply to make you think about yourself and your own creative potential. No one creative person has all these characteristics, but most creative people score high in many of them. (See page **125** for scoring.)

1. I'm skepitcal of what I hear — X — • — I believe what I hear
2. I don't pay attention to things around me — — X — — I notice everything
3. I get impatient easily X — — — ⑥ I'm very patient
4. I don't wonder about most things — — — — X I'm curious about everything
5. I have traveled a lot — — X — — I don't travel much
6. I like to watch TV — X — — — I like to read
7. I have strange friends — X — — — My friends are just like me
8. I like things to go according to plan — X — — — I like to improvise
9. I'm independent — X — — — I trust my friends' opinions
10. I like being with a group of people — X — — — I like being alone
11. I'm self-confident — X — — — I'm self-conscious
12. I tend to be timid — — — X — I tend to be assertive
13. I like surprises — — X — — I want to know what's going to happen
14. I'm cautious — — X — — I like to take chances
15. I thrive on confusion — X — — — I thrive on routine
16. I'm modest — — — X — I want credit for what I've done
17. I don't care what others think — — — X — I care what others think
18. I'm mostly serious — — — X — I'm mostly playful
19. I wear odd, unusual clothes — — — — X I try to dress in fashion
20. I'm not very funny — — — — X I like to be funny
21. I trust my intuition — X — — — I trust my logic
22. I don't dream — — X — — I can remember my dreams
23. I daydream a lot X — — — — I seldom daydream
24. When I study a text, I remember the words X — — — — I remember the way the page looked
25. I'm outgoing X — — — — I'm rather withdrawn

Figure 6-1: Do-It-Yourself Creativity Test.

A special report in *Business Week* on creative thinking also notes that creative people often have difficult—and diverse—childhoods. "Strains in family life—financial ups and downs or divorces—are common." The article explains, "Experts believe a dose of adversity gives children the ability to see issues and problems from different points of view." In addition the article says that childhood is marked by "exposure to diversity" and that "parents show greater-than-average cultural and intellectual interests and grant their offspring unusual freedom in exploring and making decisions."[12]

But most of all, creative people think differently, so let's investigate thinking patterns.

6.1 CREATIVE THINKING

Ideation

Getting ideas is formally called *ideation*. To "ideate," or create, is to imagine, to conceive thoughts. *Creativity* is the ability to produce original ideas or thoughts. In a publication of the Creative Education Foundation,[13] creativity is defined as "a quality possessed by persons that enables them to generate novel approaches in situations, generally reflected in new and improved solutions to problems." The key word here is **original**, which is described in advertising as new, fresh, or novel. Novelty, the "one-of-a-kind" approach, is what makes your idea creative.

original: novel, one-of-a-kind, fresh, new

Novelty and originality. *Creative* work is work that is characterized by novelty, originality, or imagination. *Original* work is work that has not been done before, something novel. *Imagination*, the ability to form a mental image of something, is the process by which people get ideas. Ideas can be considered original if they are unlike ideas previously produced by you or anyone else.

We've already mentioned that an idea can be original in the sense that you have never thought of it before. It also can be original on a higher level in the sense that *no one* has ever thought of it before. Just because it's an original idea to you doesn't mean it is original to everyone else. Advertising agencies look for people who produce ideas that are not only original to them, but also novel and one of a kind.

Alex Kroll, president of Young & Rubicam, has said, "We have found without a shadow of dispute that advertising that is in some way original, fresh, never before seen . . . is simply more productive than ho-hum stuff, stuff you've seen before." He explained, "Those 'originals' tend to be seen by more people, are remembered longer and motivate better."[14]

Originality means *breaking away* from old patterns. An example is an ad for Murphy's Oil Soap. Most ads for the household cleanser category show the usual housewife scrubbing the usual dingy floor. As Bob Garfield explained in an *Advertising Age* feature, Murphy's "thoughtfully, quietly differentiates itself from the humdrum competition." It broke the patterns by taking the product outside the home. The television spots show it being used in venerable buildings such as a church and an opera house. The campaign also does not show the usual housewife. In one spot the commercial opens on a dark Victorian mansion thick with dust and cobwebs.

Then comes the eerie music as the bottle of Murphy's, a bucket, and a mop float in the room.[15]

Another characteristic of originality is *juxtaposition*. Original ideas are created by linking two ideas in an unexpected association. That's also how a metaphor or analogy is formed, both of which are useful in creative thinking. An example of this process can be seen in the Honeywell ad that uses the old fable about the lion and the thorn as a visual metaphor for providing computerized information systems to hospitals (see Exhibit 6-1).

Clichés.   If originality produces something novel, then what is unoriginal? *Unoriginal* is the common idea that everyone comes up with, the obvious "pat" answer. *Copycat* advertising, which means taking someone else's great idea and using it for your own advertising, is also not original or imaginative.

cliché: an original idea that becomes worn out from overuse

A **cliché** is a particular type of uncreative idea; it is an idea that at one time had some unexpected phrasing or imagery. The first time it was used it was novel, but it quickly became worn out with overuse. While a cliché is uncreative because of overuse, a cliché with a *twist* can resurrect the original magic of the phrase and imagery.

Twists.   A *twist* is a sudden, unanticipated change. An example of advertising that uses a twist is a campaign by Mint Condition, an upscale candy that targets smokers with a line of mints. The campaign parodies well-known cigarette advertisements. One print ad uses a cowboy bearing a resemblance to the rugged Marlboro Man with the line, "Come to Mint Condition." Other ads play off the Merit seafaring image and Carlton's "If you smoke" slogan. The company's president says, "The ads make something even more original by changing it three degrees."[16] That's how a twist works.

Ways of Thinking

Many people think that creative ideas come from out of the blue. In reality, there is a process to creative thinking, too—and we'll discuss that shortly—but for now please note that when we talk about creative thinking, as opposed to strategic thinking, we are talking about an entirely different way of reasoning. So what kind of reasoning is it? There are several terms used to describe the type of thinking used to generate original ideas.

Divergent thinking.   J. P. Guilford is a scholar who has developed a complicated three-dimensional model of the intellect.[17] He sees creative thinking as extremely complex, but suggests that most of the creative thinking abilities are grouped around an aptitude that he calls divergent production. *Convergent* thinking is the logical (inductive, deductive) type of thinking that leads to what Guilford calls "logical imperatives" or conclusions. *Divergent* thinking, however, starts at a common point and shoots off in many directions, arriving at what he calls "logical alternatives" (see Figure 6-2).

Guilford's Structure-of-the-Intellect model is based upon decades of factor analysis of hundreds of traits. As a result of this work he has identified three specific types of traits that are common in people of high creative ability: fluency, flexibility, and originality. *Fluency is the ability*

Sometimes even hospitals need a little tender loving care.

Honeywell has a computer system that helps hospitals solve those thorny clerical problems.

And that gives the staff more time to concentrate on patient care.

It's called VITAL*, an advanced, computerized hospital information system.

At hospitals like Huntington Memorial Hospital in Pasadena, California, and Deaconess Hospital in Evansville, Indiana, VITAL processes admissions, discharges, transfers, doctors' orders, pharmacy orders, and test and treatment results. This data is only available to people who have a need to know—whenever and wherever they need it.

Honeywell has been helping progressive hospitals get these kinds of results for years. And with our new Level 6 family of minicomputers, we have more to offer than ever before.

Maybe that's why organizations of every kind are turning to The Other Computer Company.

Honeywell

*VITAL system software is licensed by National Data Communications, Inc.   Honeywell Information Systems, 200 Smith St (MS 487) Waltham, Massachusetts USA

Exhibit 6-1: The Honeywell ad develops an interesting creative concept through a visual metaphor playing on a children's fable. (Courtesy of Honeywell Information Systems)

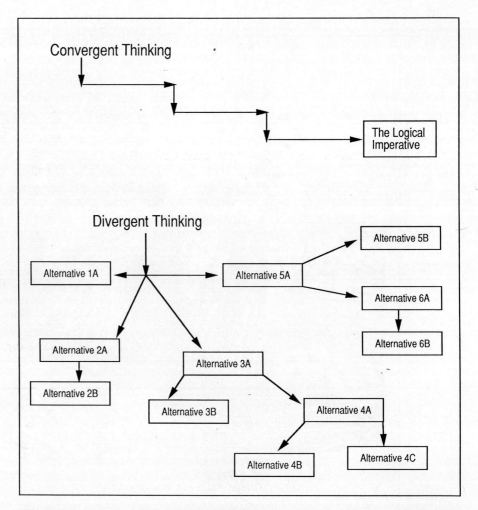

Figure 6-2:   Convergent and divergent thinking.

to produce ideas rapidly, and *flexibility* is the ability to produce original, divergent solutions in a number of categories or areas. *Originality* is a function of frequency of occurrence—how often does your idea show up on someone else's list? If it doesn't, then you have produced an original idea.

   Associative thinking.   James Webb Young's definition of the word *idea* is "a new combination of old elements."[18] He is referring to the process of seeing new connections in old relationships, or juxtaposing two previously unrelated thoughts. That's the basis of the association process. *Associative thinking*, more commonly called "free association," involves opening up your mind and expressing the thoughts as they come.[19]

   With this type of thinking the thought pattern will not be a logical one but an associational one—in other words, one thought makes you think about something else. The connection is there but it is embedded deep in your experiences, rather than in your reasoning. The associative pattern is distinctively your own, and someone else listening to the seemingly random spray of ideas may see no logic to them at all. But the ideas only appear to be random. The associations, however deep, are still there. The importance of acquiring facts for association was stressed in an article presenting a model of associative thinking in advertising.[20] The association process needs lots of facts as raw material.

Lateral thinking.   Edward de Bono in his book, *Lateral Thinking: Creativity Step by Step*,[21] develops his theory of thinking, focusing on a process that is a form of divergent thinking. De Bono describes it as *lateral thinking, or jumping around without any apparent structure*, like a dog digging for a bone. He contrasts lateral thinking with *vertical thinking*, which is reasoned, more like the thinking we have called "convergent." Vertical thinking is linear and uses either induction or deduction. People can "follow you" as you reason through a chain and arrive at a conclusion.

Everyone utilizes both types of thinking. You do it subconsciously, without even thinking about it. However, people who are considered creative have unusually well-developed lateral thinking or associative powers. They can jump around, like de Bono's dog digging for a bone, and dig in hundreds of unlikely places until they find something unexpected.

The differences between creative thinking and analytical thinking, as presented by de Bono, were summarized in an article by two Michigan State University professors, Bruce Vanden Bergh and Keith Adler.[22] Their list of differences is as follows:

Vertical thinking	Lateral thinking
1. Selective	1. Generative
2. Needs direction	2. Seeks direction
3. Analytical	3. Provocative
4. Sequential	4. Jumps, leaps
5. Judgmental—correct every step of the way	5. Not judgmental—no need to be correct at every step
6. Negative—blocks certain paths	6. Positive—investigates all possibilities
7. Excludes the irrelevant	7. Welcomes chance intrusions
8. Categorical, classifying, labeling	8. Does not categorize, classify, or label
9. Follows most likely paths	9. Explores least likely paths
10. Finite	10. Probabilistic

Analogical thinking.   Associative thinking uses metaphors and analogies. A metaphor lifts an idea out of context and uses it in another context to suggest resemblance to some other concept. When a hand is described as "fluttering in the wind," the writer is using a leaf metaphor to suggest a delicate or perhaps hesitant gesture. Bruce Stauderman found a great analogy on a billboard in France which translated as, "The telephone is the airplane of the heart."[24]

An **analogy** is similar to a metaphor. It indicates a resemblance of form, process, or relationships. An analogy can be used to help in the reasoning process because it explains steps and procedures. Many times an analogy may be a story rather than an image. Both metaphors and analogies are creative tools because they trigger the associative response.

analogy: a statement based on seeing the similarities between two otherwise disparate items

William J. J. Gordon has developed a program to train creative thinking based on the idea of forcing metaphors and analogies. His think-tank training program, called Synectics,[25] is structured around analogical approaches. The Synectics exercises are built around this simple formula: "A is to B as C is to what?" That's the foundation for analogical thinking. It becomes creative by using free association to stimulate the wildest possible connections. The credo of creative innovation through Synectics is to "make the strange familiar and the familiar strange." Gordon says that, with a structured program of metaphor construction, you don't have to wait passively until the creative muse strikes, that there are definite metaphorical weapons with which you can hunt and track down the muse.

An example of a campaign built on a metaphor is one created for a public service drug education effort. The theme is, "It's about time parents became the pushers." The Finnegan & Agec staff knew that there is a lot of antidrug clutter and kids reject most of the messages because they are too preachy. Instead, the agency targeted parents with messages that parents should steer their kids toward activities like music and sports because kids who participate in these activities are less likely to get involved with drugs. The ads explained, "Youths who are hooked on life don't get hooked on drugs."[26]

Right brain/left brain.   Another way to describe how people think is based on the physiology of the human brain. The brain is two separate compartments, or hemispheres, connected by a thin tissue. Recent research in neurosurgery has found that when this connection is cut, there are two separate brains, each capable of quite different ways of thinking and remembering. As explained in *Drawing on the Right Side of the Brain*, by Betty Edwards, the left brain is verbal and controls speech, writing, and all thinking that is logically determined. This is similar to convergent or lateral thinking. The right brain is nonverbal and controls emotions, intuition, psychomotor skills, and things that people learn *to do* and develop a *feel for*.[27]

The left brain thinks in linear and sequential steps; the right brain thinks in sensory images and grasps the "whole picture." For face recognition, right-brain knowledge and thinking patterns are used. According to Thomas Blakeslee in *The Right Brain*,[28] the right brain "manipulates complex images" rather than comparing feature by feature, as the left brain does (see Exhibit 6-2). That's why creative ideas are difficult to express; they are the product of right-brain thinking and essentially nonverbal. The left brain has to do the translating in order to communicate them to bosses and clients.

In terms of applying these theories to creativity, obviously the right brain is the center of most creative thinking. That's where the mental images are stored. Visual thinking and imagery are basic to creative thinking. Blakeslee explains, "An ability to recognize things in an altered form or context is the basis of creative thinking." He points out that "creative breakthroughs are generally a result of finding hidden relationships—patterns that are obscured by their context." Verbal thinking, he says, "is inherently limited in its ability to make these kinds of abstract connections." The right brain is also the source of intuition and inspiration. Blakeslee explains that "in most intellectual fields the real breakthroughs

21 LOGICAL REASONS TO BUY A SAAB.

In each of us, there is a tough, cold, logical side that wants to have hard facts, data and empirical evidence before it will assent to anything.

So when your impulsive, emotional side saw the exciting photograph on the facing page and yelled "Hey, look at this!," your logical side immediately asked to see some solid and relevant information about the Saab.

Here, then, are some of the more significant hard facts about Saabs, facts that make a strong logical argument in favor of owning a Saab:

1) Front-wheel drive. Once, Saab was one of the few cars in the U.S. that offered this. Since then, most other carmakers have discovered the superior handling and safety of front-wheel drive and have followed Saab's lead.

2) Turbocharging. More power without more engine displacement. Saab's third generation of turbocharging, incorporating an intercooler and Saab's Automatic Performance Control system, is still a generation or two ahead of any competition.

3) Four-valve technology. Doubling the number of valves per cylinder improves engine efficiency enormously. Yet another group of manufacturers is beginning to line up behind Saab.

4) Advanced ergonomics. That's just a way of saying that all instruments, controls and functional elements are designed so that they will be easy and natural to use. A legacy of Saab's aerospace heritage. Saab is the only car manufacturer which also builds supersonic military jets.

5) Special steel underpanel. The Saab's smooth underside improves its aerodynamics and helps shed water to prevent rust.

6) Balance. 60% of the car's weight is borne by the front wheels, to maintain a consistent slight understeer and superior traction.

7) Rustproofing. A 16-step process that's designed to protect the car from the wetness and saltiness of Sweden's long winters.

8) Climate control. Your Saab is going to be comfortable inside, whatever is happening outside. Air conditioning is standard on all models, and effective insulation helps to control the temperature as well as the noise level inside.

9) High capacity electrical system. For reliable starts in subarctic cold.

10) Advanced Sound System. When you're in the Saab, the AM/FM cassette system sounds wonderful. When you get out, it can come with you, to provide the most theft deterrent possible.

11) One of the world's safest steering wheels. Heavily padded and designed to collapse in a controlled manner in case of heavy impact.

12) Safety cage construction. Last year, the U.S. Highway Loss Data Institute ranked the safety of cars based on actual damage and injury claims. Saab 900's were safer than any other midsize sedans.

13) Fold-down rear seats. This makes Saab the only performance sedan in the world that can provide up to 56 cubic feet of cargo space.

14) Large, 15-inch wheels. They permit good high-speed control with a very comfortable ride. They also permit larger disc brakes all around.

15) Price. It's modest, particularly when you see it against comparable Audi, BMW, Mercedes or Volvo models.

16) Side-cornering lights. These show you what you're getting into when you signal for a turn at night.

17) Front seats. Firmly supportive, orthopedically shaped and adjustable in practically every dimension you can imagine. They're even heated.

18) Saab dealers. They're all over the country, waiting to help you with specially trained mechanics and comprehensive stocks of Saab parts, and...

19) Saab accessories. These may be a bit too much fun for your logical side. They let you customize your Saab with factory-approved performance wheels, floor mats, fog lights and so on. And on. And on.

20) Saab's aircraft heritage. The first Saab automobile was designed by aircraft engineers who established a company tradition of carefully rethinking problems rather than just adopting the conventional solution.

21) The Saab driving experience. Best expressed on the facing page.

SAAB
The most intelligent cars ever built.

ONE EMOTIONAL REASON.

Exhibit 6-2: In this campaign Saab picks up on the right brain/left brain theories to describe how its car appeals to both logic and emotions.

are the result of intuition." He points out, however, that "intuition itself is generally useless until it can be verified and described verbally and logically."

Intuition

intuition: knowing something without using rational processes

The ability to make estimates based on past experiences is fueled by **intuition**, a "catch-all word for thinking processes that we can't verbally explain." A calculated estimate is determined methodically—point by point. In contrast, Blakeslee explains that "intuitive judgments are not arrived at step by step, but in an instant.

An article in *Madison Avenue* says intuition is "what separates those who can consistently recognize the big advertising idea from those who can't." The article describes intuition as a "subconscious thought process" that is nonrational and sensory in nature (gut feelings). It says, "Intuition is not mystic mumbo jumbo; it is the product of experience and learning that have sunk down to the subconscious level."[29]

6.2 THE CREATIVE PROCESS

A number of advertising scholars have tried to describe the creative process, and, while the steps don't work in the same way for everyone, they at least provide some ideas on how to get started. As early as 1926 Graham Wallas developed an outline of the ideation process identifying the following four steps: preparation, incubation, illumination, and verification.[30] *Preparation* means research and study. *Incubation* means getting away from it and letting the ideas jell on their own. *Illumination* is that point where the light dawns. *Verification* is the process of applying the great idea to see if it fits the requirements of the strategy.

James Webb Young, a former creative vice president at J. Walter Thompson, wrote a little book titled *A Technique for Producing Ideas*, which outlines his theory of the creative process.[31] He believes that creative thinking is based on two factors: combining old elements into new combinations and seeing the relationships between them. We've talked about combining ideas in terms of associative thinking. His second factor, the ability to see the relationships, seems obvious, but, in fact, it is a real stumbling block to creativity. Many people come up with creative ideas (or have creative ideas presented to them) and have a difficult time comprehending the essence of the novel relationship. This is a judgment problem.

Steps in the Creative Process

Immersion. Beyond these two factors, Young also describes a five-step process that summarizes how most people "get" ideas. The first step is immersion, where you gather raw materials through background research, totally immersing yourself in the problem.

Digestion. The second step is *digestion*, where you are mentally chewing the cud. It's a type of fooling around with the information—turning it over, looking at it from different angles, doodling, making lists of features and phrases. This digestion step often ends with something Young calls "brainfag" when you reach the hopeless stage. At this point everything is probably in a jumble. That's the state of "brainfag"; this feeling of hopelessness is usually a requirement before the "big idea" can break through.

Sometimes a good idea will come easy and early, but more likely the ideas that come first are the obvious approaches, the tried and true, the common, the unoriginal, the clichés. Still, getting all these obvious ideas out in the open is a necessary first step. Let them come, sort through them looking for glimmers of possible great ideas, and dump the rest.

Incubation. Young's third state is *incubation*, where you put it all out of your mind and go for a walk. In effect, you are turning it over to your subconscious. Many people intuitively turn to something that stimulates the imagination. Sherlock Holmes used to play his violin or drag Watson to a band concert. There is debate on the incubation phase. Many creative thinkers report anecdotes about the great idea that strikes when they put the problem away for a while. Some people working in advertising believe in incubation and, when they hit the wall, they will drop everything and go walk around the block or ride up and down on the elevator. There are others, however, who feel the only way to proceed is to work against pressure.

One point of agreement is that the ideas come after a period of sustained effort. The garden must be planted and weeded before the crop can be harvested. Most creative people agree that it is hard work coming up with ideas—even though the idea itself may come at some unexpected, nonwork, relaxed time.

Illumination. Rollo May, in *The Courage to Create*, makes the point that insight not only comes after a period of effort, it also tends to come at a moment of transition—usually the transition between work and relaxation.[32] It comes at the point when the books have been put away, when starting to walk to the bus or right before falling asleep. Creative people often sleep with paper and pencil next to the bed for that reason.

In the fourth stage the door opens or the light goes on. Out of nowhere, often when you least expect it, the idea will appear—showering, shaving, half dozing, bathing. That's the "Eureka phenomenon." What happens is that you turn your attention elsewhere and let your subconscious work on the problem without all the tension and anxiety. It solves the problem while you are occupied (see Exhibit 6-3).

Reality testing. Young's last stage is the cold gray dawn of the morning after. Does the idea still look so great? Does it really solve the problem and achieve the goals? More important, in advertising, does it fit the strategy? Sometimes (often) it doesn't, and you must start over again at the beginning. Many creatives tell about getting what seemed like a really great idea, only to look at it the next day and wonder how they could come up with something so silly. It happens all the time.

Advertising is goal-directed; in the field of advertising, creativity is not encouraged for its own sake. Creative thinking in advertising is problem solving and, to be effective, it must solve some identified problem. That's the ultimate test of a good idea in advertising. Creativity without direction is like a watch with no hands.

Working Creatively   Alex Osborn's (former president of BBDO) description of the creative process[33] is similar to the process described above: Specify the problem, gather information, generate possible solutions, evaluate the solutions,

---

THE CREATIVE PROCESS

Wallas's steps
1. Preparation
2. Incubation
3. Illumination
4. Verification

Osborn's steps
1. Specify the problem
2. Gather information
3. Generate possible solutions
4. Evaluate the solutions
5. Select the best one

Young's steps
1. Immersion
2. Digestion
3. Incubation
4. Illumination
5. Reality testing

Exhibit 6-3: Creativity involves seeing connections in unexpected places. The J&B ad uses a visual pun on the phrase "on the rocks." (Copyright, The Paddington Corporation 1988; reprinted with permission of The Paddington Corporation)

and select one. His approach differs in that he emphasizes solving a problem by developing lots of options as opposed to seeking one good one.

Getting started.   Osborn describes a preliminary stage that he calls "setting the working mood." Essentially, it's a mind-opening process. Some writers use special techniques to flex or stretch their imaginations. One writer will make lists of words on a yellow pad with magic markers. Another writer takes all the pencils out of his desk, walks to the pencil sharpener, and sharpens them one by one, the grinding of the sharpener serving as a physical metaphor for the grinding of the gears in his mind. The setting-the-mood stage is as personal for most people as their signatures. It's something that you develop over time, and it serves as an internal cue to your brain that the system is on line and locked in.

Rollo May describes a mental state of intensity of awareness, a type of heightened consciousness.[34] This state of intense concentration and arousal even has neurological responses, such as a faster heartbeat, higher blood pressure, narrowing of eyelids, lessening of appetite—in general, an obliviousness to things around you. In terms of imagery, he also notes that everything you encounter in this state becomes more vivid. You are more able to see unexpected patterns in what before was mundane. The heart of the creative process for Rollo May is this intense encounter.

blocking: desperation and panic when the ideas won't come

Blocking.   When you **block**, your ideas simply won't come. To a certain extent, that's a normal and expected part of the creative process. We've mentioned the role of "brainfag," the desperation you feel as you try to trigger the flow of ideas. Most creative people report having to wrestle through that familiar phase of desperation, and all have different ways of doing it.

Real blocking occurs when panic sets in. Fear precludes creativity. That's the difference between the creative stage of "brainfag" and the dysfunctional stage of blocking. The panic has to be dealt with first. Sometimes incubation can be useful. Turn your attention to something else and let the adrenalin drop. If you have to keep working, then find something routine to do—something that's easy and rhythmic. Many writers work their way out of a block by making a list—lots of repetition of an activity that takes minimal brain effort. It's another adrenalin dropper. Another technique is to do something physical like exercising, jogging, lifting weights, moving furniture, running up and down stairs. It's a way to siphon off the adrenalin overcharge that comes from the panic.

6.3 DEVELOPING CONCEPTS

Learning to Associate

There are a number of things you can do to improve your associative abilities. First of all, practice. Free association is a loosening-up exercise, a way to become mentally limber. People are stiff when they first start to exercise, but after a few days the muscles begin to limber up and their flexibility increases dramatically. The same thing is true with creative thinking. Many copywriters doodle with words when they first sit down to write copy. All they are doing is "wordstorming"—free associating with words as a technique to "limber up" their mental muscles.

Free association is a serendipity process—anything that comes to mind is relevant. The associations are pieces of ideas, fragments—not well-turned phrases and constructed essays. Cultivate the ridiculous idea; search for nonsense. You loosen up when you laugh, so humor is a useful part of the mindset. When you feel relaxed and loose, then try for some exaggerated ideas. Push for the zany, crazy, totally unrealistic ideas. You can tone down the off-the-wall idea, but it's impossible to pump life into a tired one.

Quantity. One thing you can do to improve your free association ability is to strive for quantity. Relax and practice until your lists get longer and longer. The idea is that the more material you have to work with, the more chances you will have of finding an idea with some potential. So work fast and push yourself to come up with more and more associations.

A study of free association conducted at Michigan State University found that the more ideas people come up with, the better their chances of having "good" ideas.[35] Students were asked to come up with one, three, five, and eight ideas. The researchers found that "increasing the number of creative alternatives increases the chance of finding the 'best' creative idea."

Chains and breaks. Study how the free association process works. Look at your lists of words. Can you see the chaining process that holds the associations together? Notice how the words move along on one track and then all of a sudden jump to an entirely different topic. That's called a break in the chain.

Cultivate those breaks in the chain. When you jump tracks from one category to another, you're beginning to develop what de Bono calls "lateral thinking." There are some who define creativity as the ability to break away from conventional sequences of thought. That's exactly what happens when you break the association chain. You're in a rut if you continue to move down the same track.

Imagery. Another way to improve your associative skill is to try associating, not with words, but with visual images. What pictures do you see in your mind when you think of words like "bank," "bush," and "guide"? When you do visual associations you write down, not words that come to mind, but descriptions of the pictures you see in your mind. Obviously, what is happening here is that you are expanding your capacity for visual imagery.

Once you feel comfortable with visual associations, move through the other senses. What do you hear in your mind's ear when you think of music? What do you smell when you think of spring or the ocean? What do you taste when you think of summer? What do you feel when you think of roller skating? Tune in to your senses and develop your ability to make note of the sensations that come to mind. That's the hardest part—training yourself to make note of your own responses and then finding words to express them.

Brainstorming   The discussion so far has focused on individual thinking. Individual ideation is important, but advertising also uses collaborative teams of two—usually a copywriter and art director—and a type of group ideation called

brainstorming: creating inspiration by using a group of people to generate a large quantity of ideas

brainstorming. This concept was developed in the late thirties by Alex Osborn.[36] His agency, along with many other agencies and corporations, has used brainstorming for group problem solving and generating ideas.

Brainstorming uses the brainpower of a number of people to intensify divergent thinking and increase the number of available ideas. It's a synergistic approach using free association in a group environment. Like a chain of firecrackers, one person's idea bounces off another person's, and both ideas spark other ideas in other people's minds. It's a game of compound interest, with the number of ideas exceeding any one person's contributions in an equivalent amount of time. Both the fluency and flexibility of a group is thought to be higher than that of one individual.

There is still a very important role for individuals. Groups don't write copy or design ads. They may be able to generate ideas, but the implementation and development is still left to the lonely individual at the board or the typewriter or the computer.

Collaboration. Ideas, after all, come from one mind at a time, so the individual is still the heart of the ideation process. *Collaboration* is useful primarily as a supplement to the individual effort.

The most common collaboration is the partnership between a copywriter and an art director. Two people who work well together are teamed in most agencies, and work assignments are distributed to get the maximum use of a talented combination. Some people are on the same "wavelength" and stimulate each other; others couldn't find their way out of a paper bag together. Agencies encourage the natural teams.

Deferring judgment. Osborn outlined four rules to guide brainstorming. The first and most critical is to defer judgment. Brainstorming feeds on a positive environment and, to make it work, all criticism must be ruled out. That doesn't mean there is no place for evaluation—in fact, evaluation is very important—but it comes at the end of the process. Osborn mentions that a number of research projects have shown that a group will produce twice as many good ideas in a spirit of cooperation and contagious enthusiasm when judgment is deferred. The idea is to separate idea generation from idea evaluation. It is important to nurture a free and open climate. John Philipp, a Synectics vice president, explains that for the best ideas "you need permission to think crazy thoughts that aren't feasible, and you need external permission: 'Is it ok for me to say this in front of other people?'"[37]

Quantity. Osborn's second rule is to go for quantity. Pile up as many ideas as possible. Each one stimulates another line of thought and every one might possibly have the clue to a final solution. Brainstorming groups can easily compile 80 to 100 ideas in a 15-minute session. Hour-long sessions report ideas in the thousands. Fill the board, fill the pad, fill the wall—keep pushing your group to come up with more and more and more. Research into creativity in advertising has found that the more ideas generated, the better the final concepts. That's a basic principle in creative thinking: The more ideas there are to choose from, the better the final choice will be.[38]

Playfulness. This rule relates to attitude. Osborn insists that free-wheeling and a spirit of playfulness are welcome. Shoot wild. Push yourself and the group to come up with wild and zany, off-the-wall ideas. Remember there's no evaluation at this stage, so nothing is inappropriate or foolish. Use humor, cultivate exaggeration. The truly original solution is more likely to be developed from a wild and zany idea than from a routine comment. Work on the edge of silly.

Reprocessing. Osborn's fourth rule is a suggestion for procedure: Combine and improve. Ideas grow on one another and good ideas can become better. Every idea can be reconsidered in terms of how it can be improved. Osborn calls this "reprocessing." Can a previously considered idea be modified, combined, twisted, applied in a different context, and so on? Piggyback your ideas.

Group spirit. In addition to Osborn's four rules, there are a number of other suggestions on how to make a brainstorming session work. The important thing is the spirit of the group. There needs to be a spirit of mutual encouragement. Nothing is taken personally; no one's ego is at stake. No one is trying to show off or score points.

The group spirit depends on a delicate balance of intensity and relaxation. Osborn says it should be a mental set where everyone is relaxed but trying hard. That's more difficult than it may sound. You have to be relaxed for the free association process to work, but you need a spirit of intensity to move beyond the partying mentality. It's like getting serious about playing a game—or making a game out of hitting a target.

Group size. Most formal brainstorming groups operate with 10 to 12 members, although they can function with as few as 6 and still be productive. Most research has found that the more people there are, the more ideas there are. However, the more people, the fewer the number of contributions per person. If you're working with a larger group, try to keep the group cohesive and avoid breaking up spontaneously into small groups.

Environment. Most people, when they are trying to think creatively, try to hibernate, to get away from distractions. Tom Monohan, president of Leonard Monohan Saabye Lubars, created "Concept Hell," a room in the bowels of the agency where there are no telephones and where, once the door closes, no one is able to intrude. Once in Concept Hell, strange things happen. Sketches and words fill tissue papers which are then tacked on the wall. In hours the walls take on the appearance of the "mad artists'" lair. Finally the copywriter and art director emerge and, with a bit of luck, a great ad idea has also emerged.[39]

Leader and recorder. Appoint a leader, preferably someone skilled at leading brainstorming sessions. This person directs the effort in the beginning while you're trying to get the group momentum up as well as during the periods when the pace slows. The leader should also find ways to involve everyone as well as limit the influence of any dominant individuals who might try to take over the session. One way to control dominance and encourage participation is to use a technique called *group sequencing*, where everyone gives an idea in turn, ending the series with the person who has tried to dominate.

In terms of group composition it is useful, especially at the beginning, to have a few people in the group who are self-starters. They serve as spark plugs and their enthusiasm tends to ignite everyone else.

A recorder is needed to keep track of the ideas—*all* the ideas. Sometimes you may work with a visual recording system—writing on a blackboard, a big piece of kraft paper taped to the wall, or a newsprint pad. The public recording is useful because it stimulates the reprocessing function. You often get new ideas from something that was said earlier. The leader can function as recorder, although it is easier to have a second person doing the writing. If a visible recording system isn't available, then the recorder can make notes on a yellow pad.

Evaluation. When the idea generation session is over, then it's time for evaluation. It's a good idea to maintain the same positive attitude in this stage as well. Sort the ideas, looking for "possibles." In other words, avoid criticizing any of the ideas. Don't look for losers. There's no point in pointing out weaknesses. Focus only on the ideas that have potential. And keep sorting on that basis, each time narrowing the field.

Competition. Fallon, McElligott is an agency that has roomfuls of awards for its advertising. Pat Burnham, FM's associate creative director, believes there is something different at his agency that helps it consistently produce award-winning ads. He feels that one way FM creates its magic is "with competition—competition among ourselves." He explains, "It takes on momentum and it really does breed better work."[40]

Overcoming inertia. One of the biggest problems with group sessions is getting started. A common technique used in advertising is *attribute sorting*. By simply listing the features of the product or service, you're beginning to get everyone's mind in gear. Next, move to *benefit sorting*, which is another way of listing features, this time in terms of the user. All that is pretty dry, so you will have to throw in something to pull them away from rational "strategic" thinking. One way is to use the Synectics method of metaphor building. Take each attribute or feature and ask what it's like in terms of an analogy or a metaphor. You can force freewheeling by locating the metaphor. For example, ask how each attribute relates to something in a zoo or a garage or a schoolroom, and so on.

Fears. There are blocks to brainstorming, just like there are to free association and other types of creative thinking. Now all those personal fears are compounded by public attention. Most of the fears that gum up brainstorming relate to the group environment: "What will the others think of me?" *The Universal Traveler*[41] details the debilitating effects of these fears. Here are some of the fears listed in *The Traveler*: fear of making mistakes, fear of being seen as foolish, fear of being criticized, fear of being misused, fear of being alone (any person with a new idea is automatically a minority of one), fear of disturbing traditions, fear of being associated with taboos, fear of losing the security of habit, fear of losing the respect of the group, fear of truly being an individual. These are mostly internalized fears and have to be worked on by the individual alone.

There are a few things the leader and the group members can do in a group to help overcome the fright. First, stick absolutely to the principle of *deferring judgment*. If there's no finger-pointing, no one can be made to look foolish. Mutual encouragement may help overcome some of these fears. Lots of positive responses ("That's good") may help. Don't try to evaluate as you go, because it dampens the spirit.

Alex Osborn described a number of cramps to creativity. In addition to the problem of ill-timed criticism, he also points to lack of enthusiasm and negative attitudes. It takes lots of alternatives to find a good idea. Someone who is negative will usually give up too soon. Osborn also mentions the fear of feeling foolish, timidity, and self-discouragement.

Rollo May describes rigidity as another obstacle to creativity. Rigidity can manifest itself as a lack of flexibility in thinking. A common type of rigidity that shows up in advertising comes from an overdependence on strategy and research findings. Strategy is just a place to get started; it's rarely the expression of an inspired idea. John Fiedler, senior vice president and executive director of research at Ted Bates, recognizes the limitations of research-bound creativity: "Carefully analyzed, beautifully charted, intelligently presented research briefings rarely inspire creativity." He continues, "I don't know of a single creative problem which, when it was surrounded by research, surrendered." He explains, "Creativity often arises from and flourishes in an atmosphere of inconsistency and incongruity."[42]

Breakthroughs
One of the biggest advantages of brainstorming in groups as opposed to working alone is that it can be an exhilarating, exciting, almost surrealistic experience. When a number of people loosen up and start associating, the ideas generated will astound you. And one or two zany thinkers can pull everyone into the deep water of unself-conscious spontaneous association—an experience some individuals will never know on their own. There's something magical about being part of such a group. It's a real emotional high.

6.4 THE CREATIVE CONCEPT

The purpose of creative thinking is to develop a *big idea*, a creative concept. Behind every ad, every campaign, every sales promotion is a central idea that translates the strategy into an ad that has impact. This big idea is big because it must do several things at once. It must communicate the concept clearly and it must be attention-getting, memorable, interesting, and believable. There's a saying in advertising: "Don't sell the steak; sell the sizzle." The creative concept is the sizzle, the flash, the splash. Without a strong concept, an ad is as flat and unexciting as the strategy statement.

The Heart of an Ad
A strong creative concept is the heart of an ad. An example of a creative concept that successfully creates impact from a routine strategy is found in an ad for the Peugeot SW8 Turbo station wagon. The strategy was to focus on the car's durability and reliability. The agency, HDM, took the car to Africa and filmed it driving through a variety of stunning settings juxtaposed with shots of deadly lions and threatening rhinos and elephants. The voice-over says, "If your car breaks down here, finding a mechanic is the least of your problems." The spot continues with, "If you need a car you can rely on (a lion snarls as the car goes by), buy a Peugeot." Other copy focused on the car's past performance on the African continent and concludes, "A car, to be able to do this in Africa, has to be reliable and durable."[43]

Sometimes you can identify the central idea from a slogan or headline used in the advertising, such as Frank Perdue's "It takes a tough man to make a tender chicken." Perdue is featured in the print and television ads as a tough-talking businessman/farmer who is a fanatic about quality in his chickens. Quality, of course, is expressed as tender meat.

Understandability. You should be able to look at any ad and ask yourself: *What's the point?* Whatever the point is, that's the idea of the message, and it should be obvious in the creative concept. If you can't puzzle it out, either it isn't clearly communicated or the idea simply isn't there. Another problem is an ad that's trying to do too many things. A single-minded ad rarely has a problem with its creative concept. The creative concept should be simple and clear and obvious. No matter how involved the execution, you should be able to put your finger on the heart of the message without any hesitation. What is it that this ad is trying to say?

One example of a failed creative concept is one that ran in the *New York Times* for a carpet store. The headline reads, "The carpet that sells itself." The first sentence of the body copy says, "We don't need great salespeople to sell this carpet. Or advertising people to sell it." Meanwhile, the illustration is a close-up of the weave of the carpet and the body goes on to explain the features. Clearly the reader is being sold a carpet, and even more clearly, the reader is reading an ad. The whole concept is nonsensical.

Attention, interest, and memorability. An effective creative concept should have impact, and that means it should be attention-getting, interesting, and memorable. These factors are a product of the artistry of the execution. Creative concepts are also defined as "unique treatments," and it is the magic of the execution that makes these treatments unique.

An effective creative concept must also have pulling power and stopping power. The idea needs to be intriguing, fascinating, or involving. The Samsonite "Survivor" campaign uses "borrowed interest" to create advertising that is totally unique in the category of luggage advertising. As the Indiana Jones phenomenon spreads, this particular idea will no longer be unique. That is a common problem for truly unique ideas. They are arresting while they are fresh; they become clichés after they have been borrowed too many times.

An example of a campaign that uses a high level of gimmickry to create a novel and arresting creative concept is one by the American Museum of Natural History. This campaign used brochures, coloring books, subway posters, and other unconventional media to promote museum attendance. The idea is to create mythical dinosaurs with twentieth-century characteristics. The creatures come in parts and you can even assemble your own. Some of the creatures created by the advertising team and used in the promotions included "Thesaurus Rex," which they described with the following copy:

A dinosaur with a vocabulary of 1,000 words?

Instruments capable of detecting prehistoric sounds have recently made this remarkable discovery.

The Thesaurus Rex originated in Great Britain. During the Rococo period it migrated to the South where it quickly became Italicized.

Scientists believe its diet was rich in pronouns and probably included phrase fruit and synonym. Perhaps its most satisfying meals consisted of Grammar's Cookies and Mother Tongue.

Equipped with only a semicolon, Thesaurus Rex experienced severe difficulty with its vowels and ate itself into extinction.

Animals with large vocabularies visit the American Museum of Natural History every day. They come to see dinosaurs, minerals, and a variety of exciting exhibits, 79th Street and Central Park West.

The perfect fit.   While a unique treatment is essential in devising creative concepts, it is also important to find a "big idea" that fits the product, the audience, and the situation. Sometimes the best idea is the obvious one. You can scratch around and try to create something that is unexpected and find all your effort is going into the search for novelty. In fact, you may be looking at the idea, but it is so obvious you can't see it.

Ogilvy & Mather and DDB Needham distribute a little book to employees titled, *Obvious Adams*. The book is written in turn-of-the-century literary style and it recounts the career of an early (mythical) advertising genius whose one great gift was the ability to see the obvious solution. The point is that there is a certain elegance in an idea that fits perfectly and solves the problem neatly. Mathematicians speak of a formula as being both elegant and parsimonious. What this means is that it is a solution that fits perfectly and has no wasted effort. This doesn't mean the idea is dull or bland, it just communicates its message perfectly and economically.

For example, in an early AAF National Student Advertising Competition, where the product was Rold Gold pretzels, the San Jose State University team won with the theme "The only pretzel worth its salt." The simplest and most obvious idea was clearly the winner, and everyone in the room said to themselves: *Gee, I wish I had thought of that.* That kind of response comes when an idea fits perfectly.

Visual/verbal synergy.   An effective creative concept, then, is one that communicates a clear central idea with a unique treatment that is attention-getting, interesting, and memorable. This clever idea that makes a good advertisement original and distinctive is also a perfect package of verbal and visual elements (see Exhibit 6-4). All media use both words and pictures—including radio, where the visual is created in the viewer's mind. Both the visual and verbal are important, and in an effective message they will be integrated and interactive—one reinforcing the other.

One person who brought the verbal and visual together was Bill Bernbach, and it is clear in the work of his agency that art directors and copywriters get equal time. Some of the finest advertising ever done by Doyle Dane Bernbach illustrates the perfect marriage of visual and verbal.

The classic Volkswagen advertising campaign includes one for the VW bus that shows a group of nuns with the headline, "Mass transit." One of the greatest VW television spots opens with a man climbing into a VW Beetle on a dark snowy morning and, as he drives through the storm, the announcer asks: "Have you ever wondered how the man who drives the snowplow gets to the snowplow?"

Exhibit 6-4: "How to balance the books" demonstrates the effective interplay between the visual and the verbal content of the ad. (Courtesy of IBM)

Birth of a Concept

We'll close this discussion of creative concepts with a case history, the story about how BBDO developed the "Good things" campaign for General Electric.

Good things. General Electric has maintained its own continuous public perception research since the 1950s. In the summer of 1979, both BBDO and Young & Rubicam were asked to develop proposals for a corporate image campaign. At the time both agencies were handling GE business and neither realized that this assignment would turn into a creative shootout. The story is told in a Madison Avenue article.[44] GE research had found that, while GE products are pervasive and located throughout every home, the public didn't have any coherent perception of the breadth of the corporation's activities. Furthermore, BBDO researchers had found that more and more people looked at GE as old-fashioned and traditional. The image was flat, boring, unexciting—but nice.

Dennis Berger, the BBDO creative director, admitted that it was hard to get excited about this assignment. At first the creative team developed several concepts. One was a presenter-style "Do you believe in magic?" which endowed consumer appliances with all manner of attributes. The second was built on the line, "You ain't seen nothing yet." It was criticized because, while intriguing, it was not quite believable and suggested capabilities that GE didn't have at the time.

Their third concept illustrates thinking through the obvious. The creative team asked, "What does GE do to make life better?"; that question turned out to be the creative concept and the key to the award-winning campaign. However, it was a long way yet before the idea jelled.

Berger explained, "The one thing we knew was that we were going to use music." He went on, "Any creative person knows that music is a good tool for creating excitement, for changing an image." He added, "We also ruled out humor because it didn't seem appropriate." Len McCaron, vice president and executive art director, said, "We thought of mothers putting their children's pictures up on refrigerator doors with magnets; fathers taping baby's first sounds; kids listening to radios on skateboards."

From such images they began to compose a song starting with lines like, "We make your daughters dance, we wake you to the sun, and so on." They couldn't come up with an ending other than "We make the things that make life good." They brought the pieces of the song to Philip Dusenberry, at that time executive creative director and new CEO, who thought the ending was the "klunkiest one I ever heard." Dusenberry was haunted by it and, days later, riding to the office in a cab, he reworded it to "We bring things to life." Still unhappy, he added the word "good" just before "things." Dusenberry explained that "a good creative director doesn't shove anything down his writers' throats," so he just read it to them and asked what they thought.

This line turned out to be the "magic" that holds the entire campaign together. The executions were developed in vignettes, similar to the original images the creative team used in their brainstorming. When BBDO presented it to GE executives, the creative team knew by the look on their faces that they had a winner. The final campaign uses the vignettes to present the GE product line. The products are portrayed in scenes as true to life as possible; the viewer may see the side of the washer rather than the front, the radio is in the background, and the refrigerator is human scale rather than monumental, like so many appliance ads. BBDO came up with a creative concept that successfully links GE with the good things and the sweet moments in life.

SUMMARY

This chapter introduced the subject of creativity in advertising. The following topics have been covered:

1. People who are creative use intuition, fueled by diverse experiences; they also take risks and are independent, curious, and flexible.
2. A creative idea is original or novel; a copycat idea is one that has been used before; a cliché is an idea that has been used so much that it becomes trite.
3. Creative people use different types of thinking:
   - Divergent, or lateral, thinking to search for many alternatives
   - Associative thinking to see connections
   - Analogic thinking to see patterns and similarities
4. There are five steps in the creative process:
   a. Immersion: background research
   b. Digestion: fooling around with the background information
   c. Incubation: turning it over to your subconscious
   d. Illumination: the point where the door opens or the light comes on
   e. Reality testing: making sure that it solves the problem or achieves the goals
5. Brainstorming is used to intensify divergent thinking to increase the number of ideas available.
6. A creative concept uses a "big idea" to translate the strategy into an ad theme that has impact, flair, and excitement.

NOTES

1. Malcom D. MacDougall, "Emerging from the Creative Coma," *Adweek*, November 30, 1981, p. 2.
2. Michael Ray and Rochelle Myers, *Creativity in Business* (New York: Doubleday & Company, 1986).
3. Keith L. Reinhard, "Creative Directors Gallery," *Back Stage*, September 18, 1987, p. 18.
4. *Advertising Age*, "What's a Big Idea Worth?" June 6, 1988, p. 16.
5. Barbara Lippert, "Joe Isuzu Strays from the True Spirit of the Original," *Adweek*, March 13, 1989, p. 21.
6. Eammon Santry and Vicky Scott, "Creative versus Planners," *Campaign*, November 4, 1988, pp. 71–72.
7. Betsy Sharkey, "Dissecting the Creative Process," *Adweek Special Report*, December 5, 1988, pp. F.K. 22–23.

8. Roxanne Hovland, Gary Wilcox, and Tina Hoffman, "An Exploratory Study of Identifying Characteristics of Advertising Creatives: The Creative Quotient Test," 1988 annual American Academy of Advertising conference, Chicago, April 11, 1988.

9. Bruce Stauderman, "Creativity Is Hard Work," *Advertising/Marketing Review*, July 1985, pp. 4–5.

10. John Keil, *How to Zig in a Zagging World: Unleashing Your Hidden Creativity* (New York: Wiley, 1988).

11. Bill Moyers, "Sources of Creativity," *Members Only*, November 1982, p. 1.

12. Emily Smith, "Are You Creative?" *Business Week*, September 30, 1985, pp. 80–84.

13. David Mars, "Organizational Climate for Creativity," *Occasional Paper No. Four* (Buffalo, N.Y.: Creative Education Foundation, 1969).

14. Alex Kroll, "Let's Take the Imagination out of the Garage," *Advertising Age*, July 12, 1982, pp. M20–21.

15. Bob Garfield, "Murphy's Spots Go Against Grain," *Advertising Age*, October 26, 1987, p. 48.

16. David Kalish, "Copy-Cat Advertising," *Marketing & Media Decisions*, March 1987, pp. 22–23.

17. J. P. Guilford, "Traits of Personality," in *Creativity and Its Cultivation*, ed. H. H. Anderson (New York: Harper & Brothers, 1959); *The Nature of Human Intelligence* (New York: McGraw-Hill, 1967); "Creativity—Retrospect and Prospect," *Journal of Creative Behavior*, 7:4 (1973), pp. 247–252.

18. James Webb Young, *A Technique for Producing Ideas*, 3d ed. (Chicago: Crain Books, 1975).

19. S. A. Mednick, "The Associative Basis of the Creative Process," *Psychological Review*, 69 (1962), pp. 220–232.

20. Leonard N. Reid and Herbert Rotfeld, "Toward an Associative Model of Advertising Creative Thinking," *Journal of Advertising*, 5:4 (1976), pp. 24–29.

21. Edward de Bono, *Lateral Thinking: Creativity Step by Step* (New York: Harper & Row, 1970).

22. Bruce G. Vanden Bergh and Keith Adler, "Take This Ten Lesson Course on Managing Creatives Creatively," *Marketing News*, March 18, 1983, sect. 1, p. 22.

23. Jerry Juska, "An Evaluation of the Effectiveness of Word Association Exercises for Training Programs in Creativity," Ph.D. thesis, Northwestern University, June 1988.

24. Bruce Stauderman, "Creativity, Part II," *Advertising/Marketing Review*, August 1985, pp. 4–5.

25. W. J. J. Gordon, *The Metaphorical Way of Learning and Knowing* (Cambridge: Penguin Books, 1971); Jack Fincher, "The New Idea Man," *Human Behavior*, March 1978, pp. 28–32.

26. Jim Osterman and Philip Stelly, Jr., "Parents Become 'Pushers' in F&A Ads," *Adweek*, January 23, 1989, p. 16.

27. Betty Edwards, *Drawing on the Right Side of the Brain* (Los Angeles: Tarcher, 1979).

28. Thomas R. Blakeslee, *The Right Brain: A New Understanding of the Unconscious Mind and Its Creative Powers* (New York: Berkley Books, 1983).

29. Steve Blount, "The Big Idea—How to Find It, How to Use It," *Madison Avenue*, November 1982, p. 1.

30. I. A. Taylor, "The Nature of the Creative Process," in *Creativity: An Examination of the Creative Process* (New York: Hastings House, 1959).

31. Young, op. cit.

32. Rollo May, *The Courage to Create* (New York: Norton, 1975).

33. Alex F. Osborn, *Applied Imagination*, 3d ed. (New York: Scribners, 1963).

34. May, op. cit.
35. Bruce G. Vanden Bergh, Leonard N. Reid, and Gerald A. Schorin, "How Many Creative Alternatives to Generate," *Journal of Advertising*, 12 (1983), p. 4.
36. Osborn, op. cit.
37. Sarah Stiansen, "'Big Idea' Void Moves Firms to 'Manage' Creativity," *Adweek*, September 19, 1988, p. 30.
38. Vanden Bergh, Reid, and Schorin, op. cit.
39. Sharkey, op. cit.
40. Sharkey, op. cit.
41. Don Koberg and Jim Bagnall, *The Universal Traveler* (Los Altos, Calif.: Kaufmann, 1976).
42. John Fiedler, Panel Discussion: "Can a Scorpio Creative Director Find Happiness with a Virgo Researcher?" AAF Conference, Atlanta, May 1982.
43. Debbie Seaman, "HDM Takes a Ride on the Wild Side," *Adweek*, August 8, 1988, p. 20.
44. Barbara Mehlman, "BBDO Brings 'Good Things' to Client GE," *Madison Avenue*, November 1982, pp. 44–54.

Scoring Key (creativity test located on page 102: Creative characteristics score on the *left* side of the scale for the *odd*-numbered items and on the *right* side of the scale for the *even*-numbered items. Remember, this isn't a scientific test; it's designed for an analysis of your own creative characteristics.

CHAPTER

7

Visual Communication

KEY POINTS

- Advertising's front line of communication is the visual image.
- Words and pictures perform different, but complementary, functions.
- One of the most important creative decisions involves deciding what type of art or visual image to use.
- Composition guides the perception of the visual image.
- Color communicates; it speaks a language of its own.

7.1 VISUAL COMMUNICATION

In the last chapter we talked about the creative concept, the central idea that holds the advertising message together. The creative concept comes alive in the form of words and visuals. While words are very important in delivering the sales message and making the point, the visual in an advertising message is often the first thing seen and the last thing remembered. For that reason we'll move now to a discussion of visual communication.

The Importance of Visuals

Michael Schudson, in his thought-provoking book, *Advertising, The Uneasy Persuasion*, observed that "the importance of the visual relative to the verbal has grown." He explained, "Ads with little or no written message are reasonably common now but would have been unknown fifty or sixty years ago."[1] While there are still "talking heads" on television and

126

Exhibit 7-1: The ''snow monkey'' spot for Sony Walkman shows a monkey standing by a deserted seashore, wearing a Sony Walkman portable radio. The monkey, absorbed by the music, closes its eyes and listens. (Copyright Sony Corporation of America. Used by permission)

Ogilvy-style long-copy ads in print, more and more ads are relying on the power of the visual to attract attention and create memorable images. (See Exhibit 7-1.)

Television, of course, is a visual medium; it is also the most dominant medium in terms of aesthetic and stylistic impact. Television borrows techniques from cinema and experimental video tape (such as on MTV)—both of which use unusual visual techniques to create impact. All this experimental work splashes over other media that also use visuals, particularly magazine advertising. For example, computergraphics was pioneered by movies such as *Star Wars* and *Tron*, and was then used in commercials, and has also been adapted for print.

Clutter busting. The reason for the explosion in visual impact is the need for clutter-busting messages. Television and print are delivering more and more commercial messages—all fighting for the attention of an audience that is becoming increasingly adept at dodging the message. Advertisers are looking for high-impact advertising to break through this clutter. And impact registers first in the visual. That's the first thing that the typical reader sees and, of course, the screen image dominates the attention of the television viewer.

Mike Tench, vice president and creative director at the Martin Agency, emphasized that point in an *Adweek* special report that focused on the use of big, striking photos. He said, ''Visual ideas are becoming more important.'' He explained, ''The art directors know that the audience is harder to impress.''[2]

An intriguing visual that grabs attention is a Renault commercial that shows a man literally changing into a car. Similarly an American Motors ad shows a man riding a buffalo which turns into a Jeep.[3] These are described by their creators as attempts at ''zap-proofing,'' creative concepts that grab and mesmerize and make it impossible for the viewer to use the remote control to switch channels or skip the commercial.

Likewise in a visual presentation for Scotch videocassettes, a series of transformations take place as the logo on the package changes form repeatedly to an egg, a yolk, an olive, and a cue ball. Dick Kernan, executive vice president of creative services for Grey Advertising, described the Scotch commercial as "visually arresting."[4] "Arresting" means that viewers have been stopped in their tracks, and that's the first step in the process of getting the message across. The "Panda" ad for Busch Gardens (Exhibit 7-2) is an example of an arresting visual.

Visuals and the future. A number of experts predict that in the coming years commercials will become more and more visual, in keeping with the change from a print-oriented society to a picture-dominated society. Articles in *Advertising Age* herald "the age of the art director,"[5] where what you *show* is more important than what you say.

Dick Christian, former head of Marsteller and now a professor at Northwestern University, has said, "The culture of past generations is based on words. Tomorrow, attitudes, perceptions, and beliefs may be more important than facts." He concludes, "Tomorrow's culture, and much of today's, is based on images, concepts, and ideas."[6]

Visuals and global advertising. Visual communication is also an important trend in the developing area of global advertising, where transnational advertising by multinational companies is complicated by multiple languages. Visual communication, using universally understood images and symbols, is making an end run around language-based communication to make multinational, as well as global, advertising possible.

An article in the British mass media magazine *The Listener* described successful global advertising in the satellite age as using simple ideas, presenting strong brand images, having maximum visual and musical impact, and using a minimum amount of language.[7] In an article on 1992 (the predicted date for a single European market with no national borders), the *London Times* described a successful pan-European advertisement as "a hit American tune, strong visual presentation, and a short slogan."[8]

Dr. Ronald Beatson, director general of the European Association of Advertising Agencies, told a Finnish audience, "As the message transcends national frontiers and languages it will rely increasingly on *nonverbal* communication." Furthermore, he said, "This puts a premium on the visual and musical content of commercials; and, as brands develop more expertise in nonverbal communication, I think we shall see this phenomenon appearing in print media too, with much more emphasis on graphics than on copy."[9]

The European influence. David Ogilvy brought an urbane sophistication to advertising that reflected his European background (actually Scottish). His work was cultured and polished with beautifully phrased copy. American advertising, in contrast, was bombastic and hard-sell. During the eighties, however, there was a resurgence of interest in "European-style" advertisements. But this European influence was expressed visually, rather than in cultivated phrases—with cars that looked like birds, bottles that looked like sculpture, and bathroom fixtures that looked like wings and airplanes.

Michael Schudson explains the European emphasis on visuals: "European advertising is even more visually centered than American because advertising crosses national and linguistic barriers regularly. . . . The visual quality of ads in Europe tends to be better than that in American

Exhibit 7-2: The ''Panda'' ad for Busch Gardens uses a high-impact illustration to create visual drama.

advertising because advertising has had to be so much less reliant on words."[10]

The Concept of Imagery

image: a mental picture

An **image** is a mental picture. It's a very important part of imagination and cognitive processing. When an individual understands something, he or she typically responds with, "I see what you mean" or "I get the picture." That should tell you how important images are to the basic human mental process.

The process of thinking visually is sometimes referred to as *imagination* or *visualization*. Writers as well as artists are able to see "pictures in the mind." While artists sketch their images with pencils and felt tips, writers paint pictures with words. Imagery is the ability to recall sensory impressions—how something looks, feels, smells, tastes, and sounds. Advertising calls for imagination in all areas on all levels. Imagination means being able to see things in "the mind's eye."

An ad that relies on imagery is one for General Foods' Dutch Chocolate Mint Coffee. The picture is a huge bowl of mint ice cream with chocolate chips. The headline says, "Picture melting mint chocolate chip ice cream in a coffee cup."

The importance of images was underscored in a *New York Times Magazine* article that described the international youth market. The article said that this group speaks a "common fashion language," a style in clothing and fashion that it described as "global melange." The significance of this is that the article pinpointed *universal images* as the driving force behind this phenomenon. "It's clear that young people draw their ideas from a common image bank."[11] "Where do these universal images come from and how can they travel with the speed of a fax? The important thing is that a fashion trend like "street style" varies little from country to country, from Madrid to Modena to Mobile.

Brand images. Images are an important part of branding. What do you think of when you think of Coke? L'Eggs? Marlboro? Maytag? Pillsbury? Kool Aid? Morton's Salt? Vlasic pickles? It's probably something visual. The image can be a logo (a written version of the brand name), like the distinctive Coca-Cola name, or it can be packaging, like the unusual shape of the Coca-Cola bottle or the L'Eggs egg-shaped container. An image can also be built on a character such as Maytag's lonely repairman, the Pillsbury Doughboy, Kool Aid's smiling pitcher face, Morton's little girl with the umbrella, or the Vlasic stork with its Groucho Marx voice. All these images act as memorability anchors.

Visualization. The word *visualization* is used in several different ways in advertising. One way is to refer to a presentation piece, called a **comprehensive**, that is executed by artists to show what the advertisement will look like after it is produced. This is a visualization of the complete ad, making the idea visible so others can "see" it while it is still in the talking stage.

Visualization also refers to the process of turning the creative concept into a visual. The words are translated into an effective piece of art that is both arresting and memorable. This type of visualization calls for a sound understanding of the principles of visual communication—what

comprehensive: a sketch of the ad idea that shows what the ad will look like

can and can't be done with a visual as well as knowledge of how a visual communicates its message. The chapter discusses the production as well as the perception of visual images.

Finally, visualization can mean the process of mentally "seeing" the solution to an advertising problem. This calls for a well-developed ability to *think visually* using the powers of mental imagery.

The Functions of Visuals

Advertising designers use visuals to accomplish a number of objectives. The primary objectives are to be captivating (to get attention) and to anchor an image in memory. Of course, reinforcing the creative concept is also important. Other functions are listed below.

FUNCTIONS OF VISUALS

- Get attention
- Anchor an image in memory
- Reinforce the creative concept
- Maintain interest by presenting a mesmerizing image or sequence
- Establish a mood
- Create believability through realism
- Demonstrate product features
- Depict situations and settings
- Establish a product personality
- Associate the product with certain symbols and lifestyles
- Overcome time and distance
- Bring inaccessible processes such as historical events or microscopic changes to the audience

---

With the trend toward less dependence on words, these objectives will become even more important in many creative strategies. Will the new emphasis on visual forms work in advertising and will these messages be effective—even in crossing national borders? *The Independent*, a London-based newspaper, described the "Euro-Future" of 1992, observing that "tomorrow's adult Europeans are already better at understanding images and graphics without words."[12] That's a thought-provoking statement—particularly considering that it appears in a newspaper.

Attention.   Advertisements are more or less persuasive depending upon their ability to get attention. Starch research[13] has shown that ads with illustrations are seen more than ads without, and the more compelling the visual, the more readers will note the ad and the more they will attend to further development of the message. This shows up in the Starch "read most" scores. There is a definite carry-over effect for compelling visuals. High "noted" scores tend to generate high "read most" scores.

What makes a visual arresting? Novelty and surprise are particularly intriguing. Even understatement can be novel. Bold graphics, big and bold type, and bright colors are strong attention-getting devices. Research in newspaper advertising has proved that size is a factor—the bigger the ad, the more attention it receives. Color is important, too. In a black-and-white environment, simplicity stands out. The principle here is contrast or novelty.

ARRESTING VISUALS

- Bold graphics
- Big, bold type
- Bright colors
- Novelty
- Surprise
- Contrast
- Personal interest

Interest is still the crux of the attention dimension. For someone who is hungry, a platter of steaming fried chicken can be arresting. Appetite appeal has been demonstrated over and over as a strong attention-getting device. It is difficult to describe the taste of pizza in words, but most people will salivate when they see a steaming pizza coming out of the oven in a commercial.

Even in trade advertising, which is much more concerned with providing information and a logical selling message, readership studies have found that striking visuals have proved effective.[14]

Memorability. People file away memories as traces of visuals, indelible images that are locked into the mind. Advertising research has found that people attend more to the visuals than to the words, and they tend to remember the pictures longer than the words.[15]

You can test this by scanning magazines. Turn the pages in a slow, rhythmic fashion and note your own patterns of observation. The first thing you will probably note is that you tend to see the picture first. If you stop scanning the ad and study it, then the words will begin to register. Now close the magazine and try to remember the ads you just scanned. In most cases, you will probably find you are remembering either the visual or the way the ad looked on the page.

The body of research findings generated by Starch has shown consistently that people are more likely to remember a print advertisement if it contains a photo.[16] Other researchers have found that recall of a brand name is significantly higher if the name is integrated with an illustration. Lutz and Lutz have found that pictorial elements are stronger at changing or affecting attitudes than are words.[17]

For years Harry McMahan and Mack Kile have been studying effective television commercials. They consider a commercial to be effective if it has an observable effect on sales. They have found one consistent characteristic, which they call "the visual plus," a "memory picture" that sticks in the mind and reminds the viewer of the basic message.[18] Creatives call that "the key visual" or "key frame" and plan their storyboards around that dominant image.

Visual Learning Consumers use advertising to gain information about products and point of view as well as to master skills. All these are learning objectives. Advertisements are read, studied, filed, and recalled by consumers who want information about certain products and issues. And all of that happens without assignments, teachers, grades, or threats of tests. It's a natural form of self-motivated learning that relies heavily upon visual communication.

How does advertising use visual literacy? Advertising uses demonstrations; it shows how products are to be used and how things are supposed to look. "How-to" information is usually presented visually. A cake mix ad may include a recipe, but the dominant visual is usually the finished product showing how it is supposed to turn out. Food advertising visuals include serving suggestions as a form of unobtrusive instruction. Likewise, furniture and home improvement ads inevitably include decorating suggestions.

Realism and symbolism. Realism is used in advertising to present a literal, accurate depiction of something—a product, an event. Conviction and belief are the objectives of persuasion, and they can be addressed most effectively with a realistic image. People believe what they see, and in advertising viewers see it in color; they see the size and shape and the package; they see it performing in tests; they see it pitted against the competition. Realism is used to intensify believability.

literal: a realistic or lifelike representation

symbolic: something that represents a more abstract concept

A **literal** picture is realistic and obvious and gives all the details. A **symbolic** picture is abstract, analogous, and ambiguous, and it demands that the reader or viewer get involved in translating or creating the meaning.

Symbols are used to express abstract concepts that can't be easily communicated literally. Examples are Prudential's rock, Travelers' Insurance Company's umbrella, and Merrill Lynch's bull. Quality, value, durability, and friendliness are all abstract concepts used in advertising. They can be symbolized, but they can't be shown.

Symbols are also used to develop associations, to link the product with settings, people, lifestyles, colors, a distinctive package, or a logo. Most symbols are visual. Symbols often are used for identification information, although they can express emotional meanings as well as factual ones. Rossiter and Percy, in their *Journal of Advertising* article on visual imagery,[19] note that visual images can lead to favorable attitudes without words. Images, in other words, can affect attitudes. A picture of a kitten with toilet paper can very effectively communicate softness, perhaps better than words.

Some simple literal concepts may be difficult to communicate, too. Roominess in a car is hard to picture. No matter how it is photographed, the inside of a car is still a tight, cramped space. How can the ease of handling, the thrill of speed be depicted? There's no way in a still picture to show actual motion, so advertisers are forced into using symbols and graphic conventions such as blurred tires and hair blowing in the wind. The Maxell ad is a good example of the exaggeration necessary to depict a "blast" of sound (see Exhibit 7-3).

If the symbol works, it provides a shortcut form of communication. The symbol expresses the essence of the idea, but not the details. It sim-

AFTER 500 PLAYS OUR HIGH FIDELITY TAPE STILL DELIVERS HIGH FIDELITY.

If your old favorites don't sound as good as they used to, the problem could be your recording tape.

Some tapes show their age more than others. And when a tape ages prematurely, the music on it does too.

What can happen is, the oxide particles that are bound onto tape loosen and fall off, taking some of your music with them.

At Maxell, we've developed a binding process that helps to prevent this. When oxide particles are bound onto our tape, they stay put. And so does your music.

So even after a Maxell recording is 500 plays old, you'll swear it's not a play over five.

maxell

IT'S WORTH IT.

Maxell Corporation of America, 60 Oxford Drive, Moonachie, N.J. 07074.

Exhibit 7-3: The Maxell "500 Plays" advertisement uses an arresting visual to dramatize a "blast of sound." (Courtesy of Maxell and Scali, McCabe, Sloves, Inc.)

plifies, and because of that it can convey meaning faster than a literal depiction with all its many details. Symbolism is used in advertising for this reason. It is another technique for compressing information and presenting complex messages in short time frames.

Psychological appeals to emotions are often best expressed in symbolic visuals—love is a mother and child, childhood is a tot and a puppy, fear is a fire in the home or an auto accident or a burglar. These emotions can be put into words, but a picture dramatizes them more powerfully and strikes at the core of human feelings. The emotional "button" or "trigger" is often a picture.

Quantified relations, particularly in size and amount, are often best expressed as visuals (see Exhibit 7-4). Anyone who has had a basic course in math knows that a pie chart explains the relative size of pieces of a whole much easier than words or even numbers. Most statistical findings are graphed for presentation, and analysis using graphs shows the results far faster than columns of numbers can.

7.2 ART

Art, or graphics is a generic term used in advertising to apply to the visual expression of the creative concept. It includes photography as well as illustration. Deciding how an advertisement or commercial will "look" is the art director's responsibility.

One of the most difficult problems faced by those who work on the creative side is how to communicate a concept that exists only as a loose picture in the mind. In order to move into the "execution" decisions and make a rough idea materialize on paper, there are some basic decisions that have to be made. Generally, every visual demands decisions in the following areas: illustration or photography, color or black and white, product depiction, and style or "look."

Basic Decisions

Photo or illustration. Illustrations and photographs have an entirely different feeling. In general, an illustration (or animation in television) is more unreal, more fanciful; a photograph can be more literal and realistic. These distinctions are inherent in the way viewers perceive the two forms. Artwork is always a metaphor, an abstraction, a manipulated and constructed image. It can look like reality, but it is never real. It abstracts, it eliminates details, it focuses attention. Because it abstracts, it can communicate faster and more pointedly. It can also intensify meanings and moods. It is an ideal medium for fantasy and escape.

Photography has a reality, an authenticity, that makes it powerful. Most people believe their eyes, and when they are shown a photograph it appears to them as reality. Most people feel that pictures don't lie. For credibility, photography is a good medium. Photographs, of course, can also create evocative, abstract, and fanciful images, but, generally, photography is used in advertising because of its realism.

Research by Ogilvy & Mather shows that, in general, photographs work better in advertising than do drawings. The O&M studies found that

OGILVY & MATHER

2 EAST 48 STREET, NEW YORK 10017

907-3400

Client: HERSHEY FOODS
Product: KISSES
Title: "LITTLE KISSES/MAN"
Commercial No.: HUKI 7013
Date Approved: 4/2/87

1. (MUSIC UNDER) MAN SINGS: Little Hershey's Kisses

2. have big, big chocolate.

3. Little Hershey's Kisses have big, big chocolate.

4. Little Kisses have big chocolate

5. you're gonna love.

6. They got little silver wrappers.

7. They got tiny little flags.

8. They got big, big chocolate.

9. They live in great big bags.

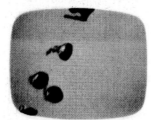

10. Little Hershey's Kisses

11. have big, big chocolate.

12. Little Kisses have big chocolate you're gonna love.

Exhibit 7-4: The HERSHEY'S KISSES® chocolates commercial uses constructed oversize models to emphasize the concept of "bigness" for a tiny product. (Courtesy of Hershey Foods Corporation. The conical configuration, the attached plume device, and the words HERSHEY'S KISSES are registered trademarks of Hershey Foods Corporation)

ART DECISIONS

When to use photos	When to use artwork
Depicting realism	Portraying fantasy
Comparing	Showing how something works (technical illustrations, diagrams, cutaways)
Demonstrating	
Showing performance tests	Relating numbers (charts and graphs)
Communicating news events	
Evoking human interest	Symbolizing
Creating a mood	Evoking humor
Exaggerating effects	When photos won't reproduce well
	When subject is impossible to photograph

---

photography increases recall 26 percent over artwork. In reporting this, Bruce Stauderman observed, "In terms of intrusiveness, photography can be more arresting, more shocking, more compelling." He concludes, "So, as an attention-getter, the 'live' photography usually wins hands down."[20]

There are a few photographers, illustrators, and designers who have become national figures. Seymour Chwast and Milt Glaser have been dominant figures in the design world since the sixties. Glaser is well known for his illustrations used in the Perrier "Earth's first soft drink" campaign. His "Full-color sound" ad for Sony (see Exhibit 7-7) is in New York's Museum of Modern Art.

Some of the best known names in photography are Irving Penn, Richard Avedon, Annie Leibowitz, and Dennis Manarchy. Avedon photographed the Calvin Klein ads, including the famous one with Brooke Shields. He has also done the celebrity-studded campaign for Revlon that asks, "What makes a woman unforgettable?" Annie Leibowitz shot the American Express "Cardmember" series with personality portrait studies of famous people like Ray Charles, Quincy Jones, Dennis Conner, Wilt Chamberlain, and Willie Shoemaker. She also shot the Arrow Shirt campaign that shows shirts, and the people who wear them, going from formal to casual. Dennis Manarchy's work appears in ads for Nike, Soloflex, and Harley-Davidson.

Color or black and white.   Another basic decision is the use of color. Print advertisements can be produced in black and white, full color, or spot color. The advertising medium has some effect on this decision. Most magazines provide quality full color, while most newspapers are more limited in their ability to reproduce quality color images. In addition, full color is more expensive in most advertising media. Spot color, the addition of a second or third accent color, is used to create attention-getting effects in what essentially is a black-and-white format. Television commercials, of course, are generally filmed in color, although black and white and sepia tints are used to create a "documentary look" in both print and video.

There are creative reasons behind the color decision, too. Black and white is dramatic and more abstract. It is used to create dramatic and documentary effects. Sometimes it is used just to be different, as in a magazine where all the other ads are in full color. The early Volkswagen Beetle ads used black and white in an era when American car advertising was bombastic and colorful. It was a technique of deliberate understatement.

Color, however, is more realistic and it is essential in literal messages. It is very difficult to create a mouth-watering effect for a pizza advertisement when it is depicted in black and white. We'll talk more about color later in this chapter.

Product depiction. Another critical decision is the depiction of the concept and the product. What will be the *content* of the visual? How does it express your big idea? You may think that describing the content is the easiest part of the proposal process. In fact, it's the hardest.

It is easy in advertising to get carried away with a great idea and forget about the product. For that reason it's important in this part of the decision making to think about how the product is to be treated. The product may be pictured alone or against some dramatic background. The product alone is frequently used with new-product introduction when name and product recognition is the primary objective. It is also used in the maturity stage as a reminder of the stature and image of the product.

An interesting example of a campaign that turns the product into a piece of artwork is the Citizen Noblia ads which turn wristwatches—and the arms they are worn on—into exotic animals. The hand-painted wrist art makes wristwatches look "as beautiful as a peacock," "as exotic as a parrot," and "as sleek as a panther."

Where the focus of the advertisement is on the product, we call the technique product as hero. Beer advertising is an area where the usual technique is to show a group of guys holding the beer. Campbell-Mithon developed a series of product-as-hero spots for Corona that broke the stereotype. One spot focuses on two bottles of Corona half submerged in a lake. A turtle and a fish swim around them with the background sounds of water gently lapping on the shore. It's like a still life. Another spot shows a fleet of inflated flamingo pool toys floating right to left across the screen. Some pool toys have Coronas resting in them; some have limes. In his review of the campaign, Bob Garfield describes them as "minimalist advertising at its best."[21]

Another technique is to show the product in use. The setting becomes very important here in terms of whatever props are necessary to make the situation credible. People are also important because they become role models, and viewers must be able to identify with them in that situation.

A variation on the product-alone treatment is the use of a product in a monumental setting. The objective is to create some kind of emotive response to the background situation that will carry over to the product. Cars, for example, are frequently shown against mountains, beaches, and setting sun scenes. Perfume ads show the bottle against exotic locales and elegant, romantic settings. The setting is used to create an association, to express symbolically the type of psychological appeal identified in the creative strategy.

Style and "look."   The tone of the design derives from the creative strategy. An illustration, for example, can be executed in a rough, loose, primitive, or tight style. Photographs can depict images that are formal or informal, casual or uptight. Execution style is particularly important for illustrations. If the artist works very tightly, then the art will be more formal, restrained, or even technical. If you ask for a loose style, the art will be more playful and free.

The "look" of an ad tends to follow design trends. The seventies saw lots of ads with a *nostalgic* look mirroring either art noveau or art deco styles. The early eighties was a period when *new wave* ads were popular—European, fluid motion, and surrealistic. MTV brought fast cuts, jerky motion, and ambiguity. The *warm and gentle* look has always been around, but it is particularly appropriate for the Bush era; particularly with the soft-focus technique. Other styles that have been in and out include *cinema verité*—"docu-ads" with hand-held camera, and tinted and grainy film. Examples are the Levis 501 Blues ads and Michelob's "The night belongs to Michelob" campaign. The *minimalist* look is simple, with a few elements artfully arranged. *Retro* is a style that picks up on the look of the forties and fifties. *Hyper-reality* focuses tight on sweaty faces and straining bodies as in the Reebok urban basketball spot.[22]

Calvin Klein has maintained a distinctive look for his products in such diverse areas as clothing, perfume, and now personal care products. Exhibit 7-5 illustrates the high-fashion but somewhat mystical Calvin Klein look in hair care products.

Medium   If you decide to use art, there are still a number of other specific decisions to be made. An illustration can be rendered (executed) using a number of different techniques. A black-and-white pencil sketch is the simplest form of line art. A sketch can also be done in color. For fine details a pen-and-ink illustration is good, particularly with cross-hatching details to create shadows.

Color can be achieved by using watercolor, tempera, pastels, and felt tip markers. Watercolor and pastels give a soft feeling. Tempera can be both soft and hard. Felt tip markers give a feeling of casualness, although they can provide edge and detail.

Other techniques include wash drawings using gray watercolors over pen and ink drawings to soften the edge and add shadows. Airbrush techniques are used to soften edges or to delete entire sections of an illustration or photograph. A scratchboard gives a rough feeling to an illustration. Both scratchboard and cross-hatching are stylized and can create feelings of age and antiquity. Cartooning is another type of line drawing that can be executed either in black and white or flat colors.

Sources of art.   Every metropolitan area has freelance artists and design studios. This is your best source for original art. Other types of art are available besides originally created work. Primitive types of art are appropriate for nostalgia or historical effects. These include woodcuts, engravings, and rubbings. These can be original works or they can be

Exhibit 7-5: While the focus of this Calvin Klein ad is clearly on hair, the use of a sepia tint technique ties in with the original fragrance ads to reinforce the Calvin Klein look across the entire brand and range of products.

reproduced from antique sources. A source of inexpensive historical art is the Dover Pictorial Archives, which reproduces illustrations that once appeared in publications for which the copyright has run out.

There are other sources of inexpensive commercial art besides original art done by an artist. A number of commercial art houses provide "clip art." You can buy a book of art or a series of small volumes of art on special topics that can be used anywhere without paying a royalty or needing permission. Of course, anyone can use the same art. There is nothing exclusive about clip art.

Photography. There are photographers who specialize in just about everything from fashion and food to architecture. Each specialty has its own techniques and effects. Food photography, for example, demands an understanding of cooking and food presentation, and shots are taken under incredibly difficult circumstances. Naturalness in food presentation is sometimes extremely difficult to achieve under the hot lights of a set. Shots of ice cream and beer in ice-covered mugs demand ingenuity and a knowledge of look-alike substances. In fashion photography it can take hours to "pin" a model so that the fit is exact, the creases fall perfectly, and the wrinkles don't show.

In addition to hiring photographers, you can also go to photo houses that will supply stock photos and stock film footage—like clip art. You buy the photo and you can use it without paying any additional royalty. Of course, everyone else can buy and use it, too. An example of stock photography is the forest shot used in the *Wall Street Journal* Radio Network ad (see Exhibit 12-1 in Chapter 12). The photo was provided by the Ibid stock photography studio.

Computer Graphics

Sophisticated computer graphic systems, such as those used to create film animation and *Star Wars* special effects, plus computer graphic slide systems like Genographics and Dicomed, have pioneered the creation of imaginative art on computer. Computer graphic specialists are using the Quantel Paint Box system to create and manipulate all kinds of images including video. Adobe Systems is producing state-of-the-art graphics software for use with personal computers.

digitizing: breaking an image into small squares that can be read and coded by a computer

Digitizing images is done by breaking the images down into a grid of tiny sectors, each one identified by a computer code. It is possible to convert still photographs to digitized graphics that can be used on a personal computer, such as a Macintosh or an IBM-PC. More sophisticated systems are available to digitize moving images for video and film. Digitized images have even been used for outdoor advertising.

Computer graphics specialists brag they can do anything with an image using a computerized "paintbox"—they can make Robert Redford look 80 and Ronald Reagan look 40. They can look at any object from any angle or even from inside out. Computerized paintboxes have 16 million colors available.[23] Photographs of real objects can metamorphose into art or animation and then come back to life again. The technology is bringing an exciting fusion of techniques that combine real-life photography with computer graphics and animation, as in the *Roger Rabbit* movie. The creative opportunities are limited only by the imagination of the artists using the computer.

As an example of what can be done, a commercial by the Charlex production company for Pringles showed six kids munching on some Pringles that they appeared to be getting out of their computer screens. The set is a marriage of live elements including such standard classroom fixtures as desks, chairs, computers, students, bookcases, and a portrait of George Washington. The scene, however, is "perfectly colorized, cloned, and totally paintboxed right down to shadows and lighting." The wide angle reveals six kids, but two of the youngsters were created by paintbox. Likewise, only three computers existed in the original scene; the rest were cloned by paintbox.[24]

Composition

composition: the arrangement of the elements in a picture

The way elements are arranged within a picture or photograph is called **composition**. Composition is based on both psychology and aesthetics. The professional is trying to compose an image that directs the eye to the significant elements and organizes the visual field, while at the same time creating an image that is aesthetically pleasing.

Planes. The vertical and horizontal are imaginary axis lines that define the orientation of the visual. A standard magazine page is two dimensional, and layouts are designed to work in the vertical plane in full-page ads. Double-page ads, however, focus on the horizontal. In television, the plane also is horizontal. Occasionally, a print layout will use the visual techniques of illusion to create the feeling of depth. Vanishing lines, creating perspective, are used to establish the illusion of a third dimension.

Rule of thirds. In most discussions of composition, one of the first suggestions is to avoid dividing things in half. In other words, if you are photographing or drawing a scene, try to position the horizon so that it is either above or below the halfway mark. Dividing a visual into two equal pieces is considered to create disinterest because there is no dominance between two equal pieces. If one is larger than the other, the relationships become more interesting visually.

Likewise, you will hear that you should avoid putting your center of interest directly in the middle of a composition. The middle is considered a dead spot, a position of minimal visual interest. It is better to locate the center of interest above, below, or to the side of dead center.

These two principles regarding equal parts and dead center are addressed in a concept developed by Kodak called "the rule of thirds." The principle is that when the horizontal and vertical dimensions of any composition are divided into thirds, an arrangement of nine sections is the result. The four points where the lines intersect are the points of maximum visual impact, and the natural location in a composition for the element considered to be the "center of interest." If you scan through a magazine and check the photographs, you will see that many of them use the rule of thirds and that the major elements are located on these intersections (see Figure 7-1).

Framing. Another compositional technique that is used in advertising visuals is the idea of *framing*. In photography, a long-distance scene will be shot using a tree and its limbs in the foreground as a frame that extends across the top and down one side. Sometimes the scene will be

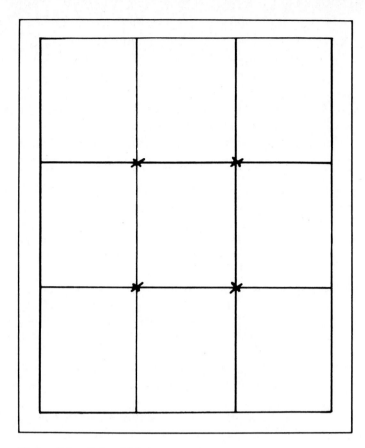

Figure 7-1: Rule of thirds.

framed by a window or by the lines of a door, porch, or column. This technique establishes a more visible distinction between foreground and background, intensifying the feeling of depth.

Most print ads are framed by a **margin** of white space which creates visual separation from surrounding text and competing ads. Sometimes in magazine advertising the frame is eliminated by **bleeding** the photo or art past the trim edge of the page. The extension, the feeling of "oversize," is used to create visual dominance and impact.

Scale.   A person, tree, car, or other identifiable figure can be used in a composition to establish *scale*. In other words, size is relative and sometimes it is difficult to know how large or small something is unless it is next to something else that serves as a visual reference. We know how tall a person generally stands and therefore a figure of a person next to a rock makes it clear just how large the rock really is. Otherwise, the rock could be tiny or huge and there would be no way to know from the visual.

Leading lines.   Elements within a composition can create a visual pattern of lines, and these lines can be used to direct the eye. A shot of a skeleton of a building under construction may contain a pattern created by the lines of the girders. These lines may converge and pull the eye to

margins: white space that frames an ad and separates it from surrounding material

bleed: a photo that runs to the trim edge of the page, allowing no margins

the center of attention, or they may move across a space creating a horizontal or vertical sweep that guides the eye just like yellow lines painted on the highway guide the motion of the car. A skilled photographer or artist has a good eye for these internal patterns that can be manipulated to direct the viewer's attention.

Lighting and shadows. The play of light and shadow creates both psychological and aesthetic effects. Bright lighting creates highlights that suggest openness, happiness, carefree moments, and freedom. The glistening image of reflected light suggests sunlight, ice, or a light shining on a wet pavement.

Colors that are saturated with light, or overexposed, can give a washed-out effect that creates the feeling of softness. A field of wildflowers, for example, might be overexposed to create this effect.

Shadows are dramatic and mysterious. "Rembrandt" lighting is a technique that lights the center of interest and lets the surrounding details fall into dark shadows. "Rim light" is a technique used to separate a subject from the background. The light is coming from behind the subject and serves as a visual outline of the figure.

There are other techniques for using lighting to create meaning. A single light from the direction of the camera or the viewer will flatten and wash out details. Light from the side, however, will emphasize texture. A diffused light on the face will soften features; however, a harsh light from above will create deep shadows on the face and create sinister effects. High-contrast lighting is harsh and creates dramatic effects. A light-colored background is softer than a dark background. Dark backgrounds often are used for dramatic effects.

Camera angles. Every visual is seen through the eye of a viewer and replicated by the artist or photographer. Every visual is looked at from some specific angle. The most common angle is direct and straight on, as if the viewer were looking at a set on a stage or in a display window from the street. This is the least obtrusive angle.

If the image is shot or drawn from below, looking up at it, its height is intensified. It appears to be taller, more monumental. People "look up" to something they respect. This visual perspective is used with people who are to be respected, and also for important buildings. In advertising, you will see this camera angle used to create a monumental image for the product. The Mobil One automobile oil can is usually shot from below. The can becomes a monumental figure. Liquor bottles are also often shot from this angle.

A viewing angle from above looking down tends to reduce the significance of the image—making the viewer feel superior. People "look down" on things that are "beneath" them. This angle is used to convey a sense of smallness for pictures of children and pets.

Another viewing angle you may hear mentioned is the "subjective camera," where the camera is in the position of the participant or user. This technique makes the viewer an actor in the visual. An ad for the title of a movie may be shot from below to create the effect that you are part of an audience. A writing pen or a watch may be shot from above, from the user's perspective. An ad for speakers shows them positioned on the floor. The camera is positioned where viewers would be if they were standing above the speakers, looking down.

The "worm's eye-view" is an angle that focuses down on the surface and dramatizes the size and the perspective of the visual. This is a technique used to dramatize scale. A shot from the plate on a baby's highchair looking up at the baby would be an example of a worm's-eye view.

Images that are shot tilted are seen as dynamic. These angles suggest movement and excitement. The image is seen as unstable or off balance and that involves the viewer or reader. There is a compulsion to right the object and stabilize it, to bring it to a position of rest. It's like a picture hanging crooked on the wall. It attracts attention by reaching out to the viewer. There is a compulsion to get involved.

The scene.   The definition of a scene is another aspect of the viewing eye that creates meaning. A scene can be shot or drawn from a long distance off—a *long shot* or panoramic shot. A shot can also be *close up*, so close that the texture in the paper or the pores on the skin are visible. A long shot is used in cinema and video as an "establishing" shot; it sets the scene by showing the entire location. A close-up magnifies and intensifies the significance of the image. It is a more "emotional" shot. It can also suggest a close, intimate relationship. Viewers are only this close to something they own or care about.

7.3   COLOR

Color has always been known to be a grabber in advertising. Research has consistently shown that color ads outpull black-and-white ads. That principle, however, has to be balanced against the principle of contrast, which says that black and white can stand out if everything else is in color. Guess, the clothing company, has been using black-and-white advertising since 1975.

The Seven-Up Company used black and white for the introduction of Cherry 7Up. The characters and scenery are black and white, such details as a tie and scarf are shown in pink, and the Cherry 7Up can is in full color. Janet Brown, account supervisor at Leo Burnett, says that "Pink on black and white really dramatizes the essence of the product." Brown explains that there's no other major soft drink out there that's pink. The campaign has been so effective that it captured 1.3 percent of the market in its first nine months, making it the most successful soft drink introduction since Diet Coke[25] (see Exhibit 7-6).

Color Theory   A discussion of color involves physics and physiology, as well as aesthetics and graphic production. Color is reflected in and through light. There is nothing *red* in an apple; it's all in how it is perceived. If you look at an apple in a dark room, for example, it may seem gray. If you look at it under a blue or green light, it will appear black. However, if you really want to make it look super red, display it against a green background.

Color is light, and the human eye sees color only as light is reflected from or passes through some object. If all light is reflected, then it is called

Exhibit 7-6: Cherry 7Up used a touch of pink on essentially black-and-white visuals to dramatize the color of the beverage. (Cherry 7Up storyboard used courtesy of The Seven-Up Company)

"white." If all light is absorbed, the object is called "black." Color is analyzed in terms of three characteristics: hue, saturation, and brightness.

The *hue* is the color: in other words, "red" or "blue" or "green." These colors are created from a spectrum of light, the familiar rainbow with colors that proceed from red through orange, yellow, green, blue, and violet. Approximately 150 separate shades are distinguishable by eye. These colors can be seen by splitting a beam of light through a prism. The position of each color in the spectrum is carefully determined by measuring the reflective properties of its light.

Saturation is the relative strength or purity of the color, for example, off-white or grayish-blue. This suggests that the saturation of color is not total. In fact, it is possible to alter saturation by changing the shade or the tint. Changing the shade is done by darkening the saturation; changing that tint is done by lightening the saturation. These modifications are created by adding shades of white or black to the basic hue.

The third way color varies is *brightness*, and this is a measure of the intensity of the light a color reflects. A bright color reflects lots of light, while a dull color absorbs light. A pink, for example, can be bright or dull in terms of its reflective capability.

The color wheel. The color wheel is used to locate the relative position of colors. Primary colors are red, blue, and yellow. The secondary colors lie directly across the color wheel from the primaries. They are orange, green, and violet (see Figure 7-2).

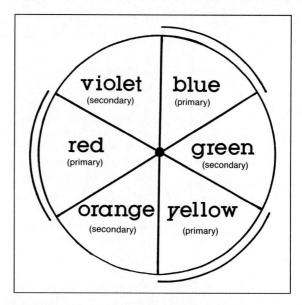

Figure 7-2: Color wheel indicating primaries and secondaries.

In addition to primary and secondary, there is another way to describe these color relationships. A complementary color is the color opposite it on the color wheel. The primary color yellow has the secondary color violet as its complementary color. The primary color red has green as its complementary color. These complementaries are natural pairs of colors. They bring out the best in each other. That is why the red apple looks so much brighter on a green background than on an orange background.

These complementaries used together are also bright and attention-getting. They make use of the strongest contrast. For example, yellow and violet, blue and orange, and red and green are used to create bold effects. When complementaries are used together, both seem to be emphasized. Neither one is dominant.

Neighboring values are the colors on each side of any given color. These are harmonious combinations of colors. They go together because they share some hue in common. Violet and green are the two neighbors to blue. Either one will be harmonious with blue.

Clashing or garish colors can be created by working with the relationships that are neither complementary nor secondary. For example, red and blue, depending upon the shades used, sometimes appear to conflict. The clashing effect can be created when two colors are used with shades that move away from the basic hue. For example, red and blue both have violet as a neighbor. If a clashing effect is desired, a shade of blue that moves a little toward green or a shade of red that moves a little toward yellow is effective.

This is the equivalent of a hard-sell use of color. This clashing effect is used occasionally in discount store advertising, because it creates this jangling effect. It's the visual equivalent of the fast-talking salesperson.

Color composition.   Another way to talk about hue is in terms of its light composition. Television uses the *additive* colors of red, green,

---

COLOR SYMBOLISM

- *Red:* Generally exciting, cheerful, defiant, and powerful. Also associated with heat, anger, passion, war, and blood. Red is stimulating.
- *Blue:* Is often considered a happy color. It means peace, calmness, loyalty, security, and tenderness. Also associated with intellectual appeals as opposed to emotional (red). Can be identified with cold, ice, distance, and infinity as well as calm reflection.
- *Yellow:* Associated with the sunlight and openness as well as radiance and vividness. Because of its luminosity, it is highly attention-getting.
- *Green:* Like blue, also associated with serenity and calmness as well as nature. It is a quiet color. It is used symbolically to suggest hope, meditation, and tranquility.
- *Black:* Associated with distress, despondency, and defiance. Used to suggest hate and death, but also can be used to express power and elegance, especially if it is shiny.
- *White:* In Western cultures, white means purity as well as sanitary and clean. By its lack of apparent color, it also conveys emptiness, infinity, and the inexplicable. White is used visually to express total silence.

---

and blue. They are called additive colors because when added together they create white. When the color on a color television screen is adjusted, the dots or lines of color appear more or less separately. When all three colors come together on the screen, the result is white. Projected visuals displayed on a white screen also use additive colors. This is the visual principle behind color slides and cinema. Stage lights, for example, are modified by "gels" of transparent color.

Printing, on the other hand, uses *subtractive* colors. The primary colors of ink, called "process colors," are yellow, magenta (a shade of red), and cyan (a shade of blue). These are transparent inks, and when they are printed one on top of another, they create black. Color prints made photographically are also composed of subtractive colors created and modified through the use of filters.

Color Symbolism In advertising, color is used for a variety of specific purposes. It creates moods, it draws attention, it emphasizes, it intensifies memorability, and it helps define foreground and background. It can also be used as a cue, to either associate with or symbolize something else. Visa ran an ad with the headline, "Why is the American Express Card green?" The Answer, "Envy." The copy explains that Visa offers a more impressive array of services. Black and white, contrasted against color, can be used to highlight changes in time or age.

Mood. The primary function of color in advertising is to help create mood and emotional responses. Color tints language with emotional connotations. We get blue when we are depressed; we see red when we are mad; we're feeling cowardly when we are yellow; we are cheerful when we're in the pink; we're in the dumps when we are in a brown mood or a brown study. These are color labels that society has attached to certain emotions.

Beyond these labels are definite color associations with moods, and these are used effectively in advertising to create an emotional foundation for a message. Some commonly accepted associations are as follows:

A famous advertisement designed by Milton Glaser for Sony tapes used the metaphor, "full-color sound," to describe audio richness. Music is described as color, and the colors are then associated with emotions and feelings. It's a multilayered example of metaphor (see Exhibit 7-7).

Temperature.   Colors can also be associated with temperature. The "warm" colors are those between red and yellow on the color wheel—including orange, gold, and shades of pink. These are high-energy colors. "Cool" colors are between and around blue and green, including turquoise and violet.

Restaurants, particularly fast-food places, use hot colors. They want to convey a feeling of "busyness" and yet friendliness. These colors help to keep people moving; they are less inclined to settle in and dawdle over their meal or coffee. Blues, purples, and silver are used in restaurants that are trying to project an elegant image. Cool colors also are used for sheets and blankets and locations where serenity and reflection are important.

Objectives of Color Use

Attention.   Certain colors are inherently eye-catching. Yellow is powerful because of its luminosity, and it is especially powerful when combined with black. The 3M Post-It Notes are yellow to get attention. That feature is depicted in Exhibit 7-8, which associates Post-It Notes with street signs that are also yellow. Red is aggressive and a strong attention-getting color. Bright colors, in general, are attention-getting—even a hue like pink will stand out when a bright shade is used.

Spot color is a printing technique used in advertising to take advantage of these characteristics of colors. For example, a strong attention-getting color can be used with the center of interest to make sure the eye is attracted to the most important element.

Emphasis.   Using strong attention-getting colors to attract the eye is another way to emphasize what you believe is the most important element to be seen. Emphasis means contrast, and to make something stand out it has to contrast with everything around it. If the other elements are printed in black or neutral tones and the dominant element is printed in red, then you have assisted the viewer/reader in the process of visually organizing the message.

Color coding.   Colors are easy to remember and, if you can create an indelible association between a color and a product, then you will be assisting the retention process. Color coding is a process of establishing visual cues.

A green ad in the newspaper with a picture of a cigarette pack will probably bring to mind the name of the product, Kools. Johnnie Walker Red has a long-running campaign that seeks to establish a link between the warm side of the color red and the product. Budget Rent A Car is

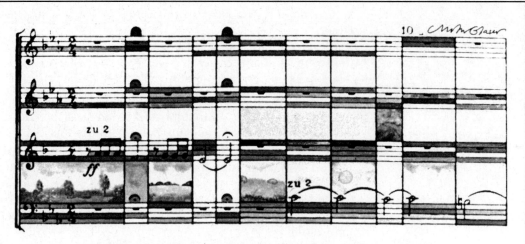

Sony Tape. Full Color Sound.

Music is full of color. Incredibly beautiful color. Color that you can hear...and (if you close your eyes) color you can almost see. From the soft pastel tones of a Mozart to the blinding brilliant flashes of hard rock to the passionately vibrant blues of the Blues.

In fact, one of the most famous tenors in the world described a passage as "brown ...by brown I mean dark...rich and full."

Music does have color. Yet when most people listen to music they don't hear the full rich range of color the instruments are playing. They either hear music in black-and-white, or in a few washed-out colors.

That's a shame. Because they're missing the delicate shading, the elusive tints and tones, the infinite hues and variations of color that make music one of the most expressive, emotional and moving arts of all.

Music has color. All kinds of color. And that is why Sony is introducing audio tape with Full Color Sound.

<u>Sony tape with Full Color Sound can actually record more sound than you can hear.</u>

So that every tint and tone and shade and hue of color that's in the original music will

be on the Sony tape. Every single nuance of color, not just the broad strokes.

Sony tape with Full Color Sound is truly different. Full Color Sound means that Sony tape has a greatly expanded dynamic range — probably more expanded than the tape you're using. This gives an extremely high output over the entire frequency range, plus a very high recording sensitivity.

There's even more to Sony tape with Full Color Sound, however. Sony has invented a new, exclusive SP mechanism for smoother running tape, plus a specially developed tape surface treatment that gives a mirror-smooth surface to greatly reduce distortion, hiss and other noise. Each type of tape also has its own exclusive binder formulation, that gives it extra durability.

Any way you look at it — or rather, listen to it, you'll find that Sony tape with Full Color Sound is nothing short of superb.

If you're not hearing the whole rainbow on your audio tape, try recording on Sony tape with Full Color Sound Then you'll be hearing all the glorious full color that makes every kind of music, music.

Exhibit 7-7: Sony's "Full-color sound" campaign developed the concept that music is colorful by relating different sounds to different colors. This campaign, by Milt Glaser, is one of the few that is signed by the art director. The original is in the permanent collection of the Metropolitan Museum of Art. (Courtesy of Sony Corporation of America)

YELLOW IS A SIGN OF IMPORTANCE.

That's why people with important business messages use our Post-it™ Notes adhesive note pads. Bright notes that stick virtually anywhere. To make sure your messages get noticed. Call 1-800-328-1684 for a free sample. Then get more Post-it Notes from a nearby stationer or retail store. And start getting the recognition you deserve.

Commercial Office Supply Division/3M

3M

Exhibit 7-8: 3M's Post-It Notes make good use of the color yellow and its association with attention-getting signs to build brand awareness. (Courtesy of 3M Commercial Office Supply Division)

building a campaign on its own color—orange. In the Chicago area, for example, the ads are headlined "The Big Orange of Chicago." Color coding can be a very strong tool in brand identity.

Depth definition. Color can be used to establish the foreground and background relationship, signifying the dominant element. A neutral or pastel color is often used as background with a brighter, stronger color used for the foreground elements. In perceiving visuals, we expect to see that relationship.

There are some unusual characteristics of color physics that also contribute to the perception of depth in the background/foreground relationship. Red and orange, for example, have been identified as **aggressive colors**—they seem to advance toward the viewer. Blue and green, the cool colors, are seen as **recessive**—they appear to retreat.

aggressive colors: colors that appear to advance

recessive colors: colors that appear to retreat

There is a physiological explanation for this phenomenon. Red falls on the rear of the retina where the lens grows convex and the result, as explained by vision expert Gerald McVey,[26] is that red and orange appear to approach the viewer. Objects in these colors appear larger. Blue and green fall in front of the retina where the lens flattens and, as a result, these colors appear to recede. Objects depicted in blue will appear to be smaller and off in the distance.

For these reasons, it is particularly important to plan your use of background colors carefully. Blue and green are natural colors for background, red isn't. If you use a blue image on a red field, the background may seem to be moving toward the viewer and fights with the image for dominance. The result is that peculiar illusion where the two colors seem to be in motion and changing position back and forth.

Color and Personality

Different people respond to different colors in different ways. Color preferences are to some extent a function of personality, but they also reflect social and cultural values. Research has found that extroverts, for example, seem to prefer the more highly saturated colors of blue, red, and green, while introverts prefer pastels.[27]

While preference by sex isn't consistent, some research has found that, in ads and displays, blue brings the highest returns from males while red brings the highest returns from females.

Favre and November report a number of experiments with people, products, and color.[28] A group of people were asked to evaluate coffee that had been poured from four different-colored pots: red, blue, brown, and yellow. The coffee was identical but the perceptions weren't. The coffee from the brown pot was considered too strong, the red pot poured coffee that was perceived as rich and full-bodied, coffee from the blue pot was thought to have a milder aroma, and the coffee in the yellow pot was considered weak.

In another experiment, the researchers reported that housewives given three different packets of washing powder, which varied only in the color of the packet, found significant perceived differences in the product's effectiveness. The soap in the yellow packet was considered too strong, the soap in the blue packet was judged not strong enough, and the packet with a combination of yellow and blue was supposed to contain soap that was "marvelous."

Advertising and Color   Obviously, color reactions are important personality characteristics. Ideally, if targeting were truly precise, professionals might be able to design ads using color patterns that would be most motivating for the particular type of personality being targeted by the message.

Color speaks to the emotions rather than to the reason. In some cases, the color and the design of the package are the only real differences between one product and another. Impulse purchases are particularly susceptible to color triggers. Red and yellow are known to be highly effective to stimulate impulse purchases.

In packaging, the first objective of the color is to command the eye. It has to be seen, to jump off the shelf, if it is to survive the intense competition of the self-service environment. Next, the package color is chosen for its ability to associate with certain desired qualities such as elegance, naturalness, softness, and so on.

Brand image is another aspect of advertising that is affected by color characterization. It goes all the way back to school colors—colors chosen to symbolize an entire group of people and all their activities. With the growth of self-service retailing, color is used as a continuity device as well as for identification. The use of a standardized color is an important part of most identity campaigns, as in the Johnnie Walker Red and Kool campaigns. And the color is chosen to reflect the personality of the brand or corporation.

Color communicates. It speaks a language of its own. Successful advertising and successful advertising campaigns use color as a powerful part of the message design.

SUMMARY

This chapter discussed the importance of the visual image and the critical role it plays in the development of the creative concept.

1. The three primary functions of a visual are to get attention, to anchor an image in memory, and to reinforce the creative concept.
2. Visuals that are arresting have some of the following characteristics: they are bold, bright, colorful, novel, contrasting, or surprising.
3. Television commercials, as well as print ads, that are effective have a "memory picture" that sticks in the mind.
4. Visuals communicate easily because they are easy to scan and comprehend at a glance and they are easy to file away in memory.
5. Visual realism is high in believability; visual symbolization is used to establish associations and abstractions.
6. Visuals are best used to prove claims, demonstrate, appeal to emotions, establish an association or mood, and show relationships; words are better for explaining abstract concepts.
7. Photos are used for realism; art for fantasy and technical illustration.
8. Composition directs the eye, organizes the visual field, and creates aesthetically pleasing images.
9. Color is used to get attention, emphasize an important element, contribute to mood, touch emotions, and color-code information to help with identification and recognition.

NOTES

1. Michael Schudson, *Advertising, The Uneasy Persuasion* (New York: Basic Books, 1984), p. 63.
2. Nancy Madlin, "Making the Photograph the Star," *Adweek*, Oct. 5, 1987, p. D12.
3. "Why TV Zappers Worry Ad Industry," *U.S. News & World Report*, November 12, 1984, pp. 66–67.
4. "Can Ad Agency Creativity Combat Zapping, Zipping?" *Television/Radio Age*, November 11, 1985, pp. 63–65.
5. Harvey Bailey, "What Happened to Copy? The Age of Art Directors Eclipsing Writers," *Advertising Age*, October 17, 1985, p. 67.
6. Richard Christian, "Can Advertising Survive Split 30s, Zapping, Globalization, High Tech, Million Dollar Minutes, Narrowcasting, and Even More Accountability?" *Back Stage*, May 31, 1985, pp. 12, 24.
7. David Bernstein, "Going for a Song," *The Listener*, August 11, 1988, p. 17.
8. "Shift from Cheek to Chic as French Tone Down Ads," *The Sunday Times* (London), December 11, 1988, p. D8.
9. Ronald Beatson, "The World's Largest Market," speech published by European Association of Advertising Agencies, Brussels, 1988.
10. Schudson, p. 253.
11. Ruth La Ferla, "It's a Small World," *New York Times Magazine*, January 15, 1989, pp. 44–48.
12. Stephen Ward, "Ad Agencies Prepare to Sell Us Our Euro-Future," *The Independent*, September 10, 1988, p. 5.
13. Philip W. Burton, *Which Ads Pulled Best* (Chicago: Crain, 1981).
14. Belinda Hulin-Salkin, "Use a Picture—and Fewer than 1,000 Words," *Advertising Age*, June 14, 1982, p. M20.
15. Julie A. Edell and Richard Staelin, "The Information Processing Pictures in Print Advertising," *Journal of Consumer Research*, 10 (June 1983), pp. 45–61.
16. Daniel Starch, "How Does the Shape of Ads Affect Readership?" *Media/Scope*, 10 (1966), pp. 83–85.
17. Kathy A. Lutz and Richard J. Lutz, "Effects of Interactive Imagery on Learning: Applications to Advertising," *Journal of Applied Psychology*, 62 (August 1977), pp. 483–498.
18. Harry McMahan and Mack Kile, "In TV Sports, One Picture Worth 10,000 Words," *Advertising Age*, April 27, 1981, p. 50.
19. John R. Rossiter and Larry Percy, "Attitude Change Through Visual Images in Advertising," *Journal of Advertising*, 9:2 (1980), pp. 10–16.
20. Bruce Stauderman, "Photography or Artwork," *Advertising/Marketing Review*, May 1987, p. 6.
21. Bob Garfield, "Corona Rises Above Sea of Beer-Ad Foam," *Advertising Age*, May 9, 1988, p. 104.
22. Mary Huhn, "Creative Trends," *Adweek*, September 14, 1987, p. FP16.
23. "Is This the New Face of Graphics?" *Advertising/Marketing Review*, March 1985, pp. 15–17.
24. William Meyers, "Psycho-Sell Looks to the Future," *Advertising Age*, January 21, 1985, pp. 18, 20.
25. Neal Santelmann, "Color That Yells, 'Buy Me,'" *Forbes*, May 2, 1988, p. 110.
26. G. F. McVey, "Putting Color into Your Visual Presentation," *Photomethods*, November 1976, pp. 57–59.
27. Faber Birren, *Color: A Survey in Words and Pictures* (New York: University Books, 1963).
28. Jean-Paul Favre and Andre November, *Color and Communication* (Zerach: ABC Verlag, 1979), p. 46.

8

Advertising Writing

KEY POINTS

- People who create ads love words—their meanings as well as their sounds.
- Advertising style differs in a number of ways from literary, or essay, style.
- Ad-ese, the use of formula copy, is a parody of good advertising writing.
- There are five basic writing techniques used in advertising: announcement, definition, description, narration, and explanation.

8.1 ADVERTISING AND WORDS

In advertising, words and pictures work together to create a creative concept. In the last chapter we discussed visual communication and the impact created by the visual; now let's consider the words and the style of advertising writing.

Most people in advertising spend their professional lives in search of the right "magic words." Copywriters, of course, are trying to find the right words to warm up a mood or soften resistance. The creative team struggles together to come up with a concept that expresses an appeal in words and pictures. The account executive tries to express the complexities of a marketing situation in a simple position statement. And—throughout the industry—both agency and industry executives are looking for the magic words to sell, defend, explain, and justify their recommendations and decisions.

Recruiters and interviewers patiently explain to students that what they look for is not so much technical knowledge but communication skills. Writing skill is required in every area of advertising. Ralph Zeuthen, a management supervisor at Compton Advertising, explained the need for good writing skills in an article in *Advertising Age:* "This year Compton people will put literally billions of words down on more than a million pieces of paper. It's a fair guess that, every day, the average word output matches the bulk of a bulky novel. Whatever else we are, we are undeniably people of the written word."[1]

The Copywriter

Advertising copywriters are excellent writers as well as savvy marketers. A former creative director at Ted Bates once said that a good advertising writer is a very competitive person—"a killer poet." A good copywriter wants to win, but wins with art.[2]

The analogy between advertising and poetry is based on some important similarities. Barbara Stern, in an article using literary analysis for advertising, explained that "Both are consciously created condensed written words that seek to affect the perceiver through evocative language." These "poets of commerce" use creative language to make the intangible tangible.[3]

The Right Word

You have to love words to be a copywriter—or even to be in advertising. Advertising is a search for the clever twist, the pun, the powerful description, the punch, the essence of nuance—for words that whip and batter, plead, sob, cajole, and impress. People in advertising get paid good money for playing very skillful word games. But you have to be good at it. You have to be an expert at words or, rather, a student of them. You know their meanings, their derivations, their moods and feelings, their sounds, and the reverberations and vibrations they create in someone else's mind.

John Caples, a legendary copywriter, was a master of words. He once made the point that a simple change in a single world can have major impact on the effectiveness of a message. For example, he wrote, "Once I changed the word 'repair' to 'fix' and the ad pulled 20 percent more."[4] Caples worked in direct response advertising and he learned to love research because it told him about the power of his words. He "studied" everything he wrote and developed an extraordinary feel for the power of English.

Literal meanings. Words have exact meanings and writers like Caples are deliberate in their search for the perfect word. A column that ran in *Advertising Age* written by Michael Gartner focused on the use and misuse of words. He quotes this headline from a *Wall Street Journal* ad: "Rid your home or plant permanently of pests and varmit with DeciMate." He wondered if the manufacturers of the product knew that the word "decimate" to the literal-minded means to kill only every tenth one. He also notes that "varmit" is a singular and "varmits" is plural; however, he speculates that the ad writer really meant vermin and that this word is both singular and plural.[5] Gartner also quoted a classified ad: "Well seasoned mixed firewood. $88 a chord." He observed that while "it struck a responsive *chord*, the wood is stacked in *cords*."

Connotative meanings. Words have meanings beyond the literal— meanings that are suggested or implied by their usage. These are **connotative** meanings. Only a sensitive writer like Caples would sense the difference between "fix" and "repair." *Fix* is something common people do; *repair* is what experts do. That's a distinction that is not found in any dictionary, but in tightly targeted advertising a shade of meaning that announced such a critical distinction in the audience could make the difference between advertising that is on target and off target.

connotation: a suggested meaning in addition to the explicit or literal meaning of a word

Writers and teachers of writing assign *personality characteristics* to words. In an article in *Writer's Digest* magazine,[6] Gary Provost described what he called "power" words. First, power words are *short*. "Rich" is stronger than "wealthy"; "rape" is stronger than "sexual assault." Power words also are specific. "Doberman" is more powerful than "dog"; "gossip," "prattle," and "chat" all have more power than "talk." Power also comes from active verbs. A passive compound verb like "was driving" is much weaker than "drove." He also suggests eliminating the "to be" verbs such as "is," "am," "was," or "will be." They are static. "Cigar smoke was in the air" is weaker than "Cigar smoke filled the air." Provost explains that, when more meaning is crowded into a short space, power is gained. The word "bully" is packed with punch and describes a person better than a phrase like a "mean person." "Wrote rapidly" can be changed to "scribbled," and "kissed lightly" to "pecked."

Provost says power words are usually the most *familiar*; obscure words just get passed by. An example of an advertisement that flirts with the unusual, obscure word is found in an ad for the Cayman Islands. The ad tries to break away from the clichés of travel promotion with a headline that says, "The climate of the Caymans is conducive to concinnity." While "concinnity" may be a perfectly good word, since it means "a harmony of fitness" and "studied elegance of design," it is totally unfamiliar. (We had to consult three dictionaries to find one that had a definition.)

On the other hand, a beautifully written ad for cashmere sweaters uses strong, distinctive words carefully chosen for their imagery. It begins: "On the slopes of the world's highest mountain range begins a remarkable journey that ends on one of life's lovely miracles." The power words are found in the second graph that continues: "Here the precious, downy fleece of the Kashmir goat is hand-plucked and taken by ox-cart to a railroad, then a coastal steamer and finally a cargo vessel which churns across the ocean to Scotland." Study the word choices and feel the richness of their imagery: "downy fleece," "hand-plucked," "ox-cart," "coastal steamer," "cargo vessel," and "churns across the ocean." Even though the end product is a delicate sweater, the writing reflects the feel of raw unprocessed fleece in transit. You can almost smell it.

Words also have *gender*. In an article on "whip words," Charles Ferguson says that men manage the language and have used typically male expressions to express power.[7] He explains that "man words carry the oldest articulated feelings of the role. Those seeking to arouse people to good causes use man words naturally, whether they are appropriate or not.'' An example is hymns, which he says "resound with battle language.'' He also notes that "in periods of national crisis the emotions of the male military tradition" are expressed in words of killing and conquest. These are used openly, he says, "to stimulate the contentious and combative side of our nature.'' Advertising talks about campaigns, targets, and strategies, obviously a field dominated by male language.

Certain products lend themselves to *atmosphere*, or *mood*, writing—namely perfume, cosmetics, and liquor. Old Grand Dad has been running a "Spirit of America" campaign that features beautiful shots of landscapes, often nostalgic, and a few lines of copy to capture the mood of the illustration. One depicts a riverboat scene through trees from the bank. The illustration caption says "Sundown on the Mississippi.'' The copy reads, "Men with imagination as big as the Delta Sky tamed the Mississippi. And at sunset, rivermen still wind down the day sipping America's native whiskey, Kentucky Bourbon.'' Another ad in the same series shows a cowboy on horseback herding cattle. Titled "Wyoming winter," the copy picks up a famous line from an early Jordan car ad: "Somewhere west of Laramie, men still ride from dawn til dusk. And settle down to a shot of Bourbon against the chill of the night.''

One of the most impressive advertisements ever was written by Bill Marsteller as a house ad for his agency. It ran in the *Wall Street Journal* under the headline "The wonderful world of words." The entire article plays with the connotative meaning of words. It starts out: "Human beings come in all sizes, a variety of colors, in different ages, and with unique, complex and changing personalities. So do words. There are tall, skinny words and short, fat ones, and strong ones and weak ones, and boy words and girl words.'' The rest of the copy illustrates the sizes, colors, ages, shapes, and personalities of words (see Exhibit 8-1).

Associative meanings. One aspect of connotative meaning is the associated meanings of a word. Lincoln Mercury got an unexpected, but fortunate, response from consumers when it used the slogan, "The shape you want to be in.'' Consumers not only interpreted it to be descriptive of the car, but of their own physical and financial states as well. Since the campaign was targeted to upscale baby boomers, the fitness message was a welcome, although unexpected, benefit.[8]

Probably the most famous sophisticated research into product names and their associations was conducted for a product that wound up with an absolutely unmarketable name, the Edsel. (Of course, some say the design was unmarketable, too.) Over a three-year period the agency came up with and tested, using association and projection techniques, some 2,000 names; then started over again with a new list of 18,000; whittled that down to 6,000, only to have the chair of Ford Motors throw them all out and use a family name, Edsel.

Sounds of Words   The sound a word makes can be a critical aspect of its choice. The noted columnist William Safire once ran a contest in the *New York Times Sunday Magazine* for the most beautiful word. He called it the "Miss Word Contest.''[9] The entries were categorized by sounds—meaning didn't count—only words that the ear of the hearer would find beautiful. The winners in some of the most "beautiful" sound categories are as follows:

Human beings come in all sizes, a variety of colors, in different ages, and with unique, complex and changing personalities.

So do words.

There are tall, skinny words and short, fat ones, and strong ones and weak ones, and boy words and girl words and so on.

For instance, title, lattice, latitude, lily, tattle, Illinois and intellect are all lean and lanky. While these words get their height partly out of "t's" and "l's" and "i's", other words are tall and skinny without a lot of ascenders and descenders. Take, for example, Abraham, peninsula and ellipsis, all tall.

Here are some nice short-fat words: hog, yogurt, bomb, pot, bonbon, acne, plump, sop and slobber.

Sometimes a word gets its size from what it means but sometimes it's just how the word sounds. Acne is a short-fat word even though pimple, with which it is associated, is a puny word.

Puny words are not the same as feminine words. Feminine words are such as tissue, slipper, cute, squeamish, peek, flutter, gauze and cumulus. Masculine words are like bourbon, rupture, oak, cartel, steak and socks. Words can mean the same thing and be of the opposite sex. Naked is masculine, but nude is feminine.

Sex isn't always a clear-cut, yes-or-no thing on upper Madison Avenue or Division Street, and there are words like that, too. On a fencing team, for instance, a man may compete with a sabre and that is definitely a masculine word. Because it is also a sword of sorts, an épée is also a boy word, but you know how it is with épées.

Just as feminine words are not necessarily puny words, masculine words are not necessarily muscular. Muscular words are thrust, earth, girder, ingot, cask, Leo, ale, bulldozer, sledge and thug. Fullback is very muscular; quarterback is masculine but not especially muscular.

Words have colors, too.

Red: fire, passion, explode, smash, murder, rape, lightning, attack.

Green: moss, brook, cool, comfort, meander, solitude, hammock.

Black: glower, agitate, funeral, dictator, anarchy, thunder, tomb, somber, cloak.

Beige: unctuous, abstruse, surrender, clerk, conform, observe, float.

San Francisco is a red city, Cleveland is beige, Asheville is green and Buffalo is black.

Shout is red, persuade is green, rave is black and listen is beige.

Oklahoma is brown, Florida is yellow, Virginia is light blue and Massachusetts is dark green, almost black. Although they were all Red, at one point Khrushchev was red-red, Castro orange, Mao Tse-tung gray and Kadar black as hate.

One of the more useful characteristics of words is their age.

There's youth in go, pancake, hamburger, bat, ball, frog, air, surprise, morning and tickle. Middle age brings abrupt, moderate, agree, shade, stroll and uncertain. Fragile, lavender, astringent, acerbic, fern, velvet, lace, worn and Packard are old. There never was a young Packard, not even the touring car.

Mostly, religion is old. Prayer, vespers, choir, Joshua, Judges, Ruth and cathedral are all old. Once, temple was older than cathedral and it still is in some parts of the world, but in the United States, temple is now fairly young. Rocker is younger than it used to be, too.

Saturday, the seventh day of the week, is young while Sunday, the first day of the week, is old. Night is old, and so, although more old people die in the hours of the morning just before the dawn, we call that part of the morning, incorrectly, night.

Some words are worried and some radiate disgusting self-confidence. Pill, ulcer, twitch, itch, stomach and peek are all worried words. Confident, smug words are like proud, lavish, major, divine, stare, dare, ignore, demand. Suburb used to be a smug word and still is in some parts of the country, but not so much around New York anymore. Brooklyn, by the way, is a confident word and everyone knows the Bronx is a worried word. Joe is confident; Horace is worried.

Now about shapes.

For round products, round companies or round ideas use dot, bob, melon, loquacious, hock, bubble and bald. Square words are, for instance, box, cramp, sunk, block and even ankle. Ohio is round but Iowa, a similar word, is square but not as square as Nebraska. Boston is, too—not as square as Nebraska, but about like Iowa. The roundest city is, of course, Oslo.

Some words are clearly oblong. Obscure is oblong (it is also beige) and so are platter and meditation (which is also middle-aged). Lavish, which as we saw is self-confident, is also oblong. The most oblong lake is Ontario, even more than Michigan, which is also surprisingly muscular for an oblong, though not nearly as strong as Huron, which is more stocky. Lake Pontchartrain is almost a straight line. Lake Como is round and very short and fat. Lake Erie is worried.

Some words are shaped like Rorschach ink blots. Like drool, plot, mediocre, involvement, liquid, amoeba and phlegm.

At first blush (which is young), fast words seem to come from a common stem (which is puny). For example, dash, flash, bash and brash are all fast words. However, ash, hash and gnash are all slow. Flush is changing. It used to be slow, somewhat like sluice, but it is getting faster. Both are wet words, as is Flushing, which is really quite dry compared to New Canaan, which sounds drier but is much wetter. Wilkinsburg, as you would expect, is dry, square, old and light gray. But back to motion.

Raid, rocket, piccolo, hound, bee and rob are fast words. Guard, drizzle, lard, cow, sloth, muck and damp are slow words. Fast words are often young and slow words old, but not always. Hamburger is young but slow, especially when uncooked. Astringent is old but fast. Black is old, and yellow—nearly opposite on the spectrum—is young, but orange and brown are nearly next to each other and orange is just as young as yellow while brown is only middle-aged. Further, purple, though darker than lavender, is not as old; however, it is much slower than violet, which is extremely fast.

Because it's darker, purple is often softer than lavender, even though it is younger. Lavender is actually a rather hard word. Not as hard as rock, edge, point, corner, jaw, trooper, frigid or trumpet, but hard nevertheless. Lamb, lip, thud, sofa, fuzz, stuff, froth and madam are soft. Although they are the same thing, timpani are harder than kettle drums, partly because drum is a soft word (it is also fat and slow) and as pots and pans go, kettle is one of the softer.

There is a point to all of this.

Ours is a business of imagination. We are employed to make corporations personable, to make useful products desirable, to clarify ideas, to create friendships in the mass for our employers.

We have great power to do these things. We have power through art and photography and graphics and typography and all the visual elements that are part of the finished advertisement or the published publicity release.

And these are great powers. Often it is true that one picture is worth ten thousand words.

But not necessarily worth one word.

The *right* word.

The Wonderful World of Words

MARSTELLER INC.

Exhibit 8-1: "The wonderful world of words" is a house ad by Marsteller Inc. that expresses the power of well-chosen phrases. (Courtesy of Marsteller Inc.)

zh: *illusion and mirage*
  s: *quintessence, celestial, crystalline, with russet and sunset as run-ners-up*
sh: *ravish*
  w: *wherewithal, wonderland, windward, dawning, and waterfall*
  m: *mom followed by madrigal, meander, and mesmerize*
  v: *lovely, evanescent, suave, gravel*
  f: *dolphin, effervescent, taffeta, daffodil*
  l: *lilacs, lullaby, laurel, lavender, lanolin, soliloquy, cellar, hollow*
m & l: *marshmallow, marmalade, melancholy, llama, lemonade, sala-mander, pell mell*

And the winner of the Miss Word Contest was from the m & l lexicographic category—"mellifluous." Incidentally, Safire also determined that the leader in the "Ugly Word Contest" was "glut."

Consonants. Advertising is particularly enamored of a sound linguists call the "plosives." These are *k, p, b, c, d,* and *g.* A Michigan State advertising professor, Bruce Vanden Bergh, described the effect of these letters: "When the sound is actually made, a small explosion is created by the sudden rush of air out of the mouth almost creating a popping noise."[10]

Vanden Bergh noted that of the top 200 brand names, 172 contained at least one "plosive." Some examples are Bic, Buick, Burger King, Cadillac, Coca-Cola, Colgate, Datsun, Delta, K-Mart, Kodak, Kraft, Pabst, Pampers, Pepsi-Cola, Pizza Hut, Tab, and Tide. He comments that "given the intent of brand names to be easily recognized (and remembered) amid the clutter of names in the marketplace (350,000 or more), it makes sense to get the greatest impact possible from the first sound you hear in the name." Nasals like *m* and *n*, for example, are much weaker and less attention-getting consonants.

The *s* sound has a number of interesting effects. It is used to create a mood than can range from soft and sultry to sophisticated or siren. In a marvelous piece of writing for Rolls-Royce, the copywriter used the *s* sound in a heavy paragraph of product attribute description. Notice how the repetition of the *s* ties the otherwise hard mechanical functions into a soft, easy flowing, well-oiled piece of machine art:

> To cite but three examples, a unique automatic air-conditioning system maintains any temperature you desire at two levels of the interior: a sophisticated rack-and-pinion system turns the humble steering wheel into a thing of ease and precision; a self-leveling suspension system lets you forgive and forget the rudest of uneven roads.

In terms of strong sounds, advertising copywriters have long known that consonants give the distinctive color to a word. Scotty Sawyer, one of Marsteller's all-time great copywriters, explained, "Consonants are what give words definition. Vowels are just connectives between consonants." He cited "scratch" as a word he considers a beautiful example of consonant/vowel ratio: "Seven letters, only one vowel. It even has an onomatopoetic effect: 'scratch' sounds like a scratch."

Onomatopoeia.   Certain words have been created as an echo of a sound: "clatter," "clang," "clink," "ping," "rat-a-tat," "ding-dong," "ticktock," "hum," "whir," "buzz," "gurgle," and "splash" are a few examples. (Notice the consonant/vowel ratio in the preceding list of words.) These words are rich in audio imagery, and their associations reverberate in the mind of the reader or hearer.

onomatopoeia: a word that imitates a sound

A wonderful example of the use of **onomatopoeia** in advertising was in the classic "Head for the mountains" campaign for Busch beer. The campaign broke with an ad that showed a close-up of a can of Busch being opened and the word "BUSCHHHHHHHHH!" sprayed across the double-page spread. The copy by Jim Kochevar read, "Introducing a new beer with a bright new taste. And even a sound all its own."

Another example of elegant copywriting using word sounds is found in the "Sounds of silence" tourism campaign for Ontario. In one, the illustration shows two fishermen on a foggy lake. Onomatopoeia is carefully worked into the first sentence, which reads: "The dip and pull and ripple of the paddle, the whistle whirring of the reel, the echo of the loon." The scene comes alive by its sounds because the copywriter has crafted an indelible audio image.

Alliteration.   Another dimension of word sounds is repetition. **Alliteration** is the repetition of the same sound—usually the initial sound, although it can be in other parts of the word. Words with high internal alliteration include "bobble," "dawdle," "bumblebee," "orangutang," and "tintinnabulation." Usually, however, alliteration occurs within a phrase or sentence with multiple words beginning with or repeating the same sound. A poetic piece of copy for Cabriole perfume ends with this description of the fragrance.

alliteration: the repetition of two or more stressed syllables

> A melding of flowers
> and more flowers
> mingled with a fresh flourish
> of spices.
> We call it Cabriole

Word Order

cadence: a rhythmic pattern

The sequencing of the words in a phrase or sentence can create effects of its own. Stress and repetition can be used to create a "beat," or **cadence**, as well as emphasis. For example, you may break the natural cadence deliberately to add an attention-getting discordant beat. In addition to calling attention, word order can add emphasis and change meaning. An example cited by William Safire in a *New York Times* column illustrates the difference in wording between the following variations on the famous song:

- I only have eyes for you
- I have only eyes for you
- I have eyes for you only
- Only I have eyes for you

Parallel construction.   Repetition of sounds can also be constructed from one phrase or sentence to another. This is a literary device called *parallel construction.* It is used for emphasis and accent. With heavy bold words, it is like pounding on the table with your fist. With softer words it is a gentle form of insistence. A Nationwide Insurance ad targeted to young career women used parallel construction in the headline: "Your own car. Your own phone. Your own place. Your dad's insurance?"

In addition to emphasis, it is also used to develop a cadence or flow and to control the pace of the reading. An example of a well-constructed parallel sentence is found in a paragraph from the Rolls-Royce ad for the Silver Wraith II. The preceding sentence talks about the engineers and artisans who build Rolls-Royce. The copy continues with this sentence:

> It is in their marrow to revere the past, relish the present and welcome the future all at once, because the driving force behind a Rolls is not merely to come and go, but to go on and on.

That passage is an inspiring example of parallel construction, alliteration, and sensitive word choice.

rhyme: repetition of the ending sounds of words

Rhyme. The most common type of sound repetition used in advertising is **rhyme**, where the ending sounds of the words are repeated. Early advertisements around the turn of the century and up until 1930 or so used full rhyme in the body copy. More recent advertising style uses copy that speaks directly to the audience in natural language, so that these old "poetic" ads now sound quaint. Occasionally, full rhyme is used deliberately for effect. Primarily, rhyme is used in radio copy for jingles.

A Beefeater Gin advertisement uses full rhyme for body copy in a parody of the famous poem, *The Children's Hour* (see Exhibit 8-2).

rhythm: a pattern of stressed and unstressed syllables or "beats"

Rhythm. Rhythm is the musical sound of words. The pattern of words with their stressed and unstressed syllables can be used to create a cadence, and the cadence can be soft and gentle, sprightly marching, or even foot stomping.

Poetry is scanned in terms of certain conventional patterns of stress, and this scanning system is useful for anyone writing copy where the beat or meter is important. Jingle writers, in particular, need to be able to use this notational system to analyze the metrical structure of their phrases. The symbol / is used to indicate a stress, and the symbol v is used to indicate unstressed or weak stress. A common pattern of two or three beats is called a "foot," and there are four common types of metrical feet. These four patterns are as follows:

Iambic: v /

Trochee: / v

Dactylic: / v v

Anapestic: v v /

Iambic is the beat of the march: *dactylic* is the beat of the waltz. Generally, two beats are stronger than three, and the stressed last syllable is stronger than the stressed first syllable. The old literary stereotype calls trochee and dactylic passive or feminine meters (*fashion* and *passion*). The unstressed first syllable is considered aggressive or masculine (*inventive, perform, assure, iconoclast*). The Beefeater hour, obviously tar-

Exhibit 8-2: The "Beefeater hour" is an unusual use of a poetic form in advertising copy. (Reprinted with permission of James Burrough and Kobrand Corporation)

geted to males, is written with an anapestic foot. The anapestic foot is also the meter behind limericks.

v / v v/ v v / v v /
The Beefeater hour: it usually comes

The most famous advertisements to use rhythm and rhyme were the Burma Shave roadsigns—perhaps the most famous and best liked advertising campaign ever. Each of the four lines was on a successive sign and created a moving billboard effect. The folksy down-home rhymes captivated road-weary readers.

He played the sax
had no B.O.
But his whiskers scratched
so she let him go.
Burma Shave

Most advertising copy is not written to a beat, although cadence can be important when you are trying to develop a well-crafted parallel construction. Where metrical scanning is more useful is in the writing of slogans and jingles. Both use meter and cadence and since jingles are set to music, the beat may, in some cases, be more important than the words.

Slogans are short and catchy. Their memorability is enhanced by the use of rhythm and sometimes rhyme. They should be easy to slide off the tongue. Notice the cadence in the following slogans:

- When you care enough to send the very best

- We bring good things to life

- You deserve a break today

- The pause that refreshes

- 99 and 44/100 percent pure

- When it rains, it pours

- When it positively, absolutely, has to be there overnight

- The wings of man

Jingle writing demands a good ear for rhythm. All songs are written to an underlying beat pattern. It is the repetition of the words to a beat that makes jingles so memorable. An example of a slogan that has been adapted to a jingle format is "Look for the union label" and "When you've said Bud, you've said it all." Once you've heard the jingle, it's almost impossible to say the slogan without hearing the beat and melody in your mind.

McDonald's has had success with rhythmic chants, including the famous "Two all-beef patties," which had all the kids in town competing to see who could say it. Another McDonald's television commercial called

"Double Dutch" has a team of four girls doing intricate fancy footwork to the old double dutch jump-roping game. The rhythmic chant the jumpers used to coordinate their split-second footwork is nothing other than a recital of the McDonald's menu: "Big Mac, Filet of Fish, Quarter Pounder, French Fries, Icy Coke, Thick Shakes, Sundaes, Apple Pies." It's interesting to see that a strong beat pattern can be imposed on something as variable as a list of menu items.

syntax: rules underlying the formation of grammatically correct sentences

Syntax. **Syntax** refers to the rules and patterns underlying the formation of grammatically correct sentences. It also refers to the aesthetics of "good" sentences. Syntax can be used to describe the variety of sentence lengths in a passage. Variety is used to create emphasis as well as interest. For example, a long explanatory sentence may be followed by a short, punchy sentence that restates the key point.

Syntax also refers to how the logic develops through the phrases and clauses. An example of body copy that has syntax problems came from a carpet ad that appeared in *The New York Times*. The first sentence says it is "a carpet whose time has come." That cliché is then followed by this sentence, which is full of awkward syntax problems: "With the versatile, non-directional, go with anything at home or office, loop pile construction that's very much now."

Euphony

"Euphonious" is a 50-cent word that means everything fits well together and the resulting sound is pleasant, agreeable, and harmonious. It is used here to summarize all the intricacies of phrasing—the exact literal meaning, the connotations and nuances, the sounds including onomatopoeia, alliteration, parallel construction, rhyme, rhythm, word order, and syntax—in short, all the aesthetic considerations of any literary work. Advertising copy, when it is concerned with using the right words, is as much of an art form as any other literary effort.

An example of advertising that can be described as "euphonious"—and also poetic—is a long-running campaign by Waterford Crystal. A typical ad from the series will feature one goblet or bowl, and the copy will try to develop the essence of this piece of crystal (see Exhibit 8-3). Notice the cadence, alliteration, and parallel construction in the following Waterford example:

> Light a Crystal Fire.
> The light of
> the stars.
> The light of
> the sun.
> The light of
> Waterford Crystal.
> A legend
> blown by mouth,
> cut wholly by hand,
> with heart.

LIGHT A CRYSTAL FIRE.

The light of
the stars.
The light of
the sun.
The light of
Waterford crystal.
A legend,
blown by mouth,
cut wholly by hand,
with heart.

WATERFORD

Photo Pesin

Exhibit 8-3: Waterford Crystal is an elegant product whose image is reflected in the elegant phrasing of its copy.

This is the copy for an ad used to introduce a book inspired by the campaign.

Waterford pours forth memories.
It conjures up fantasies,
evokes poetic imagery,
provokes the creative spirit,
celebrates life's mysteries.
It is never too early nor too late
to assume the title:
Waterford Collector.
Some begin at birth.
Others as nonagenarians.
To the collector,
a piece of Waterford crystal
is more than a drinking vessel,
more than a vase,
a decanter, a lamp, a chandelier;
more than a family heirloom,
more than an object d'art;
It is an incentive to lose weight,
to win forgiveness,
a way to attract a lover,
to distract a patient,
to symbolize hope,
to crystallize a dream,
to bid adieu,
to hail the seasons,
to raise spirits,
to diminish melancholy,
to mark events,
to start traditions,
to end a day.
It is a noble rite of passage.
Born of the breath of man,
Waterford is life's child.

8.2 ADVERTISING STYLE

Literary style and advertising style are entirely different. In literary, or essay style, writers display their unique way of looking at the world. A fiction writer's style is personal, like facial features and fingerprints. The writer's unique viewpoint colors and shades all his or her messages so, regardless of the content, you can tell by the style of the writing who the author is.

Characteristics

Anonymous. In advertising writing, however, the author is anonymous—no byline, no ego trip. There is no personal style. The good copywriter, like a good actor, can shift to reflect the product and the message strategy. The copywriter may work on an ad for tissues one day and trucks the next. The writer must be endlessly adaptable.

Rather than uniqueness of style, versatility of style is valued in advertising. The writer still uses literary style to express nuances and personalities, it is just that the personality expressed is the product's, not the writer's. Advertising copywriting demands the same high level of writing talent. Some might even say it is harder to master many styles than it is to develop one.

Vernacular language. Advertising writing does have some general style characteristics. Most ad copy is written *the way people talk*, using plain, ordinary language. A well-targeted message will mirror the natural language used by the target audience in normal situations where they would encounter a discussion of the product. For status products, like Mercedes-Benz, you might find yourself using formal sentence constructions, but for most everyday products, everyday language is used.

idiomatic: language that's peculiar to a particular situation

vernacular: plain, everyday ordinary language; sometimes nonstandard

Copywriters have a good ear for how people talk, recognizing that different people talk different ways in different situations. That's called **idiomatic** language.

One aspect of idiomatic **vernacular** language is that it is contemporary. Key phrases from the vernacular are used to establish this contemporary cue. There are phrases that peg speech as "in" or, if you are not careful, dated. Dated expressions include such phrases as "cool," "neat," "with it," "to be sure," or "spaced out." These trendy phrases were current at one time, and they now are as old as grandpa's leisure suit.

An analysis of this use of trendy language was developed by William Safire in a *New York Times Sunday Magazine* column.[11] He analyzed a popular electrical metaphor: "To turn on, as in turning on a light, was originally drug culture lingo, later gained sexual overtones, and now means 'to excite, interest or titillate'; one who is 'turned on' or 'switched on' is hip, with it, an avant-gardian."

He continued, "The latest version of this electrical connection is 'plugged in.' If you are still saying 'turned on,' you are not plugged in." He found this metaphor in a Macy's ad for Gloria Vanderbilt corduroy jeans. The ad was headlined: "Gloria Vanderbilt switches to plugged-in cords." Safire observed that "with corduroy clipped to 'cords,' the word gains an allusion to an electrical cord, which plugs in to a neat fit."

Idiomatic language doesn't sound (or look) like the formal English used to write essays. It is conversational; it sounds like the natural language you would use talking to a friend or writing a letter to your mother. Reva Korda, a creative head at Ogilvy & Mather and a member of the agency's board of directors, advises writers not to labor too long on a writing assignment because the naturalness of the writing will wither.[12] She explains that "an advertisement is not an intellectual exercise, and the longer you take to write it, the further away you will get from the person you are talking to. Because that's all advertising is—talking to a friend, and telling him, or more likely her, about a service or product."

Present and active.   Another characteristic of advertising copy is the use of present tense and active voice. *Past tense* may be found in corporate "we" copy where there is a tendency to list what has been accomplished or to explain why something was done the way it was. *Present tense* develops the feeling of immediacy, of a conversation that is happening as you read. *Active voice* is a more powerful form than passive and advertising values dynamic, assertive language. Contractions are okay also. They're a natural part of natural speech.

Succint.   Some specific characteristics of conversational language that are used in advertising writing include the use of short sentences, even sentence fragments. Conversational language is spoken in thoughts, and "thought" expressions are usually very simple sentence constructions—and short. Thoughts don't always come out constructed in full-blown sentences, particularly if they are run-on thoughts. For that reason you will see sentences in advertising writing that begin with "and."

Short paragraphs are another characteristic of advertising. Most paragraphs in advertising are rarely longer than a couple of sentences, and some are only one sentence long. There's a visual reason for that. Copy that is written in short packages looks easier to read than the long, gray, forbidding paragraphs found in textbooks.

Personal.   Advertising copy is also written in personal language with lots of "yous." Avoid the corporate "we," which sounds pompous, but use the other personal pronouns. "I" is used in testimonials. The reason for emphasizing "you" is that it forces you to think in terms of your consumer's interest and benefits. It also overcomes some of the distance and anonymity that plagues most forms of mass communication.

Simple.   Advertising writing is simple. Simplicity is valued for clarity of meaning and ease of reading. Use simple words; use simple sentence constructions. John Caples was a believer in the power of simplicity. He said, "Simple words are powerful words. Even the best educated people don't resent simple words."[13] He continued, "They're the only words many people understand. Write to your barber, or mechanic or elevator operator." The ad called "Keep it simple" is an institutional ad by United Technologies (see Exhibit 8-4).

Frank Rathbun in an article in *Writer's Digest* made the point that long, fancy words are often just masquerading for learning.[14] These pompous words are pretenders, just "pretentious words and phrases that express ordinary thoughts." The list below contains the pretentious word followed by its simpler synonym:

attempt (try)	inaugurate (begin)
purchase (buy)	incarcerate (jail)
purloin (steal)	employ (use, hire)
antagonist (enemy)	obtain (get)
veracity (truth)	maintenance (care)
prevaricate (lie)	produce (make)
terminate (end)	facilitate (help)
peruse (read)	eliminate (save, get rid of)

The tendency to use pompous words creeps into advertising copy. William Safire, in his *New York Times* column, noted that ad copy has

Keep It Simple

Strike three.
Get your hand off my knee.
You're overdrawn.
Your horse won.
Yes.
No.
You have the account.
Walk.
Don't walk.
Mother's dead.
Basic events
require simple language.
Idiosyncratically euphuistic
eccentricities are the
promulgators of
triturable obfuscation.
What did you do last night?
Enter into a meaningful
romantic involvement
or
fall in love?
What did you have for
breakfast this morning?
The upper part of a hog's
hind leg with two oval
bodies encased in a shell
laid by a female bird
or
ham and eggs?
David Belasco, the great
American theatrical producer,
once said, "If you can't
write your idea on the
back of my calling
card,
you don't have a clear idea."

Exhibit 8-4: "Keep it simple," with its emphasis on clarity of communication, is an advertisement from a corporate campaign for United Technologies. (Courtesy of United Technologies Corp.)

moved from simple nouns to elegant nouns that require elaborate adjectives.[15] He quoted the following Pentax ad:

> Sixty years of research and human engineering have given rise to a remarkable photographic instrument. The Pentax LX is a photographic instrument of such quality that it will exhilarate you.

Note the use of such phrases as "human engineering," whatever that means, and "photographic instrument" instead of camera. He also observed that Chrysler is now calling its product "America's personal driving machine" instead of a car.

Natural. These are the primary characteristics of advertising writing: idiomatic language, short sentences and paragraphs, sentence fragments, personal pronouns, direct address, present tense, and active voice. It's natural writing using simple language—not affected, not cute, not pedantic or preachy. It's a conversation about the product, service, or idea. If you can't imagine yourself saying what you've written to someone you know who fits the profile of the target audience, then you haven't written natural language.

An example of advertising style is found in an ad for Bayer aspirin. It is targeted to a businessman and shows an executive at his desk with his hand to his head and a pained expression on his face. The headline says, "Even for this headache . . . all you need is Bayer." The copy, using short sentence fragments and direct address, says:

> Too much to do. Not enough time to do it. Result? That "business" headache. Even for one that bad, all you need is Bayer aspirin.

Advertising style sounds simple—it *is* simple. But it is not simple to *write*. Few people write as they talk. The minute you pick up a pencil or strike a typewriter key, all those years of English composition will bubble to the surface and you'll find yourself writing formal English using complete sentences with multiple levels of phrases and bigger, more impressive words. Writing simple is more difficult than writing formal.

The most common complication is *strategy hypnosis*. You can study the MBA jargon and worry about positions and objectives until all your powers of imagination have been turned off. It's like throwing a blanket over the whole creative process. There's nothing wrong with studying the research and the strategy as background—you have to know the background before you know *what* to write—but don't get hypnotized by the marketing lingo.

Put all the formal documents in your bottom drawer and forget all the pompous phrasing in the creative platform. A lot of the bad writing in advertising comes from lifting the copy platform or strategy statement and turning it into the ad copy. It will never read like natural language.

Strategy hypnosis often creates "writer's blocks." You know you're not doing something right because you can't write. Reva Korda explains it this way: "If you have a lot of misery writing it, if it isn't coming naturally, something is probably wrong. Maybe what you're trying to say is too complicated. Maybe it isn't worth saying at all. You don't agonize over talking to a friend, and you shouldn't have to agonize over writing to a friend."[16]

The Right Tone

The word "tone" is used to describe a general atmosphere or a manner of expression, as in, "John speaks in an angry tone of voice." It is an elusive word that implies shades of coloring, nuances, emotion, or personality. When a creative director or a client says, "It just doesn't feel right," he or she is probably referring to the tone.

Perhaps the best metaphor is tone of voice. People modulate and inflect their words to express emotions. The same thing happens with the choice of words (and visuals) for an advertisement. Some ads speak with authority and confidence. Some are bold, brash, loud, and screaming. Others are meek, reserved, and understated. Some have fun; some are angry. Identifying the right tone for an ad is just as important as choosing the right words for the headline.

Usually the tone in advertising is positive, like one friend talking to another. Sometimes it is warm and gentle or concerned. The tone is determined by the product and its message objectives. For example, an advertisement about a relaxing beach vacation may use longer sentences and languid phrasing. In contrast, a high-energy topic may be written with short, punchy, staccato sentences and phrases. Syntax, as well as word choice, can contribute to tone of voice.

One way to control the tone is to work with a *photo file*. Keep a file of photos of people—just clippings from newspapers and magazines. Pick out a photo that looks like a typical member of your audience. What kind of language would you use to talk to this person? A variation on this technique is to ask yourself how the target would most likely hear about the product. Imagine two people having a conversation about your product. What kind of language would they use between themselves? Would they be happy, excited, enthusiastic, sarcastic, logical, joking, sincere, relaxed, assertive? These adjectives all describe tone of voice. Let the tone of that imaginary conversation determine the tone of your copy.

The Chrysler turnaround ads featured Lee Iacocca, the president, using a mildly pugnacious tone of voice. After all, this man was begging the government to save his company, fighting off creditors and critics, cajoling the unions, and trying to rebuild the confidence of his employees and dealers. You wouldn't expect him to be meek and humble.

An ad that ran in the middle of the debate over federal loan guarantees was headlined: "Would America be better off without Chrysler?" The copy is signed by Iacocca and John Riccardo, chair of Chrysler. It's tough and blunt in tone:

It's a fair question.

You've heard from all the pundits, the instant experts, and the vested interests. They all have their favorite version of what's wrong with Chrysler.

Now we'd like to set the record straight.

We've made our share of mistakes in tough competitive business. And we're willing to accept responsibility for them.

But to turn our back on 140 thousand of our own employees would be irresponsibility.

To close the doors in 52 American communities in which Chrysler is a major factor of the local economy would be irresponsibility.

To deny employment to the 150 thousand people who work for the dealers who sell Chrysler products would be irresponsibility.

To curtail the income of the hundreds of thousands who supply goods and services to Chrysler would be irresponsibility.

Another ad in an entirely different tone tries to sell Parker Brothers game of Sorry® to parents. The tone is one of a sympathetic friend who understands that parents have to play dumb kids' games whether they want to or not. The copy reads:

Your seven-year-old asks you to play a game with her. You feel bad if you say no. You feel worse if you say yes and have to play a boring kids' game for an hour.

Avoid this dilemma. Play Sorry.® It's a very amazing game. There's enough skill involved to keep you interested, and even excited.

And there's enough luck to give your kids a real chance to beat you fair and square.

An appropriate tone of voice usually adds power to the advertising message.

The Wrong Tone

There are some tones, however, that can be relatively ineffective in advertising. Pedantic, *preachy advertising* that sounds like the stereotyped schoolteacher shaking a finger at you is rarely effective. No one likes to be lectured at or to.

The "*corporate we*" is a type of announcement advertising that consistently gets the lowest possible readership scores. Advertising should speak to the reader's interest rather than to the corporate interest. The "brag-and-boast" style of advertising is full of pompous, puffed statements of self-importance. Besides being irritating, there is nothing in it for the reader that makes it worth reading.

A *negative* tone sometimes comes across in copy. In your haste to control a competitive corner, you may sometimes find yourself taking potshots at the competition. Be very careful of negative blasts; they have a tendency to backfire. If you have a positive statement to make about your product, then stick to the positive. Even strong comparative advertising can be written from a positive stance. There's something self-defeating about potshots. They not only cast your own product or client in a negative light but also undermine anything you might have to say that is positive.

There's another type of negative that creeps into copy. Sometimes you will find copy that takes potshots at the reader. It's subtly patronizing. This is often inadvertent and the copywriter doesn't even realize the tone is there, but it is there and the reader recognizes it on some subconscious level. Usually, the copywriter is trying to write to a target that he or she can't identify with and it comes off as a putdown. Keith Reinhard, a creative director who is now chair and CEO of DDB Needham, has said, "Always approach the customer with love and respect."[17] If advertising works at all, it does so because it generally makes people feel good about themselves, their lifestyles, their decision making. A negative or threatening tone of voice rarely leaves people feeling good.

Ad-ese

Earlier sections described what advertising writing *is*: this section describes what it is *not*—or at least what it's not supposed to be. *Ad-ese* is formula copy. Ad-ese is a form of copywriting that is stilted, artificial, and hackneyed. It's the kind of copy that people identify as "ad copy" because it includes sets of overused phrases like, "have a tall, cool one" or, "welcome to the world of. . . ." People remember it for its style and for its quaint form—not for its message or for the product. It's the kind of advertising that comedians parody. You probably don't realize how much these phrases have permeated your language.

Ad-ese causes a problem in copytesting, since most people carry a bundle of ad-ese in their heads as typical of the genre. When asked which one they like best, they will often choose the version that comes closest to stereotyped ad writing.[18] After all, "that's what an ad is supposed to sound like."

Formula phrases. So what do we mean by ad-ese? The first category is the *formula phrase*, the trite, stale and uninteresting phrase that is used to fill the space between ideas. Often, this is a stock opening and closing. It is the "red flag" of ad-ese because it signals stereotyped ad writing. Some typical formula phrases are:

- Introducing, announcing, presenting
- Special introductory offer
- Something we discovered
- Doctors recommend
- Your opportunity to
- Congratulations, you have just
- You can't go wrong
- Quick. Send one dollar and get
- Don't wait any longer
- Buy one today
- Replace free of charge
- For as long as you own
- Don't settle for anything less
- Backed by our unconditional guarantee
- Last chance at these low prices
- Avoid the last-minute rush

puffery: statements based on exaggeration and hyperbole

Puffery and hype. Another highly visible form of ad-ese is **puffery**, characterized by those exaggerated superlatives underscored with anonymous subjective opinions. Rotzoll and Rotfeld, two advertising professors, describe "puffery" as different from other advertising approaches in that it uses exaggerations and inflated claims that consumers are presumed not to believe.[19] In other words, it is thought that consumers see a statement like "the most beautiful" as mere "seller's talk." Rotzoll and Rotfeld found in a study of puffery that many consumers do, in fact, believe such statements, even if they are puffery.

Puffery is not illegal in advertising, but it is unnatural in writing. When *Saturday Night Live* skits make fun of advertising, they are usually parodying the puffery. It's hype, and it robs copy of believability. Some examples of puffery include:

- The most exciting, brilliant, effective, reliable, unique, perfect, important, romantic, talked about
- The only, the latest, the most, the finest, the best
- As close to perfection as you'll ever get
- An exceptional opportunity
- Better than any other
- The finest ingredients
- The best the world has to offer
- One of a kind
- Perfect for every occasion
- The ultimate experience
- Incredible, exclusive, tremendous, amazing

Clichés. Clichés are statements that were originally unique, strong attention-getters. The first time a distinctive statement is used, it can stop the audience because of its novelty or unexpected imagery. When it is borrowed and used over and over, it becomes a *cliché*. Clichés often use unexpected juxtapositions and metaphors. A statement becomes a cliché, not because of its phrasing, but because of its overuse. People tire of it easily because of its original novelty. An example of cliché ad copy appears in an ad for a rug: "Our wool color bouclé imported from Belgium is truly a carpet *whose time has come.*" Other familiar ones are:

- Talk of the town
- Out of this world
- Ripe old age
- Cold, hard cash
- Night owls, early birds
- High time
- Mint condition
- Quick as a flash

Frayed phrases. A variation on the cliché is a phrase that comes to life on a television show, in a song, or as a slogan for a character actor. Sometimes it is a catchy phrase from another ad. The phrase gets attention and comes into popular usage as a fad phrase, but usually only for a short time. During that period it appears everywhere. After the phrase wears out, becomes "frayed," it sounds terribly dated. Some examples are:

- Where's the beef?
- I can't believe I ate the whole thing
- Believe it
- Wild and crazy
- The real thing
- The new you
- Love me, love my _____
- Nobody does it better
- It's happening/what's happening
- Would you believe
- Don't look now, but . . .
- If you like _____, you'll love _____

Empty phrases and generalities. The largest category of ad-ese is one the scholars call "glittering generalities." These are empty phrases, space fillers. They may hint at some vague benefit, but without any substantiation, they carry little meaning. An example from our favorite carpet ad is a sentence which talks about "construction that's *very much now.*" Some other examples are:

- New, distinctive collection
- A sign/symbol of quality
- Choice beyond the traditional
- You have never experienced anything like it
- Intimately fresh
- Deliciously different, totally different
- Delightfully refreshing
- Years ahead of its time
- Age-old secret
- An honored gift
- The preferred taste
- Names that are synonymous with quality
- So much for so little
- Made with you in mind

Stock promises. Many advertising messages are benefit-oriented; this means that the copy focuses on the user's benefits rather than the product's features. In some cases, it makes a promise to the prospect about what good things will happen to the person if he or she uses the product or service. But even this strategy has its stock phrases—both reasons-why and promises. These phrases are used as codes to shortcut or signal the benefit. Here are some common stock promises:

- You can't go wrong
- Special protection
- Assembles in a jiffy

- Free with any purchase of _____
- Convenient locations near you
- Fits all sizes
- Fun for the entire family
- Last chance to buy at these low prices
- One week from today you'll look more beautiful
- Look years younger

Ad-ese is easy to spot when you know what to look for. The formula phrases, puffery, clichés, frayed phrases, empty phrases, and stock promises are the working tools of a lazy copywriter. Recognizing ad-ese is a form of aesthetic judgment that anyone can develop.

8.3 WRITING TECHNIQUES

There are a number of ways to write an advertisement. Most of the messages can be grouped under a set of basic categories of writing styles. These are common literary styles but they are used in advertising too. They are announcement, definition, description, narration, and explanation. A good copywriter needs to master all five writing techniques and must know when and why each approach is used.

Announcement   Copy that states a fact about a product or service uses an *announcement* style, sometimes called a straight-line style of writing. It's basically a journalistic approach, and it is used primarily for news announcements.

Straight-line style.   This style uses assertions, or statements of fact, to establish that something exists or has been reported or found. It plays it straight and sticks to the facts. Ad copy approaches that use the "now you can buy" formula tend to be announcement messages.

An interesting use of the announcement technique is found in an ad by Crest that states: "On April 6, 1976, the official publication of the American Chemical Society listed the great discoveries of the last 100 years. We're proud to be one of them." The double-page ad then lists column after column of breakthroughs in chemistry, some 80 in all. Crest's development of stannous fluoride is the first entry under 1955.

News.   A news announcement is a particular type of straight-line writing. News is a report of a recent event. To be considered "newsworthy," the event has to be of interest to the general public. The Merit cigarette campaign uses a strong news peg. The Merit ads report some new fact that has been discovered by research and treat the announcement as a straight news story.

Definition   A variation of straight-line copy is a style of writing that focuses on defining concepts, ideas, or terms. A definitional advertisement is often used with a new product or with a new ingredient. The early Crest ads, for example, used definitional strategies to explain stannous fluoride. The ads announcing major additives in gas and engineering breakthroughs in product design are often definitional. A *definition* is a statement of the meaning of a word or phrase, a distillation of the essence of the concept.

Synonyms.   One way to define is to list *synonyms* and explain the differences among them in terms of their shades of meaning. You are substituting the unfamiliar word with one of similar meaning that you think the audience might know. Another way to define is to list the pieces or components. In other words, what is included in the concept or what is it composed of? This is the *inclusiveness* dimension of definition, the significant features of the category represented by that word. Product advertising often defines what a product means in terms of its significant features or attributes. A third technique of definition is to explain in terms of *exclusiveness.* In other words, what are the discriminating features that separate this concept from all others? In advertising, exclusiveness is used to identify points of distinctiveness.

Functional definitions.   Another type of definition is *functional*— a statement of what the concept means. Often, in advertising, a product or service will be defined in terms of what it does for the user or how it is used. Definition is a type of writing used in combination with other techniques. However, one advertisement that focuses almost exclusively on definition is a service ad by General Foods explaining nutritional terms found on package labels. The headline says: "Dear General Foods. All this talk about nutrition gives me 100 percent of my daily requirements of confusion." The copy begins: "There's a tendency for people's eyes to glaze over when reading things like 25 percent U.S. RDA Thiamin. You'll find mysterious-sounding terms like this on the nutritional labels on any General Foods products." Under the subhead, "What's a U.S. RDA?" the copy reads, "It stands for United States Recommended Daily Allowance, and it tells you the amounts of various nutrients considered adequate for maintenance of good nutrition in most healthy persons in the United States." Most definitions in this advertisement are functional; they explain what the nutrients do for the consumer.

Description

Descriptive writing develops images that stick in the mind. Psychological research has found that images are often easier to remember than words. When people see things as images, they code them directly into memory. The goal in using strong descriptive copy, then, is to stimulate the images to help anchor the concept.

Experiences.   Descriptions bridge experience. In some cases, you may be writing about something entirely new. You have seen it but your audience hasn't. With your words, you make the experience of seeing it come to life for them. In other cases, you may simply be cuing their memory processes. They have had similar experiences, so your well-chosen words bring their experiences back to mind. The more experiences you have in common with the audience, the easier it is to describe the object. You can tell someone that a buffalo looks like a bull with a shaggy hump. If they have seen a bull, then the gap in experience is easier to bridge. But how do you describe an umbrella to someone who has never seen one before? Or a claw hammer? Some gaps in experience are very difficult to bridge.

Sensory details.   Description is the reporting of sensory details. You have seen something you want to tell your audience about so you describe for them what it looks like, as well as how it feels, smells, tastes, and sounds. Writers use the five senses to describe their experiences.

The following copy from an ad by the Royal Caribbean cruise line is a good example of descriptive writing.

> The decks are strung with lights that soar high above the sea, framing the deepening indigo of the night.
>
> Far below you, on the water, the reflection of a tropical moon scatters into a thousand glowing bits.
>
> When evening comes, on a Royal Caribbean cruise, you'll see that all the romantic stories you've heard about cruising are absolutely true.
>
> You'll sip a vintage Bordeaux, savor a perfectly prepared leg of lamb, indulge yourself in Cherries Jubilee flamed right at your table.
>
> You'll watch the silent passing of a freighter, far out on the horizon. And dance under more stars than you ever thought the sky could hold.
>
> And you'll find that the warmth of the islands lingers in your mind, long after the sun goes down.
>
> So talk to your travel agent about a Royal Caribbean cruise. For seven, eight, ten or fourteen days.
>
> After all, some things are just too good to be left to your imagination.

If you want to develop your sensitivities, make a habit of describing to yourself any new experience—riding a roller coaster, eating a new food, wearing a new outfit. What is it like to eat a melting ice cream cone on a hot summer day? What does the sting of a mosquito feel like? The smell of liniment, the sound that comes from an amusement park? Tune in to these experiences and relive the sensations in your words. Describe them for an imaginery friend who is unfamiliar with the experience.

Explicit details. Description that records details explicitly is analytical in tone. There are two dimensions to this type of writing: order and point of view. *Order* is the sequence used to report the sensory impressions. When looking at a picture, the viewer scans it so quickly that he or she records a number of details almost simultaneously. But you can't write details simultaneously; they have to be recorded one at a time in a sequence of some sort. As Donald Hall says in his book on writing: "The order is not critical; but it is critical that there be an order."[20]

In visual description the order is usually spatial. The details may be recorded in standard western scanning patterns such as left to right and top to bottom, or perhaps from the center to the periphery or from the periphery to the center. The order for other types of situations may be temporal; you record the first thing you observed and the next and the next and so on. The sensations may move from visual to sound, to smell and back again to visual. The logic is based on the pattern of decreasing impact—a temporal sequence of impressions.

The second aspect of explicit description is the *point of view* of the observer. If you record the details as you experience something, then maintain that orientation as you put the experience in words.

Often in advertising, the copy will be written from the viewpoint of the user. To write this you have to imagine yourself, or remember yourself, in the role of a user experiencing the product or service for the first time. What did you see/hear/smell/taste/feel first? What was the most indelible sensation? How did you move through the sequence of experiences? What caught your attention next and next and next? How did you proceed to build a layer of sensations into a total impression? Is it a coherent picture?

A good example of an advertisement that uses explicit description is an ad for Raleigh cigarettes. The headline says, "The road to Raleigh is," and the body copy continues with a description of what it is like to be a truck driver. The first section is a view from the driver's seat. The order is from close to distant, as seen through the windshield:

> Yellow lines and just laid asphalt.
> Endless stretches of black ribbon that
> run all the way to where the sun disappears.
> It's telephone poles and fence posts,
> you keep passin' 'em one by one.
> It's those rows of corn, that sea of wheat.
> Tall trees blockin' out of the sun.

Then the view shifts from the scenery outside the window to the objects noticed inside the cab:

> It's 13 speeds in an overdrive gearbox.
> And a CB handle
> when you've got the country music turned off.

Then it moves to internal reflections by the driver himself:

> The road to Raleigh is a man
> who gets up when he wants to . . .
> goes to bed when he says.
> Pushes himself to the limit
> and then relaxes with gusto.
> He doesn't give a damn what you think.

For the conclusion, the writer puts it all together as a total sensory description of what it's like on the road—in all weather, on all roads, at all times of the day.

> The road to Raleigh has
> the feel of hard rain
> and blowin' snow.
> The light of a rising sun.
> The pale of a pea soup fog.
> It's got the smell of hot coffee.
> And the stench of diesel fuel.

And finally it all wraps up with the theme and a product identification.

> It's got men.
> It's got freedom.
> It's got the flavor you can only get
> When you're on the road to Raleigh.
> Take the road to flavor—Raleigh Lights.

It's unusual to see description used in such a poetic form throughout an advertisement—particularly for cigarettes—and particularly for macho truck drivers. The Raleigh ad manages to romanticize the road without using syrupy words. That's the power of description used as a stylistic form.

Evocative. *Evocative* description moves from recording sensory details to recording feelings associated with them. It is used to create mood and to tug at the heart strings. It takes description out of the senses and into the emotions.

An example of evocative description is found in a perfume ad for Je Reviens. The headline, "The world's smallest harvest," is clearly an understatement in advertising, but it sets the stage for the description of the harvest of a rare wildflower used in the perfume. The copy describes the flower, the area where it grows, and the camaraderie accompanying its harvest.

> After the last snow has melted, the children of Lozère go with the town's old people into the mountains to gather a rare wild flower. For on the slopes surrounding this tiny hamlet the wild narcissus grows. And because it grows one here, one there, in crevices and on the steepest of slopes, to pick these fragile yellow and white flowers requires the patience of the old and the agility of the young.

The story of old folks and kids working together is supported by a touching photo of an older gentleman and a cute, curly-headed little boy with a basket of flowers.

Figurative language. A third type of description uses the power of metaphors, similes, and analogies to create total sensory impressions. A *metaphor* takes the identity of characteristics of one thing and associates it with something entirely different: for example, "a barn of a house," and "the hand is a leaf fluttering in the wind." Similes are more obvious metaphors. A *simile* states that something *is like* something else. Earlier, a zebra was described as *like* a horse, but with stripes. The word "like" cues the use of a simile. An *analogy* compares two things on the basis of a similar feature.

Metaphorical description is powerful because it impresses like a picture does—all the sensory details come flooding into the mind from the depths of imagination and memory. A metaphor is a summarizing device—it can synthesize and provide perspective because it stimulates the total experience, the whole picture.

Barbara Stern explained the power of figurative language as creating striking comparisons by saying one thing in terms of something else. Furthermore, she said, the use of imagery forms the basis for advertising's connotative power and verbal richness.[21]

Technical. Another type of description is found in *technical* writing. It uses literal descriptions with the details given in exact dimensions—the quantification dimension is critical to develop an accurate representation of the object. Technical descriptions may be useful in research reports, but they don't communicate very well. For example, "two circular plates 3 inches in diameter attached to a curved cylinder approximately 2½ inches in diameter" is hard to recognize as a description

figurative language: a comparison that isn't literal but uses figures of speech like metaphors, similes, and analogies

of the hand piece of a telephone. A metaphor described it better: "A banana-like handle squashed flat at each end."

Narrative   *Narrative* writing tells a story. Stories are little plays, anecdotes, or dramas that describe an experience, happening, or event. A story brings to life a setting, characters with their distinctive expressions, voices, and gestures, dialogue between the characters, mood, and the action as the story develops. The Je Reviens perfume ad, which we discussed earlier in terms of its descriptive techniques, is also a good example of a story.

Anecdotes.   There are several types of narrative techniques used in advertising. The most common is the *anecdote* with an anonymous voice describing some little happening. An example is an advertisement by Apple Computers that described a bizarre home disaster where an Apple got baked at Thanksgiving. The copy says:

> Last Thanksgiving, a designer from Lynn/Ohio Corporation took one of the company's Apple Personal Computers home for the holidays.
>
> While he was out eating turkey, it got baked.
>
> His cat, perhaps miffed at being left alone, knocked over a lamp which started a fire which, among other unpleasantries, melted his TV set all over his computer. He thought his goose was cooked.
>
> But when he took the Apple to Cincinnati Computer Store, mirabile dictu, it still worked.
>
> A new case and keyboard made it as good as new.

Storytelling.   Another type of narrative is the *storyteller* format; it reads like a piece of good fiction. The scene is set, characters are introduced, a point of suspense is established, the action rolls, and finally some kind of happy ending is achieved—usually because of the product.

An example of the storyteller technique is an ad for After Eight Chocolate Mints that reads like a mystery novel. The headline reads: "Lord Horace calls in the police" and the underline is "Chapter 1 of 'The Last Mint,' a baffling story of low doings in high places." This is a long copy ad. It parodies a mystery novel; a bit of the copy will give you a feel for the piece:

> Welcome to Blodstoke, the modest country home of Lord Horace and Lady Penelope Blodgett-Stokes, known to their friends as Chuff and Binky. Forty-eight bedrooms, two bathrooms.
>
> In this four-century-old house, where the dining table is a bit too long for a decent game of ping-pong, a major crisis has arisen: there is a mysterious shortage of After Eight Chocolate Mints.

Process.   Narrative copy can also be used to describe processes such as the invention, use, or production of a product. This kind of narrative may rely less on dramatic techniques, but it may be more effective at relating product features. An example of *process* narrative is found in an advertisement for Jack Daniel's. Under a photograph of two old-timers in overalls standing next to a row of wood kegs is the following copy:

> These men can tell exactly what's happening inside every barrel in a Jack Daniel's warehouse.

In the heat of summer the whiskey is expanding into the charred inner wood of the barrel. Come Halloween, it's starting to cool. And inching its way back toward the center. Over the aging period, this gentle circulation of whiskey is going on constantly. Of course, it can't be perceived by the human eye. But after a sip of Jack Daniel's, we believe you'll recognize its importance.

Plot. The concept of action and a developing story is more commonly known as plot. Plots are constructed with a beginning, middle, and end. A *plot* is a summary of a sequence of events over time leading up to some conclusion.

Dialogue. This is a technique used in narrative writing to present people talking to one another. The award-winning ad for Paco Rabanne uses a style of dialogue. This is straight dialogue, raw and without any anonymous author's commentary. It reads like a script or the transcript of a conversation (see Exhibit 8-5). It gives viewers the feeling that they are overhearing a personal, intimate conversation that they aren't supposed to hear between two literate, worldly, loving, teasing people. The dialogue records both sides of what is clearly a phone conversation (apparent from the initial word cue). The personality of the characters comes through only in their words; there are no scripting cues to tell viewers if they are angry, happy, or sad. But the copy is so well written that the euphoria of a new love shines through the sophisticated repartee.

Occasionally, *monologue* is used in advertising copy. Testimonials are the most common examples of the monologue form, particularly for television. The leading character reports his or her experiences with the product.

Storytelling tips. Here are some suggestions on how to write narrative copy. These are particularly useful when writing television commercials. First, set up the scene or scenes in your mind—better yet, find a real setting similar to what you imagine. Know your way around the set and what it looks like from every angle.

Develop the characters as individuals before you start writing. Colleen Reece, an instructor of fiction writing, uses a 38-point "character chart." It is a list of characteristics, looks, special qualities, opinions, demographics, and so on for each major character. If you're accumulating a photo file, then find a picture of the character you envision and set it up on the desk in front of you.

The photo file technique is recommended by another fiction writer, Roy Sorrells.[22] He also suggests that you close the door and "act out" the story, taking the role of each of the characters. Don't write the words, let them come naturally out of the mouth of the characters as you walk through the scene in their shoes. Get it all down on a tape recorder. Then go back to the typewriter and transcribe and revise from the tape-recorded "live" copy. If you are writing a simple story without complicated plot lines and action, then just talk it into the tape recorder. Storytelling is a verbal art form. The spirit of the story will come through more honestly if you talk it rather than write it.

Explanation   Explanation assumes that the subject of the message is unknown to the audience. You use explanation to translate the topic so that it will be as familiar to your audience as it is to you. Explanation uses all the previ-

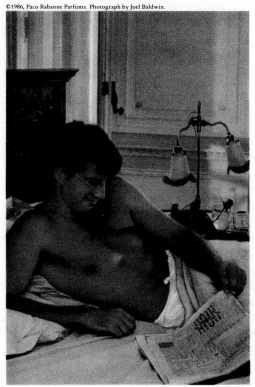

Hello?

Is this the man with the secret tattoo?

Now that you know about it, it's not a secret anymore, is it?

Your tattoo is safe with me. Were you able to get a taxi ?

I walked home.

And how was Paris while all the sensible folk were still in bed?

It was grey and drizzling and bloody marvelous. I kept making up poems with your name in them. Also a love song that, for rhyming reasons, ended up being all about your right elbow. I don't think my feet touched the ground once all the way home.

I meant to tell you. I love the way you smell. Most men's colognes make them smell like they take themselves too seriously.

I thank you. My Paco Rabanne cologne thanks you. My mother thanks you.

Your mother would never approve of what you and your Paco Rabanne do to me, so let's leave her out of this. Am I going to see your tattoo again tonight?

That's up to you, isn't it?

Paco Rabanne
For men
What is remembered is up to you

Exhibit 8-5: The Paco Rabanne campaign uses a casual conversational style with sophisticated repartee to associate language with a target.

ously discussed techniques. Sometimes unfamiliar terms are used in an explanation and they have to be defined. Before you can explain something you often have to describe it first, and sometimes in explaining something you may use narrative techniques to develop a picture of a process. So definition, description, and narration can all be used in explanation.

Unfamiliarity. The need for explanation occurs whenever we try to communicate a new idea or experience to an audience that has not confronted the idea or experience before. The newness may lie simply in a way of seeing the idea or experience. But whatever it is, you have a mental picture that they don't. You use explanation to get your mental picture to look as much like your audience's as possible. You can't simply transmit the picture. As C. S. Osgood has said, "there are no wires strung from one mind to another."[23]

You can't *transmit* meanings; instead, you have to use words to generate a mental picture from the audience's repertoire or previous experiences. Their picture will never be identical with yours, because your experiences are different from everyone else's. The best you can hope for is similarity in the essential dimensions.

These islands of experience may represent a product engineer talking about a new breakthrough, or someone who is mechanically inept trying to explain to the mechanic what's wrong with the car.

The first problem is a gap of some sort—a gap in knowledge or in experience. Most communication operates on a basic assumption of commonality of background between source and receiver. The more common the experiences and the shared meanings, the greater the probability of success in communication. Explanation, by definition, violates this assumption. If both source and receiver shared a common meaning, there would be no need for explanation.

A second problem is that people are afraid to try something new. Adults, in particular, resist new information and new experiences. Advertising copy has to overcome this barrier by providing the initial experience of trial within the ad itself. Let them experience it vicariously, painlessly, through your words and they will be more likely to buy the product. The objective, then, is to make the strange familiar.

The question. In order for an explanation to be successful, you need to stimulate the questioning process in your audience's mind. An effective explanation operates in a state of inquiry—a curious mind seeking answers. Any question can lead to explanation, but there are certain key questions that cue different types of responses. Basically, the key questions seem to be *What? Why? How?* and *So what?* The What? question is really preliminary to explanation. It calls for definition and description. The relevant question can be expanded to "What is this like?" and that, of course, calls for a description of sensory details and impressions. A TWA ad is a good example of how an explanation can be built on definition. The headline reads: "TWA redefines First Class." Then it gets serious about defining what makes first class different.

A better class of seat.

Our seats are more comfortable then ever. (Not surprising. They were redesigned with that in mind.)

In our 747s, our Sleeper Seats™ recline a full 60 degrees. Which, apart from being extraordinarily comfortable, makes falling asleep in one extraordinarily easy.

An appeal to one's good taste.

The food will come as a rather pleasant surprise. On international flights, there's domestic caviar. Chateaubriand with sauce Perigueux. Lobster Thermidor. Vintage wines from California and France. Liquors, cognacs, cordials, and more.

A Why? question leads to reasons, causes, and results. Advertising professionals talk about a type of message strategy called *reason-why* copy. This message format translates information about the product into a use or benefit to the consumer. It states the "reason why" the consumer should buy the product. Reason-why copy can be identified by certain key phrases that are used to cue this type of explanation: "because," "in order that," "the reason why," "the answer is," "the causes are," "that's why," "the advantages are," "and here's proof." The following headlines cue the use of the why question in advertising:

- Why do 28 of the Fortune Directory's top 100 manufacturers use NCR shop-floor systems?
- Aside from its having the Herman's label, here are 13 more reasons why you should buy this down parka.
- Why you should open your IRA Retirement program with a company deeply involved in retirement planning.

How? questions call for an explanation of a process. They ask, "How does this work?" or "How do I do it?" "How-to" ads are very common in advertising, and they are used principally to explain how to use a new product. Any time you see suggestions, tips, recipes and menus, a demonstration, or any other kind of process instruction, you are working with a How? question. Word cues for how explanations include: "the process is," "how it works," "how to do," "a way to," "here's what you do," "hints," "tips," and so on. Some headlines from sample How? ads include:

- How to fire someone you like
- How we're making the incubator safer for babies
- How to be sure your business makes the most of the new tax laws

A good example of an ad that walks someone through a process is one by Smith-Corona headlined, "How to buy a typewriter." The copy has 10 subheads identifying key things to look at when you try out a typewriter. Here are some excerpts:

Choosing a portable typewriter isn't hard if you know what to look for. This brief guide will help you make the best choice.

Test the feel. Check the slope and height of the keyboard. Check the size and shape of the keys. Make sure the controls are uncrowded and easy to reach. . . .

Try the touch. A responsive touch makes for better, easier typing. Look for a touch that is prompt, easy, and dependable. . . .

Listen to the sound. The typewriter is trying to tell you something. If it sounds tinny, beware. This may indicate that the construction is too light.

Note the look of the type. Lines and individual letters should be straight. The impression should be crisp, clean, and even. The print quality should not vary over the page. . . .

A So what? question asks for an analysis of significance, synthesis, and perspective. It answers the underlying question, "What does this mean?" This is the highest order of explanation, since it calls for interpretation. Words used to cue So what? explanations include: "this means that," "what happened," "don't you know," "the results mean," and so on. This type of explanation is not used as often as How? or Why? Some ads that use So what? strategies in their copy have the following headlines and copy points:

"Good news for bad knees." (Converse has developed a new feature for running shoes called a Stabilizer Bar. The copy explains what it does and why it's important.)

"Life insurance? What for? I'm still single." (New York Life explains that you should get insurance while you're young because of better rates and because something might happen that would throw you into the high-risk category.)

Explanatory techniques. The primary technique basic to explanation is *example* or *illustration*. Using an example is a way to cite an instance in order to explain the whole. It is a sample that illustrates the points being made, a concrete application of a concept that, in many cases, may be abstract. A good example functions to make the central point more clear to the reader.

Advertising copy that uses examples often will cue the reader by saying "for example." But sometimes the illustration isn't overt. An ad for American Express says, "A day can seem like a long time. . . . Let's say you're in a strange country and you lose your wallet. . . ." In this case, the content is clearly setting up a situation that illustrates the case in point.

Another technique is *comparison* and *contrast*, which points out resemblances and differences. In advertising, a simple comparison of two products as to features or uses is an effective way to make a strong claim of distinctiveness. Simple comparisons are usually signaled by such phrases as "things like" and "like . . . as" statements. An example of a simple comparison from a Panasonic ad is, "You can use a 60-minute cassette (not 30, like other microrecorders)."

Writing Problems

Dull. One of the biggest problems in copywriting is trying to make the message interesting. Too much of what viewers read, see, and hear is just plain boring. Harvey Bailey, a master copywriter, said in an *Advertising Age* column, "How come with all the bright, sophisticated advertising people I meet, there are still so many dumb commercials and ads . . . how come there is so much of the boring, insipid stuff still around?" He puts the blame on formula advertising, copycat advertising that uses the same old plots, rules, and techniques. You know what he means— "the soft drink commercials that have to be musical masterpieces, the tire commercials that have to show people driving through rain, the toothpaste commercials that have to show entire families in the bathroom at the same time."[24] They are dull because they don't say anything new and they are so predictable.

Copy hash.   This is advertising writing that is unclear, inaccurate, illogical, and/or poorly worded. It may sound well phrased when you read it, but when you think about it you realize that it is gibberish. An example of an advertisement that doesn't follow logically is from Sears. The rather obscure headline says, "You can count on Sears to look at a new product from every angle." The underline continues with this quote:

> "The first thing we did was test 16 of the top-rated running shoes," says the Sears buyer, "as well as the bare foot." Not many companies have the luxury of starting from scratch, but Sears spent nearly two painstaking years developing the 440. Here's why they spent the time:

(At this point, you are probably wondering what the product is. It's not clear from the headline. Since the 440 was mentioned at the end of the underline, one might expect that this new shoe is the product. The body copy uses a long narrative to explain the development of the 440.)

> Sears knew it took more than a good factory to make a good running shoe—one that would fit comfortably and help reduce the foot, ankle, and knee problems that runners sometimes encounter.
> They went to experts: Northwestern University Medical School Center for Sports Medicine. The doctors kept a sharp eye on stress points and suggested possible ways the 440 Running Shoe could aid in helping to prevent the problems that plague runners.
> The buyers and Sears' own lab worked closely with this team of nationally known orthopedic surgeons and the manufacturer. Prototype after prototype was discarded as not good enough.
> Not good enough because Sears wanted to go further than a shoe that would fit comfortably and minimize problems—they also wanted a shoe that would look attractive, wear well, and sell at a fair price.
> The 440 Running Shoe pleased all concerned with its innovative features. Like a cushiony insole you can remove so it will dry out between wearings. A nicety whether you wear the shoe to run the Boston Marathon or go get the groceries.

(A little wordy perhaps, but still the narrative approach is an interesting way to sell a well-designed shoe. The copy continues.)

> Finding a better way of doing things is virtually a policy at Sears. Each year, Sears lab tests over ten thousand products and, along with the buyers, keeps up a running dialogue with manufacturers with this aim: How can we make it better?

(What are we selling now?)

> Sometimes innovation means portability: the Bionic TV set has a two-inch diagonal measure black-and-white picture and weighs a spanking two pounds. It can hang around your neck like binoculars, and it's only at Sears.

(Now we are selling televisions?)

> Often, innovation means a unique feature thought up by Sears first and then patented. Like the Corrector™ key on many Sears portable electric typewriters. This clever key lets you correct mistakes without moving your hands from the keyboard.

(And now we are into typewriters?)

> These are a few in a string of product innovations and improvements from Sears. But there is one thing Sears hasn't had to improve upon in over half a century: Its famous promise:
>> Satisfaction guaranteed or your money back

And that's it, friends—an ad that starts out with a long explanation of a new running shoe, and then without so much as a transition moves to the company lab, the portability feature of a TV set, and the correcting key on a typewriter. Finally, in the last paragraph, you find out that the thread that holds this mélange together is the company's emphasis on innovation. But no, the innovation wrapup can't even stand alone—it has to take second seat to the company's policy on guarantees. There you have a classic example of an advertisement that suffers from wandering logic and large leaps.

For another example of copy hash, let's turn to a strange advertisement by Kodak. It starts off with this headline:

> The only people who are generous enough to read English themes are English teachers.
> —from *You and Aunt Arie*, by Pamela Wood, an English teacher

If the headline doesn't leave you shaking your head, then plow on into the body copy and see if you can make any sense of it.

> Foxfire was the first of them. As you can see, the idea has now spread far and wide—high school magazines where students picture the older ways of the community, and never mind teenage fantasy. Pamela Wood's book* telling how to do this advises down to the last detail of film processing, subscription list maintenance, and courteous interviewing technique how ordinary high school kids become chroniclers of lives, joys, place, reality, skills, and culture before and beyond the shopping malls that homogenize the continent. We are interested because photography and today's printing methods based on the photographic process are essential for these marvelous magazines, but anybody of the generations that stand between the chroniclers and their peppery interviewees can admire the professionalism in writing, editing, layout, and management skills that deliver such fascinating and instructive reading for the buyer's dollar. If you were going to say something about inarticulate, uppity modern youth, forget it. Could your own high school teach English this way?

Did the copywriter's high school teach English that way, you might wonder? Where do you begin critiquing something like this? First and most obvious, there isn't a single paragraph break. Given the lack of transitions, the juxtaposition of seemingly unrelated ideas makes for incomprehensible copy.

The headline, of course, was an obscure quote and the lead sentence had nothing whatsoever to do with the head. The lead also contained a reference to "them"—whoever "them" might be. "As you can see" is a ludicrous transition since nothing that came before relates to anything that follows.

There are two serious syntax problems in the second sentence, including a botched parallel construction and a tacked-on, unrelated editorial comment about today's teenagers. By chasing the asterisk, you can find out that Pamela Wood wrote a book entitled *You and Aunt Arie*, but that piece of information tells you nothing.

Then follow the two longest sentences ever to see the stroke of typesetting in an American advertisement. The sentence beginning with Pamela Wood is an unheard-of 49 words. The one beginning with "We are interested" is an even more incredible 56 words. It isn't just the length that offends, it's the circuitous phrasing that wanders undirected through a forest of kids and old folks and shopping malls, and homogenized continents, and undefined "we's," plus tours of photography and printing and magazines and interviewing and instructive reading. It all leads to the final non sequitur—the almighty "buying dollar."

The part of the last sentence that contains the clause, "but anybody of the generations that stand between the chronicler and their interviewees," is copied directly from the ad—it's not a typo, nothing has been left out—except meaning and syntax. If you were going to say something about inarticulate copywriters, forget it. This ad is, without doubt, the ultimate example of copy hash.

SUMMARY

This chapter discusses advertising style and what makes it different from literary, or essay, style.

1. Words have literal, connotative, and associative meanings.
2. Word sounds impart a distinctive color to a piece of copy, as well as cadence, rhythm, and beat.
3. The advertising writer is anonymous and a master of a variety of styles of writing.
4. Advertising writing uses vernacular and idiomatic language; it's succinct, personal, simple, and natural.
5. Tone of voice used in an ad should match the product and the message objectives.
6. Ad-ese is formula copy that uses pat phrases, clichés, puffery and hype, generalizations and empty phrases, frayed, out-of-date language, and stock promises.
7. An announcement plays it straight, sticks to facts, and emphasizes the news angle if appropriate.
8. Definitional copy explains terms, which is particularly important with new products.

9. Descriptive writing develops images that stick in the mind.

10. Narrative writing is used to tell a story.

11. Explanation answers the questions of What? Why? How? and So what?

12. The three most common writing problems are dull and boring copy, ungrammatical constructions, and copy hash.

NOTES

1. Ralph Zeuthen, "Top Notch Writing Offers Your Product or Idea a Better Chance," *Advertising Age*, April 21, 1975, p. 65.
2. Michael Becker, "Advertising in the Year 2000," *AAAA Newsletter*, December 1984, p. 1.
3. Barbara Stern "What Does an Ad Mean? Language in Services Advertising," *Journal of Advertising*, 17:2 (1988), pp. 3–14.
4. John Caples, "Caples on Copy," *Wall Street Journal*, house ad series.
5. Michael Gartner, "Words from Gartner," *Advertising Age*, April 11, 1982.
6. Gary Provost, "Pack Every Word with Power," *Writer's Digest*, February 1983, pp. 21–23.
7. Charles W. Ferguson, "How Whip Words Show America to Be Male Dominated," *National Observer*, April 17, 1967.
8. "Words of Mouth," *Madison Avenue*, June 1986, p. 11.
9. William Safire, "Miss Word of 1982," *New York Times Magazine*, June 27, 1982, pp. 9–10.
10. Bruce G. Vanden Bergh, "More Chickens and Pickles," *Journal of Advertising Research*, March 1982.
11. William Safire, "Effecticity," *New York Times Magazine*, January 10, 1982.
12. Reva Korda, "How to Break the Rules: Heresies About Writing Copy," *Advertising Age*, March 5, 1979, p. 47.
13. John Caples, "Caples on Copy," house ad by *The Wall Street Journal* that ran in *Advertising Age*.
14. Frank Rathbun, "Conciseness in F Major," *Writer's Digest*, August 1977, pp. 45–47.
15. William Safire, "By Any Other Name," *New York Times Magazine*, December 6, 1981, p. 22.
16. Korda, op. cit.
17. "ADWEEK All-Midwest Creative Team," *Adweek*, February 7, 1983, pp. 21–22.
18. Sandra E. Moriarty, "E-Z Copy," *Industrial Marketing*, January 1983.
19. Herbert J. Rotfeld and Kim B. Rotzoll, "Is Advertising Puffery Believed?" *Journal of Advertising*, 9:3 (1980), pp. 16–20.
20. Donald Hall, *Writing Well* (Boston: Little, Brown, 1973).
21. Stern, op. cit.
22. Roy Sorrells, "Ham on Bond: Using Acting Techniques to Improve Your Writing," *Writer's Digest*, July 1980, pp. 39–40.
23. Charles S. Osgood, George J. Suci, Percy H. Tannenbaum, *The Measurement of Meaning* (Urbana: University of Illinois Press, 1971).
24. Bailey, op. cit.

PART

2

MEDIA SPECIFICS

9

The Copy Package

KEY POINTS

- The display elements get attention and stimulate interest; the body copy maintains interest and explains or proves the key points.
- Headlines can be classified as either user-oriented or product-focused.
- The display copy—such as overlines, underlines, captions, and subheads—structures the reading process.
- The creative concept is developed in the lead and reinforced in the closing.
- The closing focuses on action and identification.
- The flow and logic of the body copy is controlled by the transitions.

All the topics we've discussed so far—background research, strategy development, creative concepts, advertising style, visual communication—are universal. In other words, what we've presented applies to all kinds of advertising in all kinds of media. With this chapter, we begin to look at the specifics of the various media.

The pieces that make up the copy package in print advertising can be pulled apart and analyzed separately, but they are all woven together to create a total effect. We may talk about these pieces separately but remember that the impact of the advertising message is a function of synergism—all the pieces working together. The creative concept is the thread that runs throughout and ties everything together.

The major pieces of the copy package for newspaper, magazine, and yellow pages advertising include the headline, other display copy (including overlines, underlines, captions, and subheads), the signature, the body copy (including the lead, transitions, and the wrap-up). Outdoor advertising uses some of these elements, such as the display copy or headlines, but it doesn't use body copy. All the display elements work to accomplish one of two overriding functions: to get attention and to stimulate interest. The body copy functions to maintain interest and explain or prove the key points.

9.1 THE DISPLAY COPY

Headlines   The headline is the most important part of the copy package. It works together with the visual to establish the creative concept, or theme, the "big idea" that makes the advertisement interesting and original. This is called the integration of copy and art. The synergistic effect created when both the verbal and the visual are linked with a strong concept separates the outstanding ads from the mediocre.

Attention.   Headlines have several objectives, but the primary function of the head is to get the reader's attention. It is a red flag; its job is to make the reader stop. It has to be arresting enough *to be seen* when the reader is concentrating on other matters, such as the editorial content and other competing advertisements. It also has to be arresting enough *to stop* the scanning process. Many people "read" newspapers and magazines in a rhythmic fashion that involves briefly scanning the headline and visual and then turning the page. The rhythm has to be broken before an ad can be attended to or read. It takes verbal dynamite to break through either the editorial concentration or the almost mindless scanning.

Self-interest.   The next function of the headline is to capture the reader's self-interest. That's how an "arresting" headline works—it breaks through the wall of indifference by speaking to the reader's interest. Techniques employed to accomplish this include headlines that promise something or arouse curiosity. A claim can be arresting if it is unexpected or surprising. When you write a head, put yourself in the reader's place and ask, "What's in it for me?" or "Why should I stop and read this?"

An example of an arresting head is an old one for Fiat; it used type easily half the page in size with a headline that screamed "$400 back." This is verbal (and visual) dynamite. A more restrained example is found in a trade ad for General Electric that used both curiosity and a promise; it stated, "Changing the lamps in their office saved $23,000 a year."

Strong, arresting claims make good flags. An example is a headline for Peugeot that states: "Every Peugeot goes through hell to get to America." The supporting copy explains all the tests the car goes through at the factory.

Segmenting and targeting.   Another function of headlines is to sort out the audience and select the targeted prospects. It should be immediately clear from the headline whom you are addressing. You can segment by using questions and direct address, such as: "Are you a woman who . . . ?" or "A car for those who . . . ?" The targeting can also be a function of stylistics and word choice. An ad for Smirnoff used the headline, "Chow down," to specify a macho audience.

Another example of a clearly targeted headline is in an ad for Allstate Insurance that asks, "Do you own a small business?" There's no doubt whom the ad is speaking to and, furthermore, because of the compelling question, it is unlikely that an owner of a small business could avoid reading at least the headline, and probably the rest of the ad as well. A billboard shows a four-wheel-drive car all dirty and covered with mud. The headline speaks to the off-the-road crowd: "A face only a mudder could love."

Product identification. Identifying the product or at least the product category is another function of the headline. The reader should be able to tell at a glance whether the ad is about raincoats or automobiles.

If it takes too long getting to the point, either in print or in broadcast, you may find your impatient consumer tuning the message out entirely, and turning the page. Sometimes there is a valid reason for using ambiguity, but that technique will always override product identification. You have to decide if it's worth the sacrifice. The ads that most successfully meet this objective will identify not only the product category, but also the brand. Wise old heads in advertising usually recommend that the brand name be in the headline if at all possible. Two examples of headlines that have strong brand identification are:

Old Volvos never die. They pass on.

With so many fine gins around why choose Bombay?

Sell. The final function of a headline is to start the selling message. If a head speaks to a reader's self-interest as an attention-getting device, it has already accomplished this objective. The essence of the selling premise should be clear in the headline. The Mobil One oil ad that promises "Get up to 10 extra miles out of a tankful of gas" is a good example. Strong benefit headlines are especially good at this. Lipton's ad explaining how to make solor tea—"Let the Sun brew your iced tea"—is a good example of a benefit head.

Automotive advertising is often feature- or product-oriented, but it can speak to a brand image, too. An advertisement by Mercedes-Benz breaks that mold. It promises this appealing benefit: "It is reassuring to know that the Mercedes-Benz 240D can take you farther on a tank of fuel than any other car sold in America." That's a long headline, but it fits the Mercedes-Benz personality. Another strong benefit head that uses an interesting visual demonstration is found in the ad for the IBM Displaywriter, highlighting its self-correction feature: "It makes impossibel impossible." One ad that evokes a strong brand image is by Fallon, McElligott for Porsche: "Think of it as a Mercedes with Tabasco Sauce."

Types of Heads   This discussion of headline objectives has introduced several common types of headlines. Most headlines can be categorized as either focusing on the product or the user. A third category would include those heads that play word games as an attention-getting technique. Of the headlines discussed so far, claim and demonstration tend to be product-oriented.

These can be strong heads, but intrinsically they are less powerful than heads that speak to the self-interest of the audience. Benefit and curiosity heads tend to be user-oriented. Other headline strategies include news, emotion, how-to, and wordplay.

News.   News is attention-getting if it is a subject of interest. People have a compulsive need for news and find it hard to resist reading a news announcement. That's why so many ads use the word "new" in the headline or in an overline. The word has been run into the ground, but it is still a powerful attention-getter.

An example of an entire campaign, and a highly successful one against all odds, is the Merit cigarette campaign. Merit cigarettes were introduced after cigarette advertising was banned from television. The industry predicted that there could never be another major brand introduction nationally. Knowing that the brand identity would be limited to print messages, the Merit strategy was to adopt all the stylistics of newspaper stories—a strong typographical layout, a newspaper typeface, a news announcement headline, and a long news story. An example of one of the headlines demonstrates the use of the newspaper treatment. It reads: "Twelve-year effort ends with unprecedented flavor in low-tar smoke."

Emotion.   A headline with a strong emotional appeal is user-oriented. A seasonal ad appealing to the sense of pride of an achiever is one used by Johnnie Walker Black that reads: "For those of you whose success cannot be measured by an Oscar, Emmy, or Tony."

A Phillips Petroleum ad explaining the company's contributions to medical emergency care used this head above a picture of an automobile accident. "How to save hours when there isn't a second to waste." This is a good example of an alarming head with a mild appeal to fear.

Headlines for DeBeers diamonds use a touching, romantic appeal: "For all the times I worked late and never gave you a ring—Happy Anniversary." Headlines like these try to punch the emotional buttons using such appeals as pride, alarm, fear, love, nostalgia, and anger.

How-to.   Another major category of user-oriented headlines features the "how-tos." Advertisements that teach consumers how to do or to use something are strong in both attention and self-interest. An example of an arresting "how-to" headline is found in an ad for American Savings Bonds which says: "How a minus on your paycheck can be a plus in your future." The wordplay between minus and plus adds to the interest. Another example of a how-to head, also with a twist, is one for Republic Travelers Checks that reads: "How to pay a Czech in Prague."

Wordplay.   These past two headlines also are examples of the third category—headlines that play with words. The verbal twists are used as attention-getting devices, and they can be effective at stopping the consumer from scanning. An example is the headline announcing a new pine-orange banana juice that reads: "A refreshing new taste you'll love a bunch." This can create problems, however, in that it may fail to identify the product category or to state a selling premise. If the head isn't strong enough to pull the reader into the body copy, then there is very little residual effect in terms of advertising power.

One that does effectively identify the product category is a cartoon

Exhibit 9-1: The Talon "big zipper" ad used a play on words that is reinforced in the graphics. (Courtesy of Talon, Inc.)

ad by Talon that shows a father and son out on a dark night looking at the stars. The father says, "And that, son, that's the Big Zipper." The stars in the sky, of course, spell out "Talon" (see Exhibit 9-1). Another successful wordplay is a headline for a Christmas season ad that artfully incorporates the brand name: "Dewar's unto others."

Heads with Problems Headlines can fail for a number of reasons, usually because they don't accomplish the previously stated objectives: get attention, speak to self-interest, segment the audience, identify the product or product category, or state the selling premise. They can also fail because they are poorly written and unclear.

Garbled. A garbled headline is one that is unclear. Whatever the point is, it doesn't get across to the reader. A classic example of a garbled head is one for a short-lived cigarette named Tall. In addition to creating much confusion in the market, this particular ad got rave (rabid) reviews in the letters-to-the-editor column in the trade press. The headline for the introductory ad read: "Why is this cigarette selling with no advertising and it's hard to come by?" In addition to several serious syntax problems, it also defies logic. If there's no advertising, then what is the reader reading?

An equally obscure headline appeared on an ad for Cuervo Especial. The illustration is of a woman in tennis clothes. The head reads: "I always drink Cuervo gold. Now and then." Always—now and then?

Labels. The most unarresting headlines are labels, particularly if the label is just the product name. Labels are static; they have no verbs and they have no action or impact. A liquor store in a small community ran a series of newspaper service ads on how to buy wines. The idea was good but the headlines were weak labels. One ad, for example, was headlined "Generic wines." There's just not enough content in a static phrase like that to pull anyone into the body copy. So what about generic wines?

Fred Messner pointed out another example in his column in *Adweek*. He quoted the copy for a trade advertisement that described the five steps used by the company to ensure quality control. The copy was fine but the headline was "Heiser quality." Messner commented that it was "a static label type of headline that doesn't manage to say much—yet manages to sound smug while saying it."[1]

Verbless. A problem related to label headlines is the use of verbless heads. A headline without a verb is an idea with its guts cut out. The verb adds life, action, motion, excitement, vigor, and power to thoughts. Without a verb, it just sits. A classic example of the power of a verb is the previously quoted Smirnoff headline: "Chow down." The verb, or really verb phrase, is commanding, as well as arresting. A trade ad for Triangle Engineering's ventilators demonstrates this lack of power. The headline reads: "Energy free comfort cooling." There may be a real benefit here, but it's hiding behind punchless phrasing. The response is, typically, "So what?"

Hanging heads. A hanging head is an incomplete thought—the reader has to read the body copy to get the point. It's a great device for pulling readers into the copy. Unfortunately, someone who gets impatient and turns the page after reading the head may find no usable information at all, and no product identification. Decades of copytesting research by the Starch Company shows that 80 percent of the people who read a head will not read the copy.[2] A hanging head with its incomplete thought is a real gamble.

Two ads by Heublein and Air New Zealand illustrate the problem of hanging heads that don't clearly identify the product category. Both ads use the same head—"Paradise found"—which is a twist on Milton's famous *Paradise Lost*. It's an interesting phrase and an arresting twist, but there is not enough direct link to the product category for either headline to fulfill its identification function.

Questions. Be careful of question headlines. They are used to develop curiosity and reader involvement, but they can backfire. A question that seems obvious to you (because you have the answer in your mind) can be obscure to everyone else. The opposite problem is more common. Most question heads tend to be too obvious. "Would you like to double your income? Would you like to live to be 100?" These obvious heads turn off the audience and invite "smart ass" responses. A common response to many of these heads is, "Dumb question." A negative reaction like that isn't particularly conducive to a positive product association.

Long heads. Some of the direct response research indicates that long heads work—at least for direct response ads. David Ogilvy and John Caples believe heads should be long enough to tell the story. Most copywriting books, however, recommend short, succinct, to-the-point headlines. They know that the reading public spends a very brief period with any ad, and that short heads are more likely to break and stop the scanning process. Most copywriters feel that a head has a better chance of being read if it's brief and quick.

The disagreement might lie with the nature of the message. Certain products, particularly big-ticket, high-involvement ones, speak to an audience with an already developed high level of interest. They will not only tolerate, they will welcome, long heads and long copy. Direct response ads, where the prospects have to sell themselves, also need to include lots of information in the headline. Other products, such as package goods with frequent repeat purchases, have low reader interest. For these products, short succinct headlines may be more appropriate.

It may also be a function of the message. If you have an involving story to tell, then the headline can demand more time from the reader. If the message is primarily reminder, then the reader doesn't expect to make a major time commitment.

Automotive advertising is one category where both short and long heads appear, depending upon whether the ad uses an image theme or an attribute approach with its need for explanation. For example, an ad for Datsun 20-SX is selling the image of a sporty car and lifestyle. The short head says: "Step on the exhilarator!" An opposite approach is found in an ad by Mercedes-Benz; the long headline asks, "The Mercedes-Benz 240 Diesel—is it the world's finest economy car, or is it the world's most economical fine car?"

Watch out for long heads. They do tax the reader. If you use them, make them inescapably intriguing and make them fit the tone and style of both the product and the targeted audience.

Cute and contrived. Headlines can try too hard to be attention-getting, and the result may strain credulity. Often they just sound sophomoric, like something you would find in a high school yearbook.

An example of a head that tries too hard to make its point is by West Virginia Brand Hams. Apparently, according to the picture, there are three varieties of hams offered. The head tries to pick up on that by stating: "There is only one West Virginia Brand Ham. This are it." That's the kind of headline that makes the reader wince.

An example of another headline that is too contrived is one written for Stouffer's Side Dishes. It reads: "What a diamond ring does for your finger, Stouffer's Side Dishes do for dinner." It's an attempt to stretch a metaphor, but it's stretched so far it falls apart.

Borrowed interest. One definition of a creative idea is the juxtaposition of two previously unrelated thoughts. Often, in advertising, a characteristic of the product is associated or juxtaposed with some unexpected situation to create a new way to look at the attribute or benefit. It's a technique used to add an unexpected twist. It also can be another form of a contrived head. A dull idea will hitchhike on a well-known concept, or even on a cliché, and attempt to create some excitement for the product by mere association with something else exciting. This is called "borrowed interest." Sometimes it works; more often, it backfires.

An example of borrowed interest that seemed to work is a trade ad for the electronics industry that used an Alice in Wonderland theme. The Copy Chasers evaluated this ad in their *Industrial Marketing* column as an extreme example of "borrowed interest."* A storm of protest arose with the company's president, as well as others in the industry, citing the results of the advertisement. Apparently, it was both a strong attention-getter and had very high memorability. The Copy Chasers concluded that Lewis Carroll, a famous mathematician, understood the intellectual affinity between mathematics (and electronics) and fantasy—perhaps better than the Copy Chasers did.

Another Copy Chasers example of borrowed interest that didn't work very well is an ad by EMC Controls. The picture shows Frankenstein-like characters. The head is a quote from the plant manager of USS Chemicals: "We avoided a chamber of horrors when we contacted EMC Controls." The horrible creatures might get attention but they also steal the essence of the message—even if the promise were spelled out a little more clearly.

Hype. Headline hype is found in brag-and-boast statements and puffed-up phrases. A number of ads critiqued in the Copy Chasers column suffer from this form of ad-ese. An example of pure hype is the headline for Consolidated Freightways: "The greatest thing since the wheel." The Copy Chasers chided Consolidated for overstatement and exaggeration.

Another hype head featured in the Copy Chasers column came from an ad for Micro-Plate company. It reads: "Innovative technology that improves productivity, quality, and economy." The vague, general, pompous words tell nothing about Micro-Plate's business, or about what the company has to offer its customers in terms of specific services.

* The Copy Chasers column runs every month in *Industrial Marketing.*

Other Display Copy

display copy: copy (words) that is set in larger or bolder type or set off in some way from the text of the advertisement

The word "display" is used here to mean copy that is set in type that is larger or bolder than the body copy (text) of the advertisement. The headline is the most important element of the **display copy**. Related elements include overlines and underlines, captions and subheads. The function of these secondary display elements is to establish a logical progression of attention-getting pieces of copy.

A carefully written advertisement will structure the reading process so the reader moves from initial interest to involvement and eventually to concentration on the body copy. The headline establishes the initial interest, and these other display elements create the pattern of progressive involvement until the decision is finally made to settle in and read the body copy.

Overlines and underlines.   These short pieces of copy serve as appetizers—they lead to the head or from the head to some other element. In most cases, their function is to establish and reinforce the progression. They may also be used to break a long or complicated headline into shorter, more easy-to-read segments.

FTD Florist uses this lead-in overline: "Wherever you are . . . the man from FTD will find you." The picture shows a woman traffic officer with a bouquet of flowers. The headline says: "I got it in traffic, the FTD Birthday Party Bouquet." There are lots of things going on in this overline/headline combination. It introduces the idea of personal delivery of flowers anytime, anywhere, and dramatizes it with a testimonial from someone receiving flowers in a most unlikely situation. The complexity necessitates the use of the lead-in line.

In advertising, *underlines* are more common than overlines. Their primary purpose is to pull the reader from the head down into the body copy. They also fulfill the function of segmenting long, complicated thoughts.

An example of the use of an extended headline made of multiple overlines and underlines is found in a campaign for General Foods International Coffees. The three-part heads set up a little drama:

"After going to every store in town today

"Mom and I came home for a cup of Cafe Vienna

"and realized the perfect wedding dress was in the attic all the time."

Captions.   Next to the headline, with its attendant overlines and underlines, captions have the second highest readership. Starch data show that the reading pattern is established first with the headline and then drawn immediately to the captions under the illustrations.[3] Unfortunately, captions are rarely used in advertising. Most copywriters seem to feel the body copy of the ad, in a simple layout, acts as the caption. They are missing a good bet, however, since a caption is an irresistible hook into the reader's interest.

In addition to their pull, captions serve an information function. In spite of the use of carefully contrived visuals in most advertising, there is still a need for explanation of illustrations. Journalists are aware that a photo can mean different things to different people. Photos in newspapers or magazines are almost always accompanied by explanatory captions.

Most advertising illustrations could benefit from additional explanation in the caption. But the real value of a caption is that it is one more chance to try to capture the attention and stimulate the interest of the reader. It's a shame to leave out a piece of copy with such intrinsically high readership.

An example of an ad that makes good use of captions is the Peugeot ad discussed earlier. Each of the six little photos that frame the body of the ad shows a car on a different part of a test track. The headline reads: "Every Peugeot goes through hell to get to America." Under the pictures are these short but graphic captions: "fiendish ribs," "nasty cobblestones," "wicked curves," "cruel bumps," "twisting stairs," and "mean moguls."

Call-outs.   Johnson & Johnson baby products used a caption treatment to package main pieces of the body copy. The head reads: "How to bathe a mommy." Positioned around a picture of a woman are short paragraphs with arrows pointing to various parts of her body. These "call-outs" describe the good things Johnson & Johnson does for feet, hands, makeup removal, moisture absorption, and skin softening. Starch research also has shown that call-outs have extremely high readership.

Subheads.   Display lines embedded in the body serve two purposes. First, they break up long, forbidding blocks of copy and make it appear more inviting to read. The primary purpose, however, is to stimulate interest. Most people, before they decide to read the body copy, will scan the subheads to see if the copy sounds interesting. These little subheads provide your last chance to move your target from scanning to reading. They don't just summarize the copy that follows; they package the copy to maximize its enticing features.

An example of a subhead that is carefully crafted to entice as well as to extend the thematic concept can be found in a Toyota ad. The headline reads: "The right shape for right now." The first subhead says: "Engineers say it's right." The second subhead uses parallel construction to heighten the force of the message: "Experts say it's right." The final subhead associates the product with the theme as a wrap-up technique: "Celica GT-S: the right stuff, plus."

9.2   BODY COPY

Function   As mentioned earlier, the purpose of the headline is to flag attention; the other pieces of the display copy help stimulate interest. They throw out hooks and dangle interesting bait to entice the reader into reading the **body copy,** the text of the advertisement.

body copy: the text of an advertisement

Copy point.   The body copy's function is to present the "copy points," the key points that the ad is supposed to deliver. Body copy expands on the selling premise, which should have been introduced in the headline or in the attendant overlines and underlines. The body copy elaborates, compares, explains, instructs, and persuades. It uses all the established literary techniques of definition, description, narrative, dialogue, and argument to flesh out the message.

If the display copy is successful, then it pulls the reader right into the body copy, which serves to explain and further describe the product. But as we have mentioned before, the Starch research indicates that only about 20 percent of those who read the headline will continue to read the body copy. That means 80 percent stop after the headline. That's a depressing statistic for copywriters but it certainly establishes the challenge. Here are some of the reasons why so few people read the text of an ad.

Interest.   The audience for advertising messages is largely indifferent. Only a very small part of the audience is in the market at the time they see the advertisement. The disinterest level, particularly for low-involvement product categories, is very high. If you win a reader and he or she continues on into the body copy, it's like making a religious conversion—truly a major accomplishment. Keeping the reader interested is the great challenge for the body copy.

Writing problems.   In addition to feeling disinterest, a lot of readers may turn away from ad copy because it is poorly written. It may not be targeted to the right audience. It may be confusing and unclear. It may be dull and full of artificial ad-ese. Why would anyone want to read an advertisement if the editorial copy in the magazine or newspaper surrounding the ad is more interesting? Advertising copy needs to be even more interesting than the surrounding editorial matter.

The truth is that a lot of advertising writing is dreadful. It's full of clichés, ad-ese, puffery, pompous phrases, and boring lists of product features. So those are the challenges (and the obstacles faced by every copywriter): to overcome the disinterest and to write lively, interesting, and personal copy.

The Opening   The opening, or the "lead," is the first sentence of the body copy. It marks the transition point where the reader's involvement changes from skimming to reading. The interest has been stimulated by the display copy, but it is up to the lead to establish the mood of concentration. This is a point of critical transition. The Cafe Vienna "wedding dress" ad mentioned earlier has a good example of a transition for its lead sentence. The first line of body copy reads, "Old lace, new beginnings, and Cafe Vienna."

In addition to establishing this critical change of mood, the lead has several other functions. The headline and visual introduce the creative theme, and most good leads will feature the theme and carry it into the body copy. The selling premise often gets traded off. It takes over as the primary concern of the remainder of the body copy, which continues from the second paragraph to the end.

Leads may often be "hangers." Here curiosity and ambiguity are used deliberately to force continued reading. In order to understand the point, the reader has to keep reading. Magazine articles are written this way. Interesting magazine leads are called "zingers," and certain magazines such as *Time* and *Newsweek* have turned the writing of compelling leads into a fine art. Donald Hall, in his book on writing, described zingers as "constructed to grab the reader by the hair."[4] Zingers use such techniques as questions, jarring quotes, controversies, anecdotes, and startling statements.

Buccellati isn't perfect.

If all you wanted was a perfect set of sterling, there would be no need for Buccellati.

Because any machine can stamp out the same fork over, and over, and over again. (In fact, that's the way most flatware is made.)

But to Buccellati, every piece of sterling must be more than a gracefully shaped piece of metal. It must be a work of art.

And art cannot be duplicated.

That is why no two pieces of Buccellati are exactly the same. (Notice how the forks don't nest uniformly?) Each Buccellati fork is cut and tooled and finished and polished by hand.

Buccellati makes 22 different patterns, and there is more hand detail in his least expensive one than there is in any other sterling flatware, regardless of price. In fact, it takes a Buccellati craftsman three hours to create a single hand-made fork.

Of course, there are some things about Buccellati flatware that are perfect; the weight and balance you feel when you hold it in your hand. The feeling you experience when you set your table.

But as for each piece being exactly the same? Sorry. After all, we're only human.

Buccellati

703 FIFTH AVENUE, NEW YORK, N.Y. 10022
(212) 755-3253

Only Buccellati has the nerve to turn his back to you.

Because he has nothing to hide.

Most sterling flatware puts on a pretty face. But the back doesn't seem to get quite as much attention. (Out of sight, out of mind.)

On the contrary, Buccellati believes that both sides of every piece are equally important.

You see, on the continent it is traditional to set the table with the back of the flatware facing up. So old-world craftsmen have always devoted as much care to the back as to the rest of the piece. Buccellati continues the tradition.

That is why you'll find Buccellati's unmistakable craftsmanship and hand detail on both sides of every piece of sterling.

You'll also find that Buccellati uses more sterling in his flatware. And that his dinner setting is larger: to compliment the size of your china and to give it a better balance and feel. In all twenty-two patterns, from the classic to the contemporary.

So when you're ready to choose fine silverware, be sure to get both sides of the story.

Buccellati

703 FIFTH AVENUE, NEW YORK, N.Y. 10022
(212) 755-3253

Exhibit 9-2: The concept of handcrafted silver is expressed in the headline, visual, and body copy of the Buccellati advertisements. (Courtesy of Buccellati Inc.)

One example of an interesting head and lead is found in an ad by IBM that describes the company's robotics systems. It uses a curiosity angle for a headline, "obotics," and the lead that follows is a hanger. It reads: "This story begins with the period at the end of this sentence." The second paragraph explains that the robotic arm pictured in the ad can locate a hole that size and accurately insert a pin. The robotic arm is actually holding the missing "R" from the headline. It's a strong curiosity-provoking lead that makes sense only if the reader continues on into the copy.

A good example of a strong tie between the headline and the lead is found in an ad by Buccellati silverware. The ad shows a fork with tongs down and the back of the fork facing you. The headline reads: "Only Buccellati has the nerve to turn his back on you." The lead continues the thought: "Because he has nothing to hide." The copy explains that Buccellati feels both sides of the silverware are important. The creative concept, which focuses on the back side of the silverware, is the link between the headline and the lead (see Exhibit 9-2.)

The Closing

Thematic wrap-up. We will come back and discuss the middle of the copy but first let's talk about the closing. The *closing* copy is part of the thematic package and works hand in hand with the headline and lead to establish the creative concept. Usually, these three pieces are written together. The headline introduces the idea, the lead builds on it to entice the reader into the copy, and the wrap-up refers back to it.

A good example of the relationship between these three can be seen in the previously discussed Buccellati ad. After the headline and lead duo establishes the concept of the back side of the silverware as an important sign of quality, the body copy continues with a discussion of silverware craft expertise. The closing paragraph refers back to the original theme and uses a little twist to anchor it in the memory: "So when you're ready to choose fine silverware, be sure to get both sides of the story."

Another example of theme development is in the ad for the Nissan Pathfinder (see Exhibit 9-3). The headline states the creative concept: "There are no city limits." The opening line extends that thought: "They've got traffic in Trenton. Potholes in Pasadena. And noise in New Orleans." The body copy explains that the Pathfinder offers a combination of power, comfort, and durability—on the road and off. The closing line parallels the opening: "Which means now, driving will be fun in Philadelphia. Comfortable in Columbus. And smooth in Smyrna."

Call to action.   Another function of the wrap-up is to state a call to action. The importance of the call to action varies with the nature of the ad. If it's direct response, then the call is extremely important. It's also important in local or retail advertising. Reminder and image advertising are less dependent upon an immediate response, so the call may be deemphasized.

One example of a call is the Buccellati ad, which encourages readers to look at both the front and back of silverware. That's a form of decision instruction. Other ads will give specific information on where to find the product or how to buy it. Local advertising has critical information that accompanies the call to action. This includes store address, location cues such as "corner of 15th and Baker" or "across from Safeway," phone number, store hours, and credit card acceptances.

Facilitators.   Another aspect of the closing is a category of information called *facilitators*. These are devices used to make the inquiry or purchase easier. An 800 number is a common example. Incentive offers, such as a cents-off coupon or special premium offer, are considered facilitators. An order blank and a coupon for additional information are common direct response facilitators.

Some of advertising's greatest names are strong believers in coupons. David Ogilvy, for example, used coupons for very classy products. A recent O&M campaign for Saab used long copy, ended with a coupon to get more information about the car, and generated a tremendous number of responses.

Identification.   The final function of the closing is to provide the corporate or store **signature**. This can be a distinctive logo or simply the name of the store in distinctive type. Store or product names are expected to be at the bottom of the advertisement, and usually they are found either in the center or the right corner. The right corner is the point of exit; the idea is to leave the reader with a solid product or store identification as he or she turns the page. The signature may also include a slogan or a

signature: the name of a company, brand, or store presented in a distinctive type design

Exhibit 9-3: The Nissan Pathfinder "City Limits" ad uses captions to call attention to city problems.

campaign theme tagline. These are reminder devices used to anchor the identification securely in the mind.

The Body of the Body Copy

Elaboration.   The middle section of the body copy elaborates on the selling premise. If the head was a claim, then the body provides the support or proof. If the head is a benefit, the body explains how and why the benefit is derived. The elaboration is built point by point, usually beginning with the most important feature or benefit. There should be a logical progression through this sequence of points. The points can be arranged moving from the most important to the least important, from a series of different viewpoints or uses, from one feature to another, or from one reason to another.

Unity.   The logic of the sequence of thoughts is an important aspect of the total coherence of the copy. Typically body copy discusses a number of details, attributes, substantiation points, or benefits. In spite of the variety of information presented, all the parts should be pieces of an overall picture. This conceptual unity, the perspective, is difficult to achieve but essential if the copy is to hold together.

A good example of this conceptual unity is in an advertisement for the Volvo station wagon. The concept that holds it all together refers to the safety features necessary for a family car. The headline says: "A wagon built to carry cargo more precious than groceries." The body copy features a number of attributes:

A WAGON BUILT TO CARRY CARGO MORE PRECIOUS THAN GROCERIES

Any station wagon can take a load of stuff from one place to another. The Volvo wagon, on the other hand, was designed to take a load off your mind as a parent.

Volvo realizes, for example, that it's impossible to keep both eyes on the road if you have to keep one eye on the back seat.

So to keep the kids in place, we provide you with things like child-proof door locks on all the rear doors. Including the back one.

And to virtually guarantee that you can focus your attention on the road at all times, we give you defrosters for the front side windows, and the rear window comes with its own wiper, washer, and defroster.

On the road, the first thing you'll notice is how quickly our overhead cam engine can put trouble behind you. Should trouble appear ahead, you'll appreciate the way our rack and pinion steering can help you steer clear of it. And the way our four-wheel power disc brakes can stop short of it.

In spite of all these precautions, we realize that accidents do happen. So we've planned for the unplanned.

Where many wagons may feature a front end designed to impress the neighbors, the Volvo wagon features a front end designed to help absorb the impact of a collision.

Our passenger compartment is surrounded by a protective steel cage.

Our doors have steel tubes running through their insides for added protection, instead of imitation wood running down their outsides for frivolous decoration.

There's also a padded dashboard. A collapsible steering wheel. A gas tank designed not to rupture in a rear end collision.

Look at it this way.

There's finally a wagon that shows as much concern for your children as you do.

Transitions. Conceptual integration is an important aspect of unity; a careful use of transitions is another. *Transitions* perform two functions. First, they keep the logic on track. They serve as signposts that mark the progression from one idea to another and establish the relationship between the ideas. Second, they tell the readers where they've been and where they are headed—the overall perspective. Transitions are important because without them it may be hard to follow the discussion from one point to another. Copy with poor or missing transitions appears to have jumps, breaks, or leaps in logic.

You've been in conversations where someone is talking about something and then all of a sudden switches to an entirely different topic. It leaves you confused. Even worse, your mind tends to wander away from the discussion and tries to figure out the connection—what could possibly have led the speaker to such a jump? It short-circuits the conversation and can lead to termination of the discussion. When you are writing ad copy, you desperately want your reader to stay with you, so any diversion, intended or not, is unwelcome. Attention to transitions can avoid these leaps and left turns in logic.

There are a number of devices used for transitions. Remember the objective of a transition is to link ideas and establish the relationship between them. The most basic form of transition is linking words such as "so," "and," "but," "therefore," "however." Other transitional words establish sequential relationships, such as "at the beginning," "first," "second," "then," "furthermore."

Repetition of key words is another form of transition. It establishes, or maintains, a relationship between a thought and something that preceded it. Repetition is a reminder function. (Repetition can also be annoying if the same word is used too close and too frequently.) Parallelism is another aspect of repetition that strengthens transitions. Parallel construction repeats the structure of the sentence, sometimes repeating key phrases. It is a good technique to emphasize a connection.

Short-form references to something previously discussed is another type of transition. Pronouns are a common example of this type of linkage. On first reference you speak about a person by name, sometimes by title. The next reference is to "he" or "she." The connecting link between the person and the personal pronoun is understood in context. Abbreviations perform the same function. If you refer to the American Association of Advertising Agencies in the first mention, then you can just say 4As in the subsequent references and the identity is still understood.

Study the Volvo wagon ad we just analyzed for body copy development. Notice how many transitions are used to cue point of view, location, and the logical progression from one idea to another. The copy uses a number of specific transitional phrases. In the first five short paragraphs, you will find "on the other hand," "for example," "so," and "and" all used to establish relationship between thoughts. Another major transitional phrase is used at the end to indicate transition to a summarizing activity: "Look at it this way."

Transitions are also used to cue the addresser and the addressee and indicate who is speaking. In the Volvo ad the lead two sentences address the reader in personal language as "you, a parent." The third sentence refers first to the Volvo viewpoint in the abstract. The second reference in the following paragraph changes to a personal pronoun: "we." All further references to the speaker are through this personal pronoun.

Point of view is also expressed in the transitions. The first third of the Volvo copy takes a general look at the car's features as seen through the eyes of someone sitting behind the wheel. The use of phrases like "eyes on the road" and "eyes on the back seat" establishes the relationship of the visual contact points through the rearview mirror and the windshield.

Those phrases also use parallel construction to emphasize the rhythmic transitions from looking ahead to looking behind. Using the "eyes on the back seat" as a mental reference point, the copy then moves around the inside of the car—side doors, rear doors—and then back to the side front where it talks about side window defrosters. The circular scanning is completed as the attention swings back to the rear window where the wiper/defroster feature is introduced.

In the copy you've just sat in the car, looked forward and back, and then once around the inside. All that scanning is done by transitions that serve as directional signposts. The next major directional cue announces a major change of location.

The sixth paragraph starts out with a bold transition: "On the road . . ." The rest of the copy goes through a test drive experience pointing to the features the driver notices while driving. The transitional cues include such situational phrases as "the first thing" and "should trouble appear." The signposts cue not only what the driver notices but also the typical worries that come to mind when driving a new car. Such phrases as the rather vague "trouble" and the more specific "collision" establish those hypothetical situations.

The Volvo copy is an example of good body copy development and masterful transitions. The reader's attention proceeds through a variety of features from several different situations and viewpoints, and yet the relationships are clear throughout. There are no surprising unexplained jumps. The logic is sound and the points lead from one to another as clearly as if arrows were pointing the way. And yet the transitions are subtle and unobtrusive. The only obvious one is used, and properly so, to signal a major change in viewpoint. It's really a fine piece of copywriting.

SUMMARY

1. The copy package includes all the verbal pieces that work together to present and develop the creative concept.
2. The headline is the most important element in the copy package.
3. The primary function of the headline is to get the reader's attention.

4. User-oriented heads are stronger than product-focused heads.

5. Label heads are generally unarresting.

6. Hanging heads are incomplete and may leave the reader with little or no information.

7. The different pieces of display copy guide the reading process from initial interest to involvement and concentration.

8. The body copy's function is to expand on the selling premise.

9. The lead is that point where the reader's involvement with the ad changes from scanning to reading.

10. The closing includes the call to action, facilitators (if used), and the final store or product ID.

11. Transitions in the body of the copy keep the logic on track.

NOTES

1. Fred Messner, ''Moving the Prospect One Step Closer,'' *Adweek*, April 26, 1982, p. 18.

2. Daniel Starch, *Measuring Product Sales Made by Advertising* (Mamaroneck, N.Y.: Starch, 1961); Philip Ward Burton, *Which Ad Pulled Best*, 4th ed. (Chicago: Crain, 1981).

3. Starch, ibid.

4. Donald Hall, *Writing Well* (Boston: Little, Brown, 1973), p. 210.

10

Layout and Production

KEY POINTS

- Typefaces have distinctive personalities.
- Legibility, which studies the ease with which people perceive words, is often violated in advertising design.
- Design principles visually organize a layout and guide the reader's eye through the elements.
- Of all the layout formats, the picture window is the most commonly used.
- The effectiveness of a design is sometimes limited by production considerations.

10.1 TYPOGRAPHY

At first glance, a print ad appears to be mostly just words and pictures. In reality, an ad is much more complex than that, with a number of elements carefully arranged in a layout.

Words do more than carry content. In our discussion of copywriting, we looked at the meaning of the words. In this section, we will look at the impression created by the graphic techniques used to display the words. There is meaning not only in the content of the message but also in the appearance of the type. Typography is a study of how letterforms are used to create effects, from bold to elegant, from delicate to brash. Letter forms can be design elements.

Figure 10-1: Serif and sans serif letters.

Letter Characteristics

In order to understand the differences in type, we need to look first at letterforms and notice some of the details that typographers refer to in their discussions of distinctive features. We'll be talking about details here; that's where the artistry shows up in advertising. As a well-known architect, Mies Van Der Rohe, said about his craft, "God is in the details."[1]

Serifs. One of the most important details is the *serif*. This is a little detail at the end of a stroke. If you imagine lettering the capital A, like the one shown here, you would probably start with the diagonal stroke down to the right, then make the stroke to the left, and finally make the crossbar. The serif is the finishing detail on the end of the downstrokes. In more recent times, block letters that are designed without serifs have become popular. The primary distinction in type is between **serif** and **sans serif** letters. "Sans" means without (see Figure 10-1).

serif: a tiny finishing detail at the end of a downstroke

sans serif: letters with no serifs that are blocked at the end of the stroke

There are some type designs that fit between these two categories, but primarily you will be choosing one or the other. Serif letters are traditional and considered easy to read. Your early reading books were printed in serif letters and most newspapers still are, so you are comfortable with this kind of letter.

Sans serif letters are considered more modern in appearance. They are clean and free from ornament. They may be considered mechanistic because of their simple, even lines. They reproduce well in newspapers and on cheap paper such as that found in telephone books. Reference materials are often printed in sans serif letters, but long masses of copy, such as a book or the text of a magazine, usually do not appear in sans serif. Sans serif letters are also considered highly visible or easy to read from a distance. That's why stop signs are in sans serif, as well as billboards and other signs.

Most studies of type have not found any real difference in legibility between serif and sans serif, but they have found that readers prefer serif letters. That is probably because people have grown up on serif letters and that's what they are used to reading.

X-Height, ascenders, and descenders. Some other terms that advertising designers use to describe type include the x-height, and the ascenders and descenders. The x-height is the body of the letter, the space occupied by a lowercase x. Ascenders and descenders are the tails that either stick above the x-height or hang below it. You will find ascenders on such letters as *t, h, l, b,* and *d.* Descenders are found on *p, q, y,* and *g* (see Figure 10-2).

The relationship between the x-height and the ascenders and descenders is an important factor in both the aesthetics of the type and its

x-height:	ascenders:	descenders:
cemnorsuvwz	bdfhklt	gjpqy

Figure 10-2: x-height, ascenders, and descenders.

legibility. First, we recognize the distinctive shape of a word by its pattern of ascenders and descenders. Aesthetics are important, too. Letters with small x-heights and long ascenders and descenders are delicate. They are also hard to reproduce in printing, particularly in the fast, imprecise printing used by newspapers. Large-bodied letters, however, are bold and more visible. They are thought to be easier to read.

Letterform Variations

Case.   One of the most familiar type of variations is found in the distinction between *upper-* and *lowercase* or capitals and small letters. "Uppercase" and "lowercase" come from the old typecases used in hand-set type. The capitals were located above and the smaller letters were below.

There are four ways to handle case: all capital letters (all caps), all lowercase, upper- and lowercase (U&lc), and small caps. All capitals are used to create a blocky look and give a hard edge to the line of type. All lowercase is a fashion that comes and goes. The most common treatment is upper- and lowercase, with the first letter in the sentence and first letter in proper nouns being capitalized; this is designated "U&lc."

Italics.   Most letters have an italic form that slants to the right. This is a design style that picks up the slanted characteristics of running script. It is similar to, but not the same as, cursive or script type. *Cursive* is a typeface category of its own. It leans to the right, but the letters are designed to connect and actually look like handwriting (see Figure 10-3).

The *italic* version is identical in design to the typeface; the only difference is that the strokes are tilted to the right. Italics are used to create variation while still maintaining the continuity of the same type family.

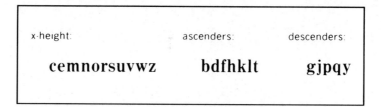

Helvetica
Helvetica Italic

Figure 10-3: Normal and italic letter shapes.

Weight.   A second letterform variation is found in the weight of letters. A letter can be designed to look light or heavy in comparison to its regular weight. This is done by manipulating the width of the strokes. A bold letter is one that has wider strokes and a light letter is one with very fine strokes (see Figure 10-4).

This is Triumvirate Light

This is Triumvirate Heavy

This is Triumvirate Black

Triumvirate Bold Condensed

Triumvirate Bold Expanded

Figure 10-4: Variations in a type family by both weight and width.

Width. Width can also be varied in the design of a typeface. Here we mean the width of the space occupied by the letter, not the width of the strokes. The letter can be condensed or squeezed to occupy less space. It can also be extended horizontally. It is still the same basic design; it is just that this basic horizontal dimension has been manipulated.

When you put all these variations together and start to combine them, you can see how complex typography becomes. A single letter, for example, can be used in its upright form in a normal (or medium) weight and width. However, it can also be italic, bold and condensed, or light and extended—or any other combination. Just the two posture variations and the three weight and width variations give a total of some 500 variations to choose from for any typeface. And when you add case, you have another four sets of variations. For one typeface you can choose from some 12,000 possible variations (see Exhibit 10-1).

Typeface Categories

You probably wonder how something so simple as a letter can become so complicated. The truth is we have just begun to scratch the surface of the variations available to the designer. Even though an *A* is an *a*, there are thousands of typefaces and each one lends a different appearance to the *a*. Typefaces have distinctive personalities; they add mood and feeling to a message. Some faces are big and blocky; others are delicate and refined. Some are elegant, some are casual. The mood of the message is enhanced by the careful choice of typeface.

Each typeface has a name, such as Century or Bookman or Bodoni or Caledonia. Most of these typefaces come in a complete set of variations. The set is called a "type family." A typesetter may have a complete range

Exhibit 10-1: Typefaces have distinct personalities and can be used to contribute to the mood, look, or feel of an advertisement. The "Variety pack" headline for TV Guide is jazzy, the "Suspension" ad for Ford demonstrates what the word means, and the Lauder's Scotch type communicates a feeling of relaxed elegance. (Center photo courtesy of Hiram Walker Incorporated, Farmington Mills, Michigan)

Sans Serif:	Oldstyle Roman:
Futura Bold	Administer Book
Square Serif:	Transitional Roman:
Lubalin Graph	Century
Round Serif:	Inscribed Serif:
Cooper Black	Optima

Figure 10-5: Common categories of typefaces.

of sizes of any one typeface and a complete range of variations, including italics, and all the weight and width variations (see Figure 10-5).

Printers' Measures

In order to specify type, you will need some skill working with printers' measures. Most measurements in the graphic arts industry are calculated in *points* and *picas*. There are 6 picas in an inch and 12 points in a pica.

The length and width of columns is measured in picas or inches. A 12-pica column width, for example, would be two inches wide.

The vertical size of type, or type height, is measured in points, a very small measure. There are 72 points in an inch. Standard type sizes of body copy include 5 or 6, 8, 10, 11, 12, and 14 points. The display copy ranges from 18 points through 20, 24, 30, 36, 42, 48, 60, 72, 96, and 120 points. For comparison, a 72-point headline would be one inch in height.

The width between lines of type in body copy is also indicated when you specify type. This space is called *leading*. In the days of hot metal type, this space was created by inserting strips of lead between the lines; hence the name "leading." Leading is measured in points, and you will normally specify one point of leading. The larger the body type, the more space you need between the lines. Likewise, the longer the line, the more leading you need.

Letterspacing

The amount of air or space around letters is both a design decision for effect and a legibility consideration. "Letterspacing" refers to the amount of space between letters in a word. The fashion is to set the type as close as possible and still keep the letters distinct. But the finesse of letterspacing also considers the shape of the adjoining letters. The amount of space between letters is adjusted to even out the mass and gaps created by letterforms. This is called "optical spacing," as opposed to the "mechanical spacing" achieved with typewriters.

A capital *T*, for example, has lots of unused air under its bars. A capital *L* has lots of air above the base. An *L* next to a *T* would create an

Mechanical spacing:	Letter spacing:
moon **little**	**moon** **little**
Normal spacing:	Kerned spacing:
Vote **PAW**	**Vote** **PAW**

Figure 10-6: Mechanically set spacing compared to letterspacing that adjusts for the shape of the letters. Below is normal spacing compared to kerned spacing where the letters are "tucked."

kerning: one element of a letter is tucked over or under an adjoining letter

TL

unusual mass of white space, more space perhaps than you might find between words, and that white space could destroy the word as a unit. To compensate for these shapes, you would pull the letters close together and let the baseline of the *L* move under the bars of the *T*. This is called **kerning**. That means one element of a letter is tucked over or under an element of the adjoining letter.

But there is more to optical spacing than just kerning. Mechanical spacing means that the amount of space between the letters is equal regardless of their shapes. Optical spacing adjusts the amount of spacing to compensate for the density of the letter. Some letters are relatively skinny, like *i*, *l*, and *t*, while others are fat, like *M* and *W*. Optical spacing considers both mass and width. The principle is to add space around the skinny letters and tighten the space around the fat, massed letters. The goal is to even out the tone of the letters by compensating for their mass, shape, and openness (see Figure 10-6).

Well-known art directors like George Lois care passionately about letterspacing. Lois takes his display type that has already been set, then razors the letters apart and rearranges them until the spacing is perfect.

Specifying the Type

You need to know about all these categories and characteristics of type because when you design an ad, usually you will have to "spec" the type—that means specify the typeface, including any variations, and the type size. A type spec is a formula that tells the typesetter how to set the type. You might say something like "36 pt. Baskerville," which, because of the specified size, is clearly display type. If you want variations, then you have to specify them, such as Baskerville Bold or Baskerville Italic or Baskerville Bold Italic Condensed. The advertising professional has available to him or her a complete book of typefaces from which to choose, an essential tool when specing an ad.

For body copy you also have to indicate the line length (column width) in picas and the leading, or space between the lines. Leading is usually stated in relationship to the type size. For example, "9 on 11" means 9-point type with 2 points of leading. Typical specifications for body copy would read as follows:

$$\frac{\text{11/12 Palatino}}{\text{24 picas}}$$ 11/12 Palatino × 24 picas

Legibility

legibility: the ease with which letters are perceived

readability: the understandability of a message

We have been talking about the effects you can create through the choice of typeface and variation. These are design or aesthetic considerations. Now let's look at the practical side of typography and discuss the principles of legibility. By **legibility** we mean the visibility of the letters, the ease with which they may be perceived (see Figure 10-7). Another word, **readability**, is often used interchangeably with legibility. For the record, readability refers to how easy it is to understand the message. Studies of readability look at such problems as sentence length and word choice.

Legibility is important to people who are concerned about the effectiveness of design. For example, David Ogilvy wrote, "You may think I exaggerate the importance of good typography." He explains, "You may ask if I ever heard a housewife say she bought a new detergent because the advertisement was set in Caslon. No. But do you think an advertisement can sell if nobody can read it?"[1]

Line length.   One major consideration in legibility, particularly for text copy, is the length of the line. If a line is too long, then readers can't find their way back to the beginning of the next line. You may see that problem sometimes with headlines that run across a two-page spread in a magazine. In body copy you will see the same problem when a block of copy is set one column wide to fill the whole page. A line length the width of a normal page is too long to read. A two-column or three-column format works better.

Acceptable line length is really a function of the size of type. Large type can be set on a wider column than can small type; the smaller the type size, the shorter the line length should be. Likewise, the spacing between the lines is a factor. Long lines in bigger type need more space between the lines than do short lines in smaller type.

A general rule of thumb for finding the optimum line length is to use 1½ times the length of the lowercase alphabet in your chosen type. If you have a type specimen book and it shows the lowercase alphabet, simply measure it and calculate the ideal line length from that. For example, if the lowercase alphabet measures two inches, then an optimum line length would be 3 inches. An acceptable range would probably be from 2½ to 3½ inches.

All caps.   Another problem noted by most legibility researchers is copy set in all capitals. The problem here is that people identify words by their shapes. An upper- and lowercase word has distinctive "coastlines" created by the pattern of ascenders, descenders, and x-height. All

1. Long lines, small size

There are six type legibility problems listed. They consist of long lines, small size; all caps; reverse; and superprinting. Italic type is also a problem, including when it is in all caps or reverse.

2. All caps

THERE ARE SIX TYPE LEGIBILITY PROBLEMS LISTED. THEY CONSIST OF LONG LINES, SMALL SIZE; ALL CAPS; REVERSE; AND SUPERPRINTING. ITALIC TYPE IS ALSO A PROBLEM, IN-CLUDING WHEN IT IS IN ALL CAPS OR REVERSE.

3. Reverse

There are six type legibility problems listed. They consist of long lines, small size; all caps; reverse; and superprinting. Italic type is also a problem, including when it is in all caps or reverse.

4. Italics

There are six type legibility problems listed. They consist of long lines, small size; all caps; reverse; and superprinting. Italic type is also a problem, including when it is in all caps or reverse.

5. Italics all caps

THERE ARE SIX TYPE LEGIBILITY PROBLEMS LISTED. THEY CONSIST OF LONG LINES, SMALL SIZE; ALL CAPS; REVERSE; AND SUPERPRINTING. ITALIC TYPE IS ALSO A PROBLEM, IN-CLUDING WHEN IT IS IN ALL CAPS OR REVERSE.

6. Italics reverse

There are six type legibility problems listed. They consist of long lines, small size; all caps; reverse; and superprinting. Italic type is also a problem, including when it is in all caps or reverse.

7. Superprinting (over pattern)

There are six type legibility problems listed. They consist of long lines, small size; all caps; reverse; and superprinting. Italic type is also a problem, including when it is in all caps or reverse.

Figure 10-7: Type legibility problems.

caps obliterates the coastline and forces the reader to slow down and scan for individual letters. The slower the reading, the less efficient it is. If you are using just a couple of words in a headline, then all caps is not much of a problem. If you are setting several lines in capitals, then you may drive your reader away.

Reverse. When letters are set "in reverse," that means the letter image appears to be white against a dark background. Reverse is used a lot in advertising because the black is dramatic and attention-getting. The only problem is that reverse letters are hard to read. The same rule of thumb used with all capitals applies to reverse letters: If it is just a little bit of copy, it doesn't matter much. If it is a lot, then you may lose your reader. The smaller the letter and the longer the copy block, the more difficult it is to read in reverse.

Italics. A long passage set in italics can be difficult to read. In an article on why so many ads are hard to read, *Adweek* mentioned the "italic-induced crick in the neck" that comes from reading long passages of italic copy.[2] Italics in reverse are even harder to read than normal type. The worst offense is all caps set in italics, which is almost impossible to decipher.

Contrast. Maximum contrast between foreground and background is another legibility principle. This is a problem involving color choice. Yellow or white on black, for example, is strong in contrast. Color combinations become a problem when you use two similar colors for foreground and background. Yellow on white is difficult to read and so is black on blue, brown, or purple. The rule of thumb is to maximize the contrast between the foreground and the background.

Surprinting. Art directors like to print type over a picture because that pulls the type and the art together and makes the layout less cluttered. In terms of simplicity, that may be a good idea. In terms of legibility it is deadly. When you **surprint** type over a picture, make sure there is no conflicting background detail. Type is made up of small details like ascenders, descenders, serifs, bowls, and counters. When you superimpose that typographic pattern over some other pattern, then the type begins to fall apart; the letters become indistinct.

surprinting: type is printed over some other image

Occasionally you will see type surprinted over a picture that has an expanse of pavement, a wooden wall, or even clouds. Within the wall or the pavement, however, there is pattern and it will conflict with the pattern of the type. Surprint type only when the area of the picture you want to use is completely empty, such as a clear sky or a white wall. Don't make the type any more difficult to read than it already is.

Type design. The typeface design, itself, can be a factor in legibility. Highly ornamented or fanciful typefaces are often difficult to decipher. Old English letters are hard to read. Uppercase cursive letters are very hard to puzzle out.

Certain typefaces interact with the printing process to create legibility problems. Newspapers are printed fast on soft paper. Any typefaces that have tiny delicate details will have a hard time surviving the newspaper production process. Bold, blocky letters work best in newspapers.

The same thing is true with visibility on billboards. The little details fade. It's better to use big and relatively bold typefaces.

Special optical effects can also create legibility problems. Given the advances in photographic and computerized typesetting, it is possible to manipulate shape, size, and even plane of the type image. Type can lean forward, backward, or to any side. It can be elongated or squished. It can squirm snake-like across the page or it can vibrate like air waves. And it is all done electronically. Just remember, the more games you play with the type, the harder it is to read. In the *Adweek* special report on legibility, a type research director at the Monotype company said, "A lot of people are thoroughly abusing typefaces today."

Type that is well set does its job and contributes to the mood and look without calling attention to itself or getting in the way of the reading. Lou Dorfsman, vice president and creative director at CBS Inc., said, "Typography should be absolutely legible and aesthetically pleasing." Helmut Krone, executive vice president and creative director at DDB Needham says he is trying to downplay the type. He explains, "I'm trying to take emphasis away from the headline. I think the picture should do more talking than the type."[3]

Copyfitting

There is one other problem with type in print: It has to fit the space. It is expensive to reset the type because it doesn't fit the layout. It is possible, with some typesetters, to tell them to "set to fit." They will play with the specifications until they get a piece of copy that fits exactly into the shape available on the layout. That's fine, but you lose control over the type specification—and it is expensive.

The solution is to estimate how much type in a certain size will fit in a given space before the type is set. If you can tell from your estimate that you have twice as much copy as you do space, then you can rewrite the copy, adjust the specifications, or redesign the layout. This is a problem with retail and catalogue advertising as well as with brochures and flyers.

Both writers and artists have to know a little something about copyfitting. It all depends upon which gets done first, the layout or the copy. If the layout is done first, then the copywriter will need to *write the copy to fit the space* allowed. This is how most catalogue copy is prepared and a lot of retail copy, too. If the copy is written first, then it's up to the artist to estimate *how much copy* there is in order to know how much space it will occupy on the layout.

Writing to fit. If you are a writer and you have to produce copy to fit a layout, there are two critical estimates you need to make before you can begin. First, you have to know how many lines to write, and then you have to know how many characters there will be in each line. Both of these estimates are derived by measuring the copy block and doing some basic calculations using the type specifications.

First, measure the copy block and write down both its width and depth *in picas*. Convert the depth to points (multiply by 12). From your type specs you should know the size of the type and the amount of leading.

Add those together and you have the height *in points* that you need to allow for a line. Now divide that line height into the total points available and you will have an estimate of how many lines you need.

For example, suppose your copy block is 7 picas deep. That is equal to 84 total points. If you are using 12-point type with 2 points of leading, then your line height is 14 points. When you divide 14 into 84, you get 7 lines. This is a neat example, with everything coming out even. However, in most cases it won't be so nice. Always remember to round down. You want the number of lines that will fit *within* the copy block.

Now to figure the character count, you will need to look up or calculate a figure called the character per pica (CPP). This is a simple estimate of how many characters will fit in a pica. It varies with every typeface and every size. Some printers include the CPP in their type spec books. If not, it is easy to calculate. You will need a sample piece of body copy set in the size and face you want to use. Measure a 10-pica length on the lines of type. Count the number of characters in 10 picas and divide by 10. (To be more accurate, you might want to estimate across several lines and then use the average.)

For example, if you have 35 characters, on the average, in the 10-pica line, then your CPP for this typeface in this size is 3.5. In other words, there are 3.5 characters in one pica.

Once you know the CPP, you simply multiply that times the line length for your copy block and that tells you how many characters there will be, on the average, in a line. If you are using a typeface with 3.5 as its CPP and the copy block is 12 picas wide, then you will type a 42-character line. Just set your margins on your typewriter for that character count, and start typing the number of lines you need.

Designing to fit. The designer goes through a similar process, only in reverse. What you need to know to lay out the copy block is how many lines the manuscript copy will set in your chosen type. Once you know that, you can simply rule in the lines to the specified line height and you are done.

To estimate the number of lines, you first will need to estimate how many total characters there are in the manuscript copy. Eyeball a point at the right edge of the typewritten lines that seems to represent the average line length. (Some lines will be longer, some will be shorter.) You can actually count the number of characters in three or four lines to find out mathematically what the average line length is, but the eyeball technique works for estimating.

Count the number of characters to that point and you will have the average character count used by the writer. Multiply that times the number of manuscript lines, and you will have an estimate of the total characters in the manuscript.

Now turn to your type specifications and find or calculate the CPP for the typeface you are using. Multiply this times the line length you have decided on for the copy block and you will know approximately how many characters of typeset copy will fit in a typeset line. Divide the line count into the total manuscript characters to find the number of lines that your typeset copy will fill.

For example, suppose you estimate that the manuscript line length averages 34 characters and the typed copy is 10 lines long. That gives you a total of 340 manuscript characters. Your specified typeface has a CPP of 2.5 and the line length you want to use on the layout is 16 picas. This means the typeset line will be 40 characters. When you divide the 40 characters into 340 total characters, you come up with 8.5 lines. Now rule 8½ lines to size.

If you are interested in reading further about typography,* there are several good books that you might consult. This is only a very brief introduction to a complicated but interesting area in advertising design.

10.2 LAYOUT AND DESIGN

We've talked about the pieces of a print advertisement—art, headline, body copy, captions, subheads, as well as product identification information such as product picture, logotype, and signature. A print advertisement is a complex piece of multielement design.

In advertising, art directors are the specialists who make visual sense of all these elements. There are art directors for both print and broadcast. In print advertising, they arrange all the elements through a process called layout, which is a visual plan. This chapter will introduce the concept of layout primarily as it applies to print advertising.

Layout

layout: a plan for the arrangement and relationship of all the elements in a print advertisement

Layout is both the process of organizing things and the plan, or arrangement, of visual elements. If all the pieces of an advertisement were dropped onto a page at random, it would be extremely difficult to make any sense of the message. It would be hard for the reader to know what is most important in the message, and where to start and end reading. Layout structures the arrangement of the pieces so that the visual is easy to read.

Layout always deals with relationships; that's how order is created. When you put a mark or a shape on a piece of paper, there is a relationship between that mark and the page. There is now foreground and background; there is a point of attention, an element that "stands out." The page itself has some basic relationships you need to consider. There are relationships between top and bottom, left and right, horizontal and vertical.

These relationships contribute to organization, emphasis, stability, and movement. The more lines and shapes you add to the page, the more complicated these relationships become. The various pieces can be separate, touching, overlapping, aligning, converging, or dispersing. They can group together or they can separate. They can form and create patterns or they can fragment and exist as discrete units. Every time you construct a layout, you are manipulating the relationships of one element to another and the individual elements to the whole.

Design Principles

There are a number of different ways to discuss the visual principles used to construct a layout. Some of the principles are primarily functional, and they give order to the perceptual process. Others are primarily aesthetic,

* *Designing with Type* by James Craig and *The ABC's of Typography* by Sandra Ernst.

Big things come in little packages.

© 1986 Hershey Foods Corporation

HERSHEY'S KISSES.

Exhibit 10-2: These two ads for HERSHEY'S KISSES® chocolates illustrate the impact of white space when it is used as a design element to set off the product. (Courtesy of Hershey Foods Corporation. The conical configuration, the attached plume device, and the words HERSHEY'S KISSES are registered trademarks of Hershey Foods Corporation)

IN CASE OF EMERGENCY,

PULL.

HERSHEY'S KISSES.

and they create arrangements that are pleasing or interesting to the eye. The *functional* principles that will be discussed here are unity, simplicity, contrast, and balance. The *aesthetic* principles are proportion and harmony.

Unity and grouping.   We have defined layout as a process of organizing visual elements, so it makes sense that the most important aspect of layout is the organizing function. That is discussed in design literature as unity or grouping. The idea is that figures and patterns take on meaning only if they are grouped so the elements that belong together are seen together. Likewise, space is used to force things apart that don't belong together. Joining and disassociating are the two basic tools of organization.

Disassociating elements is done by separating things that don't belong together. For example, four separate photos can be arranged around a page so that there is no visible relationship between them. **White space** can be used to create "alleys" of space that push the photos apart (see Exhibit 10-2). Rules and boxes can be used to separate one element from another. Rules and alleys of white space are barriers. Likewise, boxes enclose some pieces while excluding others (see Figures 10-8 and 10-9).

More commonly, in layout, the problem is one of joining things together that belong together. White space is an important element in creating unity. The white space is the area between and around the elements—the background, in other words. But white space is more than

white space: area in a layout that is unoccupied by other elements such as type or art

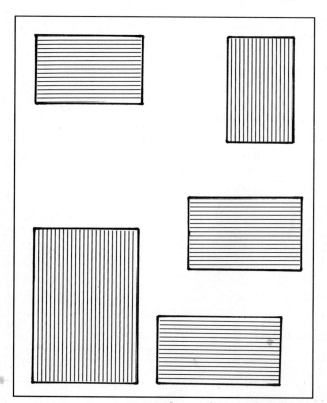

Figure 10-8: Alleys and pockets of uncontrolled white space.

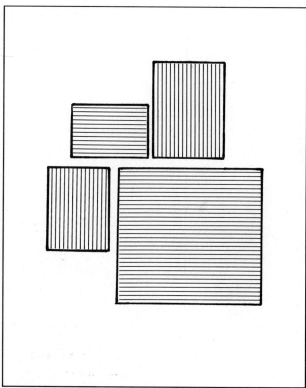

Figure 10-9: Group the elements, pushing white space to outside.

just background. It can be massed or used as a frame, at which point it becomes an element too. By decreasing white space, you visually pull elements closer together. The less white space, the closer the fit. That's how letterspacing and word spacing are manipulated to group letters into recognizable words.

In terms of unity, if you want to make the most effective use of white space, then push it to the outside. Ineffective use of white space creates pockets and alleys of trapped space that inadvertently push elements apart that you intended to group together. The rule of thumb is: Push the white space to the edge.

Joining is also done by creating *alignments*. If the four pictures mentioned above are dispersed with no visual relationships, they are seen as separate elements. If they are grouped so that there are obvious alignments along their edges, then they create a pattern. If they are aligned and pulled together, then they create a group. Four separate elements can become one group. That's how visual cohesion is created.

We discussed **rules** and **boxes** earlier as separation tools, but they can also be used for organizing. Rules frame and contain. Rules across the bottom or top, or even along an edge, provide a plane to hang or stack the elements on or against. In this sense, a rule can be an important organizing tool. A box around an element or group of elements clearly pulls those pieces together and separates them from the other elements on the page.

rule: a line

box: four rules enclosing a space

Simplicity and clutter.   These are two other terms related to unity that you will hear in critiques of layouts. *Simplicity* means use of the least possible number of elements, thereby making the arrangement easier to read as well as more dramatic. An old architectural maxim is: Less is more. The idea is that *the fewer the elements, the greater the impact.*

If you have four separate photos, then the viewer's attention is divided, and there is automatic conflict in terms of where to look first. If you group the four, then you can create one element, although it is more complex. If you use only one photo, then you have the sole attention of the viewer directed at that one element. The more elements you use, the more fragmented the impact. Any time you can group elements, you will be simplifying the layout.

A cluttered design has a thousand elements all fighting for attention. The elements aren't grouped to make perception easier; there are no obvious alignments, and every element seems to be separate. There is no visual coherence. Discount store advertising will sometimes use clutter deliberately to convey the idea of diversity and of a profusion of products. But even with deliberate clutter, there is usually some sense of organization to help readers make their way through the design.

Contrast and dominance.   Whenever you construct a layout, you are making a series of decisions. The most important one is how things should be grouped to create a unified impression. The second most important decision is what element should be emphasized. Emphasis in visual communication is created by contrast.

As a designer, you must study the elements and decide what *one* element is the most important element, and then what element is next in

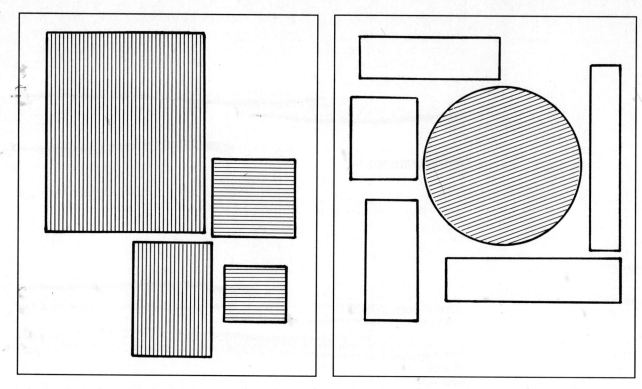

Figure 10-10: Size and position can create dominance.

Figure 10-11: Novelty and color, or tone, can create dominance.

importance, then next, and so on. Every designer ranks the elements in his or her mind intuitively. This is the editorial or decision-making side of the visual design process. Just like journalists order facts in a news story, you have to order the elements in your layout in terms of their significance.

Once you have decided what one element you want to emphasize, then you manipulate the layout so this pattern of stress becomes obvious. You do this by creating contrast. If one element is to stand out, then the other elements have to defer. What you are doing is creating a pattern of dominance. Visual dominance is created by contrasting size, shape, color, and tone, or position. The biggest element will stand out. So will the one at the top or the most colorful element or the one with the most unusual shape (see Figures 10-10 and 10-11).

If you create patterns of conflicting contrast, you create visual confusion. For example, a large element at the bottom of the page will fight with a smaller element that controls the top. There is a conflict between size and position.

Contrast is a form of visual logic. One and only one item can dominate because if there is more than one big item or an unusual item, then there is no clear pattern of contrast. The rule of thumb is: If everything is bold, then nothing is bold. Likewise, if everything is big, nothing is big. The other elements have to be reduced in significance in order for one element to dominate. If several items are competing equally for attention, then all you have is confusion.

The decision on what to emphasize should be based on the strategy. For example, if this is a heavy copy message, then the headline will probably dominate. But if there is art, then extraordinary contrast has to be used to make the head dominate the visual. Illustrations consistently overpower headlines unless something is done in the layout to give additional visual weight to the words. Being at the top of the page isn't enough because it is still easy for the eye to be drawn to the art. The head will need to be extremely large to hold its own against the art.

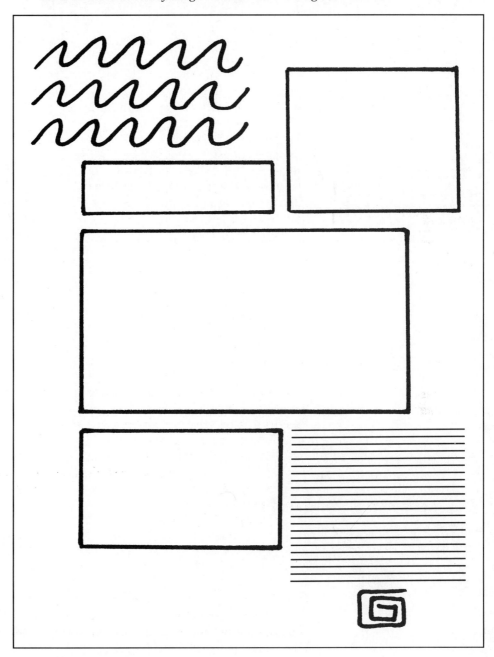

Figure 10-12: In asymmetrical balance, counterbalance the weights around the optical center.

focal point: the point of balance around which the elements are grouped

optical center: the point on a page seen as the center-point by the eye; it's actually above the mathematical center

Balance. When things are organized, they are usually grouped around a **focal point**. This is the fulcrum of the layout; elements are positioned around this fulcrum to maintain a feeling of visual balance.

When the professional analyzes a layout for balance, he or she looks at the optical weights of the various elements and notes how they are balanced or counterbalanced one against another. Optical weights are derived from the same factors that create contrast. A large element is visually "heavier" than a small one, color is heavier than black and white, unusual shapes are heavier than regular ones, and so on. A mass of white space can even be a heavy element (see Figure 10-12).

These weights are positioned around the focal point, or fulcrum, of the arrangement using the old teeter-totter principle for counterbalancing: lighter weights to the outside and heavier weights to the inside. It's the same technique used when a parent sits close to the fulcrum on a teeter-totter to counterbalance a child who sits way out on the far end of the board.

Sometimes this fulcrum is positioned on the center of the page, although it doesn't have to be. There is a natural focal point of a layout, called the **optical center**, that is located slightly above mathematical center. (Mathematical center is found by drawing diagonals from the corners. The mathematical center is the point where the diagonals cross.) (See Figure 10-13.)

Research has found that when an individual is asked to put his or her finger on the exact center of a sheet of paper, the individual will place it slightly above this mathematical center. That's the natural optical center, and the position best used as a point of balance for most layouts. Psychologists speculate that the optical center is positioned higher than the mathematical center because of the natural dominance of the top half of the page.

The focal point in advertising layout usually contains some element that serves as a visual center—in many cases it will be a product. Not all layouts use an obvious focal point, but even if the position is not accented with some critical element, there is still an underlying point of balance, an unstated or imaginary focal point, around which the elements are arranged.

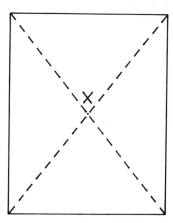

Figure 10-13: Locating the optical center.

A layout that is out of balance has the heavy weights on one side with no counterbalance on the opposite side. The elements appear to "fall off the edge" when a layout is out of balance.

There are two primary strategies for creating balance in a layout. A symmetrical layout is one where all the elements are centered around a vertical, and sometimes horizontal, axis. You could fold it in half and the edges of the elements would form a mirror image. The Hershey ads are good examples of symmetrical balance (see Exhibit 10-2). The other type of balance is asymmetrical. Here the elements are informally grouped around the optical center, carefully using the techniques of counterbalancing (see again Figure 10-12).

A symmetrical layout is considered formal, conservative, stable, and sometimes a little dull. An asymmetrical layout is considered more visually interesting, more active, more dynamic. It's more difficult to create asymmetrical balance, but the visual excitement is usually worth the effort.

The type of balance used in the layout should depend upon the execution strategy. If you have described the style as formal, then a symmetrical layout may be appropriate. If you are using a casual or informal tone, then an asymmetrical layout might work better.

Movement and direction.   Balance deals with the stability of a layout; movement and direction are concerned with the visual path created for the eye to follow. They create dynamics and action (see Exhibit 10-3). A layout is like a road map. It tells the reader where to begin, where to go next, and where to end. A layout is always dynamic because the eye is never at rest when looking at (reading) a visual. Successful layout controls the eye's gaze. Visual signposts are used to direct the eye through the course. If the layout is successful, then the direction of the eye's movement through the arrangement should be obvious.

The visual paths used in advertising are based on natural *scan sequences* used by westerners when they read. The two primary scan patterns are top to bottom and left to right. In addition, the power of contrast can be used to direct the eye to read from big to little, dark to light, color to noncolor, and unusual to usual.

The top to bottom, left to right scan pattern has been called the "Gutenberg diagonal." It summarizes the fact that people normally enter

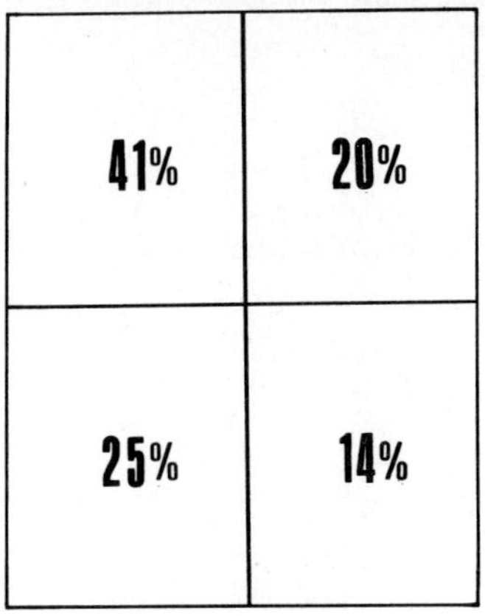

41%	20%
25%	14%

Figure 10-14: Natural entry points by quadrant.

Exhibit 10-3: The splash of nail polish knocking against the bottle creates a tremendous feeling of dynamic motion and carries the eye directly to the label.

a visual in the upper left corner and exit from the lower right. Most horizontal movement in a layout, then, is to the right and most vertical movement is toward the bottom. Research into reading habits has found that most people will look first at the upper left quadrant. It is the natural entry point for a visual (see Figure 10-14).

The *diagonal* is the simplest scan pattern. A more complex variation on that is the *Z pattern*, where the eye enters in the upper left, moves across the layout in the left to right pattern, then drops down diagonally to the lower left, and scans once again from left to right. In essence, that's the standard reading pattern for lines of type. The Z pattern can be made even more complicated by adding sets of zigzag patterns.

Sometimes the focal points will serve as the beginning point. In that case a common pattern is a *spiral* movement, with the eye beginning at the center, then circling up to the right, back across to the left, and then down the left edge and across the bottom. The same pattern can spiral to the right. The spiral to the left reverses the normal movement in the sweep across the top of the page, so it is not a good design to use with a long headline, or any headline, at the top. The right spiral ends in the left corner, which is also an unusual ending spot (see Figure 10-15).

Another simple pattern is a straight *vertical* line beginning at the top and dropping to the bottom. A formal, symmetrical layout will often use this sequence. The structure of the emphasis has to match the downward sweep. For example, in most layouts like this the most important element is at the top, then comes the next most important element, and so on down to the product signature at the bottom. Usually that includes a dominant piece of art, then the headline, then the body copy.

When the headline is above the art but not clearly dominant, this is a problem: The reader is tempted to look first at the art, then up to the headline, then turn the page. Generally speaking, it is usually a good idea to keep the headline directly above the body copy; that way it can serve its function of enticing the reader into the body copy. If the art separates the head and the body copy, it is easy to read the head and stop.

If the layout is effective, the scan pattern should be obvious. A good exercise to use in evaluating your sense of movement in layout is to take a magazine and some sheets of tracing paper, and try to draw the scan sequence of the advertisements. You will soon see that some are easy to follow and others are confusing.

Direction can be built into a layout in other ways. Rules are often used to indicate movement. They can serve as pointers. Such an obvious illustration as the woodcut "pointing finger" is another unmistakable way to establish direction. Signs of all kinds can reinforce the pattern. Alignment of the elements can be used to create movement. For example, a series of illustrations and masses of type all aligned on a strong invisible horizontal line will create an undeniable horizontal sweep.

Sometimes there are direction cues within the composition of the art. For example, a football being kicked creates a tremendous movement message. Likewise, the position of an elbow or the angle of the legs in midstride can also direct the eye. A pointing arm in the art may, in fact, be pointing directly at the headline and serving as the leading line from one element to another.

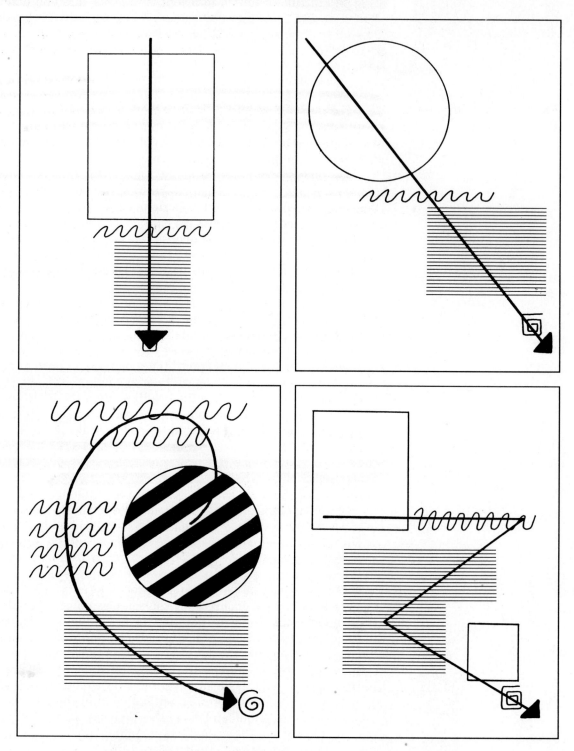

Figure 10-15: Four common visual paths.

An old rule of thumb in layout is to make sure you don't have the eyes looking out of the layout, because the direction of the gaze may cause the reader to look away. It's also considered a directional cue to turn the page. It's a subconscious response, but these cues do work on a preaware level.

Function and Aesthetics   These five principles are the basic functional guidelines for print layouts. There are other principles, such as proportion and harmony, that are best described as aesthetic; their function is to create layouts that are pleasing or interesting to the eye.

Proportion.   Proportion is a mathematical concept; it states relationships of size in terms of mathematical proportions. When you analyze proportion, you are looking at the relative size of one element to another and of each of the elements to the whole. The idea is that there are certain relationships that fit together better for no reason other than that they look good together. This is not a functional concept; it is totally subjective, and it is the basis of the set of aesthetic standards used by someone with a well-trained sense of design.

The concept of "perfect" or "divine" proportion goes back to the early Greeks. Classical archaeology is a masterpiece of proportion. The Greek designers knew that in nature certain dimensions or ratios occur frequently; others seldom. They tested these ratios and developed such concepts as "The Golden Mean" to express these aesthetic ideals. This ratio is *one to the square root of two, or 1:1.41.* For practical use, this is standardized at 3:5.

These classical designers discovered that most proportions in nature are based on the 3:5 ratio. You will rarely find a perfect square in nature, for example. A square is considered too perfect, too mechanistic, and, because it is based on a 1:1 ratio, it is predictable visually. If a relationship is predictable, it is not as interesting as a relationship that is more distinctive. The 3:5 ratio is not one the eye can predict at a glance. The 1:1 and 1:2 relationships are obvious, and therefore not as interesting.

Most quality books and magazines use page sizes that are close to a 3:5 ratio. The amount of type on the page relative to the overall page size is roughly 3:5. The proportions of the page margins to the text are also 3:5.

In fine bookmaking, the most generous depth is established at the bottom margin of the page and then moves to smaller margins around the page from the outside to the top and then to the gutter. The proportions are decided relative to the overall size of the page. For example, on an 8½-by-11 sheet the bottom margin may be 2½ inches while the top is 1½ inches. That means the margins occupy approximately 40 percent of the vertical depth, which is right in keeping with the 3:5 proportion.

Edmund Arnold, in his book *Ink on Paper*, gives a technique to use for establishing page margins.[4] Start by establishing the outside margin, then use half that width for the inside margin (the gutter). Now draw a diagonal line through your sheet. The points at which the diagonal crosses the two lines identifies the top and bottom margins. It's a simple way to develop a well-proportioned set of margins for your layout.

In layouts based upon an underlying structure of grids, the size of the grid is usually based on the 3:5 ratio. If you cut a page in half horizontally, then you have created two equal spaces—a monotonous arrangement. But if you cut the page at the 3/5th point, you will have created two distinctive rectangles. Cut both these rectangles at their 3/5th point, and you will have four rectangles, all perfectly in proportion to one another. A layout grid for page design is developed with all possible combinations of the 3:5 rectangles.

This does not mean that a square, for example, is forbidden in layout. Other proportions can be used effectively, depending upon the creative strategy. A square will be used for brochures and annual reports because the shape is rarely used and that makes it distinctive—even if the basic proportion is considered uninteresting by itself.

Harmony and tension. The term *harmony* is used in discussion of design to mean that all the design decisions fit together—in style, in concept, in tone, in effect. For example, you might ask yourself if the style of type fits the content of the headline. Does the basic layout approach match the style of art, the concept, the product? Thus, a formal symmetrical layout might not match a warehouse sales ad for a department store. Does it make sense to use a circus banner style of design for a funeral home?

Generally speaking, your objective as a designer is to make all the design decisions work together, to create a unified and coherent visual statement. Ideally, all the design decisions are mutually supportive. There is one problem, however, in that some design principles have different objectives leading to a type of creative tension.

You may find it necessary to sacrifice one principle in favor of another. For example, you may need to deemphasize contrast in order to strengthen unity. These decisions are made very carefully by a designer who is intuitively sensitive to these questions of design interaction.

Layout Formats

The discussion of layout principles gives you an understanding of the decision making that lies behind different arrangements. In advertising there are some fairly common layout patterns. These are arrangements that have been used over and over again and have been found to be highly successful in handling all the different elements in an advertisement (see Figures 10-16 to 10-25).

Picture window. The most basic layout style, and the most commonly used, is a form called the *picture window* layout. The NW Ayer agency used this style with great success in such classic breakthrough advertising as the early Volkswagen campaign.

Basically the layout uses a large dominant piece of art, followed by a headline, then the body copy, and finally the product signature information (see Figure 10-16). It is a vertical sweep and fairly symmetrical. It is the simplest layout to do as well as to read. A large proportion of the ads in most magazines use the picture window format.

Copy-heavy. Another common layout style is the *copy-heavy* format (see Figure 10-17). It begins with a strong dominant headline and is

Figure 10-16: Picture window layout.

Figure 10-17: Copy-heavy layout.

followed by a large block of copy usually set in two columns. This is basically a news announcement style, and it takes its appearance from the editorial side of a newspaper or magazine. If art is used, it is small and often inserted into the copy. Art is used to illustrate points being made in the copy rather than as an attention-getting element (see Exhibit 10-4).

Frame.   A variation on the copy-heavy format is a *frame* layout (see Figure 10-18, page 241). This is a highly disciplined layout style that encloses the copy with some kind of artistic border or frame (see Exhibit 10-5). It can be just rules, but often the frame will be a product-related illustration. Sometimes a photo will serve as a frame with the copy dropped inside the photo. But essentially a frame layout is a way to provide ornamentation or attention-getting graphics to what is, otherwise, a heavy-copy layout.

Bleed.   A bleed layout uses art that "bleeds" to all four edges of the page (see Figure 10-19, page 241). The photo defines the visual field. Usually there isn't much copy and what little there is is surprinted (printed over or on top of the photo). This creates the illusion that the photo has become the background, that it is "behind" the copy. The bleed, however, is a large photo and creates an image that dominates the surrounding environment, so this is a very graphic layout format (see Exhibit 10-6, page 243). This technique is particularly appropriate for image or mood advertising that relies more on the visual than on the words.

We're exterminating one of the nation's most destructive pests.

Potholes are to cars what gopher holes are to horses. Yet for many years, these sudden, violent little boobytraps have been a part of our streets and highways as familiar as the white center line. Because lasting repairs just cost too much. Until Phillips invented Petromat® fabric, a tough underliner for roads that reduces damage from cracks and holes.

Makes roads easier on cars, safer for the drivers. And cuts taxes spent on road repair to a fraction of former costs. That's a big bump taxpayers will be happy to miss. Phillips Petroleum. Good things for cars—and the people who drive them. **The Performance Company** PHILLIPS 66

Exhibit 10-4: Phillips has been using an interesting *copy-heavy* layout format for its corporate "Proof of performance" campaign. Notice the use of large type wrapping around the centrally positioned art. (Part of Phillips Petroleum's Proof of Performance campaign)

Figure 10-18: Frame layout.

Figure 10-19: Bleed layout.

Grid. Another layout style is the *grid*. With this format there is an underlying grid that structures the placement of all elements (see Figure 10-20). It is used to organize ads that have a lot of elements, particularly many pieces of art. Grid-based design is used for department store and discount store advertisements where a multitude of products is featured. It can also be used to standardize a layout format, so that various ads in a campaign or across a variety of product lines will all look the same.

A Mondrian layout style is a variation of grid-based design. Piet Mondrian was an early twentieth-century painter who experimented with perfectly proportioned shapes as an art form. The various-sized rectangles in a Mondrian layout are fitted together like a mosaic. Occasionally, a Mondrian-based design will be used in ads where there is a need for a structure to bring order to a variety of elements.

Panel. A panel is another variation on the grid design. *Panel* designs use strips of similar-sized blocks running either horizontally or vertically (see Figure 10-21). A horizontal version would be a format that looks like a comic strip panel. This format is good for process explanations when you need to show things in steps. It is also good for showing several views of the same product or a variety of product styles (see Exhibit 10-7).

Every Spring almost as soon as the days get a little warmer, you'll see the color coming back into your lawn and it will probably look nicer than it really is.

Your grass is now producing chlorophyll, which is where that color comes from. And this is when your soil needs all the help it can get — not just to make your grass greener, but to help thicken up your lawn with lots of new grass while the weather's fine for growing.

All this is hard work for a lawn.

How Turf Builder helps thicken your lawn with thousands of new grass plants.

Grass plants start new grasses growing around them by sending out tillers, rhizomes, or stolons which form new "branch" plants that send down roots of their own. It takes a lot of energy on your lawn's part and your soil alone just can't come up with enough nourishment to do the job right.

But about thirty minutes with your spreader and some Scotts® Turf Builder® will give your lawn the nourishment it

needs. In fact, one feeding will help grow thousands of new grass plants in a few weeks. We've done it ourselves on different grasses (from bermuda to St. Augustine to bluegrass) on our grass research farms around the country.

Turf Builder gives grass a prolonged feeding because it holds some of its nitrogen back for later. We worked out a kind of timing process that releases this food slowly, so that it will work on those thin spots for up to two months.

And you might also like to know that this same slow feeding action also keeps Turf Builder from burning your lawn. All you have to do is follow the directions on the label. In fact you could accidentally put on four times too much this Spring and it still won't burn.

We put out a quarterly booklet called Lawn Care® that's filled with tips for lawns. It's free and you can get it just by writing us here in Marysville, Ohio 43040. You don't need a street address. We're the Scotts people and everybody in town knows where we are.

Scotts Turf Builder
America's favorite fertilizer for developing thick green lawns

Exhibit 10-5: Scotts uses different *frames* for the various ads in this campaign. This one, for Turf Builder, shows a frame of grass around the ad.

Exhibit 10-6: This ad for Kleenex® Facial Tissues demonstrates two different layout formats. The basic layout can be considered a *bleed* with the photo covering the entire page to the edge of the sheet. It is also a good example of a *mortise* layout with the inset picture of the Kleenex® box and the body copy.

Figure 10-20: Grid layout.

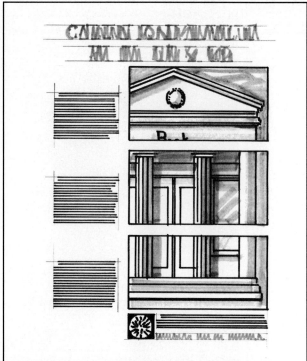

Figure 10-21: Panel layout.

Mortise. A mortise layout uses a picture embedded, or cut into, another larger picture (see Figure 10-22). Position isn't particularly important; the embedded picture can be located anywhere. Size is important, however. The embedded picture needs to be clearly smaller, in other words, visually subordinate to the primary, or dominant, picture. Often the mortise technique is used for a close-up picture of the product (see Exhibit 10-6).

Silhouette. Another common layout style, described by Roy Paul Nelson in his book on advertising design, is a *silhouette* layout.[5] Nelson is referring to an informal, or asymmetrical layout, where the art and copy together create a visually interesting arrangement or shape (see Figure 10-23). The elements are grouped internally to create some irregular shape other than the more common rectangle imposed by the internal margins. The grouping seems to be "floating" in the visual field rather than locked into a clearly defined rectangular space. If you take an asymmetrical layout and trace around the dominant elements, both art and type, you should be able to see this irregular shape created by the grouping. White space is also very carefully controlled, usually by pushing it to the outside and letting it serve as a frame.

Angular. An angular layout is a type of asymmetrical design with elements arranged to contrast with the normal perpendicular arrangements usually found in advertising layout (see Figure 10-24). In an angular layout the art, copy, or both may be positioned in oblique lines (slanted

Exhibit 10-7: The vertical *panel* layout used for Longines shows four different watch styles.

Figure 10-22: Layout with two mortises.

Figure 10-23: Silhouette layout.

or canted) or Y and V shapes. The purpose is to intensify the feeling of dynamic motion. This layout format is often used with things that move fast, such as automobiles (see Exhibit 10-8).

Jumble. A casual, busy, layout style is called a *jumble,* or *circus,* format (see Exhibit 10-9). This style of layout is playful and uses a lot of elements in something like a maze effect (see Figure 10-25). There is a visual path but it wanders through lots of pieces of art and copy blocks. This is a very difficult style to design because the whimsical effect can easily turn to clutter and the visual path can get lost in the confusion.

Doing a Layout

thumbnails: miniature sketches showing major elements

Thumbnails. There is a fairly standard visualization process followed in the development of an advertising concept. In the initial conceptual stage, the art director and copywriter will usually kick around ideas using rough sketches called **thumbnails**. These are small sketches that are used to depict the basic elements of the idea: key words, a rough sketch of the visual, the approximate size of the copy blocks, the logo or signature, and so on.

During the talking stage, many sheets of paper or newsprint are covered with these miniature sketches—by both the artist and the writer. Many creatives find that making thumbnails tends to stimulate the creative process—it's a functional form of doodling.

Exhibit 10-8: The Dodge Lancer ad uses an *angular* layout format to create the feeling of motion and flying.

Exhibit 10-9: This ad positions Hawaii as a great place for a wide variety of outdoor activities. The *jumble* layout is used effectively here to create a feeling of diversity and fun.

Figure 10-24: Angular layout.

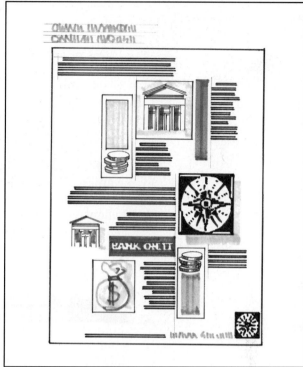

Figure 10-25: Jumble layout.

Semicomps. Thumbnails are used for getting ideas and, when several approaches begin to sound possible, then you will move to a visualization stage called "roughs" or **semicomps**. These roughs are used to show to other members of the team for critiquing. Sometimes they may be presented to the client representative if this person operates closely with the creative team in the idea development stage.

The purpose of roughs is to mock up the idea in enough detail that others can understand the message and critique the approach. Usually, there are several roughs developed so there are approaches to compare. The layouts in Figure 10-25 are executed in the semicomp style. This is the form in which most ads are presented for review and discussion.

Semicomps are executed by *lettering* in the display type, *sketching* in the visual, and *ruling* in the body copy. The idea is to show what the approach looks like without spending a lot of time and money on finished art. There are still a lot of decisions (and changes) to be made at this stage of the game.

Most of the assignments you will be doing in advertising classes will be executed in the semicomp form. Semicomps are called "roughs," but this doesn't mean sloppy. These still need to be executed as carefully and professionally as you can. Money is not spent on typesetting and hiring an artist, but time should be spent to make them look as professional as possible.

Comprehensives. When the creative people and account team decide upon the approach, an artist will develop the **comprehensives**. These

semicomps: rough layouts done to size

comprehensives: full mark-ups

are detailed visualizations of the final approach. Comprehensives look as much like the finished advertisement as possible. The art is carefully prepared, in color, if appropriate. It is usually sketched or painted using felt tips or watercolors.

The type may be "greeked" in—in other words, you use the same size and type as you have specified but without actually having it set. It may be cut out of some other publication or you may use "nonsense" type available in different type styles in transfer type. The idea is to make it look like the actual type without the expense. After all, the copy hasn't received final approval at this point, so undoubtedly there will be changes.

Most agencies have artists who specialize in doing "comps." It is a peculiar art form. These comps are then used in the official presentations to the agency's review board, if it uses one, and to the client. The comprehensive is the final stage in the visualization process. Corrections and changes are still being made, even at this stage. After the comps are approved, then the planning period is over and production begins. The work of the "keyliners" who turn the comps into "mechanicals" is discussed in the production section.

Comping type. Comping the type means the display type will be rough-lettered and the body type will be ruled in. The rough lettering should be done as close as possible to the type specifications. If you can't letter at all, it is possible to do credible roughs by tracing letters from transfer type or type spec books (see Figure 10-26).

Generally, the body copy only suggests the type size and column width. There are three different ways to comp body types. One way is to use a chisel point pencil or pen and rule in the lines of body copy, using a line that is the approximate width of the x-height. The width of the lead in a chisel point pencil can be adjusted by sandpaper block so that it matches the x-height of the letter.

Another technique is to rule the x-height of the type using two lines, one for the upper edge and one for the bottom. A third method is an extension of the x-height ruling. With this technique, you fill in the space between with a squiggly line, which indicates a little more clearly where the type will go (see Figure 10-27).

Most writers, as well as designers, can prepare thumbnails and rough comps, so it is important to understand how these forms are constructed. These are the thinking and talking pieces used in advertising in the preliminary decision stages. Anyone working on the creative side should be able to develop usable thumbnails and semicomps.

Computer Design and Graphics

The Apple Macintosh has been the leader in design and graphics, but the IBM-PC and its clones are now beginning to catch up. The Macintosh can be used to create art using software programs like Adobe Illustrator and Aldus FreeHand. Ads can be created, including typesetting as well as laying out the various elements, using software programs like Aldus PageMaker, Quark Xpress, and Ready-Set-Go by Letraset. It is possible with art and layout programs like these to do an entire ad right on the computer screen.* Most recently the software makers for the IBM-PC have

---

* For a great discussion on how to use the Macintosh in ad-making, see Chapter 19, "Making Ads on the Macintosh," in *Advertising Resource Handbook* by Keith Adler (East Lansing, MI: Advertising Resources, Inc., 1989).

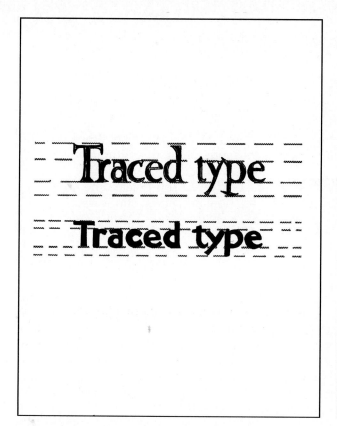

Figure 10-26: "Comping" display type by tracing.

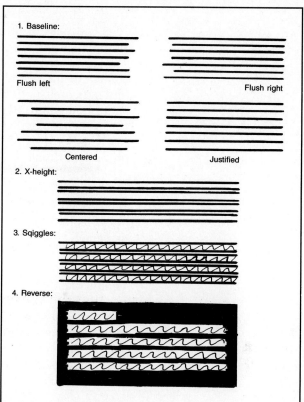

Figure 10-27: "Comping" body copy.

developed a desktop publishing program that is an ensemble of word processing, graphics, and layout, called the IBM Interleaf Publisher. New programs will continue to evolve in this exciting area of computer graphics.

10.3 PRINT PRODUCTION

The following is a very brief explanation of some aspects of print production that must be considered in the design process. There are a number of good books available as references for the various production processes, if you are interested.* Most designers find that their effectiveness is limited by their understanding of the production method and its strengths and limitations.

Halftone Reproduction

line art: a solid image or line

halftones: images, like photographs, that have a full range of gray tones

Art can be **line art** or **halftone**—or a combination of both. Line art is created by drawing on white paper with a solid line. Everything is solid on a plain background. Halftones, in contrast, imply shades of gray. The most common use for a halftone is to reproduce a photograph. When looking at a photographic print, the viewer is able to see a range of images

* *The Design of Advertising* by Roy Paul Nelson, *Art and Reproduction* by Raymond Ballinger, *Advertising Agency and Studio Skills* by Tom Cardamone, *Production for the Graphic Designer* by James Craig, *Graphic Design and Production Techniques* by Peter Croy, *Studio Tips for Artists and Graphic Designers* by Bill Gray.

from faint gray to deep black. Photographs are referred to as "continuous tone" because of these middle values. It is these middle tones that cause problems in printing.

In order to create halftones for printing, the image is shot through a screen, using a pattern of tiny dots. These dots break the image into light and dark areas; otherwise, there would be no way to create the gray areas in a photograph. Black ink, after all, is black. It doesn't come in shades of gray. The gray that you see when you look at a printed halftone is really just smaller dots of black with a lot more white area around them. It is an optical illusion.

Line art is an image that is created from a solid black line. There are no shades of gray as in photographs. Line art can be shot directly, since there is no reason to screen it. However, if you are using watercolor or wash techniques, then the art does have shades of gray and it has to be screened.

When we speak of "line screens," we are talking about how many lines of dots there are per inch. The more dots there are, the finer the details that can be reproduced. Newspapers use a relatively coarse screen, usually 65 to 110 lines, while most magazines use 110 lines or finer. Fine printing will go as high as 300 lines. Because of the better quality of paper and the more controlled printing processes, magazines can use a finer line screen than newspapers and reproduce a much better image, although many newspapers are moving toward better quality reproduction—similar to that of *USA Today*.

Color and registration. A one-color printing job means that there is only one color of ink printed, whether black, blue, green, or some other color. Two-color printing usually means black plus a "second" color, although it can be any two colors of ink. Printers call full color "process color" or "four-color process." The reason they say four colors is because the full-color effect is created by using four specific process colors: cyan (a shade of blue), magenta (a shade of red), yellow, and black. Printing inks are transparent, and all the other colors can be created by mixing and overlapping these inks.

For every color, a separate negative and printing plate is made. The inks may be printed on separate runs through the press (on small presses), or they may be printed by different rollers on the same press. These colors must align perfectly. This is called **registration**. Color registration is particularly difficult for process color, where there are four separate images that have to align perfectly.

registration: exact super-imposition of colors

Printing Processes

A word is needed here about printing processes. Historically, newspapers were printed with a process called *letterpress*. With letterpress printing, a raised surface gets inked. When it strikes the surface of the paper, the image is transferred. Type is set in metal and the art and photographs are all engraved (etched) in metal.

In the last 20 years, most printers have switched over to *offset lithography*, a type of printing that uses a smooth-surfaced but chemically treated plate to transfer the image. The offset plates are produced photographically. The original art is called "camera-ready." This means it is ready to be shot in the process, or graphic arts, camera. Everything on the

a mechanical: the pasteup, with everything perfectly positioned, that is, given to the offset printer to be shot photographically on a printing plate

mechanical (the pasteup) is pasted in place and anything that can be photographed can be printed. There is no heavy metal type, no engravings. It's simpler, cleaner, and faster.

Gravure is a type of printing that uses an incised surface. The images are engraved into the plate and ink collects in these little wells. When the plate strikes the surface of the paper, ink is transferred from the wells to the paper. In order to create this grid of wells, the entire image is screened. It's a fine screen, 150 lines or finer, but that means it is perfect for photographic reproduction. It is also good for long runs, since there is no wear on the printing surface. The limitation of gravure is that the type is screened, too, and that creates fuzzy letters. Gravure is used for fine magazine printing and for newspaper inserts that use color photography.

Another type of printing used in advertising is screen printing. Sometimes called "silk screen," the process uses a porous screen of silk, nylon, or stainless steel mounted on a frame. A stencil image is made either by hand or using a photographic process and the stencil is applied to the screen. The nonprinting areas are blocked by the stencil and the areas to be printed are left open. Using a squeegee, ink is forced through the screen onto the printing surface.

Screen printing is useful because it is versatile. Any surface can be printed on—metal, cloth, glass, wood, and so on. And the surface can be in any shape—round, curved, flat, or irregular. In advertising screen printing is used for containers, packaging, decals, transit cards, table and counter displays, point-of-purchase displays, posters, even billboards.

Special Effects

As advertisers become more concerned about getting their target's attention in an increasingly cluttered environment, many are using exotic and expensive special printing effects. Scratch 'n sniff ink is almost required now for the launch of a new perfume and is also being used for other products such as toothpaste and mouth rinse. "Sound sheets," small, flexible plastic records that can be bound into a magazine, are used to deliver musical and spoken messages. Day-Glo inks are used to create bolder and brighter effects. Heat transfer ink can be used for images that can be transferred from the magazine or newspaper to some other surface such as a T-shirt by ironing it.

An ad for Bounty paper towels used an unusual gate fold (the ad, which is printed to look like Bounty paper towels, opens up from the middle) to display a microwave meal that had been cooked in the paper towel. Liquor companies use tiny microchips to play Christmas carols when the reader opens the magazine page with their ads. Absolut Vodka used a plastic envelope over its ad containing a liquid medium and snow-like crystals that create a "blizzard" when the page is shaken. Transamerica Insurance startled magazine readers with a three-dimensional pop-up (like those found in children's books) showing the San Francisco skyline with the distinctive Transamerica pyramid as the focal point. A pop-up in *Business Week* for Honeywell cost $1 million, more than a 30-second Super Bowl spot on television. All these effects involve specialty printing by the advertiser. In many cases the preprinted piece is then sent to the magazine where it is "tipped in" (glued to a neighboring page at the spine).

New Technology

Desktop publishing. The era of desktop publishing has brought low-budget typesetting right into the office. The type quality may not be as good as what can be ordered from a real type house, but it is usable for many types of advertising, and it is fast and cheap.

We discussed the computer graphics "paintbox" systems that allow designers to create art and special effects at their desks for either print or video. These systems are expensive, but they are available in specialty design and production studios and they are beginning to move into agency art directors' offices. Many newspapers and magazines are now doing pagination, or page layout, on computer. Soon these pagination systems will be used to lay out ads, too.

Prints and proofs. Color proofs (called "C-prints") and reproduction copies of color ads with color separations are expensive and have always been produced by outside suppliers. Now, that production is moving in-house. For example, the Canon Laser Copier is running an ad explaining how the copier is used at the Fallon, McElligott agency for producing C-prints and other presentation materials. The copier is a creative tool; it can be used to change colors on visuals, marry any number of images including type, and enlarge or reduce at will—as well as make prints and color separations. Color separations can also be created on desktop publishing systems.

Satellites and lasers. A number of publications, like *USA Today* and the regional editions of many national magazines, are being printed by satellite. In other words, the page is assembled electronically at headquarters and then uplinked to the satellite and downlinked to local offices where the final printing is done. That saves time and distribution costs. Someday advertisements for these publications will be sent across the country or around the world by satellite.

Laser printing techniques are already eliminating the pasteups and plates used in offset printing. Soon newspapers and magazines will be printed directly from the image on the screen using laser-controlled ink jets—eliminating the messy and time-consuming prep steps in printing.

Some professionals speculate that it might be possible in the future for the consumer to have a custom-designed magazine or newspaper printed specifically for him or her on a home printer (like those hooked up to personal computers) with the articles and ads the particular individual wants to read—eliminating editors, media buyers, the distribution system, and the printing industry. In such a situation, will anyone choose to read ads? What will advertising look like in the day when the reader has total control over the select button?

SUMMARY

This chapter discusses the three areas of typography, layout and design, and print production. We have covered such points as:

1. Type varies by face, size, weight, width, and slant.
2. Legibility problems are found in the areas of line length, all caps, reverse type, italics, contrast, surprinting, and inappropriate typeface choices.

3. Layout is the process of arranging things; it organizes the arrangement so the visual is easy to read.
4. The functional design principles are: unity, contrast, balance, and movement; the aesthetic principles are proportion and harmony.
5. Most ads are developed and reviewed in the "semicomp" format.
6. Line art is a black image on white background; halftone art has shades, or midrange tones, that have to be converted to black and white dots in order to be printed.
7. Full-color photographs are reproduced using the four-color process; the process colors are magenta, cyan, yellow, and black.

NOTES

1. David Ogilvy, *Ogilvy on Advertising* (New York: Vintage Books, 1985).
2. Noreen O'Leary, "Legibility Lost," *Adweek*, October 5, 1987, pp. D7–D10.
3. O'Leary, op. cit.
4. Edmund Arnold, *Ink on Paper* (New York: Harper and Row, 1963).
5. Roy Paul Nelson, *The Design of Advertising*, 5th ed. (Dubuque, Iowa: Brown, 1985).

11

Print Advertising

KEY POINTS

- Magazine advertising is glossy, slick, and uses high-impact visuals and interesting writing.
- Newspapers are dominated by local retail advertising which is price-oriented and succinct.
- Yellow pages is directional; it locates businesses for people who are already ready to buy.
- The design of the format is critical to the development and effectiveness of a brochure.

In previous chapters we discussed the basics—such topics as creative thinking, strategy, writing, and visual communication. These topics are fairly universal in their application across most advertising media. Now we look at print advertising specifically. First we discussed the copy package, then we looked at layout. Now let's look at the copy and layout considerations of the various print media. Newspapers and magazines, for example, have entirely different creative needs even though they are both printed publications. The yellow pages present an entirely different challenge to creative planning. Brochures, catalogs, and the various other forms of collateral materials are also distinctive in how they are created and used in advertising.

They are grouped together here because they all, in one way or another, use a printed format. Beyond that, they are all distinctive in terms of how professionals create messages for them. Every medium has its own needs, and every medium puts a particular type of constraint on the creative process. For that reason, we will review briefly these various types of media in terms of their creative requirements.

11.1 MAGAZINES

Magazine advertising is the glitter and gloss of print advertising. Magazine advertising is primarily national, although regional buys are possibly, and primarily, brand-oriented. The paper is slick, the color is vivid, the reproduction is excellent, and many advertisers will usually spend whatever it takes to produce the best image they can for their product.

Special interest.   There are certain characteristics of the medium that affect how you will develop messages for magazines. Magazines appeal to special interests. With the exception of a few large general interest publications, most magazines are now highly segmented. They are designed to appeal to groups of people who share some interest such as an area of business, jogging, skiing, auto mechanics, science fiction, hair styling, and gourmet food.

Although many of the large mass magazines have all about disappeared, smaller, special interest publications are dynamic and growing. Consequently, there are a tremendous number of magazines available and the number is continuing to increase daily. In this age of mass media, the magazine industry has survived and grown on special interest messages.

Because they are published less frequently, magazines are read at leisure and over time. They are one of the few media available to advertisers where you have some time with your reader and where you can expect readers to come back and review the magazines and possibly your ad.

The Audience

Reflective.   The audience mindset is considerably different for magazines. We have already mentioned that magazines are read at leisure and that readers will extend their reading of a magazine over time. What this means is that readers are in a more reflective, less hurried frame of mind when they read magazines. For that reason, they will read longer copy than in newspapers and you can develop more complicated messages than in television or radio. This is an important characteristic of magazine advertising—it can convey a lot of information.

Personal relationship.   Often, people's self-concept is expressed through the publications they read. You may have been in an interview situation where you were asked what magazines you read—that's because magazine reading is a clue to your personality. Hanley Norins talks about this personal relationship with magazines in his book on copywriting.[1] He says that readers have a sense of confidence in and respect for the publications to which they have subscribed. There is a loyalty factor, too. Some people have been subscribers to their favorite magazines for decades. Magazines are the only media that have this personal relationship. Information read in magazines tends to have a higher level of relevance than that in other media.

Creative Considerations

Given the special interests of most magazines, obviously magazine ads should be oriented toward the interests of that segment of the market. The first thing to remember in writing and designing ads for magazines is to address the audience with a special appeal.

Service. Another characteristic of advertising in magazines is that it is highly service-oriented. People read magazines to find out information—and to a lesser degree for entertainment. News is important, but not as much as in newspapers. People read magazines for ideas—new ideas, ways to do things they have never done before, and new ways to think about things. The magazine is an idea medium rather than a news medium.

A successful magazine ad will often speak to this service angle. Readership studies have shown time and again that the highest scores go to ads with tips and recipes and ideas on new uses. That's why people read the editorial side of a magazine and the interest carries over to the ads.

Feature writing and stories. Magazines specialize in a style of writing called "features." These articles tend to be interesting, colorful, anecdotal, and helpful. The writing is good, and your ads will have to compete with these articles for the readers' attention. That means your ads have to be just as interesting, colorful, anecdotal, and helpful as the features.

An example of an ad that successfully competes with feature material is one for Fantastik Spray Cleaner that ran in women's magazines. A large white "swipe" obliterates what looks to be editorial text. When you start reading what's left of the copy, you find that it's fanciful tongue-in-cheek stories that have Fantastik carefully worked into the plot. This campaign has generated an unusual amount of letters to Dow Chemical complimenting the company on the interesting campaign and its agency, Henderson Advertising of Greenville, South Carolina.[2]

High-impact visuals. Magazines also use dramatic graphics to express the idea of the article and catch the attention of potential readers (see Exhibit 11-1). Magazine ads generally do an excellent job of using a dominant visual to capture attention and communicate the essence of the message. If you page through most any magazine, you will notice that most ads use a strong visual. In some cases, like the classic Merit cigarette campaign, the ad is designed to be copy-heavy and look like editorial matter. In that case, the all-type layout is being used as a graphic and its message conveys news. Magazines are also the home of national brand advertising, so magazine ads often convey visually a product's brand image. Images and imagery are very important in magazine advertising.

Production Considerations

Reproduction quality. One of the big advantages of magazine advertising over newspaper is the excellent quality of the reproduction. The quality of the paper is much better. Some magazines use clay-coated paper that is especially good for reproduction of fine details. The printing process is highly controlled so there is less of a problem with register of color than with newspapers. Photographic reproduction is particularly good in magazines because they can use a much finer line screen.

Lead time. Another characteristic of magazine production that affects the design of the message is the long lead time. The deadline for your ad may be six to eight weeks before the publication date. That obviously eliminates anything that is tied to breaking news. You can do seasonal tie-ins, but you may be working on a Christmas appeal in September so you have to be mentally flexible to adjust to the mood.

Page domination. One of the advantages of magazines over newspapers is that the competition is less obvious. There may be just as many ads in proportion to the editorial copy, but the smaller page size of magazines means there aren't as many ads competing for attention. You can buy half a page, for example, and not have another ad on the page.

Because of the smaller page, it is more likely that you will be working with a full-page ad. In that case, you are able to totally dominate the space. The only competition might come from an ad on the facing page but that's less serious. Furthermore, you may even be able to buy a spread and control both facing pages, which gives your message maximum impact with no competition.

Total control of the page is achieved with the use of a "bleed." That means the ad is designed to run past the normal margins and right off the edge of the paper. By ignoring the margins, it breaks through the formality of the publication.

Since the environment is less directly competitive, magazine advertising can be a little softer in tone and style than newspaper ads. The display type doesn't have to be as big; the headlines don't have to scream. There is more room for subtlety and ambiguity in magazines. Ads that tell stories have more space to develop the narrative.

Special arrangements. While most magazine ads are full page, there are some interesting effects that can be created by manipulating the size and placement. A one-column ad in a three-column magazine will give you a highly vertical space that is interesting just because of its extreme shape.

Gatefolds are available in some magazines, usually in conjunction with the inside front cover. This is a way to expand beyond a double-page spread and create a spread equivalent to three or four pages in width.

You can also plan a message that evolves by using successive pages. This is used occasionally with ads that tease, surprise, or in some way develop from page to page. This same technique is used with partial pages. A checkerboard effect is created by using quarter pages in succession. The message can be repeated with variations or it can evolve across the series. These are all techniques used to involve the reader and build memorability.

Ziploc® has used an interesting quarter-page buy in outdoor magazines like *Outside* to present Ziploc's "Protection from the great outdoors" campaign. One ad shows a flashlight in a Ziploc bag half-submerged in water. The headline is "Prevent a power failure." On another page is a picture of a first aid kit in a Ziploc bag with the headline, "Save your first-aid kit from drowning." Continuing to provide ideas for campers and boaters, the campaign includes an ad headlined "How to separate the men's from the boy's," with a picture of a man's pair of boaters shoes in a bag next to a pair of tiny boaters shoes in another Ziploc bag. It's a great use of repeating small-space ads by the Della Famina, Travisano agency.

Guess who didn't send it by Federal Express.

Federal Express deliver 900,000 parcels daily in 180 aeroplanes and 18,000 vehicles, to over 85 countries worldwide. And we don't just promise to get there, we get there on time. In fact, our unequalled track record has made us the No.1 air package carrier in the world. Because we understand that if we don't meet our deadlines, you won't meet yours. See Yellow Pages for your nearest Federal Express Office.

Federal Express. When it absolutely, positively has to be there on time.

Exhibit 11-1: The Federal Express ads use high-impact visuals to get the attention of magazine readers. The campaign ties in with sponsorship of the Olympic Games to position Federal Express as a premier international delivery service.

Guess who didn't send it by Federal Express.

Worldwide Sponsor

Federal Express deliver 900,000 parcels daily in 180 aeroplanes and 18,000 vehicles, to over 85 countries worldwide. And we don't just promise to get there, we get there on time. In fact, our unequalled track record has made us the No.1 air package carrier in the world. Because we understand that if we don't meet our deadlines, you won't meet yours. See Yellow Pages for your nearest Federal Express Office.

Federal Express. When it absolutely, positively has to be there on time.

261

11.2 NEWSPAPERS

Retail and local.   Newspapers are different from other types of advertising media because they are primarily retail-oriented and local. The emphasis in most newspaper ads is on *the local store* and its merchandise or service, as opposed to magazine or television advertising, which is primarily brand-oriented. In newspaper advertising, information about the service or merchandise is featured, particularly prices. But the store has to be included in the message too—memorability is particularly important for the store identification. So while it is product-oriented, retail advertising is also image-oriented. The emphasis, however, is not on the brand, but on the image of the store.

Of course, there are the more traditional national and brand product advertisements placed in local newspapers. For example, cigarette advertising by brand is common in newspapers. Also, there are several national newspapers such as the *Wall Street Journal* and *USA Today.*

Not only are newspapers local, they are also affected by their geography. Communities in different parts of the country have different climates, lifestyles, values, and political orientations. Some areas are more conservative than others; some are more outdoors- or wilderness-oriented. Some areas are more industrial, some are suburban, others are rural. Communities are different and these differences are reflected in the personality of the newspapers that serve them.

The advertising message strategy will reflect the distinctive values of the community. National ads run in local newspapers will often be revised to reflect the personality of the community. A campaign by Kent III cigarettes was built on the well-known symbols of various cities. Each city had its own version of the introductory ad, with a headline and graphic that stressed the distinctive feature of that community.

News.   In addition to local and retail, another characteristic of newspaper advertising is its emphasis on news. News is the medium's reason for existence, and advertising that mirrors this function will be the most successful. While some of the national advertising may be image or reminder advertising, most of the local ads announce something or give information about something. The "news peg" is always close to the surface in local advertising.

Newspapers are informative, rather than entertaining. True, there are some entertainment sections in newspapers, but most people read papers for news. Newspaper ads can mirror their surrounding editorial environment and provide lots of information. For example, in an unusual series of ads the United California Bank educated consumers about banking. The long copy ads had provocative headlines like, "Is it safe to write a check on Wednesday when you don't get paid until Friday?" and "What to do when you can't pay your bills?"

Ed McCabe, the copy genius at Scali, McCabe and Sloves, says that "people have always needed information about products" and that "it is easier to do a thorough selling job in print than in broadcast." He explains, "We get about 15 minutes worth of commercial time in one newspaper ad."[3] Readers *want* information, facts, details. This is one medium where advertising copy can be long because it is in context with the medium.

Newspaper information is fleeting. By definition, news is timely. What happened yesterday is no longer news. That means the information in newspapers is constantly changing and being replaced. Advertising in this milieu is also short-lived. In some cases an ad may be cut out and saved, but generally the objective is to register information about something that is happening *today*. Yesterday's ad, like yesterday's newspaper, is old news. Most newspaper advertisements build their strategies on this factor of immediacy. You will see copy that emphasizes now, today, and immediate action.

Competitive and cluttered. Another characteristic of newspaper advertising is its heavy competitive environment. True, there are other commercials on television and other ads in magazines, but none of them occur simultaneously the way they do in newspapers. An inside page of a newspaper may have 5 to 10 ads, and if it's the entertainment section you may be staring at 15 to 20. On television and in magazines, the ads follow one another (except for the small-space ads in magazines). Few advertising situations are as intensely cluttered as those involving newspapers. Television worries about "zipping" and "zapping"; that same tendency to skip over ads can and does happen all the time with newspapers. And yet advertising response levels can be very high, even with the competitive clutter.

Graphic limitations. Newspapers are printed fast on a soft, spongy, but strong paper that accepts ink easily and dries quickly. The quality of the image reproduction, given the speed, ink, and paper, is very low. A few papers, like *USA Today*, are using a better grade of paper, but generally you have to design your ads to reflect the production process and the materials used in newspaper printing (see Exhibit 11-2).

The Audience

Newspapers are read by 76 percent of the adult population and, among the well educated, the figure jumps to 88 percent, according to the Newspaper Advertising Bureau (NAB).[4] Most newspapers are read by two or more people who will spend approximately 30 minutes with the paper. Most people read their local paper in the morning, and 67 percent say they actually look forward to the advertising in the newspaper. Newspapers are the most credible media source for most people.

Receptive. That last sentence is what makes newspaper advertising different from just about every other medium. In most media, advertising is an intrusion. In newspapers it is just another form of news. People read newspapers to check the ads. Homemakers use it as a shopping guide, a quick way to see what is available, and what the current prices are. It's the local marketplace's number one source of comparative shopping information. Newspaper readership studies have shown that most readers do not consider advertising any different from editorial content—it is all news to them. That makes newspaper ads more credible and believable, as well as more sought out, than other media. The success of "shoppers," tabloid newspapers with nothing but ads, proves that advertising is valued as news, too.

In every other medium you have to worry about catching the attention of an inattentive audience, but in newspapers you have an audience

Exhibit 11-2: The Rocky Roccoco ad uses a comic strip art technique that reproduces well in a newspaper. It also has space for the local store to drop in a coupon offer.

that is interested, searching, scanning—an audience that has chosen to read the paper and your ad. That's a tremendous psychological advantage. Newspapers provide the only medium where your ad is not intrusive. This doesn't mean that your ad will automatically get read. As a matter of fact, most people don't really *read* their newspapers, they just scan them, and there are lots of competing messages on a newspaper page trying to get the reader's eye.

Heterogeneous.   Another characteristic of the audience is that it is heterogeneous. The one thing that holds this group of people together is that they all live in the same geographical area. The newspaper's readership will include women and men, old and young, black and white, rich and poor, white collar as well as pink and blue collar, and every other demographic range found in any city.

This heterogeneity limits the amount of special interest advertising found in most newspapers. It also means that there are lots of people reading who may not be interested in your product. The NAB estimates that "hot prospects," people who are actively in the market for your merchandise, make up less than 2 percent of the newspaper's readers. "Warm prospects," those who *might* be interested, make up 8 percent of the readership. That leaves 90 percent of the newspaper readers as nonprospects. That's why it is so important to telegraph your message in an instant to those 10 percent who are in the market.[5]

Everyone buys shoes and groceries and keeps their money in a bank or savings and loan. Those kinds of stores and services find it profitable to run big ads in local papers. Fashion ads will be found in the women's or home section of the paper, and tire ads will run in the sports pages, which is about all the targeting that newspapers can do. Stores that sell computers and business supplies may also advertise in newspapers, but their ads will probably be smaller because of the inability of newspapers to target by special interest. Targeting occurs in the newspaper in the sections such as sports and lifestyle, and in the classified advertising section, where you have people who are interested in looking for a certain product or service.

Types of Ads   **Display and classified.**   The two primary advertising distinctions in newspapers are between display and classified advertising. *Display* ads are boxes of space bought by the advertiser that run on the same pages adjoining the editorial copy. *Classified* ads, the "want ads," are all-copy notices placed by individuals announcing things they want to sell or buy. Usually, they run in a classified section and there is no concern about having them adjoin editorial copy. Classified ads have a tremendously high readership among the ideal target—people who are actually in the market and ready to buy (see Exhibit 11-3).

Small-space and omnibus.   Two other terms are used to describe types of ads in newspapers. A *small-space* ad usually occupies one column. In newspapers, a series of these small ads may be used instead of a large one. Size is sacrificed in favor of repetition (see Exhibit 11-4).

omnibus ads: large ads with many items from different parts of the store

Omnibus ads are used in department stores and discount store advertising. They are multiple-item ads, and usually they are not related thematically. A discount store, for example, will run a full-page ad with

PROOFREADER
Are you an avid reader?
Find the mispelled word!
EMBARRASSED
OCCURRENCE
ACCOMMODATE
Circle the word, spell it cor-
rectly, & send this ad with
your resume immediately to:
John, 41757 Paseo Padre
Parkway, Fremont CA 94539

LOS ALTOS—Midlife Crisis
garage sale—Part II. He was
the crabgrass on the lawn of
my life. My lawyer & I have
done the gardening. Now for
sale—the last blossoms of love
that was pledged forever.
Good-buys & goodbyes. Sat. &
Sun. 1522 Julie Lane.

Exhibit 11-3: These two ads by the *San Jose Mercury-News* demonstrate the compelling power of classified advertising. The "Midlife Crisis" ad won the Newspaper Advertising Bureau's Athena Award.

15 items, each representing a different part of the store. They may include what's called "loss leaders," which are used to build traffic by discounting the price. Omnibus ads are complicated to design and can be highly cluttered if there isn't a special effort made to organize them visually.

Creative Considerations

Strategies. There are two primary kinds of creative strategies used in most local newspaper advertising: image and news. *Image advertising* is used to develop the store personality. Stores have personalities just like people do, and these distinctive personalities are created by the advertising as well as by the interior design of the store. Macy's is different from Saks Fifth Avenue. K-Mart is different from Gibsons. Stores can be chic, classy, budget, professional, friendly, or haughty and that should be apparent in the design of their ads. This is discussed in more detail in the discussion of retail advertising.

Price advertising. Probably the most common and the most effective news announcement deals with price. Local newspapers are filled with ads announcing price reductions and special sales. Value advertising may be the most common appeal used in local newspaper ads. Price advertising may be supported by copy explaining what the value is. For example, during a period of coffee shortage, Nescafé ran ads explaining that, even though the bottle of instant coffee looked small, there were as many servings in a 10-ounce jar as in 2½ pounds of roast coffee.

"Peg" advertising. Another type of news strategy is one that uses a "peg" such as a season, holiday, or special event (see Exhibit 11-5). Strohs ran an ad in Detroit celebrating the opening of the baseball season, and Alka Seltzer has run ads lamenting national income tax day, April 15.

Breaking news events can also be used as pegs for advertising. During periods of crisis, such as the oil embargo, ads were running in local newspapers on such topics as mass transit, sharing rides, and the virtues of bicycles. An award-winning ad was developed when the Christie cookie factory in Canada went on strike. There wasn't an Oreo cookie to be found

SKILL TRAINING AND EXPERIENCE COME TOGETHER.

If you've applied for a job and been turned down because you don't have experience, we know you're going to like how Army training works. You're on the job, getting experience as you train with us.

This list contains just a few of the skills the Army trains qualified people in:

☐ Musician ☐ Machinist ☐ Mechanic ☐ Printer ☐ Accountant ☐ Plumber ☐ Electrician

The list could go on and on. Talk over your interests with an Army Recruiter. Something good will come of it.

ARMY. BE ALL YOU CAN BE.

2 col. (4¼" x 7")

SKILL TRAINING AND EXPERIENCE COME TOGETHER.

If you've applied for a job and been turned down because you don't have experience, we know you're going to like how Army training works. You're on the job, getting experience as you train with us.

This list contains just a few of the skills the Army trains qualified people in:

☐ Musician ☐ Machinist
☐ Mechanic ☐ Printer
☐ Accountant
☐ Plumber ☐ Electrician

The list could go on and on. Talk over your interests with an Army Recruiter. Something good will come of it.

ARMY. BE ALL YOU CAN BE.

1 col. (2" x 5")

Exhibit 11-4: These two ads demonstrate small-space advertisements for the Army that were designed to run in one column.

Exhibit 11-5: The Tulsa Philharmonic used this newspaper ad to announce an abrupt and unavoidable change in its schedule.

anywhere in Canada. The agency's creative team solved the crisis by running an ad with a recipe for the vanilla filling that could be used with two chocolate wafers to create a "spare parts Oreo."[6]

Writing style. Advertising writing in newspaper ads reflects news writing. It is straightforward. You will rarely find a collection of adjectives and adverbs stacked in one sentence in a news story. It's bare-bones writing and it's powerful because it communicates the essentials quickly and to the point. News writing is also succinct. Sentences and paragraphs are short. The writing is sparse and no extra words are used. You will see this reflected in advertising in the use of "bulletin" copy. The major points are simply listed without the ands and buts. It's very difficult to explain benefits with bulletin items, but it is a good way to give such information as sizes, colors, and other product features.

While some ads in newspapers use long copy, many local ads, particularly those for retailers, use copy that is short, succinct, and tightly focused on price and a few key product features. Because of the clutter and the way people scan newspapers, the simpler and better organized the ad, the more effective it will be. Most readers are scanning, rather than reading, so the message, as well as the design, need to be uncomplicated. The NAB uses the phrase, "telegraph the message" to describe the immediate communication necessary when the reader is immersed in rapid but intense scanning.[7]

Design. Given the tremendous competition in newspapers, your ads need to be simple in concept and design to avoid adding more confusion to the clutter. Newspaper pages are the most cluttered environment in which you will ever place an ad. Any ad that will stand out in this environment has to be very simple or very well organized or both.

There are tricks of the trade for designing newspaper ads that get attention. The first is to dominate the page. A full-page ad isn't as affected by clutter, and a half-page ad cuts down considerably on the ability of any other ad to compete. Another technique is to use spot color. Consistently, those ads with a careful use of color will dominate their black-and-white competitors.

In terms of contrast, either be bold or be simple—depending upon your product and concept. Bold headlines and bold art are attention-getting, the visual equivalent of a yell. At the other end of the spectrum, however, is a quiet, simple ad using lots of white space. This approach stands out because it is so different from everything else in the newspaper environment.

With smaller ads on competitive pages, always use a rule around your ad to define your space and then plan internal margins around the ad copy to provide a white space frame. This helps to isolate your ad from the confusion around it.

Incentives. Another characteristic of newspaper advertising is the heavy use of special incentives such as coupons. The function of a local retail ad is to build store traffic; coupons and special price deals for a limited time are good techniques to bring people in. Coupons are also useful for trial purchases and, since the newspaper ad is frequently announcing something new, it makes sense to use coupons to stimulate trial.

Newspapers serve as a shopping guide for local purchases, and price-conscious shoppers often search the newspaper specifically for coupons. Of all the coupons used in advertising, approximately 70 percent are in newspapers.[8]

STANDARD ADVERTISING UNITS (in inches)		
	Broadsheer	Tabloid
Page Depth	21	14
Page Width	13	$10^{13}/_{16}$
Number Columns	6	5
Width of Columns	$2^1/_{16}$	$2^1/_{16}$

Production

Size. A display ad can be a full page, half page, or a smaller size. Display ads are measured horizontally by the number of columns they fill. Most standard newspapers use from 6 to 9 columns. Tabloids (half the size of a standard newspaper page) can be anything from two to five columns. The number of columns and their widths are only now becoming standardized, through the Standard Ad Unit (SAU) program. In 1984 there were 400 different page formats in newspapers in the United States. By redesigning according to the SAU formats, most major market newspapers can now accept standardized sizes of advertising. For example, for newspapers, the standard ad page is 21 inches deep and 13 inches wide, with 6 columns, each $2^1/_{16}$ inches wide.[9]

To specify the size of an ad, then, you would give first the number of columns (width), then the number of inches (depth). For example, you might specify a 2-by-6 ad, which means you will get a display space that is 2 columns wide by 6 inches deep.

Design considerations. Production problems also influence design for newspaper ads. The spongy newsprint soaks up ink and makes it very difficult to reproduce fine details. Delicate typefaces are hard to reproduce, so type tends to be heavier and blockier. The middle tones in a halftone are also hard to reproduce. For that reason most newspaper ads use line art or high-contrast photographs.

Another way to solve the problem of poor quality reproduction is to use preprinted inserts. These are usually national ads in a tabloid. They are printed on coated paper using the gravure process, which gives excellent color reproduction. A national advertiser will produce the insert and then, for a fee, have it inserted in the local newspaper. Sometimes they are mailed directly to the home, but generally it is cheaper to let the newspaper handle the distribution, because the content usually fits the newspaper environment. In other words, inserts are often announcing special sales, and people turn to newspapers for this kind of information.

Color registration is another problem with newspaper printing. The printing process is so imprecise that it is very difficult to guarantee perfect alignment of additional colors. If you use spot color, use a loose application of color so that the registration is not critical.

Mats and proofs. Once an ad is finished by an agency, it has to be distributed to all the various newspapers scheduled in the media buy. Newspapers printed offset receive "reproduction proofs" that are camera-ready. They are pasted onto the paper's page and then shot. For color ads, a set of color separations have to be sent.

11.3 DIRECTORY ADVERTISING

Directional Advertising. One of the most underrated local media is the phone book. If you have an ad in the yellow pages, then you are advertising every day of the year to every person in the community who owns a phone and who is interested in your product or service. That's a tremendous reach as well as a highly selective one. In effect, you've blanketed the community. While other media try to create awareness, or a desire to buy, among a basically disinterested audience, yellow pages advertising tells the interested where to go to buy. For that reason it is called a "directional" medium; it directs people who have already decided to buy. Research by the American Association of Yellow Pages Publishers found that 98 percent of consumers use the yellow pages and 97 percent find them helpful in locating businesses when they are ready to purchase a product or engage a service.[10]

This is one of the few advertising media that people consult voluntarily and deliberately for commercial information. You have an audience here that is making an effort to search out your store or service. Your ad is not intrusive, it is welcome, and the more information you give, the more they will read.

Directories include more than just yellow pages. Many associations and organizations publish directories of their members, and many of these also accept advertising. These offer a highly segmented audience.

Uses of yellow pages. The yellow pages perform three functions; they serve as a shopping guide, a business reference, and a crisis consultant. The shopping guide role to locate businesses is the most important. For example, many people turn to the yellow pages when they want to go out to eat. It's a quick way to refresh their memories on what restaurants are available and nearby. This is a particularly important function for people who are new in town or for visitors. These people have no familiarity with your previous media advertising, so you can't rely on previous ads in other print media, such as the local newspaper.

The business reference function is important to the user. If you want to take a suit to the cleaner, it makes sense to check ahead of time to see if the store is open. In other words, people consult the yellow pages for certain types of basic information such as location and hours that they probably can't recall from advertising, no matter how much money you might spend advertising in the local paper.

The crisis consultant role is important in times of emergency. If your plumbing fails or you need to call a doctor or your insurance agent, the telephone book becomes your most reliable adviser. The phone book is highly dependable in times of stress.

Creative Considerations

Size. In terms of the shopping guide function, the primary consideration is the size of the display ad. A simple listing is rarely effective as a shopping guide clue. People tend to evaluate the success or reputation of the business on the size of the display ad. The bigger it is, the more credible the business is.

Regardless of the actual size, it is best to treat the design of a display ad in the yellow pages as a small-space ad. This kind of ad has certain characteristics. It is simple and straightforward. You don't need tricks to catch people's attention because you already have their attention. You can use a strong benefit strategy, however, to separate your store or service from that of your competitors who are all around you.

Message design. An illustration is useful to depict your product line or to establish the image of your store. Impressions created by the graphics are very important for those people using the yellow pages as a shopping guide. Body copy is used to identify the scope of your product line or services. If someone is looking for a particular brand, then you should list the brands you carry in the ad. Credibility statements are also important, such as memberships, citations, or performance achievements.

Reference information. The most important information, however, is the address, phone number, and hours. This information is run at the bottom in small type in most newspaper ads, but in the yellow pages it should be easy to find. In many cases your location information is best expressed through a simple map. People will choose stores on the basis of the one they think is the easiest to find. Having a map in the phone book is sometimes more important than the address itself.

Always give the hours. When the phone book is used as a business reference, that's just as important as the address. The phone number is used by those people who might want to check on special information, like service provided or whether you carry a particular line.

11.4 BROCHURES

Collateral materials. In advertising, the term *collateral materials* is used to describe a group of miscellaneous publications including handbills, broadsides, folders, flyers, and brochures. The two characteristics that define this category are that they are all printed and that they are all noncommissionable media. In other words, they are used in advertising as support media and the client is billed for their production costs.

Brochures may be utilized in a variety of ways. Product literature is the primary use. People who intend to make a major purchase, such as a car or a personal computer, will probably visit stores and dealers and pick up literature on the various lines. This material is used as part of the deliberation and comparison process. If you are introducing a new product, then you may want a point-of-sale brochure near the product that explains how it works or how it is used. Special promotions may include flyers on contests or premium offers. Direct mail letters often include folders that explain the product, service, or cause in more detail.

Formats   There is a wide range of publication formats available in this category. The simplest is probably a *handbill*. It is usually small and often printed on only one side. A *folder* is a single sheet of paper that has been folded in half or in thirds. It is designed to be mailed, so it will usually fit in a standard envelope. Handbills and small folders are also called *flyers*. A *broadside* is a folder that unfolds to a large sheet of paper and is read either as a poster or as a newspaper page. *Brochure* is a general term used to describe more involved pieces that usually have multiple pages assembled and bound as well as folded. A *booklet* is a small brochure, usually less than 8½ by 11, with from 8 to 48 pages.

    Pieces of publications.   There are some other common terms that need clarification. A *sheet* of paper is the entire piece of paper, both front and back. A broadside, for example, is one sheet, regardless of how many times it might be folded. Folders are described as having *panels*, rather than pages. A piece of paper folded in the middle will create a four-panel folder; folded in thirds, it will be a six-panel folder.

    A booklet, on the other hand, may be made up of four sheets folded together and stapled. The word "page" is used to refer to one side of a sheet of paper that has been assembled into a brochure, booklet, or book. To create pages in a book, a large sheet of paper is folded in half and then in half again, then stapled in the middle and trimmed on the edges. These two folds make an eight-page **signature**—four pages on each side of the sheet. Try it and see. Take any piece of blank paper and fold it in half, then fold it again opposite the original fold. You will have created a signature of eight total pages. Staple it in the middle and cut the fold and you will have an eight-page booklet.

    Likewise, three folds equals a 16-page signature, four folds equals 32 pages, and five folds equals 64 pages. Obviously, to get 64 total pages, you would be working with a huge sheet of paper. Most long-run magazines are, in fact, printed in 32- or 64-page signatures.

signature: a printed sheet folded to page size which creates a set of pages (always in multiples of four)

Design Process   *Writing.*   The copy for most brochures is usually written first, although it might be written with a rough layout in mind so there is some idea of how much copy is needed. Brochures are the ultimate in long-copy advertising. Often there is room for long stories and elaborate explanations. These tend to be pieces that interested people read and study.

    Dummying.   The word **dummy** is used a lot in the design of brochures. The "dummying process" is a phrase used to describe how the publication is designed in terms of folding and assembling. "Dummy" also refers to a particular piece constructed at one step in the process as a mockup of how the final piece will look.

    The dummying process is important because brochures of all types are complicated pieces to design and present. The message is affected by physical decisions relating to size, folding patterns, and binding techniques. The format itself is a message factor, and the design of the format is as important as writing the copy or preparing the art.

    The first decision in dummying involves the major decision on format, size, and folding. Do you want a handbill, broadside, or booklet? You

dummy: a mockup showing how the final piece will look

can see the tremendous range in formats available to you. Then what size will the final piece need to be? Will it be mailed? Does it need to go in an envelope? Will it be placed in a pocket as part of a display? Finally, what kind of folding pattern is appropriate and how will it be assembled?

Reading patterns. If you are designing a book or a booklet, then the reading pattern is fairly simple, just page by page. If you are designing a handbill, then it's a question of one side or two, and if it is two-sided then how do you get the reader to turn it over? But if you are working with a folder or broadside or a brochure that uses folds, then the reading pattern can become complicated.The objective in brochure design is to control that reading pattern and make sure it is obvious from your design where the reader is to look next (see Exhibit 11-6).

To demonstrate the problem, take another piece of blank paper and fold it in thirds. (You have to do this physically or you won't understand the point.) Now you have created a simple six-panel folder. The side facing you is the cover—*but* either side can be the cover. Do you want it to open from the right or the left? Or are you using it horizontally? Let's assume you follow normal reading patterns and open the folder on the right (fold on left). Now, which panel is read next as you open it up? The panel on the left or the panel on the right? You would probably assume that the normal reading pattern is to start on the left and read to the right. However, with folders, that panel on the right is the first one you see as you open the folder and it will get first attention. Furthermore, if you read from left to right on the inside three panels, how will you ever get back to this flap?

Production Process

Thumbnails and dummies. The first step in designing a brochure is to fold up little pieces of paper and create a number of roughs. You can go through a pad of scratch paper during this early design stage when you are working through alternative formats. This is the stage when you decide the folding pattern, reading pattern, and location of the basic message elements.

As these critical physical decisions are made, then you will move to a semicomp dummy. This is a dummy the size of the actual brochure that is produced using semicomp techniques. The art is sketched in place, the display type is lettered, and the body copy is ruled in. Semicomp dummies are used for approvals and for making the final specifications for typesetting and art sizing.

If the approval process is more formal and elaborate, then you may move to a full comp. Here the art is done as finished as possible, the display type is set, and the body copy is "greeked." "Greeking" body copy means you use letterforms that look *like* the type you want to use, and yet you have not gone to the expense of typesetting.

Mechanical. Keylining is another name for the final step in the production process when the actual mechanical is prepared. A mechanical is a finished pasteup with every element perfectly positioned that is photographed for offset printing. People who prepare this very exact pasteup are called **keyliners** because their work involves exact alignments. The printing plates are made from the negatives. A mechanical is not a presentation piece and should not be shown to the client. It is strictly for production.

keyliner: a pasetup artist who specializes in producing mechanicals

Exhibit 11-6: This brochure for American CoinPhone demonstrates the complexity of the message design and how the designer must consider page turning and reading patterns. (Reproduced by permission of Jehs & Wallis, Inc., Indianapolis, Indiana)

Production Specifications

Bids and estimates.   You will need to draw up a formal set of specifications for your brochure in order to get estimates and bids and to guide the final printing process. Sometimes it is hard to get the specs ready at the estimate stage because some of the critical decisions haven't been made. That doesn't help printers; they have to have answers to certain key factors before they can give you an estimate on the price.

An estimate is a rough guess of the cost. Most printers will eyeball a figure for you, but you have to remember that it is nonbinding. A bid is binding on both you and the printer. All the specifications have to be nailed down; if you change anything, you pay the price for change orders. Likewise, if the costs are higher than the printer bid, the printer has to absorb the difference.

Quantity.   The most important element in writing up a set of specifications for a brochure is quantity. In some cases, this may be the hardest specification to determine because you may want to print as many copies as the budget will allow. Unfortunately, printers start with quantity and all the other decisions vary around that factor. The number one principle in printing is that the cost per unit decreases as the total quantity increases. In other words, the more you print, the cheaper the cost per unit. That's because most of the cost in printing is in the initial step—typesetting, negatives, and plates—and those costs are high if you are printing only 100 copies, but they may be insignificant if you print 100,000. Eyeball a number to get started. You can get an estimate based on 5,000 and then ask your printer to tell you what the cost will be if you increase the run to 10,000. Chances are the cost will not be double, even though the quantity is.

Size.   This is the second most important piece of information the printer needs. When you give size, it is normally the size of the finished piece. Let the printer figure what the sheet sizes might be that will arrive at that finished size. You might remember, also, that paper comes in standardized sheet sizes. Your printer will figure how best to cut the sheet so it can be folded and trimmed to the size you need. In some cases, you may have created a format that is extremely expensive simply because there is no way to cut it out of the sheet efficiently; in other words, there is a lot of waste. Ask your printer about that; you might be able to save lots of money just by redesigning one of the dimensions.

Colors.   As discussed in the explanation of color, one-color printing means that there is only one color of ink printed, whether it be black, blue, brown, or some other color. A two-color job usually means you have black plus one spot color. Two colors, however, can be any two colors you might want to use. Full color, of course, is process color or the four standard process inks: cyan, magenta, yellow, and black.

On the smaller presses used for short runs, each time a color is added, that means a separate run through the press. Obviously, the number of colors becomes a cost factor. On these presses, four-color printing may demand four passes through the press. The larger presses used for long runs can print four colors of ink at one time. For extremely high-quality printing, you may even specify six-color printing; there are six-color presses capable of laying down that many inks at one time. If you are running 100,000 copies and your job is being printed on a press capable of handling four colors at once, then there is no reason to design for one color. The cost of additional colors is insignificant. Ask your printer about that when you get the estimate.

Paper.   Another big factor in printing is paper. You will need to have some kind of paper in mind when you talk to your printer about estimates. Often an art director will specify a particular type of paper, knowing that the paper is a critical factor in the impression being created by the piece. If not, then you may want to ask to see the printer's books of paper samples. You may even see some other publication printed on a paper you like and take that to your printer as a sample. They may not carry exactly the same paper, but there are often other brands that are close. You will need to specify texture, weight, and color.

Folding and binding.   We discussed folding patterns earlier in this chapter as an important part of the basic design decision. Obviously, it is important to the printer to know the format of the piece and how it folds or is assembled. The best way to make sure the printer understands what you want is to provide a dummy. This dummy should include the folding pattern as well as the layout of the pieces.

Special effects.   There are a number of techniques available to create special effects in publications. The **die cut** process is a way to cut unusual shapes. The tabs on file folders, for example, are cut using a die. Dies are thin, sharp pieces of metal. The paper is placed on the metal, pressure is applied, and the die cuts the shape out of the paper. That's how holes are cut in the covers of report forms.

die cut: a process of cutting irregular shapes with dies made of thin, sharp metal

The same technique is used for *embossing*, which creates a raised design on the surface of the paper. *Debossing* creates an indention. In both cases a die is made that has a softer edge than the one used for cutting. The paper is placed over the die (or under, for debossing), pressure and heat are applied, and the paper is stretched and molded to take on the shape.

Foil stamping is a technique used to apply metallic leaf to designs. These thin sheets of metallic leaf may be silver, gold, or bronze. These leaves of metal are placed on the paper and then a die is applied with heat. The leaf transfers to the surface of the paper and bonds to it because of the heat.

SUMMARY

This chapter has discussed magazine, newspaper, and directory advertising as well as brochures and other collateral materials.

1. Magazine advertising is:
   - slick and glossy
   - high in relevance
   - highly segmented
2. Magazine advertising uses:
   - more information
   - new ideas and services
   - interesting writing
   - high-impact visuals

3. Newspaper advertising is:
- local
- newsy and informative
- timely
- competitive and cluttered

4. Newspaper advertising uses:
- price advertising
- store image advertising
- news announcements
- simple, uncomplicated messages
- simple, bold, easy-to-reproduce graphics

5. Directory advertising is:
- highly selective
- a shopping guide
- a crisis consultant

6. Directory advertising uses:
- business reference information
- size to telegraph store credibility
- design to cue personality of store

7. Brochure design is:
- diverse and uses a variety of formats
- in control of the reading pattern, which can be complex
- built on a dummy, which helps visualize the final piece

NOTES

1. Hanley Norins, *The Compleat Copywriter* (New York: McGraw-Hill, 1966), p. 170.
2. Debbie Seaman, "Readers Say Henderson's 'Swipe' Campaign was 'Fantastik,'" *Adweek*, August 22, 1988, p. 32.
3. Newspaper Advertising Bureau, "Ten Creative Opportunities in Newspaper Advertising" (a slide show script), New York: NAB.
4. Ibid.
5. Newspaper Advertising Bureau, "INAE Copy and Layout Workshop—1, How Advertising Works," New York: NAB for INAE.
6. Ibid.
7. "Ten Creative Opportunities," op. cit.
8. Ibid.
9. *Editor & Publisher Standard Ad Unit Directory*, June 23, 1984, p. 2S.
10. "Yellow Pages . . . Is It Advertising?" *Yellow Pages Update*, 3:1 (Spring 1988), pp. 2–5.

CHAPTER

12

Radio Advertising

KEY POINTS

- Radio is a memorability medium.
- Audio imagery is involving and uses the listener's imagination to create a theater of the mind.
- Radio advertising uses three tools: music, voices, and sound effects.

12.1 THE POWER OF THE EAR

Radio is an aural medium. It speaks to the ear, and the way it speaks is entirely different from the communication patterns of other advertising media. Which do you think is the most powerful—the printed word or the spoken word? You probably said print, since American culture is dominated by printed forms. Al Ries and Jack Trout, chair and president of the ad agency Trout and Ries, disagree. In an article in *Advertising Age*, they claim the "eye is driven by the ear."[1] After all, spoken language is learned first. Reading and writing are secondary communication forms that only imitate visually what happens in speaking and listening. And there is no persuasive tool more powerful than the human voice.

Parker Seal Company, in Berea, Kentucky, found out how powerful radio can be when it tried to kick out the local union. Parker, which makes rubber parts for heavy industry, had agreed earlier to let its assembly-line workers wear radios. But when Parker mounted a campaign to decertify the local union, radio became the union's most important defensive weapon. The local union president wrote a series of ads defending the union and taped them. He identified himself in his gravelly, down-home voice before an overlay of country music began. After asking for another 32 years of representation, he said, "If it ain't broke, don't fix it," a phrase that was famous as the plant manager's canned response to most inquiries. The union distributed the schedule to the workers and just about everyone tuned in their radios to sing along with the commercial. Thanks to skillful use of radio and its ability to target narrow segments, the union won the vote.[2]

Attention

The radio audience is inattentive and listening with only half a mind. What this means to you as a message designer is that you have to plan a message that pulls the audience out of its inattentive state and focuses its attention. The first three seconds in a radio spot are critical. Chuck Blore, an award-winning radio commercial producer, calls his commercials "cluster busters." Skillfully planned and produced commercials can break through the clutter and the disinterest basic to this medium.

You have about three seconds to create this audio "slap in the ear." Words can do it—some powerful phrase or interesting question that compels attention. People respond to voices. Sound effects are particularly good grabbers. Music can be used either as a mood statement that separates the commercial from the other music being played or as an attention-getting audio theme, as in a clarion call or stage announcement.

Memorability

One of radio advertising's greatest strengths is memorability—the ability to make consumers remember the product's name and selling point. Radio advertising is not effective for transmitting complex information, but it does work well for reminder and identification. Charlie Moss, vice president of Wells, Rich, Greene, pointed to the four most famous notes in the history of advertising music to explain how audio helps memorability. He was referring to the long-running theme song, "I Love New York." The commercial was developed by WRG, with music and production by Steven Karmann.[3]

The reason radio can be highly effective in creating memorability is repetition, and the repetition primarily comes from music. Slogans, brand and store names, and key selling points can be repeated in a song without boring or irritating the audience. With the right words and music, radio ads can have great "staying power." Think how many radio commercials you can hum along with.

Identification

You don't have a visual to show, and that can be a real problem for product identification. For that reason audio often is used as a product theme, a distinctive piece of music that is highly recognizable. Some spots will start and end with this theme as well as use it in the body of the spot. A short piece of music or sound effect that is repeated often is called a **hook**. It's used deliberately to stimulate attention.

hook: a short piece of music, sound effects, or distinctive phrasing used to snag attention

Because store and product identification can be a problem with radio, you have to introduce the name as early as possible and then find ways to keep repeating it. A copywriter's rule of thumb suggests that five mentions is a minimum. Make sure the pronunciation of the product name is clear; spell it if it is hard to understand, and avoid playing the product name over background music or sound effects that might overpower it.

Location is another aspect of identification that demands careful treatment. Addresses are impossible to remember when heard over radio. It's better to give a location peg such as "across the street from K-Mart" or "on the corner of 13th and Grand." Phone numbers are impossible over radio. If you have to give one, then repeat it several times and allow time during repetitions for your listener to search for a pencil. Remember that a phone number is of no use to someone driving a car, so you are losing part of your audience right there.

Sid Woloshin, a veteran jingle producer who is known for his long-running tunes, feels advertisers should build brand *equity* by developing proven, popular pieces of ad music. He suggests that advertisers should ask, "Will this music provide equity over time, and set me apart from the competition?"[4] For example, Anheuser-Busch used "When you say 'Budweiser' . . ." for 15 years before it switched to "This Bud's for you," and the original jingle still shows up in research—that's equity.

Audio Imagery

The Radio Advertising Bureau uses the line, "I saw it on the radio" as its slogan. The idea is that images created by the audience in its "mind's eye" *are* more powerful than images presented visually. Audio imagery can be even more powerful than visual imagery. Images generated by audio suggestion will have more cross-sensory details than will visual messages. For example, you can use audio to create a picture in the mind (see Exhibit 12-1). If someone says "mountain" or "beach," you probably think of those words in terms of some image of a mountain or a beach. Unlike visual images, audio creates sensations easily in other sensory channels.

Association studies have found that certain words can generate feelings as well as sensations of smell, taste, touch, and related sounds. For example, you describe a new pair of shoes and mention the smell of leather and most people can respond with a sensation of smelling new leather, maybe even with the feeling in their feet of trying on a new pair of shoes. A picture of a pair of shoes will seldom generate those missing sensations.

"Image transfer," a concept explained by Bruce Stauderman in his advertising column in *Advertising/Marketing Review*, is another dimension of audio imagery. Imagery transfer is a technique that uses radio to make people "see" in their mind's eye a television commercial that they have previously seen. With careful writing the listener will translate audio images into video ones. Stauderman says, "The radio commercial takes on the power of the TV commercial—or more—since it involves the viewer's recall in an even more active way." He concludes, "You get virtually a TV exposure for the price of a radio spot."[5]

The plays you create in your mind as a result of audio suggestion are more real than any print or video image can ever be. They are real because they use your own experience as a platform. Your memories, your experiences provide the settings and the characters. Radio is a listener participation medium. The audience is also the author. No other medium stimulates the imagination in the way radio does, involving the audience in the construction of the message.

As an example of the power of imagination to involve listeners, read the script below. It is from a classic radio spot developed by Stan Freberg for the Radio Advertising Bureau. Admittedly, reading is not as good as

Exhibit 12-1: This print ad for the Wall Street Journal Radio Network uses audio imagery as a creative concept. (Reprinted by permission of The Wall Street Journal Radio Network, ©Dow Jones & Company, Inc., 1989. All Rights Reserved Worldwide)

hearing, but as you read this try to imagine the produced version. Exercise your skill at audio imagery and actually hear the announcer's voice and the sound effects.

[Handwritten: By Stan Freberg for Radio Adv. Bureau]

FREBERG: Okay people, now when I give the cue, I want the 700-foot mountain of whipped cream to roll into Lake Michigan, which has been drained and filled with hot chocolate. Then the Royal Canadian Air Force will fly overhead towing a ten-ton maraschino cherry which will be dropped into the whipped cream to the cheering of 25,000 extras.

FREBERG: All right, cue the mountain.

SFX: (Creaks, groans, prolonged splash)

FREBERG: Cue the Air Force.

SFX: (Propellers roar into and past mike; wing struts whine)

FREBERG: Cue the maraschino cherry.

SFX: (Screaming, whistling fall, and large plop)

FREBERG: Okay, 25,000 cheering extras.

SFX: (Prolonged and tumultuous ovation)

FREBERG: Now—you want to try that on television?

SPONSOR: Wel-l-l-l—

FREBERG: You see, radio's a very special medium because it stretches the imagination.

SPONSOR: Doesn't television stretch the imagination?

FREBERG: Up to 21 inches—yes.*

Intimacy Audio suggestion is much more powerful when presented by a live voice than by a printed word. Burt Manning, chair and CEO at J. Walter Thompson, describes the radio as a friend. He says that radio is "uniquely a communication to friends, to people with the same tastes, the same interests, the same language."[6]

He points out that 99 percent of the homes in the United States have radios, 77 percent have four or more, and 95 percent of the cars have radios. Radio is everywhere—from the beach to the bedroom. And the audience listens to it one on one; it's like a conversation between friends.

In the golden days of radio, the whole family would gather around and listen to radio programs. Now radio listening is strictly an individual activity, something done alone. It's an intimate relationship just between the listener and the voice on the radio. The message is personal—someone is speaking directly to the listener. That's why there is such tremendous suggestive power to these audio messages.

Bruce Stauderman gives an example of the power of voices and intimate conversation over radio. His agency was asked to develop a radio spot for a ski rental shop in Avon, Colorado. The store was hidden in an odd angle of a shopping center. Stauderman wrote a commercial in which a police car stops a suspicious car that has been circling the town. The passengers are, of course, looking for the ski shop and the good-natured cop gives the couple directions. One morning after the commercial had been running several months, the store's owner saw a police officer in a car with its flashing light talking to a person in a car which had pulled

* Courtesy of the Radio Advertising Bureau.

into the store's parking lot. The cop later explained to the owner what happened. It seemed that the driver was listening to the commercial and was so intent on making the right turn at the right place that he failed to notice the light had turned. The officer thought it was rather funny—a case of life imitating art.[7]

Emotion

Another characteristic of radio that sets it apart from other media is its emotional impact. Because it is intimate and because it uses personal participation and imagination, it has the power to stroke the emotions more effectively than any other medium.

People respond emotionally to the audio channel. When a person is moved to tears in a movie, it is rarely because of some emotional image; more likely, that person is responding to something that is being said and that is embellished by dramatic use of music and sound effects.[8] The look on a child's face may be "moving," but the tears come when the child speaks. It's the dialogue that tears at the heart. Words, music, and sound effects create mood, and mood generates emotion.

Ronald Travisano, creative director at Della Famina, Travisano, points to musical slogans such as "Reach out and touch someone," "I love New York," and "We bring good things to life" as good examples of emotional appeals. He said, "More than just good music with good lyrics, they capture something inside you that leaves you feeling very positive about what they are selling"[9] (see Exhibit 12-2).

Humor is a type of emotional appeal that is particularly effective on radio. People are used to listening to their friends tell jokes and funny stories. Radio presents this kind of material in the same way a friend does—primarily using words in a one-on-one situation. Also, there are humorists who do or have done commercial comedy. They include Stan Freberg, Bob and Ray, Dick and Bert, Stiller and Meara, and Dick Orkin. Humor, of course, is tricky. As we've discussed in previous chapters it needs to be relevant to the product and broad in its appeal.

The budget motel industry has had success using humor. Tom Conway leads listeners to off-beat tourist spots before directing them to Econo Lodges. In one he says, "Tonight I'm talking to you from the cavity of a two-ton molar in a health education museum in Cleveland." He continues, "When I'm through here, I'm going to put the bite on high prices by staying in Econo Lodges, the premier economy motel where you spend a night, not a fortune."[10] This kind of appeal originated with Tom Bodett doing his folksy, deadpan delivery for Motel 6, ending with his signature line, "We'll leave the light on for you." Now Martin Mull has signed up for Red Roof Inns to make fun of the differences between a $60-a-night motel and Red Roofs.[11]

In advertising, radio has been downplayed as a creative medium compared to the glamour and glitz of television. Radio commercials are assigned to junior copywriters. The radio budget is the first thing to be cut when money is tight, since, after all, it is just a "support medium." That kind of attitude is unfortunate because radio in many ways is more creative than television and can create a more powerful impact. There are a few executives in advertising like Burt Manning of J. Walter Thompson and Joel Raphaelson at Ogilvy & Mather who are sympathetic fans of radio

H A L R I N E Y *&* P A R T N E R S
I N C O R P O R A T E D

735 Battery Street, San Francisco, California 94111, (415) 981-0950, *Telex:* 755811

DH:TT

client	EDY'S	*Date*	MAY 4, 1987
Product	GRAND ICE CREAM	*Job No.*	7S 1045
Title	"WONDERFUL THINGS I" (ALTERNATE)	*Status*	AS PRODUCED (REV. 1)
Length	:50 RADIO	*Code No.*	(12-EDY-8)

ANNCR VO: We hear reports. Reports of wonderful things happening in a small town not far from here.

Wonderful things happening when people started eating Edy's Grand Ice Cream.

A little girl came home from school and found a Palamino pony in her backyard.

The voters voted overwhelmingly to give up driving and start roller skating to work.

The tax collector, after eating a big dish of Edy's Rocky Road, gave everybody a tax refund.

And the Democrats called up the Republicans and asked them if they'd like to go to a movie.

And it takes an awfully good ice cream to make things like this happen.

But then this isn't just ice cream.

It's creamy, it's rich, it's wonderful. It's Edy's Grand Ice Cream.

Exhibit 12-2: This Dreyer's ad uses evocative writing and emotional appeals to develop the concept that wonderful things happen when you eat Dreyer's (Edy's) brand ice cream.

and appreciate its effectiveness. Also, there are some people in agencies who do dynamite work with radio. Copywriter Ginny Redington has a number of hits to her credit, including "Coke is it" and "You, you're the one" for McDonald's. Jim Hartzell at Campbell Ewald wrote that nostalgic classic, "Baseball, hotdogs, apple pie, and Chevrolet."

And the industry is alive with really talented people working in production houses. Chuck Blore is known for his work with K-Mart and AT&T. Steve Karmen is known for all the Budweiser commercials through the years, including "When you say Bud," as well as "Weekends were made for Michelob," "Sooner or later you'll own Generals," "Hershey's "Great American chocolate bar," the long-time classic, "You can take Salem out of the country but. . .," and more recently the commercial that became a state song, "I love New York."

Sid Woloshin is well known for his string of hits, which include, "You deserve a break today" for McDonald's, "Come to think of it, I'll have a Heineken," and "Like a good neighbor" for State Farm Insurance.

And then there's Barry Manilow. Who knows where he would be now without his initial work for Kentucky Fried Chicken, State Farm, Dr. Pepper, Pepsi, and McDonald's? Such memorable lines as "It's not a cola; it's not a root beer," and "It's the Pepsi generation coming through," were created by Mr. Manilow.

In an area separate from music, Ken Nordine does some of the most creative work in the industry. He has created the phrase "Stare with your ears" to describe his experiments with concepts like interior speech and multilayering of sounds and thoughts. He is well known as a writer and producer, but he is probably best known as the voice on the Levi's commercials.

12.2 THE AUDIENCE

Segmented

narrowcasting: reaching a tightly targeted and highly segmented audience

A primary characteristic of radio is the configuration of the audience. Radio is a special interest medium rather than a mass medium. It practices something called **narrowcasting** rather than broadcasting; this means that various stations reach different types of audience groups, based upon what type of programming interests them. The local union in the Parker Seal example at the beginning of this chapter used radio and a country western station to reach the 300 workers on the assembly line. That's tight targeting. The chart below illustrates the variety of interests served by radio programming:

- Nonmusic
  Religion
  All news
  Talk
  Ethnic and foreign language
- *Predominantly music*
  Beautiful music
  Middle of the road

Rock/Top 40
Album-oriented rock
Adult contemporary/soft rock
Country and western
Big band/nostalgia
Classical
Jazz
Black urban

The typical audience for any of the formats above is clearly definable in terms of demographic and lifestyle characteristics. There is a major difference between people who listen to album rock and those who listen to middle of the road or country.

The rather pinpointed audience makes it much easier to speak the language of your listeners. Furthermore, you speak only to those you want to talk to. The communication can be more personal, more oriented to their interests, more direct.

Preoccupied   The other characteristic of radio listeners is that they tend to be doing other things while they listen to radio. Maybe they are driving, watching for other traffic and road signs, while they listen. They may be at home working in the shop or the kitchen or studying in their bedrooms. Some people listen to radio while they jog or ski.

Radio functions as a background for daily life. People listen with half a mind, partially tuned in but not concentrating. When something catches their interest, their attention becomes more focused on the message. Listeners constantly move in and out of the attentive state. While radio is turned on and tuned in continuously, attention isn't.

12.3   FORMATS

jingle: a piece of verse set to music, a song

There are a number of standard approaches to radio commercials that you might consider. **Jingles** or music-oriented commercials make up a high proportion of what is heard on radio daily.

We've already mentioned a straight *announcer*. That format is used with news announcements. An announcer might also be used as a storyteller in a narrative format. *Dialogue* involves two people, as an interview, panel, or participants in a little drama or "playlet."

Dramas include the "slice of life," made famous by Procter & Gamble. The "slice" usually involves overhearing some conversation, such as between a woman and her hairdresser, or between an executive and a cab driver. These little dramas can represent mundane daily life, humorous situations, or highly exaggerated fantasies. Humor works well over radio and is produced as dialogues, monologues, stories, and skits.

donut: a commercial format that opens and closes with a jingle, leaving space in the middle for a voice-over

A **donut** is a particular type of commercial form that opens with standard music; the music then fades, an announcement is dropped in, and then the music swells at the end to close. The music is often prerecorded and the local station announcer will drop in the message announcing current sales and events.

12.4 AUDIO TOOLS

Music

Because of the peculiar nature of the medium, radio advertising is heavily dependent on the use of music. You will notice in the list of formats that most of them are music-oriented. Primarily, people listen to radio for music. Advertising that takes advantage of this special characteristic of the medium will be more appreciated. And, as Sid Woloshin says, "Nothing makes a quicker impression than music."[12]

You have two basic options with music. You can either write a jingle, which is a music-dominated commercial, or you can write a word-dominated commercial where music is used as a background. Music playing in the background is called a "bed." A "voice-over" uses an announcer over some kind of background such as a music bed or sound effects. In some cases you may use a straight announcer with no music, but those commercials are rare and demand a legitimate news announcement message. The human voice on radio without music sounds naked.

An example of a successful jingle is the Armour hot dog song which played throughout the 1960s and has been brought back in the late 1980s. The 20-year-old song has been updated with Springsteen-like feel but the lyrics are original: "Hot dogs, Armour hot dogs, what kind of kids eat Armour hot dogs? Fat kids, skinny kids, kids who climb on rocks. Tough kids, sissy kids—even kids with chicken pox."[13]

Words that are written to a hummable melody are more memorable. You can get more repetition in a message when it is sung than when it is spoken. That also aids retention. Jingles are ideal for reminder advertising because of this memorability feature. A catchy tune will stay in the memory longer than a catchy phrase.

Music can also be used as a form of audio highlighting. In movies, the dramatic moments usually are underscored with changes and crescendos in music. Tension builds as speed picks up. Crisis is announced with frenzied arrangements. Quiet, melodious music signifies relief after a problem is resolved. The music speaks its own language and cues a story.

Bernard Richards, a music critic for *The London Times*, observed that the use of classical music in commercials "picks up associations like flypaper." He calls music "incredibly powerful" and "the most potent of all arts."[14]

Voices

Music is the number one characteristic of radio advertising because radio is a music-oriented medium. Voices, however, are still essential as message deliverers. An all-music ad—no words, not even lyrics—is rare. Voices carry the message content through the words of singers, announcers, narrators, interviewers, and people in conversations. Furthermore, voice can be the most persuasive of all audio tools because it is intimate and compelling.

The tone and character of the voice is a critical design decision. Little children, old men, teenagers, movie stars, busy executives—they all have distinctive voice characteristics and patterns of speaking—gruff, soft, sexy, tough, sad. Voices are emotional, too. And they all create different mental images in the minds of listeners.

When you cast a voice, it doesn't matter what the person looks like. The Valentino company records sound effects and production music. They tell a story of needing the sound of a crying baby. In trying to tape real babies and real crying, they couldn't reproduce the sound to their satisfaction. Finally, they hired a middle-aged actress who executed the finest baby cry the Valentinos had ever heard.[15] The sound is everything; its source doesn't matter.

A popular radio format is the "girl-and-guy-giggle." The Molson commercials are a good example of this "au naturel" dialogue. It's very real, as opposed to the "slickness" of many productions. It's an easy, natural give-and-take with a spontaneous giggle that punctuates the phrasing perfectly.

Little kids' voices have been found to be especially attention getting on radio. K-Mart has been highly successful advertising its photo department with its two "goof-proof" kids (see Exhibit 12-3).

Sound Effects

Sound effects (abbreviated SFX) are distinctive to radio. They are used on television, but the sound there is reinforced by a visual referent. In radio the sound effects have to tell their own story.

In fact, a story can be told with nothing but sound effects. For example, picture this: loud voices arguing, door slams, feet running down the steps, screech of tires, thump. You don't need words to develop a little drama in your mind of someone running away from an emotional argument who isn't watching traffic and gets hit.

Here's a little test of your ability to fill in the blanks in the previous audio drama: Was it a man or a woman? Was he or she hit by a car, truck, or some other vehicle? What make? What color? What was he or she wearing? What kind of building was he or she leaving? Who was he or she leaving? Why? Most listeners add details to the story—maybe not all the details, and maybe they vary from listener to listener—for the imagination is compulsively inventive.

sound effects: life-like imitations or recording of sounds

Sound effects are the cues people use to create mental dramas and the settings in which they occur. They signify things. The listener provides the links and the associations that create stories from these discrete sounds. Sounds anchor the setting—a collapse; the chirping of crickets; the roar of an auto race; the clink of glasses, silverware, and china in a restaurant; an organ in a church—they all speak to images in the mind's eye. It's pretty amazing how the whole process works, and yet it does work. Storytellers use sound effects to stimulate mental images in their listeners. They know intuitively that some experience-based images are extremely difficult to simulate with words alone. Sound effects are available from radio libraries and production studios.

Electronic Audio

The synthesizer has been manipulating music electronically for many years now. With it, a composer or performer can imitate all the conventional instrumental sounds. A more complicated piece of equipment is a Synclavier, which can do everything a synthesizer does and more. A Synclavier is a computerized digital sound machine with a 32-channel memory recorder. Sounds can be created and manipulated to the limit of the imagination. The user can create a beer barrel polka band, the sound of

RADIO *copy by*

ROSS ROY INC.

2751 EAST JEFFERSON AVENUE
DETROIT, MICHIGAN 48207
TELEPHONE 313-961-6900

CLIENT	K mart	PROGRAM	60 Seconds
PRODUCT	"The Opposite Sex" Photo Processing (Xmas Photo Card)	STATION/NETWORK	
JOB NO.	23454-2	SCHEDULE	KM-678-60
DATE TYPED		PAGE NO.	As Produced

DAVID: Okay ... this is gonna be a really good commercial. Are you ready?

JAMIE: Yes.

DAVID: Okay, when I say, "action," you say, "You get a "goof-proof" policy on picture processing at K mart."

JAMIE: I can't say all that. My mouth is too little.

DAVID: Well then, just say, "You only pay for the prints you like ... like those good shots of loved ones or ... members of the opposite sex."

JAMIE: Aw, Jeffrey, (LAUGHS) I can't say all that ... (FADES UNDER)

ANNCR: Show off your loved ones with Christmas photo greeting cards. Take your favorite photo to the K mart Camera Department and order personalized cards that carry a special message to family, friends, and to members of the opposite sex. The price is special, too ... just $6.96 for 25 cards with envelopes.

JAMIE: Jeffrey?

DAVID: What?

JAMIE: Are you the opposite sex ... or am I?

SUNG: (JAMIE & DAVID) K MART IS THE SAVING PLACE.

Exhibit 12-3: The "Opposite Sex" script uses the universal appeal of little kids with their cute voices and distinctive phrasing. The spot was designed with an announcer "bed" that can be revised to feature various K-Mart camera department merchandise. (OPPOSITE SEX created and produced for K-Mart by CHUCK BLORE & DON RICHMAN INCORPORATED and protected by copyright)

someone blowing across a bottle top, and the sound of a flip-top can whooshing open—all on the computer. The computer also can change conventional sounds such as instruments or voices into other effects. One Synclavier performer describes an assignment that required him to create sounds resembling Gregorian chants performed underwater—something impossible to record from a normal choir session. For another assignment a composer plugged the sounds of singing whales into a Synclavier and then turned those sounds into melodies. The creative opportunities for such equipment are only beginning to be explored in advertising.

12.5 SCRIPTING

script: the manuscript form which contains all the auditory descriptions and instructions as well as the content of the message

A **script** for radio contains all the auditory descriptions describing source and content of the message.

MUSIC:	(MELODRAMATIC MUSIC UP, THEN UNDER)
PROF:	Sometimes a script is written in paragraph form (PAUSE) . . . but most professionals use a format with the source indicated down the left side of the sheet and the content on the right.
STUDENT:	(SPOKEN REVERENTLY) And aren't scripts also typed double space?
PROF:	Right.
ANNCR:	And ALL CAPS is used to indicate instructions and descriptions, things that are not to be read. (STAGE WHISPER) Everything in lower case is to be read by someone—the announcer, the characters, the interviewees.
STUDENT:	The rule then is: If you don't want it to be read over the mike, then type it in all caps (DRUM ROLL BEHIND THE WORDS "ALL CAPS").
SFX:	(CHEERING EXTRAS)
PROF:	For music and sound effects the script should include some description of what the voice, sound effects, or music actually sound like (SPOKEN IN A LOUD VOICE THAT GETS QUIETER AS IF SPEAKER HAS FORGOTTEN WHAT HE IS TRYING TO SAY)
ANNCR:	Words in music are often indicated in a printed script by italic letters. *In a typed manuscript you can* underline *the words.*
PROF:	(INTERRUPTING) But underlining is also used to indicate words to *emphasize.*

Timing   Most radio commercials are recorded at certain standard lengths such as 10 seconds (a short ID), 30 seconds, or 60 seconds. When you write a script, you will usually write for a time period that is several seconds shorter than air time. In other words, a script for a 30-second commercial should time out to 28 seconds; a 60-second spot will time out at 58 seconds. That gives a little time to get the spot on and off air. Radio time is very exact. Above all, you don't want the commercial to run over the allowed length of time. A little under is okay, but never let it go over.

Some scripts are set up with a word estimate down the left edge of the sheet. That gives you some idea of how long the script will be in terms

CLIENT   U.S. Army

PRODUCT   Active Army

MEDIA/
LENGTH   Radio :30

TITLE   Dear Dad (QYAY 87-11-30)

DATE   3/29/88   WRITER

YOUNG & RUBICAM NEW YORK
285 MADISON AVENUE
NEW YORK, NEW YORK 10017-6486

AS PRODUCED SCRIPT

SFX: typing. It fades as VO begins.

SON: Dear Dad,
We made our toughest parachute jump at dawn.

JUMPMASTER (under): On your feet!

SFX: boots on pavement, soldiers hustling.

SON: And I remembered when you said that courage is putting your fear aside and doing your job.

SFX: jet takeoff.

SON: Y'know, putting off college for the Army was the right choice for me.

JUMPMASTER (under): Stand in the door! Go!

ANNOUNCER: To find out how you can earn more than $25,000 for college with the G.I. Bill and Army College Fund, call 1-800-USA-ARMY.

SFX: typing in, and fade.

SON: Now I'll get the most from college...

SINGERS: Be all that you can be.

SON: ...and the best from myself.

SINGERS: Get an edge on life in the Army.

ANNOUNCER: Paid for by the U.S. Army.

S590B Rev. 10/86

Exhibit 12-4: This "Dear Dad" commercial for the Army demonstrates how a script is formatted and how the terms and instructions are presented. (Courtesy U.S. Government, as represented by the Secretary of the Army)

of word count. Word counts are useful only if you are writing straight announcer copy or if you allow space on the script for the music and sound effects (see Exhibit 12-4). The guide below will give you some rough estimate of the length of your writing.

WORD COUNTS

Time	Words
10 sec.	20–25
20 sec.	40–45
30 sec.	60–65
60 sec.	120–25
90 sec.	185–90
2 min.	240–50

Words and Sounds

Listen to the sounds you use when you speak. Even though you are *writing* a script, words are used differently in spoken language than they are in written language. People speak in thoughts, and those translate into incomplete sentences. In an English class you would be criticized for that, but it's perfectly okay in radio work. Elaborate sentences with complicated phrases and clauses are found only in written English, rarely in spoken.

Keep your sentences simple. Radio announcers prefer short sentences, but there is one thing to remember: Short sentences become monotonous if they are stacked together. Vary the length and the construction so you don't set up a pattern of three- and four-word chunks.

Certain combinations of sounds are extremely difficult to pronounce or to understand over air. Some linguistic combinations sound the same even though they are spelled differently—"white shoes" and "why choose," for example. With sound-alike phrases, the secret is to use them in a context that makes the meaning clear—and don't focus on that phrase for repetition.

The sibilants sound like hissing over the air, particularly when several of them are grouped together, as in, "so sensitive it's simply sensational." The stream of s sounds obliterates the other letters in between. It's not only uncomfortable to listen to but also hard to understand.

The aspirants are sounds created by the expelling of air, and they are equally discomforting to listen to when used in a group. The puff sounds like p and the barking sounds like ack and ark are troublesome. The puffs and popping sounds of a phrase like "people-pleasing pleasure" are amplified through a mike, as are the barks in "back behind the barracks." In print, you would never know there is a problem with such phrasing.

Tongue-twisters are another problem. These are created by repetition of sounds complicated by combinations of sounds that move the tongue up and down or back and forward rapidly. A phrase like "sensitive, sensory experience" will leave an announcer frowning.

How can you know if you have written an unreadable piece of copy? Obviously, the answer is to read it aloud—over and over. Another way is not to *write* the copy in the first place. If you are developing a lot of radio copy, you might find your work improves if you "write" it into a tape recorder. In other words, use a tape recorder rather than a typewriter. Automatically, your copy will be in the form of spoken language and you won't have that artificial problem created by written forms.

Terminology Radio production has its own set of terms to communicate within the industry. If you are writing scripts, you need to become familiar with these production terms.

- *Fade in/fade out:* Fade in is a gradual increase in sound level starting at no sound. Fade out means sounds are gradually reduced until nothing can be heard. Fade in and fade out are used at the beginning and end of most commercials and sometimes in the middle to indicate a passage of time.
- *On/off mike:* Sounds and voices that are on mike are spoken directly into the microphone. Sounds that are off mike are spoken at a distance from the mike. They sound off in the distance.
- *Segue:* Pronounced "segway," this term is used to indicate a gentle transition from one sound or piece of music to another.
- *Cut:* An abrupt and instantaneous change from one piece of music to another.
- *Crossfade:* One sound gradually fades into another, with the two mixed for a short time in the middle of the fade.
- *Up, down, and under:* Used for background music to indicate change in level of music. Up means it gets louder, down means it gets softer, and under means it continues as a soft background.
- *Stinger:* A distinctive sound used as an audio punctuation point, like the twang of an out-of-tune guitar to indicate indigestion.
- *Tag:* An audio logo that is played at the end of a commercial. Sometimes it might be an audio theme, or perhaps just a reminder line "tagged on" the end.

Production Radio commercials start on paper as a script. Then they are produced in a rough form as demo, concept, or "scratch" tapes. These are simple versions of the commercial, using maybe just a piano or guitar and one voice. It's the equivalent of a "rough comp" in the layout stage. Enough of the concept is there for the listener to get an idea what the final will sound like, but none of the expenses of the final production have been incurred. Skilled audio producers like Chuck Blore can do demo live, playing the piano and talking through the copy and music. It's quite a performance, and very persuasive.

Most commercials are recorded on 24 tracks, and that means the producer is able to mix and edit the various voices, instruments, and sound effects. If the soprano is too loud, the sound can be toned down. If you don't like the sound of the synthesizer, eliminate it. Recording in the studio is a complicated engineering problem, but much of the real artistry shows up in the post-production editing of the tracks.

12.6   TIPS

1. Watch out for vampire creativity. If you are too cute, then your listener may remember the spot, but forget the product.
2. Background should be background. Don't let it overpower the message.
3. Keep it simple. Focus on one idea and build it through repetition.
4. Repeat and repeat. Your audience can't go back and reread. If they tune in halfway through the message, give them another chance to get the point and identify the product.
5. Leave them humming. Steve Karmen, a well-known jingle writer, said it best: "People don't hum the announcer."
6. Don't get bogged down in details.
7. Break up long sections. A long, involved sales pitch can lose your listener. Bring in music. Use a donut format, or some variation on it.

SUMMARY

1. Radio commercials must grab attention in the first three seconds.
2. Radio commercials are memorable because of the high use of repetition through music.
3. Radio music helps identify a product and build long-term brand equity.
4. Audio imagery engages the mind and involves the listener.
5. Radio is an intimate, one-on-one medium with tremendous power of suggestion.
6. The radio audience is highly segmented, and listeners are preoccupied with other activities.
7. Music is hummable, memorable, establishes mood and atmosphere, speaks to the emotions, and creates audio highlighting.
8. Voice is the most persuasive tool.
9. Sound effects anchor the setting and cue the details of a mental drama.
10. A script is used to give instructions, describe the source of sounds, and give the content of the message.

NOTES

1. Al Ries and Jack Trout, "The Eye vs. the Ear," *Advertising Age*, March 14, 1983, p. M27.
2. "How One Local Won with Radio Ads," *Adweek's Marketing Week*, August 1, 1988, p. 31.
3. Christy Marshall, "Old Ad Jingle Strains Show How to Create Atmosphere," *Advertising Age*, August 30, 1982, p. 48.
4. James P. Forkan, "Jingle Producer Fears Advertisers Forget Equity," *Advertising Age*, March 31, 1986, p. S7.
5. Bruce Stauderman, "Magic of Image Transfer," *Advertising/Marketing Review*, January 1985, pp. 6–7.

6. Burt Manning, "Friendly Persuasion," *Advertising Age*, September 13, 1982, pp. M8–M9.

7. Bruce Stauderman, "Anecdotes of Destiny," *Advertising/Marketing Review*, January 1987, p. 8.

8. Sandra Moriarty, "Getting at the Gut with Appeals to Pathos," *Madison Avenue*, April 1983, pp. 26–30.

9. Merle Kingman, "And Now, A Few Words That Sell," *Advertising Age*, June 16, 1983, p. M8.

10. Gary Bond, "Formats for All Seasons, All Tastes," *Advertising Age*, June 7, 1982, pp. M6–M7.

11. Christy Fisher and Ira Teinowitz, "Budget Motels Take to Humor Ads," *Advertising Age*, November 14, 1988, p. 65.

12. Forkan, op. cit.

13. Julie L. Erickson, "Frankly Speaking," *Advertising Age*, May 23, 1988, p. 86.

14. Bernard Richards, "Music's Soft Sell-Out," *The London Times*, November 19, 1988, p. 10.

15. N. R. Kleinfield, "The Valentinos Can Supply Sounds of Grunting Gorillas or an A-Bomb," *Wall Street Journal*, October 21, 1974, p. 12.

13

Television Advertising

KEY POINTS

- Television is a powerful medium because it offers action and high-impact imagery.
- Planning a commercial revolves around identifying the key visual.
- In some commercials casting is 50 percent of the job.
- Technology is bringing more and more special effects into the production of commercials.
- A commercial is planned and approved on the basis of a script and storyboard.
- Copywriters must understand optical commands, the language of filming.
- Production includes getting bids, hiring a production house and other specialists, making arrangements for and conducting the "shoot," and postproduction editing.

Television is a *visual* medium; however, it is also an *audio-visual* medium, which means that, with skillful use, you can have all the strengths of audio, plus the impact of visual communication. Good commercials are often written without words or with words only as a reinforcing tool. If a good television commercial is written for maximum visual impact, then it should make sense when you turn off the audio and just look at the video. The audio is still important; it provides the persuasive power of the human voice, the mood of music, and the excitement of sound effects. With a television commercial, these tools are used in support of the visual.

Television has power because of its use of action and dramatic imagery. A comparison of print and television advertisements was quoted in a *Journal of Advertising* article on visual imagery.[1] The study found that television commercials were able to produce more favorable product attitudes than comparable print ads. The authors explained that "TV commercials with their succession of visual elements provide more opportunities than print for engaging the consumer in product-related visual imagery which enhances the product attributes."

An example of a high-powered visual effect is a commercial for Peugeot titled "Africa," shot in Kenya by noted wildlife photographer/conservationist/filmmaker Peter Beard. Beard took his crew into the thick of things looking for images of Africa, shooting herds of wild game from distances that were too close for comfort. Beard believes the challenge in shooting commercials is "visual economics—the ability to show something powerful in a very limited space of time."[2] These powerful images were shot on the run—they couldn't be scripted, timed, or controlled. When Beard saw animals he wanted to shoot, he would position the car in front of them and shoot until they left. It was up to the editor to combine the images effectively into a 30-second package. In the final version of the commercial, the Peugeot wagon drives through a variety of stunning settings, juxtaposed with those incredible shots of wild animals. The announcer says, "If your car breaks down out here, finding a mechanic is the least of your problems. That's why on the African continent, where there are few roads and fewer mechanics, Peugeot has sold more cars over the past ten years than any other carmaker. If you need a car you can rely on (a lion snarls as the car goes by), buy a Peugeot."

13.1 PLANNING A COMMERCIAL

This chapter will discuss both the planning and production of a television commercial. As you approach an assignment to do a commercial, think about the types of messages that work best on television, the key visual, and the most effective use of the tools of television.

The Key Visual

key visual: an image that sticks in the mind as a visual cue

The secret to planning effective visual communication in television advertising is to think in terms of a **key visual**. Harry McMahan, a long-term agency producer and developer of many techniques used today, calls this "The Visual Plus," a visual designed to stick in the mind as a memory cue.[3] This one dominant scene is the focus of the entire commercial. It summarizes the whole point of the message.

McDonald's instructs its agencies to plan television commercials around something the company calls the "magic moment."[4] It is a key visual but with an added ingredient. The "magic moment" in McDonald's commercials is the point that creates an emotional response. For example, in a spot titled "Mary Ryan" a young teenage girl has a crush on a guy at school. She keeps running into him in different places and gets flustered and embarrassed. Finally, when she and her friends are at McDonald's, this guy joins them and sits down next to her. That key "magic moment" happens, of course, at McDonald's.

To get the most impact for your money with television advertising, think in terms of these indelible images, the key visual that summarizes the heart of the message. In radio you leave them humming; in television you leave them humming *and* with a picture in their mind.

What TV Does Best   Television is best used for any message that involves action and motion. Demonstrations and torture tests are particularly effective on television. Demonstration creates believability, so demonstrate a new feature, a benefit, a promise. Demonstration is also good for how-to information, so demonstrate how the product works, how the product can save time or money, how it makes a person more attractive, or how easy it is to use (see Exhibit 13-1).

Television is also an entertainment medium, so messages that entertain as they sell both fit the medium and reward the viewer. The Coke and Pepsi extravaganzas with performers such as Michael Jackson, Madonna, Whitney Houston, and George Michael are successful because they are entertaining.

Because it is a cinematic form, television also lends itself to drama and emotion. Storytelling, particularly stories that touch people's emotions, can be very effective on television (see Exhibit 13-2). The Michael

Exhibit 13-1: Mobil One uses a man walking through flames in a fireproof suit to demonstrate the oil's better protection against friction, wear, and extreme conditions.

Exhibit 13-2: The "father-daughter" commercial for AT&T Long Distance Lines is an example of the use of emotion in television advertising. This series of commercials was powerful enough to survive most zapping. (Courtesy of AT&T)

J. Fox commercials for Pepsi and the Bud Light wordplays tell interesting stories that involve the product and the viewer.

In a major research effort that resulted in a book entitled *Effective Television Advertising*, David Stewart and David Furse found that the single most important factor in effective television advertising is "the presence of a brand-differentiating message." The authors suggest that television works best when it concentrates on unique selling propositions and brand images.[5]

Zap-proofing. We touched on this topic in an earlier chapter. Viewers, particularly those with remote control devices, are becoming very particular about what they watch. If they don't like the way the commercial begins, they "zap" it by switching channels. If it's prerecorded, then they "zip" past it. A recent study found that 50 percent of households use remote control, and of those, 20 percent are considered heavy channel-changing households—on the average they change channels once every two minutes.[6] "Grazing" is a term used to describe the activity of viewers who flit from channel to channel.

In order to survive the threat of zipping, zapping, and grazing, commercials have to be designed to be mesmerizing—they have to be just as entertaining as the surrounding programming, perhaps more so. Other techniques include making the ad sound or look like a program. General Foods, for example, has developed "Shortcuts," a series of spots that look like a cooking program.[7] Some commercials, particularly in Europe, are being developed as soap operas with a continuing plot and a long-running cast of characters. The product (say, coffee) is an integral part of the action.

Effectiveness. The big question now is, "Does television advertising work?" It is undoubtably the most expensive medium and it reaches the largest audience. But does it deliver? Gerald Tellis, a University of Iowa professor, stirred up a hornet's nest when he claimed that his research couldn't support the idea that television advertising works. While the comments made a lot of people in the advertising industry mad, many of them generally agreed with Tellis's findings. However, defenders said the problem isn't television advertising, it's *bad* television advertising. Robert Schmidt, chair of Levine, Huntley, Schmidt, Beaver, said, "Great advertising works. But only 5% of commercials are reasonably professional, and even less than that are terrific."[8] Another study mentioned in a *Wall Street Journal* article by Information Resources found that TV advertising does work, but that it works only 50 percent of the time. About half the time, more TV advertising does lead to increased sales.

On top of questions of effectiveness come reports that consumers generally dislike television advertising. For years, the research company Video Storyboard Tests has been testing viewers' opinions of television. Consumers are becoming increasingly skeptical and irritated by TV commercials. They especially complain about commercials that make exaggerated claims about product performance and ads that insult their intelligence. In spite of the bad news, viewers do think that commercials are becoming more informative and more entertaining. Here is how the viewers' view television commercials[9]:

	1986	1987	1988
Misleading	27.6%	28.5%	33.4%
Insulting	29.4	29.2	32.0
Boring	20.0	22.2	32.0
Informative	15.7	19.4	21.0
Entertaining	14.4	18.6	18.9

With all the clutter and competition on television, with the remote control in the impatient hands of disinterested and bored viewers, and with the skeptics questioning the very purpose of television advertising, it is easy to see that the challenge is to do *only* breakthrough work. If you want to work with television advertising, then you must accept that challenge and not be satisfied with the other 95 percent of ideas that are ho-hum, copycat, clichéd, or infinitely forgettable.

Television Tools

The raw pieces of a television commercial first can be grouped under the two basic categories of audio and video. We have already described the use of voices, music, and sound effects in the chapter on radio advertising. Television uses exactly the same audio materials. The only difference is that these audio materials are used to support a visual rather than to create one. In that respect, television is more exact and makes less demand on the viewer's imagination. But we can't downplay the importance of the audio. Hooper White, a consultant in commercial production, says, "In most cases the sound track is at least 50% of the effectiveness of your television commercial's selling force."[10] Music is particularly important in contemporary commercials.

Video. The video advantage that you get with television that you don't get with any other advertising medium is action. Motion commands attention; motion mesmerizes. The images are not static, as they are in newspapers and magazines. They can walk right off the screen. Television is an offspring of cinema, and that means all the advantages of "movies" are also available to television.

Even though television is a broadcast medium, it still uses graphics. *Letters* on screen can be created electronically in a variety of typefaces using a character generator, or they can "crawl" across the bottom of the screen like a news bulletin. They may even be set in type on a posterboard and shot as a still.

Stills and *stock footage* are two other forms of raw materials used in making a television commercial. Stills would include photographs, slides, and artwork mounted on posterboards. **Stock footage** is film or tape created for some other use that is being worked into the visual message. For example, shots of a rocket taking off are not taken by the agency specifically for a commercial. Instead, it can use stock footage of such scenes from NASA. News footage, obtained from a network or local TV station, is sometimes worked into a commercial.

Action. Commercials are shot using living action or some form of animation. On rare occasions, you might create one that is shot "live live."

stock footage: film or tape created for some other use that can be incorporated in a commercial

Most of the commercials you see on television are live action. That means they include real people, tangible settings, and real action. Even though the production is shot on film and edited to create the final version, this is still described as a live-action commercial.

"Live live" is a commercial that is shot live before an audience right on the air. There is no filming, no editing. When Ed McMahon does an Alpo commercial on the Johnny Carson show he is doing a live live-action commercial. If there are bloopers, they are generally unretractable. When Betty Furness couldn't get the refrigerator door open in the famous commercial from the early days of television, she was being filmed live. (On network broadcasts there is a short lag of from 15 to 30 seconds before the videotape is aired, so technically nothing is "live live.")

The Schlitz taste test that aired during the 1981 Super Bowl was produced live live.[11] It took an incredible amount of planning and coordination to bring off a commercial that showed an actual taste test between Schlitz and Michelob using 100 people randomly selected from New Orleans households. The point of doing the commercial live was to stress the believability of the test—no one could question the results. The results, incidentally, gave Schlitz 50 out of the 100 first preferences—which isn't bad for a challenge campaign.

animation: objects are sketched and then shot one frame at a time

In contrast, **animation** is fiction that has been drawn by an artist (or possibly a computer) (see Exhibit 13-3). The characters are cartoons. The action doesn't exist; the viewer sees only the illusion of movement. A character is drawn on acetate, then a series of "cels" are drawn, each one depicting some slight change in arm, leg, or head position. Animation is

Exhibit 13-3: Equalactin is an over-the-counter preparation for treating both diarrhea and constipation. To symbolize these less-than-pleasant subjects, the commercial used an animated spot by cartoonist R. O. Blechman to illustrate how a person feels like a tortoise on some days and like a hare on other days.

traditionally shot at 12 or 16 drawings per second. Low-budget animation uses fewer drawings and the motion looks jerky. More recently the drawing has been streamlined by the use of computerized images. Only the beginning and the end of the action is drawn and the computer fills in the points between, which has eliminated much of the costly handwork involved in animation. The drawings are shot using an Oxberry camera, a large rig with a camera mounted on a tube. Both the camera and the platform on which the drawing rests can be moved up and down.

When the drawings pass in front of the eyes quickly, viewers think they see movement. Of course, that isn't so very different from live-action film. Actually, those 24 frames that pass in a second all are stills. The audience *thinks* it is seeing movement in "movies." That's because of an optical illusion called the "persistence of vision," which means the individual retains an impression until a new image replaces it.

Some types of action cross over between live action and animation. You can shoot live action with Kodalith film (an extremely high-contrast film that makes the images look like drawings), play with the color, and come up with something that looks like a drawing even though it started out as real action. A famous commercial for Levi's, called "the stranger," used that technique, called *posterization.*

Puppets, dolls, and models can be made to move using the same technique that animators use. If you want the Pillsbury Doughboy puppet to dance, then you shoot him one frame at a time and each time move his arms and legs a little. You have created the illusion of movement from a static object. This is called **stop action** or *freeze frame.* Both posterization and stop action will be discussed later in a section on special effects.

Claymation, the technique used in the Raisin Board dancing raisins commercials, also uses a form of stop action. The characters are created from clay and then photographed one shot at a time. These manipulated clay figures are the product of Will Vinton Productions, Portland, Oregon. The inspired use of Marvin Gaye's "I Heard It Through the Grapevine" was the idea of Foote, Cone & Belding's San Francisco office. For claymation, animators use a special clay that never hardens, laboriously sculpting the figures frame by frame. Production takes an average of 12 weeks for a typical "Grapevine" spot. Vinton's claymation technique has also been used for Domino Pizza's "Noid."[12]

Pixilation creates the feeling of watching a series of stills. In fact, the effect may be created from either still or moving images. With movie film, it is achieved by skipping frames and then holding an individual frame longer than normal. It gives a jerky movement to the film.

Rotoscoping combines live action with animation. The commercials with Tony the Tiger talking to real kids were created using rotoscoping. The *Roger Rabbit* movie was filmed using rotoscoping. Piggly Wiggly, a pudgy pig used as the animated mascot of the regional Piggly Wiggly grocery stores, has been seen in live commercials dancing around the supermarket, cheering up babies, and giving advice to tired shoppers. The Albuquerque animation studio, Bandelier, did the spots using the rotoscoping technique.[13] Disney characters are shown cavorting with a child in a spot for Ultra Pampers Plus and are also appearing mixed with live action in a commercial for the Chevrolet Lumina launch. When a product

stop action: inanimate objects are filmed one frame at a time, creating the illusion of movement

claymation: characters are molded in clay, shot, and then remolded, creating the illusion of movement

pixilation: a jerky style that looks like a series of stills

rotoscoping: an animated figure is combined with live action

appears to be spinning through the air toward the viewer, most likely the effect has been created using rotoscoping and freeze frame action. Hooper White, in his book *How to Produce an Effective TV Commercial*, points out that this is a very expensive technique.[14] In effect, it has to be produced twice: First the live action is shot and edited, then the graphic effects are added frame by frame.

Casting.   Some of the other tools of video include *characters*. A television commercial is a very short drama, but within it the writer must develop personalities that are huggable or hateful. The product itself takes a role, becomes a character, and develops a personality. The character of Clara made the "Where's the beef?" commercial for Wendy's so memorable. Without her and her distinctive diction and appearance, the spot would never have been so successful. Many professionals feel that casting the commercial is the key to its success (see Exhibit 13-4). McDonald's commercials are known for their clean-cut, all-American teenagers—the kid with the freckles, the redhead, the one with braces or a missing front tooth.

Hal Riney is known for using nonactors in his commercials—and for his ability to spot these personality types. Frank and Ed, the lovable down-home farmer duo for Bartles & Jaymes, are not actors—one of them was an acquaintance of Riney's. Riney builds many of his commercials around "characters" like these with distinctive personalities—not the slick, clichéd advertising "types" that normally show up for a casting call.

Joe Sedelmaier, one of the hottest commercial producers in the business, is also known for his wacky characters. He believes that casting is 50 percent of his job.[15] He is famous for using nonactors—plumbers, bodyguards, lawyers, architects—people he sees on the street and in the store who become part of his repertory company. Sedelmaier is best known for his fast-talking man in the Federal Express commercial. He also developed commercials for Mr. Coffee, which involved disgruntled coffee drinkers hurling cups and saucers out windows, and for Pacific Southwest Airlines, in which a harried business traveler is trying to get to Phoenix.

Sedelmaier's commercials are instantly recognizable; they are funny and odd because of the casting and character development. In an article on commercial directors, *Esquire* described Sedelmaier's commercials as "slightly surreal 30-second dissertations of the fears of daily life."[16] In many of Sedelmaier's commercials some poor guy keeps a straight face while his life shatters around him. An example is the Federal Express ad in which the chair of the board assures a meeting of big shots that all is well because Bingham has sent their extremely important bid via Federal Express. Bingham, who clearly has done no such thing, stares blankly— and hilariously—as his life passes before his eyes.

Costumes.   Costuming is another element of character development. In commercials set in the past (or the future), period costumes are a necessity. Costumes can also cue lifestyle, such as golf clothes, baseball or soccer jerseys, or employment-related uniforms such as those worn by doctors, nurses, waitresses, mechanics, bus drivers, and hair stylists.

Costumes can also become a central part of the story (see Exhibit 13-5). In the "Feed me" commercial for GE's Rechargeable Battery System,

RIGHT GUARD SPORT
"ANIMALS"—MARVIN HAGLER (NEW)

GSGC 7013

30 SECONDS

(MUSIC UNDER)
Odious...contemptible...deplorable...I'm speaking of "offending" in the personal grooming arena...

Something I would of course consider quite beyond the pale...

So I give you new Right Guard Sport Stick...Anti-perspirant and deodorant.

When one has to seek maximum protection...and a fresh new scent,

one should grab oneself one of these Right Guard Sport Sticks...

Because one would hate to be considered malodorous by one's chums...wouldn't one?

New Right Guard Sport Sticks from Gillette.

Anything less would be uncivilized.

The Gillette Company
Personal Care Division

N W Ayer Incorporated

Exhibit 13-4: In an unusual bit of casting Right Guard used boxer Marvin Hagler and football pro Brian Bosworth to speak on behalf of civilized living—focusing on the deodorant which "sports" new contemporary fragrances and packaging.

RIGHT GUARD SPORT STICK

"BOSWORTH'S BOOK OF ETIQUETTE"

GSGC 8013

30 SECONDS

(MUSIC UNDER)
BOSWORTH: Now the final chapter, students,

in Bosworth's Book of Etiquette.

"Personal Hygiene."

How will you separate yourselves from those barbaric hordes that exude

a most malodorous air?

New Right Guard Sport Stick from Gillette.

Maximum protection and a fresh new scent. A veritable olfactory medley.

New Right Guard Sport Stick.

Anything less would be uncivilized.

Raise your glasses

gentlemen,

to "civilization."

 The Gillette Company
Personal Care Division

NW Ayer Incorporated

Exhibit 13-5: "Sexy salmon" designed for the Seattle Aquarium and "A formal clarinet" designed for the Seattle Symphony are exotic costumes used by their organizations for both advertising and promotion. (Jennifer Q. Smith of Avant Garb Costumes—Indianapolis, Indiana. Sexy Salmon was used by Seattle Aquarium for opening ceremonies and throughout first year. Clarinet—Seattle Symphony)

a "transformer" toy, in a takeoff on the *Little Shop of Horrors* movie and play, comes alive and demands to be fed by other battery-operated toys in the toy shop. The ravenous robot and the other toys were created in BBDO's in-house production studio using a Spielberg technique. In reality, the toys were costumes worn by actors. The human "toys" were filmed on an oversized set and shot at different speeds to make sure their movements would come across as toylike.[17]

Sets. The location, or setting, is another important aspect of the commercial. Commercials can be shot in a studio on a set that is constructed or "on location" at a setting that is real. Directors have books of properties that can be used for commercials, and they can often find the perfect house or storefront without having to resort to the cost of building a set. Filming at exotic locations, such as the Caribbean or the Sahara, is particularly costly and cumbersome.

Calet, Hirsch & Spector created an eerie set for Toshiba—a symbolic "graveyard" for televisions.[18] The purpose was to dramatize the concept that Toshiba is revolutionizing the engineering of televisions and that televisions by other manufacturers are being tossed aside.

The commercial was shot at Vasquez Rock in the desert northwest of Los Angeles. The spot opens with a rock video playing on what appears to be a fragment of a TV set. As the camera pulls back, the audience sees that it is a TV picture tube partially buried in a desert, surrounded by hundreds of other TV tubes in a similar state of demise. In the eerie light they are broadcasting everything from old movies to cartoons and sporting events.

The commercial was shot using a "Louma" rig, which suspended the camera on a boom. Operated by remote control, the Louma could float above the location and pull back on the entire area without the dolly tracks below becoming visible. Finding the location was difficult enough, but then the crew found that the area chosen for the shoot was part of a national park. That meant the crew was not allowed to dig up the ground to bury the wiring for the live tubes. The solution was to bring in 100 tons of sand along with additional indigenous plants, all of which had to be approved by the park rangers. The 300 TV sets were positioned and buried in the 103-degree heat, which was also playing havoc with the video van where 20 VCRs were feeding the film footage to the live picture tubes.

Props. Props for TV commercials can sometimes present a challenge. For example, in the Toshiba commercial, Toshiba contributed some of the old tubes, others were from repaired sets that customers had never retrieved, and the production house found a company that buys used TV sets from motels and hotels and sells them cheap.

Props were also a problem for the GE Rechargeable Battery commercial. Since the toys were people and the set was oversized, that meant the props were to scale. A "toy" car, for example, was a real Ferrari, and the GE battery recharger that the "toys" push across the floor to the robot was a giant model constructed for the filming.

When the Lowe Marschalk agency developed a Grey Poupon mustard commercial that showed a couple dining in a gondola on the canals of

Venice, the props were Limoges china, Baccarat crystal, and antique silver. Disaster struck when the props fell into the murky waters of the canal. The director turned white and almost went into the water himself before a young Italian dove into the canal and retrieved every piece.[19]

Lighting.   Lighting contributes to the mood of the commercial and can be another central factor. For example, in the GE Rechargeable Battery commercial, the action takes place at night after the little old toymaker has gone upstairs to bed. That means the set has to look dark—and yet there had to be enough light for the cameras to record the action. The Toshiba "graveyard" spot had to be filmed during a seven-minute period around sunset when the director determined the light was "correct" for the impression the spot was trying to create. Many directors, such as Joe Sedelmaier, feel that lighting is extremely important and insist on doing it themselves.

Special effects.   There are a number of other optical effects available in television production. These manipulate image, motion, or time. Time, in particular, can be speeded up, slowed down, or "jumbled." Since this is a highly innovative area, it's hard to keep up with the latest developments.

matting: shooting two images separately and then combining them

Matting is a mainstay of both television and movie production. The *Star Wars* movies have made excellent use of matte shots to create the appearance of action happening in exotic locations. Matting is also used on television; for example, it is used to create the illusion that a weather forecaster is standing in front of a satellite picture or a weather map. A matte shot is complicated to produce. It involves shooting both the object and the background in live film, but separately. A special film is then used to shoot the object against a blue background—the film is not sensitive to blue; that film becomes a mask used to combine the two previous images. Using double printing, the object is printed through the mask over the new background, eliminating the original background.

The California Raisin Board's "Grapevine" spot used the matting technique to create the long line of raisins. Actually there were only four models, but they were cloned and repeated using matting.

Timex created a series of commercials showing enormous digital watches that are the center of other action. In one, a Timex sitting up on its side appears to have joggers running up one side and across the top. Matting was used to remove the background from the watch shot and superimpose it on another shot which contained the action.[20]

Another way to manipulate the background is to shoot the object against a *rear projection screen.* The background image can be still, like a slide of a mountain or castle, or it can be in motion. It saves shooting at impossible locations or building expensive sets.

Polarity reversal is a technique used to change the image from a positive to a negative form. *Posterization* involves making several exposures of the film, each shot at a different exposure. Then the images are combined and each exposure is assigned a different color or shade. It creates an arty effect from a photographic original.

The image can also be manipulated through lenses. A *fisheye* lens is used to create the appearance of an extreme wide-angle view. In other words, viewers appear to see the image wrapping around them (if rear projection) or wrapping around a globe in front of them (if front projection).

Soft focus is done by shooting slightly out of focus. *Defocusing* means the image is taken out of focus and then brought back in. *Filters* can be used on lenses to intensify different colors or to desaturate the colors, creating overexposed or washed-out images. A *lens prism* creates multiple images from one subject. It can also be used to tilt or slant a horizon line as in a shot of a car turning a corner. A *canted* shot is where the camera itself is on an angle to create an image that is not horizontal.

There are a number of techniques used to manipulate time. *Reverse speed* means the frames run backward. There is something intrinsically funny about reverse motion, and it is used to create absurd, comic images.

Speeded-up motion is another technique that is used to get laughs. This is done by running the film faster, shooting at less than 24 frames per second, or editing out every other frame. It gives the effect of old-time movies.

Time lapse shoots the action with long periods of time between each frame. It speeds up the action so the viewer can watch something that takes days or years to happen replayed in a short time frame. For example, you might use time lapse to show a house being built or a caterpillar turning into a butterfly.

Slow motion is half speed, and it is created by repeating frames, thus extending the motion. *Freeze frame* or *stop action* appears to have stopped the action in midair. The film may continue to run, but it is simply projecting the same image on successive frames.

New advances.   More art directors are turning to computers to design and produce their ads, television as well as print, and many are using computers for storyboarding. At a conference on computers in design given by the San Francisco Art Directors Club, 85 to 90 percent of the 450 designers in attendance said they had been working with a computer for an average of two years. Of that group, 90 percent used a Macintosh.[21]

Houston artist Ron Scott explained how he produced three-dimensional (3-D) models of a golf ball and a watch with their reflections shown on a shiny surface. He said they were drawn in the manner of papier-mâché, using a one-dimensional "wire frame" image. Then he instructed the computer to produce its mathematically perfect 3-D representation. To create the pitted surface on the golf ball, Scott created just a single pit, and duplicated it over the image using "texture mapping." He then "painted" his 3-D wire frame with the picture of the pitted surface. Finally he made reflections by duplicating the golf ball and watch, inverting their images, and making them transparent.

These same techniques are being used in 3-D animation with even more sophisticated equipment. Texture mapping and painting are used along with "camera capture," a technique employed when shooting a live, single frame picture and using it within the 3-D image. This is how images are "cloned." Animators can also use painting to clean up pictures by adding colors; amending scratches, blemishes, or wrinkles; or adding details like a full head of hair or a mustache. Painting and 3-D animation are the fastest growing segments of video. New equipment and software programs come out daily, and the equipment list of a house that specializes in video animation can scare a banker to death.

Coke was the first national advertiser to use 3-D commercials. The big splash spot ran during halftime at the 1988 Super Bowl after 20 million 3-D glasses were given away with Diet Coke six-packs. Coke uses a special 3-D process called Nuoptix which Coke developed. Supposedly it eliminates the double-vision distortion normally associated with 3-D at theaters.[22]

The *Star Wars* movie technology is also making inroads into television commercial production. Bajus-Jones, a Minneapolis animation and graphics studio, is using computerized cameras operated from a computer keyboard. By pushing certain combinations of keys, the target surface shifts, as in a video game. Bajus-Jones also has a boom-arm camera, like the one that filmed the *Star Wars* chase scenes, that can move through complicated, precise, and repeatable motions. This camera is particularly good for shooting through, inside, and around models.[23]

Stereo TV has made it necessary to record quality audio tracks for commercials in stereo. The music, for example, in the Lipton Tea "Little Old Ladies" commercial was a critical element in the repositioning strategy (see Exhibit 13-6). Digital recording for audio is also becoming more important, as there is more recognition of the need for quality sound. All this has to be matched to the video recording technology—whether film or videotape—which is becoming easier as digital recording moves into both audio and video production.

High-definition television (HDTV) is the latest technological improvement to move into the mass market, bringing very sharp, wide-screen images to the home TV. It will also challenge production techniques because it can produce images end-zone to end-zone. It brings five times as much detail as a conventional video image at up to 30 percent less cost. David Niles, director and CEO of an HDTV production house, says, "Ordinary video compared to high-definition TV is like comparing a bicycle to a Rolls-Royce."[24]

Sony, the creator of HDTV, and Reebok have already made high-definition commercials, even though the audience can't detect the differences on ordinary TV sets in the United States. Today's television system in the United States has 525 horizontal lines; the Japanese-developed HDTV more than doubles that to 1,125 lines. This advance provides a much higher degree of clarity and detail—the viewer can see every pore on the skin. Color can be reproduced more faithfully, also. The picture can be shown on a big screen without the degradation familiar to viewers of big-screen sets in bars and airplanes. HDTV combines the ease of editing videotape with the picture quality of 35mm film. It will cut postproduction costs by eliminating film and the separate creation of special effects, because the new HDTV cameras will be more able to create multiple-image illusions without the fuzzy images that presently appear when two images are blended.

Reebok's agency, Heller Breene, used HDTV production because it needed to overlay two scenes in a commercial featuring complicated stunts in a shoe store plus a crowd scene outside the store window. High-

Exhibit 13-6: The "Little old ladies" spot, directed by Leslie Dektor, tries to dispel the myth that tea is only for the old by showing contemporary men and women, young and old, drinking tea. The shots are juxtaposed against high-energy original music with upbeat lyrics. "Look at all those little old ladies drinking Lipton Tea . . . now that's gentility." (Lipton is a registered trademark of Thomas J. Lipton, Inc.)

definition video allows such shots to be shot and overlapped (matted) more accurately. The camera operator and director can see the scenes combined as they are being shot.[25]

It will be awhile before HDTV is a reality in the United States because of confusion over standards for transmission. In Japan and Europe the debate over standards was avoided because transmission is by DBS satellite direct to a small dish receiver in the home. There will still be a need to convert or replace home televisions in the United States to receive these new images.

Interactive television is another aspect of the digital revolution. "Interactive" means the viewer can respond to what is happening on the television set. For some years now, experiments have been conducted using "black boxes" that attach to television sets or push-button telephones. Home computers can also be hooked up to televisions to provide a response system via the keyboard.

Coca-Cola is experimenting with an interactive device that works like a remote control—a box with a keyboard and a small video screen. The screen prompts viewers to answer questions, enter contests, or request coupons. Coke hopes to work with major league sports to involve viewers in predicting football or baseball plays as they watch the games—turning the home TV into a live video game. The interactive system could tabulate a winner who might get championship tickets or a cash prize. Coke sees this technology as a way to hold the attention of viewers and stop the zapping and grazing.[26]

13.2 SCRIPTING A COMMERCIAL

Television ideas are hard to communicate while they are still in the "thinking stage." There are so many things to be covered—the images, the motion, the sound, the sets, colors, acting, and so on. It's very difficult to extract the essence of the idea you see in your mind and put it down on paper so it can be presented, reviewed, debated, and approved. There are three forms used for expressing the concept before moving to actual production: the key visual, the script, and the storyboard.

We've talked about the key visual before. It is the heart of the concept, the one image that best expresses the message. This is used in initial copytesting when you want to check the concept. It's also used as a planning device. Key visuals also work like thumbnails, rough sketches of ideas developed during brainstorming.

The Script

TV script: written version of a television commercial with description of both audio and video content

The **TV script** is an outline of all the critical pieces. It is divided in the middle, and the audio goes in the column on the right and the video goes in the column on the left. The relationship of your typed lines back and forth between the audio and video should give a rough idea of how these two dimensions interact. In other words, if the announcer is describing a product feature, then exactly opposite the lines would be the video instructions identifying how the product feature is to be shot (see Exhibit 13-7).

The audio part of the script gives all the audio information—voices, music, and sound effects. The lines to be read are typed in upper- and lower-case. The instructions and descriptions are typed in all capitals. Every critical detail should be described on the script, such as the type of voice or the type of music.

The video column gives the four categories of optical information: distance, camera action, transitions, and special effects. The distance cue plus the camera action or transition and the subject will be included in most video instructions. For example, you will write something like: "zoom back to a MS of anncr" or "cut to ECU of trembling hands." Use abbreviations where possible. Script writing is a tight language and uses lots of codes to communicate complex information fast.

The purpose of the script is to present the narrative and to describe all other significant aspects of the commercial. It should give you a clear idea of what the relationship is between audio and video, and also how the action tracks across time. What happens in the beginning, the middle, and the end? And how much time do different pieces of action occupy?

TV SCRIPT

Client __National Ecology Center__   Writer __Reising, Grzelewski__

Length __:30__   Title __"America the Beautiful"__

Video	Audio
ROLL FILM. CRANE IN ON LITTLE GIRL AT WATER'S EDGE. SHE'S PLAYING WITH A PAPER SAILBOAT AND SINGING SOFTLY TO HERSELF..."OH BEAUTIFUL..."	MUSIC: SOFT GUITARS IN AND UNDER ON CUE. LITTLE GIRL: For amber waves of grain...
2. CUT TO CU OF GIRL'S HAND MOVING BOAT THROUGH WATER	2. GIRL: For purple mountain's majesty... above the fruited plain ...
3. TILT UP TO CU OF GIRL'S EYES-- EXPRESSION IS HAPPY	3. GIRL: LOUDER...America, America, God shed his grace on thee (SINGING FADES)
4. MATCH DISSOLVE TO CU OF GIRL'S EYES IN SAME POSITION BUT NOW SHE'S AN ADULT	4. WOMAN'S VOICE: and crown thy good with brotherhood....(LOUDER)
5. TILT DOWN TO CU OF SAILBOAT IN POLLUTED WATER	5. MUSIC COMPLETES LAST BARS OF SONG
6. ZOOM OUT TO LS OF WOMAN AND HER SON STOPPING OVER WATER'S EDGE. SUPER TITLE TO MATCH ANNCR'S CLOSING STATEMENT	6. MUSIC...UNDER AND OUT ANNCR: You can help. Call your local Ecology Center. We need you.

Exhibit 13-7: A sample script.

The Storyboard

storyboard: a pictorial diagram of a TV commercial showing a series of frames representing scenes and tabs below the frames with audio cues

The **storyboard** is a pictorial diagram, a frame for the sketch of the image; under the frame will be a box called a "tab," for the accompanying audio. The audio cues are important on the storyboard because they coordinate the images with the audio track. In the storyboard there is less emphasis on the descriptive elements than you find in the script. The critical role of the storyboard is to help those involved in the approval and production visualize what the creative people saw in their minds when they developed the concept. It should be clear from looking at the frame sketched in the storyboard exactly what the script means when it says "MS of package on table" (see Exhibit 13-8).

One of the critical decisions in storyboarding is how many frames you need to sketch. If the commercial features a stand-up announcer, then you may need only two or three—the opening shot, the middle with its elaboration of the sales message, and the closing shot. On the other hand, if the commercial is a fast-paced, flash-cut sequence, then you may need 12 to 15 frames to depict how the action develops.

Generally, the rule of thumb on frames is to use a frame for every scene. If there are six major scenes in the commercial, then there need to be at least six frames in the storyboard. The thing to remember with storyboard frames is that all they do is freeze a sequence of moving action. And a scene is composed of many shots. For example, your script may say "zoom to CU of product in anncr's hands." Does your frame show the beginning, middle, or end of that shot? Is that shot the important one to define the major action of the scene?

Think back on the previous discussion of the "key visual." There should be one visual that comes to mind when the commercial is over. Obviously, that should be one of the frames used in the storyboard. But you can also think in terms of every scene having a key visual—and it will usually be the end of the action, the point of resolution. Those key visuals are what you build your storyboard around.

How long should a storyboard be? Use only what is necessary to communicate the essence of the idea. Don't overstoryboard an idea. You want your instructions to be clear, but leave the producer some room. For example, if you have a clearly defined piece of action but it can't be filmed in the amount of time allowed, then the producer is going to have to be able to adjust elsewhere. It's a delicate balance; you have to communicate what you want without ham-stringing the producer. But do tell the producer what you want. Effort, time, and money are wasted on reshooting scenes simply because they weren't clearly described.

Generally, a 30-second commercial will have 4 to 6 scenes that average from 4 to 6 seconds apiece. Rarely will you see a 30-second commercial with 8 or more frames. A 60-second commercial will have twice that number of scenes and usually no more than 15 frames. These are all rough estimates because the nature of the commercial determines the number of frames needed.

When you make a storyboard, you are usually working with a large horizontal piece of posterboard or newsprint. These sheets should be big enough for presentation to a group of people at a conference table. The frame is usually drawn in a proportion of 4:3 and with rounded corners to represent a TV screen. A box the same width is ruled underneath the frame and a short version of the audio and video information from the script will be included there (distance, transitions, music, SFX, dialogue, supers, etc.). Normally, you will have three or four frames across and two rows of frames.

For presentation to a client or a review board, it is advisable to record the audio track on a tape. You may even want to shoot slides of the storyboard, so you can advance the slides in sync with the audio track. For presentation in a plans book, the same format is used but scaled down to

TV STORYBOARD

Client ___National Ecology Center___   Writer ___Reising, Grzelewski___

Length ___:30___   Title ___"America the Beautiful"___

ZOOM IN ON LITTLE GIRL
PLAYING WITH SAILBOAT

MUSIC: IN AND UNDER ON CUE

GIRL: For amber waves of
grain...

CUT TO CU OF GIRL'S HAND
PLAYING WITH BOAT IN WATER

GIRL: For purple mountain's
majesty above the fruited
plain...

TILT UP TO CU OF GIRL'S
EXPRESSION

GIRL: America, America, God
shed his grace on thee...
(SINGING FADES)

MATCH DISSOLVE TO CU OF WOMAN'S
EXPRESSION

WOMAN: and crown thy good
with brotherhood....(LOUDER)

TILT DOWN TO CU OF SAILBOAT
IN POLLUTED WATER

MUSIC COMPLETES LAST BARS

ZOOM OUT TO LS OF WOMAN AND
SON STOOPING OVER WATER'S EDGE

SUPER TITLE

MUSIC: OUT

ANNCR (VO): You can help. Call
your local Ecology Center.
We need you.

Exhibit 13-8: A sample storyboard.

fit on a standard sheet of paper. Sometimes only three or four frames will be shown per page and two pages will be used to reproduce the series. A foldout page is another way to solve the problem of paper size.

Keith Reinhard, CEO of DDB Needham, predicts that with the use of computers and "paintbox" programs, we aren't far from the day of electronic storyboards. He says, "Not only will television commercials of tomorrow be created on computers, but storyboards will be a thing of the past."[27]

Optical Commands

You need to understand the basics of film language in order to write a script for a television commercial. The terminology can be grouped into four categories: type of shot, camera commands, editing commands, and special effects. All four pieces of information are included in the script.

Distance and angle of shot. The camera operator and the director need this information so that they will know how to set up the shot. It indicates the composition of the visual image. The following are common terms.

- *Medium shot (MS):* The subject fills the screen, but not tightly. You can still see context.
- *Long shot (LS):* A shot used to show the entire setting—all the context. A variation is a *medium long shot (MLS)* or an *extreme long shot (ELS).*
- *Wide shot (WS):* Like a long shot, this shot is used to show the entire setting, but here the emphasis is on the panorama, the wide-angle view.
- *Close-up (CU):* A shot that comes in close on the subject. It might just show the face or hands. The subject fills the screen. A variation is a *medium close-up (MCU).*
- *Extreme close-up (XCU or ECU):* This shot is so close it shows only part of the subject—for example, tight on the face, you can't see the rest of the head, or tight on the fingers and you can't see the rest of the hand.
- *Full shot (FS):* This shot shows the full figure, head to toe. Variations on this shot are *shoulder shot* (shoulder and up), *waist shot, bust shot, chest shot, knee shot,* and *hip shot.*
- *Boom shot:* This is a camera angle shot in the studio from above the set with the camera mounted on a boom.
- *Helicopter shot:* A shot from above outdoors. Usually extremely high and shot from a helicopter.
- *Zero-degree angle:* This shot is taken from the angle of the user, as if seen through his or her eyes.
- *Worm's-eye view:* This is a view from a surface. For example, you might shoot a package on the table with the camera sitting right there on that level.

These shots are used to communicate different effects. In the discussion of editing, we introduced the idea that different angles and distances have different meanings. The long shot, for example, is often used as an establishing shot; it identifies the location and context for the action. A close-up is dramatic and an ECU is very intense. Close-ups are used a lot in advertising because most products are small. Don't be afraid to come in tight on them.

The concepts of objective and subjective camera are a result of the angle of view and the distance of the shot. An objective shot is from the point of view of a neutral observer, while a subjective angle is from the viewpoint of a participant. If you use a shot of someone's hands typing on a typewriter and the hands look as if they are your own, that is a subjective camera angle. A "tracking shot" is a type of shot that puts the viewer in the position of someone following something—a trail, for example.

A Nike commercial uses a dog's-eye view of race walking with his Nike-wearing owner. The visuals, as seen from pavement level, are jerky and jokey (fire hydrant, car tire). The dog's voice is suitably crabby. His last line is "Dogs were meant to lie in the sun and sleep."[28]

Camera commands.   These commands are also for the camera operator. They explain what action happens to the image as it is filmed. This is very important, since television's basic advantage is motion. These commands control the presentation of motion.

- *Pan left or right:* The camera follows the action by swinging the camera head. The tripod or "dolly" (tripod with wheels) is stationary. The head of the camera swings to the left or right with the action.

- *Zoom in or out:* The camera follows the action in or out by adjusting the focal plane of the lens. The dolly doesn't move.

- *Truck left or right:* The camera follows the action by moving left or right with the action. The dolly itself moves and the head of the camera stays stationary. Camera is in parallel motion to the subject.

- *Dolly in or out:* The camera follows the action by moving with the dolly closer or farther back. The lens stays stationary while the whole camera moves.

- *Tilt up and down:* The head of the camera swings up toward the ceiling or down toward the floor. This may also be called a "dutched" camera angle.

These basic camera actions create different feelings in the viewer. When the camera stays steady and the action moves past, the pan gives the feeling that the observer is standing still and watching. When the camera moves with the action, the truck or dolly motion makes the observer feel as if he or she is moving with the action.

For example, if you are filming a scene of some action on a motorboat, you can have the camera stay steady as the boat zips past. You have to swing your head to see anything; the pan creates that same kind of view. However, if you were in a second boat traveling alongside the boat with the action, then you would feel that motion and be able to study what was happening in the neighboring boat. They are two entirely different orientations to the observer's point of view—and they create much different effects.

Transitions. In videotaping, much of the editing happens as the film is shot. A director is controlling the way the images are recorded from several different cameras and, in particular, specifies what kind of transition will be used to move from the image of one camera to the image of another. In film the same kind of transitions are needed, but they are produced as part of the editing process when the two pieces of film, representing shots, are edited together. Some of the common terms used to describe these transitions are as follows:

- *Cut:* An instantaneous switch from one picture to another. It's like an eyeblink; it is hardly noticeable because it is largely unobtrusive. Variations include a *match cut,* where the two images are matched in shape and size, and a *flash cut,* where a series of very rapid cuts are stacked together.
- *Fade in and out:* The image begins to appear from a blank screen or it fades to a blank screen.
- *Dissolve:* One image fades to black as a second picture comes up from black. The fades are superimposed to create the impression that one image is fading into another. A variation is a *match dissolve,* where the shapes of the two images are matched—for example, the company's round logo may dissolve into a spinning globe. Dissolves can be fast or slow. A *lap dissolve* is a slow dissolve where the overlap is held for a short time. *Ripple dissolve* creates a shimmering image as one picture replaces the other.
- *Superimposition:* A super is a shot where two images are on the screen at the same time, one over another. It's created by holding a lap dissolve at the midpoint.
- *Wipe:* Like a window shade, one image comes down over the other and replaces it. In addition to top to bottom, wipes can also be right to left, left to right, bottom to top, or corner to corner. Ornamental wipes, such as a diamond, box, circle, or spiral, are also available on most special effects generators. The *flip wipe* shows the new image flipping over and over as it moves toward or away from the viewer. A *clock wipe* shows the image changing as the hand on a clock sweeps around the face.
- *Swish pan:* This transition begins as a fast pan but in the middle the image is completely blurred, then becomes a pan again with a new second image.
- *Split screen:* Two different images are displayed side by side on the screen. With a *quad screen* four images are possible, one in each corner.

These editing commands also create effects. A fade is usually used at the beginning and end of a commercial to separate the spot from what's happening on screen before and after. It's like putting rules around a newspaper ad. Fades are also used to indicate a passage of time or a flashback.

Dissolves give a dreamy feeling, particularly a lap dissolve, and they can also be used for flashbacks. A ripple dissolve is used for cuing before and after scenes, a type of a flashback. A swish pan is used to jump ahead in time. A clock wipe is another way to manipulate time. You will see it in recipes and instructions where the announcer says, "And now, five minutes later . . ." Split screens are often used for before-and-after scenes or product comparisons.

A typical use of superimpositions is to add the name of the product on screen, either over some key visual or beneath the package. These titles can "pop up" or be "zoomed in" or "zoomed back." They can also "crawl" from left to right across the bottom of the screen.

13.3 PRODUCTION OF A COMMERCIAL

Once the commercial is planned, scripted, and approved, the actual production process begins. This involves making production decisions, getting bids, hiring a production house and other specialists, and making all the arrangements for the shoot.

Filming

All these raw materials are assembled into some sort of visual image by recording them on either film or videotape. Both film and videotape are shot in color. Rarely is black-and-white film used commercially, except for special effect.

videotape: a type of recording medium that electronically records sounds and images simultaneously

Videotape records sound and picture simultaneously on magnetic tape. It's just like an audio tape. You can make a recording and play it back and see what you have recorded. This immediate feedback is useful because you can change lighting, camera angles, action, and so on and then reshoot. Videotape offers a much shorter production and editing time, which makes it faster and cheaper. Videotaped commercials are produced more for local than national use.

Until the eighties videotape was thought of as an inferior alternative to film; however, the quality of videotape has improved dramatically. Now most television commercials are shot in 16mm or 35mm film and processed, then the image is transferred to videotape. This is called *film-to-tape transfer.* Innovations in editing have also improved the quality of videotape production.

Most of the videotape production is done in the ¾-inch U-Matic format. Some television stations have moved to the ½-inch VSH format for their local news filming, but the industry standard still seems to be the ¾-inch cassette for taping and duping. The ½-inch Beta format is rarely found in professional use. Recent developments in miniaturization, however, will probably make all these standards obsolete. As systems become lighter and more portable, the tape also is becoming smaller and its quality is improving. Sony is doing to television production what the Walkman did to stereo sound.

Film is shot in three sizes: 70mm (2 inch), 35mm, and 16mm. You are familiar with 16mm film; that's what your elementary school teacher used to show you movies on rainy days. The 35mm format is larger and equivalent in size to the film used in 35mm cameras. The 70mm film is twice as large as 35mm film. The principle here is that the larger the film, the better the quality of the recorded image. Movies are produced in 70mm and then shot down to 35mm for commercial distribution. Some ultra high quality movies are shot and distributed in 70mm and shown in specially equipped movie houses. Most commercials are shot in 35mm, although cost-saving efforts are demanding that more and more spots be shot in 16mm or videotape. The distribution to local television stations may be either 16mm or a videotape duplicate made using the *film-to-tape transfer* process.

With film, the sound is recorded separately from the picture. The voices, instruments, and sound effects are all recorded on separate tracks and mixed. The film is recorded separately, edited, and then combined with the sound track. It is a much more complicated, time-consuming, and expensive process than videotape.

Lengths.   Most television commercials are produced as 10-, 15-, 20-, 30-, or 60-second messages. The 10-second spot is used for a quick reminder. Its only objective is identification. The 60-second spot used to be common but, with the increase in costs, most commercials are now being produced as 30-second spots, although many major high-budget commercials will be produced with both a long form (:60) and a short form (:30). Occasionally, a 20-second spot will be produced as a short form of a 30-second spot.

The trend is moving to more use of 15-second spots. Those ads are being used as a way to stretch a budget and make more impressions. They are a challenge to create because there's barely enough time to develop any message at all. J. Walter Thompson experts suggest that 15-second commercials be used for reminder advertising when a brand and campaign are well established. Alan Webb, executive creative director, suggests that creatives should focus tightly on the "big idea" and use a high-impact visual. Alice Sylvester, media research director, says, "Get used to using them well. They're here to stay."[29] Creatives agree that the :15 is a discipline of its own and will force advertising back to basics. The key is to be simple and tightly focused.

Longer commercials in the 2- and 3-minute range are also being created. They are run on advertiser-sponsored programs such as the *Hallmark Hall of Fame* and the *GE Theatre*. These "infomercials" are also being used on cable television and in theater advertising.

Scenes and shots.   The underlying structure of television commercials—and movies—is scenes and shots. The shot is what is recorded as a piece of film passes through a camera for a short time. It is the point of view seen by the camera lens as a stand-in for the human eye. As another camera records the action from a different angle, another shot is being created.

A scene is more complex. It is a series of actions usually occurring in one place. Several different cameras may record different views of various aspects of the action, but it is all built around this one event in this one location. A scene, then, is made up of one or several shots. Most scenes in commercials are four to six seconds long, although they may be shorter or longer to create a special effect. In rare cases, you may see a commercial that is all one shot with no breaks for different views or different scenes.

Editing   Filming is only the beginning of the production process. In actuality, thousands of feet of film or videotape are shot for every 30-second commercial. That includes multiple angles of every piece of the action as well as different forms of action. When the filming is done, the actual commercial is created through a process called editing.

Individual shots are assembled to create a scene and then the scenes are assembled to create a story. The shots may be taken at different times in different locations in different parts of the world. But it all holds together as a coherent message because of the skill of the editor. The actual footage used is only a tiny part of what was shot. The rest winds up on the floor of the "cutting room."

Film is projected at a standard speed of 24 frames per second, and that means a 30-second commercial will have approximately 720 frames. The editor is working with groups of these frames—as shots and scenes—and can cut them apart or join them anywhere between two frames. In that sense, editing on film is a tangible, physical activity.

Other devices such as character generators (which create letters on the screen), digital video effects, and audio machines have also helped to spur more editing on videotape, rather than on film. Today, videotape editing is called "an electronic optical process," and clients have come to rely on film-to-tape transfer as an integral part of the production.

Film meanings.   Editing involves more than physically joining two pieces of film. Suppose your script calls for a scene of two people sitting at a restaurant having a conversation. They start off happy and end up angry. How does an editor effect the perception of that scene? One thing the editor can do is take the piece of film from the camera that is shooting front and center and use it as a straightforward record of the event.

Another technique is to assemble various shots of this event to emphasize the action and its meaning. The editor may start with an "establishing" shot from a distance that shows the table, the people, and enough of the surroundings so that it is recognizable as a restaurant. Then a shot may be used that moves closer and tightly frames the two people on each side of the table. Next, the editor may use a shot of the speaker's face to focus the attention of the viewer progressively tighter and tighter.

Now the editor may insert a reaction shot of the other person, showing what effect the speaker's words are having. Now back to the speaker who is making a point with his hands. That means the shot has to back off and show most of the upper body. Now another reaction shot, and this can be an extreme close-up that might even be able to catch a tear in the eye. For added dramatic impact, the next shot may be of the listener's hands nervously twisting a napkin. Then back to the speaker, who has built up to the emotional climax of the scene. This can be an extreme close-up to focus attention on the anger in the eyes and the taut, thin lips.

The scene ends with a closing shot showing the entire table and both people, but now you can see the change in body positions as the speaker turns away from the table and the other person sits slumped over the table, shoulders bowed and head down.

The point of this scenario is that the editor uses the language of film to create and highlight meaning in the visual message. Skillful editing can make a scene far more powerful than a static shot may be. The editor is constantly asking: How can I show stress or anger or love? What details communicate the essence of those emotions, and how can I use filmic techniques to highlight those details? It's an art form.

Production Notes   In addition to the script and the storyboard, there is a third document developed specifically for the production stage called "production notes." The primary use of this document is during the bid stage to give the producers and technical suppliers a clear idea of what will be involved in producing the script. All the details are spelled out. If you are using a house for the setting, then describe the house, describe the rooms, the decorations, the furniture—whatever is necessary to create the feeling and mood.

There are certain categories of information that are included in a set of production notes. Some of these things are included routinely, while other pieces of information vary, depending upon the special needs of the commercial.

- Summary of strategy: target audience, message objective
- Creative dimensions: mood, tone, action
- Filming technique: live, animation, freeze frame, and so on
- Product treatment: package, label, brand name
- Casting: voices, parts of body, costumes, makeup
- Location and sets: lighting, props
- Music and sound effects
- Special optical effects
- Graphics: art, slides, stock footage, typography

Describe as many details as possible. Will you provide the music? Is it a jingle? Will it have to be composed? Can you use something from a music library? Then describe the kind of music. Describe the beat, the type of sound (rock, country, R&B), singers, instrumentation, and so on. Give every little clue you can. And do this for every category. The production notes may be a 15- to 20-page document by the time you are through.

There are a lot of decisions and a lot of details involved in making a commercial. It's better to think through all this before you actually start into production, and make sure everyone involved understands the approach and agrees with the decisions. That's one of the roles of the production notes.

Another role is to nail down cost items. The bids are made on the basis of the production notes. If some little detail is forgotten, it may turn out to be a major cost item. Hooper White describes a commercial that was to be filmed in Jamaica. The entire crew was assembled on location, and then the producer found out that the white horse described in the script wasn't available on the island. It had to be air freighted from the States while the crew stood around and waited.[30] If the details are worked out ahead of time, then there will be less opportunity for these little surprises to pop up and break the budget.

Production Sequence

1. *Strategy sessions.* The first step is to get the advertiser, the account management people, and the creative people together to discuss the overall strategy of the commercial. Sometimes this involves two levels of meetings: First, the advertising manager meets with the agency account team, and then the account team meets with the creative people. Most creatives appreciate being involved with the initial client meetings so they have a better picture of what the client wants.

2. *Creative sessions.* Whatever it takes to come up with the idea—background research, brainstorming sessions, demonstrations, comparative tests, product focus groups. Usually the creative team, which may involve a creative director, copywriter, art director, and agency producer (depending upon the size of the agency and the talent available in-house) will kick around a hundred approaches. Finally, a few possibles begin to surface.

3. *Informal critiques.* At this point, the ideas are still in a "rough" state. Scripts and storyboards are developed and they may be tried out on other staff members, the agency review board (if one exists), top management, the advertising manager, and anyone else who can provide feedback, including a focus group.

    Concept testing can be developed at this stage using a sketch of the key visual and a paragraph description of the action. It's rough but it does give you structured feedback on the concept independent of the execution. It can take anywhere from four to eight weeks for this initial idea development stage.

4. *Revisions and final approvals.* A final script and storyboard are developed for official review. This involves sign-off by the agency review board or top executive, legal approvals, and finally the client approvals. Approvals and revisions may add on another two weeks. For copytesting, slides or rough videotapes of the spot may be developed or a film may be made by shooting the frames from the storyboard and using the film with a rough tape.

5. *Production notes.* When the script and storyboard have been officially approved by everyone involved, the production notes are developed. Depending upon the complexity of the concept, the production notes may take from one to two weeks to develop.

6. *Bids.* The script, storyboard, and production notes are sent to producers, studios, production houses, talent agencies, and all supporting vendors. Sometimes particular producers, artists, or musicians are specified because they create distinctive effects. Usually, however, the contracts are awarded on the basis of low bids. Bids often take 10 days to 2 weeks.

7. *Preproduction arrangements.* Sets have to be built, actors auditioned, music composed, props located, and a thousand other details worked out. Some of this is done by the agency; some by the producer's studio. This can take two to six weeks, depending upon the complexity of the commercial.

A preproduction meeting is usually scheduled three to four days before the actual shoot. The creative people, along with the account manager and the advertising manager, meet with the producer and key production staff. Every detail of the script is talked through, every action walked through, every arrangement verified. Of all the hundreds of meetings involved in the development of a commercial, this one is the most important.

8. *The shoot.* The actual production activities are in the hands of the producer, although agency and client are usually represented on the set. Shooting for a 30-second commercial may take from 1,000 to 4,000 feet of film—even though only 45 feet is needed. Sometimes extra footage is shot because the director is trying to capture just the right piece of action. In other cases, extra footage is shot so that there are different angles to choose from in the editing process. The "shoot" may take one to two days or as long as a week. This is expensive time, since it involves a large and expensive professional crew.

   Action is rarely shot in sequence. Some scenes may be shot in the studio, while other bits of action might be shot on location. Also, the film is shot separate from the audio. The two don't come together until the last stages of the postproduction process.

9. *"Dailies" or "rushes."* Direct copies of the footage shot that day are available for viewing that evening. The director can decide if the film shot is what is needed or whether it needs to be reshot.

10. *The "rough cut."* The first step in the postproduction editing process. Here the scenes are edited together and the audio is assembled on a separate tape. For initial viewing they can be played simultaneously, even though they are still separate.

11. *The "work print" or "fine cut."* A version that is compiled after all the changes and revisions were made from the rough cut. All editing has been approved and the visual sequence is finalized; however, the special effects are not included yet. The shots are assembled into scenes and the scenes are edited together—the sequence has been assembled, but the more complicated transitions are yet to be done.

12. *An "interlock."* Produced after the "work print" is approved. The opticals are added and the audio and video are synchronized together on one piece of sound film. Any changes made in the interlock are presented on a "corrected print."

13. *The "release print."* The final step, a duplicate transferred onto 16mm film or videotape for distribution to television stations. Depending upon the media buy, there may be hundreds of release prints produced.

This postproduction process may take 3 to 4 weeks. The entire commercial process will often take 16 to 18 weeks, and maybe as long as 6 months. It is a complicated, expensive, and time-consuming process.

Production Costs Certain kinds of commercials cost bundles; other approaches are cheaper. A 4A's two-year study of commercials (for 1987 and 1988) found that a national TV commercial costs, on the average, 50 percent more to produce than a regional spot, and almost three times what it takes to make a local spot. The average cost for a national commercial came to $156,600 compared to $102,200 for regional and $57,000 for local. The study also found a wide range in the costs of commercials by product category. In national advertising, packaged-goods spots averaged $119,500, beauty and fashion averaged up to $223,800, and fast food, beer, soft drinks, and snacks averaged $241,900. There were differences, too, depending upon the type of commercial. The interview/testimonial averaged $77,400, followed by monologues at $88,200. Spots that used "special effects" cost an average of $207,600 to produce, while "multi-storyline" commercials averaged $265,000. Song-and-dance spots were the most expensive of all, averaging $277,700.[31]

Some advertisers are now hiring cost consultants to police production costs. Campbell Soup, Kimberly-Clark, the Matchabelli's division of Chesebrough-Ponds, and General Foods have all saved money by introducing cost consultants into the commercial planning process. In some cases they review the production notes as well as the bids and may appear on the shoot as the advertisers' representatives. The issue of soaring production costs should be the concern of everyone involved in television commercial production.[32]

You may think that budgets are strictly the responsibility of the accountants, but the cost factors are derived from the script and that puts the creative people in charge of the bottom line. It is possible to produce a script for $80,000 and a similar and equally effective version for half or twice that amount—just by varying certain aspects of the specifications.

Here are some things to remember:

- It's usually cheaper to film in the studio than on location.
- Exotic locations are particularly expensive, no matter how much you might like a trip to New Zealand.
- Sets can be expensive to build (depending upon their complexity).
- Simple locations are sometimes cheaper than sets—such as a real house in the same city (most producers have files on available locations, but you have to be flexible to use something that already exists).
- Every person that appears on camera earns residuals every time the commercial is shown. Do you really need six people?
- The less you show of a person, the less you pay. Hands are cheaper than faces.
- Cheap music is available from music libraries and production houses. Do you really need to have original music composed, arranged, and performed?
- Can you shoot a "pool" of commercials while you're at it, rather than just one?
- Do you need to shoot at night? That means overtime.
- Do you have to fly everyone from New York (or Detroit or Dayton)? Can you shoot here? Or hire them there?

- Can you gang up your productions? If this is one of a series, can you shoot scenes for successive commercials at the same time? You don't have to start from scratch each time.
- Do you really need the children? It varies from state to state, but often they have to be accompanied by a welfare worker and you have to allow them time to go to school.
- Do you need the dog? That means a trainer and often a representative from the humane society.
- 16mm and videotape are replacing 35mm. Will the difference in quality be fatal to your production?

The biggest budget buster is lack of planning, according to Hooper White in his *Advertising Age* column.[33] Insufficient time is allowed for every step of the production process and things have to be done in haste. Inevitably, there is waste when you are in a hurry. He points to the problems of insufficient time to work out the production notes and details of the bids.

Likewise, poor communication and explanation is another source of unexpected costs. Having to reshoot because it didn't come out as you wanted usually means that you did a poor job of communicating what you wanted. It's your problem, not the producer's. Production people can't read your mind. Agencies must have creative people who can visualize what they want and communicate it with a storyboard. Hooper White says the most expensive creative person is one who says, "I know exactly what I want and the minute I see it, I'll let you know."

SUMMARY

This chapter has discussed the planning and production of television commercials. You should know:

1. A key visual is a visual image that sticks in the mind.
2. Television advertising is best used for action, demonstration, entertainment, touching emotions, and storytelling.
3. The most effective television advertising uses a brand-differentiating message.
4. The primary tools of television production include audio, video, action, casting, costumes, sets, props, lighting, and special effects.
5. Television action is live, animated, or a combination of both.
6. Special effects manipulate image, motion, and perception of time.
7. A script describes the audio and video in detail; a storyboard is a visual diagram of the scenes and shots.
8. Optical commands are used to describe the distance of a shot, the angle of a shot, camera movements, and the transitions between shots and scenes.
9. Film used to be the standard recording medium, but with film-to-tape transfer and electronic editing, videotape is becoming more important.
10. Production notes summarize all the production decisions and specifications.

11. Production costs are skyrocketing but they can be controlled by good planning at the creative end.

NOTES

1. John R. Rossiter and Larry Percy, "Attitude Change Through Visual Imagery in Advertising," *Journal of Advertising*, 9:2 (1980), pp. 10–16.
2. Dottie Enrico, "Out of Africa: Peter Beard Ventures into U.S. Advertising," *Adweek*, August 22, 1988, p. 17; and Debbie Seaman, "HDM Takes a Ride on the Wild Side," *Adweek*, August 8, 1988, p. 20.
3. Harry McMahan and Mack Kile, "In TV Spots, One Picture Worth 10,000 Words," *Advertising Age*, April 27, 1981, p. 50.
4. Marianne Paskowski, "Filmmakers Hear McDonald's Ad Recipes," *Adweek*, December 14, 1981, p. 9.
5. David W. Stewart and David H. Furse, *Effective Television Advertising* (Lexington, Mass.: Lexington Books, 1986), p. 119.
6. "Clearer Picture of Viewing Habits on the Horizon," *Marketing News*, August 29, 1988, p. 26.
7. David Kalish, "Advertisements That Aren't," *Marketing & Media Decisions*, July 1987, pp. 24–25.
8. Joanne Lipman, "Don't Blame Television, Irate Readers Say," *Wall Street Journal*, March 1, 1989, p. B6.
9. "Advertising's Image Problem," *Wall Street Journal*, March 10, 1989, p. B4.
10. Hooper White, "Countdown to Airtime: How Schlitz Went Live," *Advertising Age*, April 20, 1981.
11. Ibid.
12. Marcy Magiera, "Claymation Wiz Molds Winning Business," *Advertising Age*, November 14, 1988, p. 4.
13. Janet Meyers, "Piggly Wiggles Down South in Grocer's Animated Spots," *Advertising Age*, July 25, 1988, p. 42MW; and Ron Gales, "More 'Roger Rabbit' Offspring in Offing," *Adweek*, March 20, 1989, p. 67.
14. Hooper White, *How to Produce an Effective TV Commercial* (Chicago: Crain Books, 1981).
15. Lynn Hirschberg, "When You Absolutely, Positively Want the Best," *Esquire*, August 1983, pp. 53–61.
16. Ibid.; and Geoffrey Colvin, "The Ad Game's Buster Keaton," *Fortune*, June 13, 1983, pp. 115–120.
17. Debbie Seaman, "GE Charger Feeds Imaginations of BBDO," *Adweek*, December 5, 1988, p. 26.
18. Debbie Seaman, "Toshiba's Agency Takes Hellish Trip to TV Graveyard," *Adweek*, November 28, 1988, p. 24.
19. Debbie Seaman, "Grey Poupon's Unsinkable Series Charts Canals of Venice," *Adweek*, July 13, 1987, p. 28.
20. Robert Garfield, "Re-creating Those Nifty Effects That Make Commercials Special," *USA Today*, June 17, 1983, p. 5.
21. Watson Saint James, "Art Directors Drawn to Macintosh," *Advertising Age*, March 13, 1989, p. 50.
22. Patricia Winters, "Coke Pops First 3-D Spot," *Advertising Age*, January 11, 1988, p. 1; and Michael J. McCarthy, "Coke Looks to Score at the Super Bowl with 3-D TV Spot," *Wall Street Journal*, January 20, 1989, p. B5.
23. Dan Wascoe, Jr., "Boom-Arm Camera Gives Company All the Angles," and "It's All a Blur with the Track Camera," *Minneapolis Star and Tribune*, July 14, 1985, p. 1D.

24. Joanne Lipman, "Firms Use High-Definition Ads but Viewers Can't See Effects," *The Wall Street Journal*, March 23, 1989, p. B6; and "Super Television: The High Promise—and High Risks—of High-Definition TV," *Business Week*, January 30, 1989, pp. 56–66.

25. Ibid.

26. Joanne Lipman, "New Attempt at Interactive TV Planned to End Passive Viewing," *Wall Street Journal*, February 23, 1989, p. B6; and Lenore Skenazy, "Interactive TV Gets a Crack at Baseball," *Advertising Age*, April 3, 1989, p. 53.

27. Keith L. Reinhard, "Advertising: Yesterday, Today and Tomorrow," Speech to the American Marketing Association, Montreal, Canada, May 28, 1987.

28. Barbara Lippert, "Nike's 'Revolution' is Over and Everyone's a Winner," *Adweek*, August 22, 1988, p. 19.

29. Wally Wood, ":15s: Half-Priced or Half-Baked?" *Marketing & Media Decisions*, March 1987, p. 138.

30. Hooper White, "How to Avoid Foul-ups Leading to Shopping for Bags and Nags," *Advertising Age*, February 12, 1979, pp. 58–61; and Hooper White, "Ad Groups Analyze Spiraling Production Costs," *Advertising Age*, March 31, 1986, p. S2.

31. Ron Gales, "4A's Study Details Production Costs," *Adweek*, March 6, 1989, p. 17; and Gary Levin, "Cost of TV Spot Pegged at $145,600," *Advertising Age*, March 6, 1989, p. 68.

32. Janet Meyers and Laurie Freeman, "Marketers Police TV Commercial Costs," *Advertising Age*, April 3, 1989; and J. Max Robins, "Windsong Was on His Mind," *The New York Times Magazine*, April 2, 1989, pp. 34, 62–64.

33. White, op. cit.

14

Other Advertising Media

KEY POINTS

- The poster is a key medium, the foundation for outdoor, transit and in-store advertising.
- Outdoor advertising must be bold, succinct, and to the point.
- Packaging's primary objective is to stimulate action.
- Store displays bring advertising and merchandising together.
- Theater advertising has to be even more entertaining than television advertising.

14.1 POSTERS

Almost any kind of posted notice can be called a poster, including several types of media that we will discuss separately—such as transit and outdoor advertising. The reason for a separate section here is to call your attention to the poster, itself, as an advertising medium—in all its various sizes and shapes. The poster is the foundation for outdoor, transit, and subway advertising.

Poster space can be rented at locations where people use most forms of mass transit, such as bus stops and shelters, taxi stands and subway platforms. Posters also enliven the walls in bus depots, train stations, and airports. You'll even find them on rented space on trash cans and grocery carts. In addition to rented spaces, posters will also be seen on bulletin boards, kiosks, fences and walls, and telephone poles, and even free-standing on their own stakes—such as campaign yard signs.

Poster design has always been a highly creative area of graphic design. In the late 1800s, some of the most exciting design of the century was being produced in poster form by people like Aubrey Beardsley, Will Bradley, Eugene Grasset, and Alfons Mucha. These posters advertised products like bicycles, chocolate, books, and special issues of magazines, as well as special events like expositions, theater and opera performances, and the follies. Even today there are poster design competitions, and well-designed posters are sold in galleries as well as in stores.

Recent award winners in the British Design and Art Direction (D & AD) competition included a poster for the United Way showing a grandfather and his little granddaughter holding hands as they walked down a path. The headline read, "This may be the last time he'll see his granddaughter. She has cancer." A Volvo poster showed line drawings of pieces of a human skeleton. The headline read, "Drive a Volvo because replacement parts are hard to find." Posters can be short reminder messages like billboards, and they can be posted in high-traffic areas where people are passing by, such as supermarkets, airport terminals, and shopping malls. These messages give quick facts. Posters also can present more involved messages and can be posted in places where people wait, like subway stations and bus stops. People at a bus stop are a captive audience and they will read, even study, anything while they wait. The type of design must be appropriate to the location.

Another use of posters is for tearoff. This is a pad of coupons, recipes, or additional information. Readers can take one with them. Most often, the tearoff stimulates some kind of further response.

14.2 OUTDOOR

Outdoor advertising is the primary way to reach consumers who are traveling. Outdoor advertising goes back to the ancient Egyptians, and probably beyond that. It includes any form of posted notice. Billboards came into being in the late 1800s when traveling circuses leased wooden panels on which printed "bills" or notices could be posted. With the development of paved streets, highways, and interstates, the importance of outdoor advertising has increased.

Travel is an important part of modern life, and that has made the street and highway a convenient vehicle for commercial messages. Furthermore, people who travel are often looking for information about such necessities as gas stations, motels, and restaurants. Even if they are not actively searching, they may still be interested in advertising along the highways, because it helps break up the monotony of driving. In cities, outdoor advertising can also be used in the form of signposts, giving travel information and location of certain services.

Types of Outdoor Recognized companies that are members of the Outdoor Advertising Association prepare billboards in standardized sizes. The *poster panel* billboards are the most common. They use preprinted strips of posters and are identified by the number of "sheets," or strips needed to paper the board. The outside board is generally 12 feet high by 24 feet long. The design area varies with the size of the preprinted poster. There are three sizes for the preprinted posters: *24-sheet: 8'8" × 19'6", 30-sheet: 9'7" × 21'7", and bleed: 10'5" × 22'8".*

The 30-sheet poster panel is the most common size. The dimensions given above are the image areas. For example, the 30-sheet poster has an overall size of 12 feet by 25 feet. The difference allows for a border of white space around the image area. The bleed poster is bigger because it eliminates most of the border area. The 30-sheet poster has approximately 200 square feet of image area. The proportion is roughly 1:2¼.

Preprinted posters are used for national advertising where it makes sense to print thousands of copies using either silkscreen or lithography. The printing is done from camera-ready art, like that used for a magazine ad. For local advertising, however, printing on this scale is too expensive for one or a few billboards. Boards produced in limited numbers are called *painted bulletins;* they are painted by hand by skilled artists who work for the outdoor companies. The original is designed on a piece of layout paper and then projected onto larger sheets of paper the size of the boards. The projected image is transferred in outline form, using "pounce patterns," onto the panels and then the artists fill in the color, shading, and lettering. (A "pounce pattern" is a perforated sheet through which the image is transferred onto the panel.)

The standard size of painted billboards is 48 feet long by 14 feet high. That's a proportion of 1:3½, which looks long and narrow when you work with a painted billboard layout. It is nearly three times as large as a poster panel. The overall image area is approximately 600 square feet.

Creative Considerations

Because of their "bigness" and the mobility of the audience, billboards demand special creative considerations. Primarily billboards are used for a memorable visual.

There are two characteristics of billboards that influence the way they are designed. First, they are seen by people who are moving. Unlike other media, the outdoor image is stationary and the viewer is in motion. Second, they are seen at a distance. Some billboards may be located at intersections where traffic stops and there might be a little time to study the message, but generally they are on the street or highway and they are seen by people moving past in a hurry. This logically calls for bold print and quick communication. Clarity and simplicity are required in all elements of the design.

In his column in *Advertising/Marketing Review*, Bruce Stauderman says that he has always felt that outdoor is "probably the most difficult of all advertising media. To capture the essence of a product and communicate it in two or three seconds is a tall order."[1]

Few words. Whenever readers are moving, you know they don't have time to study a complicated message. They can only glance, they can't read. The creative concept has to be very strong, very clear, and very brief. The point must be communicated instantaneously; there is no time to repeat or elaborate. Most people who work in outdoor advertising advise to keep the copy short and succinct—very few words, a short message that can be seen in a quick glance. These messages are designed to give a quick impression, not details. All copy is display. There really isn't such a thing as "body" copy on a billboard. The concepts have to be simple to be understood at a glance—one single strong idea. There are no frills, no extra verbiage in outdoor copy. It has to get right to the heart of the message immediately. The rule of thumb is to use no more than seven words.[2]

Bold art.   The art is usually graphic and dramatic. The lettering and the visual should be large enough for easy identification. It has to catch the attention of an audience that may not be deliberately looking for that particular message. Since people are reading the message at a glance, there needs to be a strong integration of art and copy—that is, they must work together to register the message quickly. The layout needs to be simple, with a visual path that can be scanned at a glance. There's no time to go back up and start over again. The art, as well as the type, is executed in heroic proportions—in other words, it's huge.

You have to rethink your whole approach to size and scale when you design billboards. They are designed to be read at distances from 100 feet to 300 feet. The greater the distance, obviously, the smaller the message will appear to be. You can test your own response to this distance/size relationship. If you design a layout that is roughly 4 inches by 9 inches and view it from four feet away, you will have the same viewing relationship as that of someone looking at a 24-sheet poster at 300 feet. Art that may have looked big on the 4-by-9 layout, up close, shrinks to the size of a postage stamp at 300 feet. That's why we talk about "heroic" art and type.

Legible type.   Legibility is absolutely critical for billboards. Use type that is big and bold. Sans serif faces are particularly legible for outdoor. Avoid delicate details and letters with extreme contrasts in thick and thin. Heavy typefaces become blobs and fine strokes fade. Ornamental faces are often hard to read under the best of circumstances, but impossible at 55 mph. Use normal letterspacing. Close-set letters will blur together, and wide-set letters will fall apart. Avoid all capitals. Your fast-moving audience needs all the help it can get to scan those words, and the coast-lines are essential in fast scanning (see Exhibit 14-1).

Color.   Color is important for its attention-getting power as well as for establishing associations. In choosing color combinations, think about

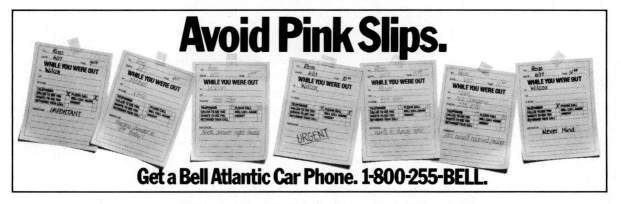

Exhibit 14-1:   The "Pink Slips" billboard for Bell Atlantic Car Phone uses a familiar reminder of what happens when a professional is out of the office and out of touch.

the contrast you are creating. If you have type over color or colored art over a colored background, maximize the contrast. Yellow and black provide the greatest contrast; white and yellow create the least contrast.

Innovations

Outdoor is a very creative area, and there are a number of experiments going on in the industry. One interesting approach is to create a figure that extends beyond the conventional frame of the billboard. The Marlboro man, for example, extends above the frame on many of the Marlboro boards. Breaking the border with these *extensions* is a technique used to create an attention-getting visual. It is unexpected. It also adds impact to the already heroic figure. The industry has standardized the sizes allowed for these extensions. You can go 5½ feet above the board and 2 feet to either side or below.

"*Geometrics,*" a technique developed by Fred Farrari, creative director at Pacific Outdoor Advertising, creates the illusion of 3-D. Even though the image is painted on a flat board, the use of perspective and shading creates the image of objects that appear to be three-dimensional. In some cases they appear to be moving toward the viewer. Once again, this is a strong attention-getting device.

Rotating panels have been around for awhile. It is possible to create a board with panels that move and change. This is used in some cases to fit multiple messages in the same space. In cities that are trying to control the proliferation of outdoor boards, "tri-vision" signs are replacing conventional boards. A tri-vision sign carries the messages on louvered panels and rotates them every 20 seconds—that's equivalent to a very short TV commercial. Rotating panels can also be used as an intriguing device to show change or growth, with a figure in the illustration growing bigger or smaller or moving from one side to another.[3] The Corvette board has motor-driven extensions that show the trunk, hood, and doors being opened. Motion in a message, particularly in a static form like billboards, is very hard to ignore (see Exhibit 14-2).

Panagraphic billboards are prepared on a translucent material that is lit from behind. This creates an image that is brighter and more intense. It looks like the projected image that audiences might see in a movie house.

Spectacolor is a company that specializes in computerized electronic display boards. The most famous one is located in Times Square in downtown Manhattan. These boards can flash color animation as well as logos and headlines.

Inflatables are a form of outdoor display. Winston has a 70-foot pack of cigarettes that floats over major events like golf tournaments. They can even be combined with more conventional billboards to create some eerie effects. Golden Lights cigarettes uses a huge inflated hand that appears to be taking a cigarette from a pack that is painted on a regular billboard.

The term *spectacular* is used to describe billboards that do everything. They have extensions, they may be designed in 3-D, they have moving parts and sometimes electronic messages. They are custom designed and custom built for a particular advertiser and left up for a much longer time than the usual 30 days.

Exhibit 14-2: The Corvette billboard used motorized extensions that showed the car "opening up." (Courtesy of Chevrolet Motor Division)

14.3 TRANSIT

Transit advertising is a general category that includes all forms of posters and advertisements developed for the different types of transit and transportation systems.

Exterior Transit

"Moving billboards" is a phrase used to describe a type of poster or billboard that is mounted on some vehicle. The *exterior* panels on buses and cabs are considered moving billboards. Poster panels also appear on delivery trucks that can be rented for a commercial message. Buses usually rent space on the top and rear. Delivery trucks provide space on the side. In transit advertising, these exterior posters are sometimes called **dash cards**.

dash cards: exterior advertisements mounted on the sides of subway cars, cabs, and buses

Buses follow scheduled routes, usually on main thoroughfares. Their message can be targeted somewhat by "buying" a certain route. Taxis and delivery trucks travel randomly through the city, and targeting is impossible.

These messages are designed to be seen by people who are outdoors—pedestrians and drivers of other vehicles. Like billboards, they are seen in a flash. There is no time to study the message unless the vehicle happens to be stopped at a stoplight. The idea has to be simple and clear and the copy has to be short and sweet.

Painted buses. An innovation in exterior transit advertising is the "painted bus." In some cities, the local bus company will let a company rent the message space on an entire bus—the exterior as well as the interior. This bus travels a regular route and also can be used by the advertiser for appearance at and transportation to special events. Some transit companies will even let you paint the entire bus. Your message is not limited to standard panels on the front, side, rear, and top of the bus. That's a real creative challenge to a designer.

Trucks. A new concept called "Truck 'n Display" has been developed by a Phoenix firm. This company has a fleet of independent truckers who will rent the side panels of their trucks for commercial messages. These messages can be planned according to the truckers' regular routes— east coast, west coast, cross country, and so on. They are seen by highway drivers as well as by residents in the cities they pass through.

Another variation on truck display is used by the Advan company in San Francisco, Los Angeles, and Seattle. Advan contracts with local delivery truck companies making regularly scheduled runs. Predictably the trucks are on the highways during morning and evening rush hours and at shopping malls, the financial district, and commercial areas during the day. Advertisers have also found that the trucks give visibility in areas that restrict outdoor boards, like Marin County.[4]

Interior Transit

Car cards. We've described the exterior transit signs under the heading of moving billboards. Now let's talk about the interior signs, or **car cards**. Buses rent space in racks above people's heads and down the side of the doors. The space above is generally standardized at 11 inches by 28 inches, although some cards are as long as 84 inches.

car cards: smaller advertisements mounted inside buses and subway cars

Interior transit is entirely different from exterior in concept and use. Car cards are viewed by a captive, and often bored, audience. They will read these messages as a relief from the tedium of the trip. The messages don't have to be short; they do have to be read at a distance, so legibility is important.

Car cards reach an unusual audience—people who aren't traveling in personal cars. They are usually the young (students riding to school), the elderly, and the poor. In major metropolitan areas, particularly those with subways like New York and Boston, the audience makeup may shift radically. These commuters are often white- and pink-collar workers, as well as executives—a much more upscale audience.

Electronic panels. A new type of interior advertising medium is electronic panels, which are located in taxis mounted behind the driver and facing the passengers. These electronic panels can change and may someday be interactive. To avoid complaints from an unhappy captive audience, many of these systems now carry announcements of events and traveler's information as well as ads.

Subway advertising. The New York City subway greets 5 million adults an average of 34 times a month. Subway or some other form of mass transit advertising exists in New York as well as Boston, Washington, DC, Atlanta, Chicago, and San Francisco. The "metro" in Paris or the "tube" in London is an essential means of getting around the city. Thousands of riders are exposed to subway advertising every day.

Experts suggest that short ad copy should be used for posters in the underground hallways, while longer copy can be used on platforms where people stand to wait. Since the average ride for people on the New York subway is 25 minutes, lengthy copy can be used in the cars. Jodi Yegelwel, director of advertising for New York's subway system, also recommends that the copy be oriented to the subway environment.[5] An example is an ad for NYNEX Yellow Pages which said, "The only thing it can't help you find is a seat on this train." Another successful poster showed a tired man with the line, "When it's 102° in here . . ." followed by a second panel showing two cans of Miller beer on ice with the line, "it's nice to know that it's 42° in here."

14.4 PACKAGING

Packaging is your message's last chance. It confronts the shopper right at that moment of purchase. The importance of packaging has grown with self-service retailing where people pick and choose their own products. Prior to the spread of supermarkets in the fifties most ads instructed shoppers to "ask for" a product; now they are told to "look for" a product. That means the package takes the place of the salesperson; this applies to a wide variety of shopping situations from supermarkets to discount stores, convenience stores, department stores, and even hardware stores.

The New Shopping Environment

This retail revolution has spawned a whole new generation of self-directed shoppers who know what they are looking for and how to compare products on the basis of information given on the shelf and package. The self-service trend has developed along with an increase in new product development. The modern supermarket, according to the Food Marketing Institute, stocks some 17,459 items, with 2,200 new products added each year. Shoppers move through this crowded environment scanning at the rate of 300 items a minute.[6]

facing: the location and size of the position a product occupies on a shelf in a store

Shelf facings.   Most supermarket shelves aren't infinitely expandable, so there is tremendous pressure to get on the shelf and to get a good **facing**. Gerron Vartan, senior vice president of S&O Consultants, says, "The grocery aisle could well be the most competitive marketing environment in the world."[7] Experts claim that 80 percent of the buying decisions are made in the store and they occur at the shelf where the shopper is scanning all the products in a category at one time.

Immediate imagery.   While advertising lures shoppers to the store, the actual decision is made on the basis of the product's impression. R. Overlock Howe, president of a package consulting group, said, "In the store, immediate imagery takes precedence and the well designed package will sell itself to its targeted customer right there at the point of purchase."[8]

Packaging can be even more effective than advertising as a sales stimulus. According to Meredith Blau, a packaging consultant, "Effective package design will generate many more impressions in its lifetime than the most expensive advertising campaign."[9] She explains that this is because packaging works continuously, 24 hours a day, 7 days a week, at home and in the store. Anthony A. Parisi, director of the corporate design center of General Foods, agrees and says, "At General Foods, we realize we have more packaging impressions in the marketplace than we have advertising impressions."[10]

Strategy   ***Communication.***   The most important function of packaging is fast and easy communication. It creates identification and recognition. It has to convey instantly what the product is and what category it is in. Allan Glass, a package designer, says, "The package has to communicate quickly what the product is." He explains, "Let's say a customer wants to buy Instant Quaker Oatmeal. There are 11 or 12 different flavors to choose from. People should be able to find Instant Quaker Oatmeal and then find the flavor they want. If they want maple and brown sugar, they shouldn't get home and find they bought raisins and cinnamon." He concludes, "It's really the job of the package designer to make the consumer's decision as easy a task as possible."[11]

Consumer problems.   Packages can solve marketing communication problems. Frederick Mittleman tells a story about the redesign of the package for the Danish national drink, Aalborg Akvavit.[12] The product is supposed to be poured from an ice-encased bottle. The distributors found that, while sales were increasing, American consumers weren't serving it correctly. A new design by Mittleman's firm used a picture of an ice-encased bottle to explain how to serve the product. The package became an important element in the distributor's education program for the brand.

Action. The primary objective of most packaging is to stimulate action. Walter Landor, a famous packaging designer and president of the company named after him, says, "The continuous challenge to us is not only to create something that looks better to most people, but to make the product action-oriented."[13] He says the package should stimulate an active desire to buy the product, even when seen for the first time.

Appetite appeal is particularly useful for food products and impulse categories such as snacks, ice cream, and cookies. Packaging for impulse categories often incorporates devices creating high appetite appeal. Cookies generally use clear wrappers to show the appetizing product or printed bags whose visuals of chunky chocolate chips or flaky coconut convey the appeal of the product. A special report on packaging in *Marketing Communications* observes that "A mouthwatering photo or illustration can turn an indecisive shopper into a hungry snacker."[14]

Targeting and segmenting. Packaging can also be used to cue targeting and segmentation decisions. Originally grocery products were aimed at the same mass market of women 18 to 49. Now, according to Michael Purvis, president of a San Francisco design firm, "Most products are created with smaller target groups in mind, so food categories are segmented by such things as price, diet, and value-added benefits."[15] Even such basic markets as frozen vegetables, beer, soft drinks, detergents, and ice cream have become highly segmented.

In an effective segmentation strategy, the package is a key factor in sorting out the audience. For example, Nabisco Brands consulted Lister Butler,[16] recognizing that several of its cookie products were not reaching the right audience. The products had more sophisticated appeal and higher cost than the average brand and were all managed separately with different packages and advertising. Lister Butler created a common graphic message that said the brands were luxury products and well worth the higher price. A golden background immediately communicated quality. A standardized product line identifier, "Dessert Cookies," in an elegant typeface suggested that the products were a treat for guests, rather than for the kids. The new packages projected a mass of gold clear down the cookie aisle and the brand was no longer lost in the crowd.

Price and quality. One important role of packaging is to cue the price-value relationship. As in the Nabisco example, the design of the package, in particular, should reflect the price. The distinctive package used by "generic" products is a good example. The black and white package with its emphasis on product category and lack of brand identification is one of the most easily recognized packages in the store. It's lack of expensive graphics broadcasts its low-price message.

Brand visibility. The impact of a line of products with a consistent look is called **billboarding**, and it is used in package design to create visibility for a brand. A billboard effect is created by rows and rows of packaged goods with repeated facings and with clear product identification using color, graphics, and distinctive brand names. Nabisco's "wall of gold" on the cookie aisle is an example of how packaging can be used

billboarding: creating visual impact by massing a line of products with a consistent brand image to create a billboard effect. Massing products with consistent design images across a variety of lines creates a strong brand presence.

Differentiation and positioning.   Most products have to stand out even when they stand alone surrounded by competitors. The objective here is positioning and brand differentiation. The package must cue the distinctiveness and uniqueness of the product by highlighting such copy lines as "Cottoney soft," "Keeps you drier than all other antiperspirants," "Cleans hard water stains," or "Offers ten times the cleaning power." These short, powerful pieces of copy use the package to advertise the primary selling point or USP.

Product personality.   Another part of positioning through packaging is the communication of a product personality. Mrs. Butterworth's distinctive brown bottle with its human figure shape says this is a thick, rich syrup that someone cares about. The Keebler packages with the tree-house logo and Ernie the Elf communicate the fantasy developed in the advertising.

Personality is one of a set of emotion-based attitudes that are conveyed by packaging. An article in the British magazine *Campaign* says that because of its emotional impact and its important role in establishing brand personality, "Packaging is a far more powerful communication tool than even its enthusiasts realise." The author, Francis Lancaster, managing director of the London Design Partnership, explains that packaging is like "body language"; the consumer intuitively decodes the package to arrive at an understanding of the brand.[17]

Lancaster explains that people match their "attitude to the task" to the product's personality. Targeting and product personality are very much interwoven. For example, people who are essentially combative in their attitude toward housework—in other words, they "declare war" on dirt—will actively seek out brands with packaging that reflects this aggressiveness. Bold, confident color combinations (like red and blue), industrial-type products, and hard lines match this consumer attitude. For others for whom cleaning is a continuous process of polishing up, a more gentle approach might be appropriate. Furniture polish and dusting sprays, for example, might have pictures of antiques, while floor cleaners would show kittens and little kids on the floor.

Visual Equity

Brand.   A long-time brand has equity built up in its visual image. The little girl in yellow under the large umbrella has symbolized Morton Salt for a hundred years. The symbol is instantly recognizable (see Exhibit 14-3). That's brand equity. Marlboro's red-and-white package and Hershey's brown wrapper are other classic examples. More recently the L'Eggs egg-shaped hosiery container and the Celestial Seasonings tea box have created brand equity for their products. The most famous example is Coca-Cola, with its distinctive typeface, the use of red and the "wave" Coke graphic on the can, and the unusual bottle shape—all important aspects of Coke's brand equity.

Kodak has gone to great lengths to protect its brand equity. It has done everything in its power, including litigation, to keep competitors from introducing yellow film packaging. Jonathan Prinz, executive vice president of the Schechter Group in New York, explains that Kodak's vigilance makes sense. "Film is generally packaged in very small cartons and then viewed by consumers at a distance, making color the single most important graphic element for brand distinction." He concludes, "If Kodak were to lose control of its yellow, it might very well lose control of its leadership position as well."[18]

Category.   There is a visual language operating behind many product categories. Green, for example, is taboo on bread, where it would signify mold (except for Italian bread, where it is used with red and white to connote the Italian flag). Green *is* commonly used with vegetables, where it signifies *fresh*. Green also means lemon-lime in soft drinks, menthol in cigarettes, and decaffeinated coffee. Warm colors like red, gold, yellow, and ochre are commonly used for crackers and cookies. Terra cotta red is used for Mexican products. A white background in soft drinks means a diet or sugar-free beverage. Blue is used for laundry and cleaning products to signify a whitening agent.

These color equities for the category are usually established by the brand leader. Jonathan Prinz points out that General Foods' Sanka created the decaffeinated coffee market and then lost control of it because of a color change in the category designation.[19] Sanka was originally introduced with a predominantly orange package. Then, after decades of dominance, its competitor Nestlé introduced both its Nescafé and Tasters' Choice decaffeinated entries in green packaging. Despite Sanka's former position as leader, General Foods lost control of the segment's visual language as other players adopted the segment's new language. Most decaffeinated coffee packaging, including General Foods' own Maxwell House, is now green.

Package Design   *Construction.*   Technological change has had a major impact on the packaging industry, and packages are no longer limited to tin cans that have to be opened with can openers and to rectangular cardboard boxes. Packages can be made of plastic or Styrofoam, as well as cardboard and aluminum. They can be clear, shrink-wrapped plastic or they might contain a plastic "window" that reveals the product. Recent innovations include pull tabs (see Exhibit 14-4), plastic squeeze bottles, boil-in-bags, crush-proof bags for fragile things like potato chips, Ziplock bags, unbreakable bottles like those used with shampoos, vacuum-seal plastic bags, and "blister cards" that seal small products under a clear plastic bubble.

Order.   The primary role of design is to bring order to the confusion of elements that are found on a typical package. Roy Parcels, founder of Dixon & Parcels, explains that surface designs must encompass quite disparate elements: trademark and brand name designs, typography for package copy, illustrations, trade characters, advertising slogans, neck bands, closures and instruction panels, as well as color schemes and color coding.[20] Ivan Chermayeff says that graphic communication in package de-

No salt salts like Morton Salt salts.

Exhibit 14-3: The Morton Salt package has built tremendous visual equity for the brand retaining the little girl in yellow, the oversize umbrella, the blue background, and the famous slogan through a number of package redesigns over the years. (Courtesy of Morton Salt Division of Morton Thiokol, Inc.)

Exhibit 14-4: The "Buschhh" campaign ties the name of the product to the sound of the pull-tab on a can being opened. The package itself becomes the focal point of the creative concept. (Courtesy of Anheuser-Busch, Inc.)

sign "is essentially one of creating order, or at least a semblance of order, in a most complex situation."[21]

The complexity of designing one package is compounded by the need to establish a consistent look, a design system, for a line of products within a brand. The Keebler line includes all kinds of cookies and crackers and yet there is a distinctive format for the brand. The same thing is true for the various Green Giant products and their packages. Here the designer's challenge is to create differentiation for the line without destroying consistency for the brand.

Testing. Most package design is studied and evaluated by placing dummy boxes on shelves in stores and using them in focus groups. These studies test visibility, consumer choice, and consumer attitudes. Clive Chajet describes a testing method called T-scope testing, in which consumers view slides showing various aspects of the existing product package and then identify the product after viewing just one segment. Chajet explains that a designer can determine from such information which are the most memorable elements of the package.[22]

flexography: a type of lithography used for printing on irregular surfaces

holography: a laser-produced image which is photographically reproduced in three dimensions and appears to move

Production. Most packaging is printed using either silkscreen or lithography. High-quality graphics may even call for six- to seven-color lithography. **Flexography**, a type of lithography used for printing on irregular surfaces, is often employed in packaging.

The latest advance in packaging is laser-produced **holography**, which photographically reproduces three-dimensional images that appear to move. At present this technology is being used on credit cards because it makes the cards hard to counterfeit. Some experts predict that this technology will soon be in use on packages.[23]

Bruce Snyder, a Londoner, who is the owner of a holography company named Holomart, hopes to bring animated three-dimensional pictures to items as commonplace as food packages and candy bar wrappers. Snyder predicts that when you reach for the breakfast cereal in a few years, a life-size face of the latest pop idol could turn toward you from the package and smile. A sunflower could wave at you from the margarine lid, and an animated cartoon could draw your attention to a pot of yogurt.

14.5 DISPLAYS

Display advertising includes a variety of categories of media designed to get a message "on display" in some special kind of environment, such as a retail store or a trade show. Displays are not measured media, they are not standardized, and they are as different as creative inventiveness allows. In a retail store, displays are either merchandise-oriented or designed to support a special theme. The theme may be seasonal, like back-to-school, or it may be topical, like fix-up or clean-up. Store displays bring advertising and merchandising together.

point-of-purchase displays: displays designed by the manufacturer and distributed to retailers in order to promote a particular brand, line, or special promotion

Point-of-purchase (PoP). **Point-of-purchase displays** are the most common form of product displays. Typically, the manufacturer provides them to the retailer as a way of getting special treatment for the display and shelving of the manufacturer's product. Typically, they wind up in the back room or dumpster because most retail stores are filled to overcrowding with signs and displays. In order for the local merchant to agree to use point-of-purchase displays, they must be well constructed, easy to maintain, and attractive. In addition, retailers will be more willing to use a PoP if there is some kind of incentive such as a special price deal.

Point-of-purchase displays can be any size, shape, or design. "Dump bins" contain special merchandise on sale. Another variation is the shelf basket, which is frequently used for paired merchandise; thus, a display of crackers might be attached to the cheese section of the cooler. Display racks and freestanding posters will be found at checkout counters. End-aisle displays are large, freestanding constructions. Display islands can be set up in the middle of an aisle or open area and also are self-contained (see Exhibit 14-5).

Point-of-purchase displays are unique in that customers are confronted with the message in the store at a moment when they are in a buying mood. Like the package, the display is the last chance for the manufacturer to stimulate the sale.

An example of a combined package and point-of-purchase display is the highly successful L'Eggs hosiery system. The combination of the words "legs" and "eggs" stimulated the idea of a small egg-shaped container that protects the hosiery. The innovative package was highly differentiating and also impossible to display in a normal hosiery section. In order to handle the innovative product, retailers also had to accept a freestanding display which was designed to handle the unusual shape, as it separated L'Eggs from the surrounding competition.

Swatch watches have used the same idea and designed separate counter and display sections to go into department stores. These resemble a booth or exhibit—an environment decorated to project the unique Swatch personality and graphics.

Signs and banners.   Retail stores exhibit a variety of different signs. Window posters announce special sales; they attract customers into the store and increase store traffic. Window posters also appear inside the store in glass cabinets—for example, coolers and freezers in grocery stores. Window displays contain arrangements of merchandise in an attractive setting. Also, large banners may hang overhead; they may even be outside on the face of the building. Banners are often used to provide thematic support for special sales events.

The Campus Source® pairs your advertisement with campus-relevant news

Exhibit 14-5:   The "Campus Source" is an electronics communication center developed by MarketSource for use on college campuses. The center is located in high-traffic locations and provides monthly campus-relevant activities plus a moving LED message about current events. Backlit, full-color advertisements are presented dramatically as part of the center.

Shelf displays. "Shelf talkers" are signs attached to shelves where merchandise is located. Often, these give only special price information, but they can also be used for thematic messages and merchandising tie-ins. They may be constructed with a simple fold that is tacked or taped to the top of the shelf. In some cases they may be mounted in metal frames. Sometimes they are elaborate forms that even contain prerecorded taped messages.

14.6 THEATER ADVERTISING

trailers: advertisements that precede a movie's feature film

Many movie theaters are now accepting commercials to run before the feature film. Called sponsored **trailers**, these advertisements are similar to television commercials, only longer and more entertaining. A 60-second spot is the minimum length used in theaters, and some trailers may run 90 seconds or even 2 minutes. The Screenvision Cinema Network is the nation's largest cinema advertising sales company, offering 5,000 screens in 185 markets from coast to coast.

Creative Dimension

The difference between a television commercial and a trailer, according to Terry Laughren, president of Screenvision, is a creative requirement written into the contract. He says, "We have storyboard approval and final cut approval of what goes on our screens." Laughren says that the company actually turns away advertisers who want to run typical television advertising on the big screens. Laughren tells them, "It's probably going to be very successful for your client, but it isn't going to play well in front of a paying theater-going audience."[24]

According to Laughren, theater advertising must be something very special; it must be entertaining and very visual."You won't see supers in our commercials. You won't hear any voiceovers. Typically, you'll see great visuals and hear great music." Screenvision commercials offer high drama, comedy, and toe-tapping music. Laughren insists that the audience doesn't consider them to be commercials. Among the major advertisers who have used trailers are Pepsi, General Electric, Kodak, Dr. Pepper, and Toyota.

The Theater Audience

Theater advertising captures an audience that is hard to reach by conventional television advertising, such as teenagers and young, active people who are generally out of the home and on the go. However, the important audience factor is the attention and concentration generated by the theater environment. The projection of larger-than-life images in a darkened theater is totally unlike the experience of watching television. The impact of the large screen makes for a compelling image that commands total attention. It is very difficult for the audience to turn off or tune out whatever is happening on the screen. Screenvision says it offers "recall that is outrageously effective."[25] That is also one of theater advertising's biggest problems and the reason Screenvision maintains such tight controls on the nature of the message. Some people resent the compelling nature of the message. Because they have paid money for entertainment, they dislike being forced to watch a commercial.

14.7 INNOVATIVE MEDIA

New and novel media are constantly being developed as vehicles for advertising messages. This is one of the most creative areas in advertising. "There's no question that more of our ad dollars are going to nontraditional media," says George Mahrlig, Campbell Soup Company's director of media services.[26] One reason is the dramatic rise in the cost of television spots while the network audience is steadily shrinking. Another reason is the clutter problem in conventional media. On television this is aggravated by the increase in the number of 15-second spots. But the primary reason is that these new media reach segments that are difficult to reach otherwise.

Alternative Media
Skywriting, airplane banners, balloons, blimps, race cars and drivers' clothes, sports outfits, sandwich boards, bill statements, and matchbook covers have been around for a long time. Now ads are appearing on parking meters, pay phones, subway clocks, postage meter indicia, postage stamps, airplanes, sailboats and yachts, and even Russian spaceships and astronaut suits. Anything that can carry a message and commands the attention of a valued audience can function as an advertising medium (see Exhibit 14-6).

Ski slopes have toyed with the idea of installing billboards next to the lifts. Motorboats with billboards mounted on the side race up and down in front of public beaches. Flatbed trucks with inflatables (like those used for floats in parades) cruise metropolitan streets. In Britain recording groups are selling paid ads on their album covers.

Shopping carts in many stores now have advertising panels mounted on the front of the cart. These confront other shoppers who are passing by. Shopping carts are also going electronic. The videocart, with a small screen attached to a grocery cart, is becoming popular in many stores as an electronic point-of-purchase medium. The cart has a laptop computer screen on its handle which provides information about merchandise on sale in the store. With a keyboard or touch screen, it could become an interactive information source. As shoppers push videocarts down the aisles, they could trigger ads for brands on the shelves they passed. Tie-in promotion ads could also be used—for example, a special on hot-dog buns when the cart is near the hot dogs.[27]

National Indoor Advertising is a company that specializes in "captive-audience" advertising. There's no escaping these magazine-page-sized ads that are placed in clusters of four on the doors of restrooms, a location NIA feels is a totally boring environment. The company's slogan is "The ad you can't ignore." The ads are tastefully framed and mounted in Plexiglas on the plaster, metal, or tile walls and doors of restrooms. The ads are graffiti-resistant, and the patented panels can be removed only by NIA personnel with a special solvent.[28]

Video
The video revolution is sparking a number of innovative opportunities for presenting advertising messages. Hotels are offering spots on their in-house television systems and receiving interest in sports, stocks, travel,

Blow up your ideas.

Macy*s Parade Spider-Man® Balloon: ™ & ©1987 Marvel Entertainment Group, Inc.

Whether the assignment is creating a presence at a major sporting event, commanding buyer attention at the point of purchase or influencing important prospects at key trade shows, Aerostar professionals can help you accomplish your objectives.

When it comes to the extraordinary, we are privileged to work with designs and models created by Macy*s Parade, constructing giants that float down Broadway on Thanksgiving Day. This willingness to meet imaginative challenges carries Aerostar into the future.

Call or write for details now.

AEROSTAR™
INTERNATIONAL, INC.
"Ballooning's Leader Since 1960"

A Subsidiary of
RAVEN®
industries, inc.

1813 "E" Ave. • P.O. Box 5057 Sioux Falls, SD 57117-5057 • (605)331-3500

Exhibit 14-6: Aerostar International designs and manufactures helium inflatables, cold air product replicas, and hot air balloons. These attention-getting media provide ''high'' product visibility and awareness.

and tourist information and extremely high-class classifieds. "Most businesspeople who are in hotels are curious about other job opportunities," says Rob Kircher, CEO of Targetvision, an executive recruitment company.[29]

Product placements in movies are also becoming very important.[30] Reese's pieces appeared in *E.T.*, *Bull Durham* had some 50 product references including Miller beer, Budweiser, Pepsi, Jim Beam bourbon, and Oscar Mayer. *Ghostbusters II* included references to Kraft Miracle Whip, Hefty trash bags, and Windex. Lark cigarettes appeared in the James Bond film *License to Kill*, and Marlboro appeared in *Superman II*.

These new adaptations of the video medium are also moving into the home. Spots are showing up on the beginning of videotaped movies. Diet Pepsi started it all with its *Top Gun*–inspired commercial that appeared on the *Top Gun* video. Nestle's "Sweet dreams" spot for its Alpine White chocolate bar was placed on the *Dirty Dancing* videotape.[31]

These advertisers and Vestron, a leading distributor of videocassettes, believe that video rentals represent a new ad medium; some are even calling it "the fourth network." Riding on this momentum is Videotagg, an advertisement that is designed to fit in either a horizontal or a vertical format on the outside of rental video plastic boxes. ADcorp, the company behind Videotagg, estimates that the rental for these boxes ranges from 12 to 18 times per quarter per movie.

Some companies are actually producing their own home videos as extended commercials. Marshall Field & Co. has used the medium for a direct marketing campaign to announce the opening of its San Antonio store. Cadillac has used videocassettes to introduce Allante, General Motors' first ultraluxury car. Soloflex has also used a 22-minute informational cassette to market its $900 home gym machine to potential buyers who request it through an advertised toll-free number.[32]

A lot of the excitement in advertising today is found in nontraditional media; advertisers are continuing to search for media that are highly targeted and less cluttered than traditional media.

SUMMARY

This chapter reviewed the other important media of advertising, media other than print and broadcast.

1. Poster design is a respected art form.
2. There are two types of outdoor boards: poster panels and painted bulletins.
3. Billboard features include few words, bold graphics, legible type, and functional uses of color.
4. Transit advertising is designed with short copy for people on the move, with longer copy for people waiting, and with more lengthy copy for riders.
5. Because of the power of immediate imagery, packaging can have more impact on a sale than advertising.

6. Packaging has many roles: communicate and identify, solve problems, stimulate action, target and segment, establish price and quality levels, ensure brand visibility, differentiate and position, and establish a product or brand personality.

7. A package expresses brand equity and the visual language of the category.

8. Point-of-purchase displays are unique three-dimensional designs.

9. Theater advertising is entertaining and uses high drama and comedy and great music, and it is highly visual.

10. Innovative media are being used to hit hard-to-reach segments and to avoid clutter in traditional media.

NOTES

1. Bruce Stauderman, "The Great Outdoors," *Advertising/Marketing Review*, February 1986, pp. 8–15.
2. Ibid.
3. Melanie Johnston, "City Limits Curb Outdoor Ads," *Advertising Age*, October 31, 1988, p. 42MW.
4. Alice Z. Cuneo, "Boards Hit the Road on Bay Area Trucks, Plan Move to L.A.," *Advertising Age*, August 17, 1987, p. 36.
5. Barbara Watson, "How to Reach a Very Specific Market Target Rather Efficiently," *Madison Avenue*, November 1985, pp. 98–99.
6. Lori Kesler, "Successful Packages Turn Medium into Message," *Advertising Age*, October 13, 1986.
7. Ibid.
8. Lori Kesler, "Shopping Around for a Design," *Advertising Age*, December 28, 1981, p. S1.
9. Meredith Blau, "Package Design Becoming a Lost Art," *Advertising Age*, November 16, 1987, p. 18.
10. Frederick Mittleman, "Design: Part of the Total Package," *Advertising Age*, December 28, 1981, p. S8.
11. Allan Glass, "A Great Design Will Only Sell a Bad Product One Time," *Chicago Tribune Magazine*, February 19, 1989, p. 38.
12. Mittleman, op. cit.
13. Andjela Kessler, "Walter Landor's Design for Living: Subtlety Sells," *Adweek*, October 18, 1982, p. 34.
14. C. Gerron Vartan and Judith Rosenfeld, "Winning the Supermarket Wars: Packaging as a Weapon," *Marketing Communications*, May 1987, pp. 31–34.
15. Kesler, October 13, 1982, op. cit.
16. Vartan and Rosenfeld, op. cit.
17. Francis Lancaster, "Body Language in Packages," *Campaign*, September 29, 1988, pp. 29–30.
18. Jonathan J. Prinz, "Controlling Visual Cues Forces Category Foes to Play Catch-Up," *Marketing News*, September 12, 1988, p. 17.
19. Ibid.
20. Roy Parcels, "Ten Steps to Profitable Packages," *Advertising Age*, September 5, 1977, pp. 31–33.
21. Ivan Chermayeff, "Attitudes in Design," *d/a*, 53:3 1963, pp. 24–29.
22. Theodore J. Gage, "Designs for the '80s: Bold, Simple," *Advertising Age*, December 28, 1981, p. S2.

23. Jane Bird, "Holograms to Bring Life into Packaging," *The London Sunday Times*, November 27, 1988, p. 9.

24. Robert Goldrich, "BJK&E's Frankfurt on Cinema Ads and Home Video Prospects," *Back Stage*, December 12, 1986, pp. 1, 39.

25. "Big Screen Ads Put Showbiz First," *Television/Radio Age*, May 26, 1986, p. 169.

26. "'Ad Space' Now Has a Whole New Meaning," *Business Week*, July 29, 1985, p. 52.

27. "Videocart Shopping Cart with Computer Screen Creates New Ad Medium That Also Gathers Data," *Marketing News*, May 9, 1988, p. 1; "Hard-Sell Shopping Carts," *Newsweek*, July 18, 1988, p. 46; and Brian Egli, "Go-Carts to Help with the Groceries," *The London Times*, October 4, 1988, p. 32.

28. Bruce Stauderman, "New Channels to the Mind," *Advertising/Marketing Review*, May 1986, p. 6; and David Luhman, "Captive-Audience Advertising Gets 'Up Close and Personal,'" *Boulder Camera/Business Plus*, April 21, 1987, p. 5.

29. Lenore Skenazy, "Forget Blue Flicks: Want Ads Bow on Hotel Room TV Sets," *Advertising Age*, October 27, 1986, p. 102.

30. Joanne Lipman, "Outcry Over Product Placement Worries Movie, Ad Executives," *Wall Street Journal*, April 7, 1989, p. B6.

31. "Nestle, Vestron Deal a Dream Come True," *Advertising Age*, January 11, 1988, p. 55.

32. Christopher Colletti, "Videocassettes Flex Their Marketing Muscle," *Advertising Age*, November 17, 1986, p. S20.

SITUATIONS AND DECISIONS

15

Advertising Situations

KEY POINTS

- Direct advertising acts as a salesperson and sells directly to the consumer.
- Retail advertising is local and focuses on the store.
- Institutional advertising focuses on the corporate image.
- Business-to-business advertising sells to the trade.
- Public service advertising is created for good causes.
- Promotion stimulates immediate action and encourages support by the trade.
- International advertising focuses on similarities in needs among people, rather than national differences.

We've talked about the basics of creative advertising in discussions of such topics as creative thinking, strategy, copywriting, and design. We also discussed the various media and the implications each medium has for the development of the message. Now we are going to look at various advertising situations and analyze them in terms of the implications for the development of your advertising message.

A number of situations are clearly identified in advertising as specialized areas needing specialized handling. *Direct advertising* is a huge business and, in some ways, is the most exact and successful of all areas of advertising; *retail advertising* focuses on the store in a local community; *institutional advertising* deals with such topics as corporate image and public service advertising; *business-to-business* advertising is a specialized area on which many creative people and agencies concentrate; *public service advertising* is run for the good of the community; *promotion in-*

cludes publicity as well as the merchandising messages created for sales promotion programs; *international advertising* is a developing area because of the increase in global marketing programs.

15.1 DIRECT ADVERTISING

direct response advertising: advertising that solicits a response from the prospect without the intervention of a store or salesperson

Direct advertising is both a type of advertising situation and a type of advertising media. It uses the shortest communication route to the consumer. The message is beamed directly from the marketer, bypassing any sales or retail staff. Its objective is to stimulate an immediate response to the message. The response may be in the form of buying the product, sending in for more literature, calling to place an order or request information, or visiting a sales location. The message is totally controlled by the advertiser, and it is addressed to a carefully defined audience who is thought to include primary prospects for this message.

Direct response demonstrates, more than other media, how a message can sell a product by itself. Because direct response is a self-contained sales message, it has to deliver all the information and all the incentives needed to make the sale.

What we are calling "direct advertising" is also known as direct response, direct mail, mail order, or direct marketing. **Direct marketing** is the broadest term and involves factors other than communication. **Direct mail** and **mail order** focus on the role of the postal service as a delivery medium. *Direct response* comes the closest to including all of the relevant media. We will discuss direct response advertising, catalogs, and direct mail.

direct marketing: a selling method that establishes a one-on-one relationship with the customer

direct mail: a form of advertising that uses the mail to carry the message

mail order: a form of marketing that uses the mail to deliver the product

Direct response can be used in all kinds of advertising situations; the critical characteristics include a carefully targeted audience, controlled communication from the advertiser to the prospect, a direct response, and no intermediate sales staff (although one of the responses may include getting prospects to visit a dealer or showroom). The advertising message is the primary communication with the consumer.

Direct response is used for all kinds of advertising: consumer, business, or institutional. It is addressed to individuals at home and at work. It is also addressed to businesses and institutions. It may sell a product, service, or idea. It is common in business-to-business marketing.

Growth   Direct response is a dynamic area and a high-growth one within the advertising industry. For example, Leo Burnett reported that one-third of its print production was for direct response advertising. The agency got into direct response in order to provide a full range of services to Marlboro. Burnett's message to its staff is, "You had better learn direct."[1]

More women are working, and their time is too precious to spend on shopping trips. People who work would rather spend their free time at home or in some kind of interesting leisure activity. That's true for men as well as women. In terms of lifestyle changes, direct response advertising is popular because it permits the convenience of *armchair shopping*.

There are some other technological changes that have contributed to the growth of direct response advertising. One is the *credit card ex-*

plosion of the sixties. Another is the *800 number*, which permits toll-free ordering. Direct response research has found that using a toll-free number will increase the response rate by as much as 20 percent.[2] The last, and perhaps most important, technological change is the *computer*. It is possible for marketers to select extremely small but tightly targeted audiences for their products, a type of search and select process that would be impossible to do by hand.

The Audience

Selectivity. One of the advantages of direct response is that it uses a rifle rather than a shotgun. Lists of prospects are available in SRDS, although that is a limited service. A good list house will have considerably more choices. For example, one major house has over 3,500 occupational classifications on file and over 6 million establishments. Advo, one of the nation's largest direct response companies, has a database of 98 million households from which it can custom tailor lists. With the power of computer sorting, lists can be cross-compiled, merged, and purged to create a list designed specifically for precision targeting to the interested.

Stan Rapp and Tom Collins see the computerized database as revolutionizing advertising and marketing. In their book *Maxi Marketing* they explain, "The trend is as clear as the name on your checkbook. From mass marketing to segmented marketing to niche marketing to tomorrow's world of one-on-one marketing—the transformation will be complete by the end of the eighties."[3]

This "personal selling" is another of the direct response advantages. However, many professionals feel it is not being used to its full advantage. Alexander Kroll, president of Young & Rubicam, U.S.A., told a group of direct marketers that "In this most personal of all media . . . only a few direct marketers are engaged in truly personal selling." Kroll also pointed out that "direct marketing—by magazine, mail or TV—can fill the void of personal selling created by the extinction of the corner store."[4]

Clutter. Consumers are not only operating on impulse, they are also inundated. Most households get several pieces of direct response mail every day. Some find it offensive, others welcome it. Those who object to this mail can have their names taken off the lists. However, Sid Bernstein reported in his column in *Advertising Age* that there were more than twice as many people contacted who wished to be put on lists than to be taken off.[5]

The result of this overwhelming use of direct response advertising is clutter. In this case, advertising is a victim of its own success. In truth, most consumers see little and remember less. It may take several mailings to make an impression and thousands of impressions to generate one response.

Accountability

Direct response advertising is the most accountable of all because the effect of the ad is immediate sales. Every ad is its own test of pulling power. If you run the same ad with two different headlines or two different visuals, you receive concrete information on which one works best. There are no hunches, no guesswork about direct response advertising. And every direct response copywriter knows his or her work will be measured in the mail. It's not a business for the thin-skinned.

Exhibit 15-1: This ad that explains direct response television advertising is part of a self-promotion campaign by Precision Marketing Associations, a direct response marketing and advertising agency.

Because of the measuring power of direct response advertising, there are some fairly well established principles. While these findings are compiled from direct response advertising, they still represent the basics of good advertising. David Ogilvy, long a student of direct response, suggests that all creatives can improve their work by studying the techniques used in this area.[6]

Rules of thumb for direct response TV include be clear—let the people know exactly what the offer is and make the offer compelling. Without the offer, you have nothing to sell. Ask for the order—repeatedly. Show the phone number on screen as long as possible with TV advertising.

Another complication in planning a direct response piece is the need to estimate the total costs of the promotion as opposed to the total income from it. Every campaign is planned with a *break-even point*. The original testing is done to determine if the pulling power of the piece is strong enough to meet and pass that break-even point. This is fiscal planning, but it is still a reality that the creative staff has to keep in mind when planning direct response advertising.

Media   Direct advertising is found in all media—in magazines, television, newspaper, and radio. In all cases the advertisement contains some kind of device for facilitating a direct response by the consumer—a coupon, cutout and mail-in blank, or telephone number. Typically the copy is long because it has to deliver the full sales message, and the sales message is highly benefit-oriented.

Direct advertising works on radio and TV, too (see Exhibit 15-1). You're familiar with the TV ads for record sets. They run because they work. Now more upscale marketers are using direct response broadcasting. For example, Shearson Lehman Hutton has been running spots on golf tournaments to sell such offers as Zero-coupon Treasury bills. "As soon as the 800 number is given, the company has found that the phone starts ringing off the hook."[7]

Catalogs   Catalogs are specific types of direct response advertising. The Sears and Ward catalogs pioneered the techniques in the field. Even now most creative directors will tell you the best training a copywriter can have is to work for Sears writing catalog copy. More recently, the action in the catalog field has been with special interest publications produced by such marketers as L. L. Bean (sporting goods), Horchow (expensive collectibles), Victoria's Secrets (lingerie), Nieman-Marcus (exotic gifts), Williams-Sonoma (kitchenware), Hammacher Schlemmer (unusual home items), and Caswell-Massey (apothecary) (see Exhibit 15-2). Many of these books are works of art, in some cases coffee table pieces. A Christmas lingerie publication by Bloomingdale's, called *Sighs and Whispers*, became a collector's item.

Catalog copy.   The first thing to note in looking through a group of catalogs is that the copy must sell. As Richard Dubiel said in a paper on catalog advertising, "The emphasis on selling takes the blitz and glitter out of copy." He describes the "interplay" of the copy benefit and the accompanying selling points. "The selling points must support the benefit

BIANCA JAGGER'S SILK GOWN
Purchased November 19, 1987.

When it came time to go shopping one afternoon last fall, Bianca Jagger didn't hop into a limousine. Or even a taxi cab.

Instead, she hopped on her exercise bike. And after pedalling a mile with the Spiegel Catalog resting on the handlebars, she found just what she wanted.

To receive your copy of the current Spiegel Catalog, simply call toll-free 1-800-345-4500 and ask for catalog 888 ($3.00).

Exhibit 15-2: The ''Bianca Jagger'' ad for Spiegels is a print ad that ran in women's magazines. It defines the personality of the catalog as it targets a particular segment of the women's market.

and make the copy believable.'' He calls this approach ''nonflamboyant and disarmingly simple.''[8]

L. L. Bean got started with the Maine Hunting Shoe®. Here is how its construction is described in the L. L. Bean catalog:

> Since 1912, we have been steadily improving our Maine Hunting Shoe®. Today we have the advantage of modern tanning techniques to produce the soft, easy-to-wear leather tops. The durable bottoms are specially compounded for us of tough, ozone-resistant rubber for longer wear. Full-grain cowhide uppers. Crepe rubber outsole permanently vulcanized to the vamp features Bean's famous Chain Tread.

The second point is brevity. Catalog copy, unlike other forms of direct response advertising, is written tight. An example is a short piece of copy for the Remington Fuzz-Away Shaver which appeared in an issue of the Campmor catalog. The copy identifies the benefit and then gives information about operation and important features:

> Shaves and saves cloths, drapes, upholstery, etc. Precision blades remove unsightly pills, lint, fuzz and frayer. Cordless, battery operated (uses 1 ''C'' battery not inc.) Wt. 3 oz. w/o batt. 4″ × 3″ × 1½″.

The need for brevity is complicated by the third characteristic of catalog copy—that it must be complete. You have to tell your audience as much as it needs to know to make a sale—no more, no less. Here's a sample from a fashion item in the Spiegel catalog. The copy describes a $90 coatdress:

> Subtly shaped in a career-wise blend of linen and cotton. With a painted, notched collar; rounded, padded shoulders and gold-tone button trim on front and sleeves. By Ambria®. Fully lined. Dry clean.

Another example for a Cordura Briefcase from the Campmor catalog demonstrates how a number of features can be described in a very limited space:

> A three compartment brief. Center section is unzippered, allowing easy access for both letter and legal size materials. Front panel has two compartments, both utilizing self-repairing nylon coil zippers. Cordura nylon 17″ × 12½″. Color: Royal. Wt. 10 oz.

Catalog copy is often written to a character count. The copywriter measures the block and estimates how many characters will fit on a line and how many lines will fit in the block. The copy is then written to fit those specifications—no more, no less. The editing is ruthless; every word must pay its way.

Bob Stone describes a catalog writer who was given the task of selling a toy lie detector in a Christmas toy catalog. The space allowed four lines of 22 characters each, but two of the lines had to be used for article number, shipping weight, and price. That left two lines. The writer's very successful copy was: ''It works! Measures emotions to spot fibs.''

Catalog design.   Catalogs are very graphic, and photos are an extremely important part of the message. Most people want to see what they are buying.

Bob Stone, in a column in *Advertising Age*, gave some suggestions on how to organize and design contemporary specialty catalogs.[9] His first suggestion is that you develop a theme for the book. Sometimes fashion books will use an exotic location such as the Isle of Capri or Marrakesh as a visual theme.

Then he suggested that you "lead with your best." In other words, find the most fascinating item in your list of merchandise and play it front and center. Strong positions, called "the hot spots," include front and back cover, inside front and back cover, middle spread, and pages before and after the order blank.

Direct Mail   Direct mail pieces can take several forms. They can be letters from a store to its customers or they can be from a major national marketer, like an insurance company, to anonymous names on a series of mailing lists. They can be postcards or eight typewritten pages. They can include samples, coupons, product literature, or any number of other inserted materials.

Direct mail usually uses a letter format, and the letters are written in a personal tone. The consumer is addressed personally and by name if possible. Informal address using lots of "yous" is also common. John Tighe, a specialist in direct mail copywriting, opened one letter for *Popular Mechanics* this way: "Good friend, this invitation isn't for deadbeats, rip-off artists or 'gentlemen' who hate to get their hands dirty. It's for the rest of us. It's for the guys who aren't afraid to get down under the sink with a pipe wrench. Guys who don't mind sticking their hands in the toilet tank to adjust the ball cock (because they know it's going to save a $16 plumber's bill).[10]

The pieces of a direct mail message are similar to the steps in the sales process. First it has to get attention, then create a need, show what the product looks like and how it works, anticipate questions and answer them, and inspire confidence and minimize risk. Finally it has to make the sale—explaining how to order and pay.

The message starts on the envelope with some kind of curiosity-provoking thought. To give you some idea how important the envelope is, Bill Jayme reports that he spends one-third of his time working on the envelope message.[11] He uses big, bold one-word teaser headlines that crystallize the sales appeal. For a *Business Week* mailing aimed at business people frustrated by better-informed associates, he used the word "DAMN." The word "MOUSETRAP" worked well for *Inc.*, a publication aimed at entrepreneurs. For over two decades, *Esquire* has been running one of Jayme's mailings with the word "PUZZLE" as a teaser on the envelope.

Direct mail copy.   While short copy is a hallmark of catalogs, long copy is typical of direct mail. Letters will often be four, six, or eight pages long, and research finds that people will read the entire letter. Another well-respected direct mail copywriter is Bob Jones. He wrote an eight-page letter offering reproductions of American pistols priced at $2,500 a pair. Sales from this letter hit $5 million.[12]

The message revolves around something direct response writers call ''The Offer.'' According to Bill Jayme, the offer is the reason-why theme that runs throughout the entire package. He suggests that when you plan a direct mail piece, you start with the envelope and then move to the order form. Those two pieces will force you to crystallize the offer. He says this sequence ''helps us to review the offer, analyze the offer, understand the offer and verbalize it.''[13]

Some other tried-and-true techniques have been outlined in direct response columns in *Folio* magazine written by Eliot DeY. Schein, president of Schein/Blattstein Advertising.[14] These techniques include always using a real stamp on the envelope rather than a printed indicia. An inner envelope, like those used with invitations, says this is an exclusive message. The signature should be handwritten and printed in blue ink; the more it looks like a real signature, the better. Include a free gift or some kind of incentive. Get them involved by having them insert a token or scratch off a number.

If you are asking them to buy something, specify that it is a no-risk offer, and that their money will be refunded if they don't like it. Include a P.S. at the bottom and use it to wrap up the appeal of the message and hit them again—no one can resist reading a P.S. If there's a special incentive, mention it in the P.S. If it's a donation, mention that it's tax-deductible.

Use inserts in the envelope as a way of reintroducing the selling point. A second letter can work like a testimony confirming what was in the first message. A separate brochure is a good way to present product facts. The order form should be separate and, once again, it should refer to the main selling point. This is your last chance to anchor your sales. Of course, you need to include either a business reply envelope or a business reply card with prepaid postage. Make it as easy as possible to place the order. If readers have to look for a stamp, you are likely to lose them.

15.2   RETAIL ADVERTISING

Retail advertising is primarily *local* in orientation. Even if the advertising is prepared by a giant national chain, the ads will still be run in local media for an audience that is selected primarily on the basis of its proximity to a local outlet. The ads focus on a store rather than a product or brand.

Media   Retail advertising is dominated by newspapers. Newspaper advertising is fast to produce, carries a tremendous amount of information, and is relatively inexpensive. It's the ideal medium for most retail marketing.

Direct mail is also used, both for merchandise news and store image advertising. Most major retailers prepare catalogs of their merchandise that are available in stores and mailed to their regular customers. They also mail ''stuffers'' to their credit card customers. These are image pieces or they announce a special sale or new line. Frequently, they give the regular customer advance information, which helps to build loyalty.

Television may be used—particularly by large retailers. Large and small stores use radio, which is good for frequent announcements of special events, such as grand openings and major sales. The radio jingle is also useful as an image-building message. It reminds the audience of the store and its distinctive personality, which should be clear from the style of the music.

Television is also good for news announcements describing special promotions. If a store can afford to use television for general merchandise advertising, it is also an excellent medium for depicting the product line. You can show what it looks like in motion and in living color. You can demonstrate how it works and what its benefits are.

Occasionally, retail advertising may also use outdoor and transit cards. These media are more enduring than newspaper or television advertising, so they are more appropriate for image advertising. A large department store, for example, may place an outdoor board on a major freeway or street leading to the store in the hopes of reaching customers who are on a shopping trip.

Merchandising support materials are also important, such as point-of-purchase displays, shelf talkers, store signs and banners, window posters, and shopping bags.

Objectives

Retail advertising operates directly on purchase behavior as its primary objective. It utilizes immediate action appeals such as price deals and special promotions.

Traffic. Surprisingly, the number one objective of most retail advertising is to build traffic. The goal is to get as many potential customers in the store as possible. They may come to look at the advertised merchandise, but while they are there they will also see unadvertised specials and products they had forgotten they needed, as well as items that appeal to spur-of-the-moment purchasing. Retailers use advertising to *get them in the store.*

The strategy underlying this objective of building traffic is to develop compelling reasons for the customer to hurry down to the store. This builds on the news and deadline orientation of local media. An ad may announce fashions for the upcoming season or holiday, using the seasonal peg to stimulate a shopping trip. Sales are the number one draw for most store advertising. A big sale with large markdowns will have a definite effect on store traffic. Special promotions can also draw a crowd.

Store image. The second major objective of retail advertising is to develop the store's personality. This image advertising may be a general institutional ad describing some key distinctive feature such as selection or quality of the lines carried. It may promote a general product category rather than specific merchandise. But the purpose is to differentiate the store in the competitive marketplace.

Every ad that runs speaks to the personality of the store. Stores such as Saks Fifth Avenue, Bloomingdale's, Nieman Marcus, Macy's, J. C. Penney's, and K-Mart all have personalities that have been carefully shaped over many years. Every ad looks like the store it represents; they all have a distinctive layout, use of art and type, and phrasing of copy. Even if the signature is covered, you can still recognize the store from the design of the ad. It doesn't matter whether the ad contains barbeques or business suits, there is a continuity in the design in print that mirrors the personality of the store, and it continues in broadcast advertising too (see Exhibit 15-3).

Price-quality relationship. Retailers have learned from years of doing business that there are certain pieces of information that consumers look for in retail advertising. The quality of the merchandise determines the respect the store will carry in the consumer's mind. An exclusive women's store is considerably different from a department store.

Most consumers understand the price-quality tradeoff: the higher the quality, the higher the price, and vice versa. Stores are positioned on a mental matrix that measures these two dimensions. For example, stores may be categorized as expensive but high quality, affordable but good value, or low price and either quantity sales or dubious value. The goal of most consumers is to get the best value they can afford, so they use both dimensions.

Creative Considerations

Big art. In designing print ads for retail advertising, the most important thing to remember is to play the art big. If you are selling merchandise, then the consumer wants to see it. Since this form of advertising functions as a respected shopping guide, you don't have to do anything cutesy to get the consumer's attention. The big decision is how best to depict the merchandise.

In retail advertising, the art dominates and the head and copy are supporting. The head should play up the news value. In other words, ask yourself, "What do I need to know or want to know about this product?" The headline points to this information of value. The body copy is for details. Explain the essential points that will affect decision making, such as durability, quality, construction, and style. Keep it factual. Be specific and avoid generalities.

Price. In retail advertising the price demands special attention. Consumers expect to find the price cited in every merchandise ad. Not only that, there is a whole visual language built on the treatment of the price. If it is printed in a typeface that is the same weight and size as the body copy, then the assumption is that you are trying to downplay the price. In other words, the price is not a selling point.

If price is an important angle, then it needs to be bigger and bolder than the rest of the type—the bigger and bolder it is, the more it signals a major savings. With sale prices, you need to give both the regular or suggested retail price and the reduced price.

To emphasize further the savings angle, also spell out the amount of the savings, preferably in the headline or in a subhead. Be exact. Don't say just "Big Savings"; instead say, "Save $5.00." Whenever you deal with value as a benefit, specify precisely what the value is. Nobody is impressed if you use a generality like "Good value" or "Best values in town" (see Exhibit 15-4). Pricing can also be employed to move the merchandise faster. Sale prices are a big draw, but multiple pricing is even stronger. For example, if an item is on sale for $3.50, you can put even more punch in the appeal by advertising three for $9.00.

Exhibit 15-3: The purpose of this ad is to heighten awareness of Marshall Fields' designer collections, rather than to sell specific merchandise. The art and copy reinforce the general mood of the collection with allusions to exotic settings and whimsical imagery. The ad successfully achieves a sense of mystery, intended to bring people into the store for a closer look.

Layout.   The store image is signaled immediately by the style of the layout. If it is busy, crowded, and cramped with lots of items and big bold type, then it is probably a discount or drug store—the kind of store that can discount prices by moving lots of inventory. In contrast, an ad that uses a delicate illustration, old-style Roman type, and lots of white space is probably for a store that sells expensive, high-quality merchandise. The layout speaks a language of its own.

Identity.   Store identification is another important part of the creative effort. In retail advertising, it isn't enough to promote merchandise; you also have to sell the store. It's not good if the audience remembers there is a big shoe sale but can't remember where.

Store identification, however, is not a selling premise. People untrained in advertising tend to stick the name of the store up at the top of the ad and let it serve as a headline. That violates the findings on how people read ads. True, they do start at the top and read down, but there has to be something interesting at the top to get them started reading. A store name won't do. The store name can be interwoven with the design and appear in the middle of the layout, but the most common position is at the bottom—for good reasons.

signature: the name of a store in distinctive typeface or style of lettering

Most stores have distinctive logos, called **signatures**. Like your own signature, the design is intended to reflect your distinctive style. Like all signatures, it is expected to be found at the bottom of a piece of communication. It's your last chance at the end to impress your audience with the name of the source or sponsor. That's a very valuable position and a very effective strategy. Every retail ad message, whether print or broadcast, should end with the name of the store—even if it was used earlier in the message. In television it is a good idea to superimpose the store name or signature at the very end, so that you have a visual reference to reinforce the name people heard.

Reference information.   In addition to the name of the store, there are certain other critical pieces of information that are part of the ID package and critical to the decision process. Location is very important, and usually it is better to give a location cue as well as a specific address. For example, you may want to say: "On the corner of 13th across from Safeway." That way your audience can develop a mental picture of the location and file it that way. It's much easier to remember than an actual address.

Store hours are another critical piece of information. How many times have you found yourself on a Saturday morning wondering if a certain store was open yet—or if it is open at all on Sunday. If you want people to shop at your store, give them all the information they need. You don't want to inadvertently turn away a customer at the door—and have the person go away disgusted. Credit card acceptance is an important part of the close.

And don't forget the phone number.

A Special Relationship

Product involvement.   People who work on the creative side of retail advertising have a special relationship with their products. Usually, the buyer will provide you with a sample. You can use it, feel it, try it

Cotton argyle sweater. $246. Sweep brim straw hat. $74.50. Floral cotton/linen scarf. $72.50. Double buckle canvas bag. $194.

The Woman's Shop at

Paul Stuart ®

Madison Ave. at 45th Street, New York City. 212•682•0320.

Exhibit 15-4: The Paul Stuart ad is a stylized still life that reflects the personality of the store as well as depicting specific clothing and accessories. Even though this is an upscale store, it still uses prices in its advertising.

on, and get to know the product intimately. The buyer will also provide you with the manufacturer's copy, with specifications and photographs. You can walk into the store and watch customers evaluating the product and even talk to them about what they want and don't want.

Feedback.   Furthermore, you have immediate feedback on the success of your ad. You can go back into the store the day it runs and see if there is any increased traffic at the counter. Most retail copywriters have fantasies about throngs of people lined up at the counter, all of them holding their clipped-out ad. The moment of truth is usually less exciting as you stand there and wait for someone, anyone, to ask about the product you described in last night's ad. But still you have the opportunity to see the actual results of your work and to notice the little increase of activity and the smile on the face of the buyer because the action at the counter is faster than normal.

15.3   INSTITUTIONAL/CORPORATE ADVERTISING

Institutional advertising focuses on the reputation of the corporation, association, or organization. Aside from advertising by institutions like universities and churches, this category includes corporate advertising to the financial or investment community, the business community, customers, and consumers. In addition to corporate image, institutional advertising includes advocacy or issue advertising.

Institutional advertising is one area where the professional concerns of public relations and advertising overlap. The corporate image is usually the concern of the public relations staff, and advertising specifically oriented toward corporate image usually is prepared by the advertising staff or agency. Obviously, there is a need here for maximum coordination. Progressive companies are establishing "marketing communications" departments to coordinate all advertising, promotions, and public relations activities with particular attention to the presentation of coordinated corporate images.

In general, most institutional advertising is geared more toward ideas, images, and attitudes than toward the sale of specific products (see Exhibit 15-5). The objectives are different for institutional and product advertising. That doesn't mean there is no bottom line or return on investment for corporate advertising. It does mean that the measurement is different. Corporations using institutional advertising measure success in terms of opinion change rather than sales.

Institutional advertising differs in another dimension: the time frame. Corporate campaigns run for decades rather than days. The advertising waves are often planned in terms of years. Research is conducted over long periods, using tracking methods to establish benchmarks and norms and to spot the changes. Corporate identity is a long-term investment.

Types of Institutional Advertising

Identity.   There are many reasons to develop institutional campaigns for a corporation, and just as many types of institutional advertising as there are reasons. One of the most common is *identity* advertising,

2000 years later, Christianity's biggest competition is still the Lions.

Before you sit down for an afternoon with the Lions, Bears, Dolphins, Rams, Cowboys or Vikings, come spend an hour with some very nice Christians in the love, worship and fellowship of Jesus Christ.
The Episcopal Church

Exhibit 15-5: The Episcopal Church Ad Project is an example of institutional advertising for an organization. The Ad Project has been creating hard-hitting ads like these since 1979. The project began at an Episcopal Church in Minneapolis, and church member Tom McElligott has been a major creative force in the development of the campaign. The ads feature bold, dramatic headlines with strong visual images. They seek to provoke questions and address particular groups, such as single people. (Courtesy The Episcopal Ad Project, St. John's Episcopal Church, 4201 Sheridan Ave. South, Minneapolis, MN 55410)

You can't meet God's gift to women in a singles' bar.

If the singles life sometimes leaves you feeling alone and empty, remember that God's gift to all women and men is Jesus Christ. Come join us in worship this Sunday in the Episcopal Church.
The Episcopal Church

where a company is trying to register who it is and what it does. This has become a serious problem with all the corporate buyouts, mergers, acquisitions, and diversifications. Beatrice has a long-running campaign with the slogan, "You've known us all along"; it highlights the various companies and brands under the corporate umbrella. ITT has an ad with the headline "All in the family" that features the logos of its various subsidiaries.

A company may elect to change its name, and that necessitates a new identity campaign. Likewise, a new company has to establish name recognition in the marketplace. All the "Baby Bell" companies had to undertake separate name campaigns after the big split-up. Navistar International, formerly International Harvester, created an ad entitled "Miracles still happen," which told how financial experts had written the company off but its employees pulled the company up by its bootstraps and put it back on its feet. The name change was the event on which the advertising was pegged.

Image. Closely related to identity advertising is *image* advertising, which attempts to develop a personality for a corporation, such as a good neighbor, a leader in technology, an innovator. For example, the US West ads all feature aggressive western symbols such as a group of cowboys riding thundering horses or two buffalos in head-to-head conflict. Hewlett-Packard uses people stories with the headline "What should you expect from a working partnership with Hewlett-Packard?" to personalize its computer business.

Advertising that focuses on accomplishments and potential is called capability advertising. Mike Turner, vice president and creative director of Ogilvy & Mather, explained, "Although it features a product, the intent of capabilities advertising is to sell the company. The logic is that if the products are good, so is the company, and vice versa."[15] The campaign for Goodyear Tire and Rubber, "The blimp's behind you," is an example of corporate advertising that says, "The company stands behind its products."

Crisis. Advertising sometimes has to deal with the unexpected—the Bhopals, the Three Mile Islands, the oil spills. Waldenbooks ran a full-page advertisement in the *Wall Street Journal* to explain its position on selling Rushdie's *Satanic Verses.* In a brochure on corporate advertising, *Business Week* observed, "Corporate advertising done only when there is bad news about your company or when the company is under attack may provoke skepticism, based not upon facts or the merits of your argument, but upon the circumstances of your presenting it." The brochure continues: "Most corporate advertisers agree that the time to be depositing 'mental money in the bank' is in advance of the need."[16] Progressive companies have a plan for handling disasters, but the best plan is to have already established goodwill.

Service. Ads that help people learn about something provide a service to the consumer. For example, International Paper Company has run ads on "How to listen" and "How to read an annual report." People feel more positive about a person or company who has provided them with useful information.

Good-citizen ads focus on the activities a corporation supports (see Exhibit 15-6). Philip Morris has run a series of ads depicting the art exhibitions it sponsors. Likewise, AT&T sponsors concerts and traveling art exhibits and features them in its advertising. Corning has spent more than $37.5 million in grants to communities where its employees live, as well as to higher education and special innovative social projects.

Financial.   Many corporations undertake institutional advertising in order to make themselves more attractive to stock analysts and potential investors. This is a very tightly directed form of advertising to a clearly defined target. A study by Yankelovich, Skelly, and White found that three out of four active investors say that they have taken specific action with respect to a company as a result of corporate advertising.[17]

In an indictment, Terry Haller, chair of Financial Communications Strategy Center, criticized most financial advertising as having the "intellectual content of baby talk."[18] He observed that most creatives don't understand security analysts or understand the thought that goes into investment decision making. He said, "So-called creatives don't care much for analytical types and probably hate them as much as their own research departments. This shows in their work." He concluded that most financial advertising is vapid and humdrum.

Financial advertising needs to be built on facts, solid information—not fluff, not vague copy extolling technological breakthroughs and glittering bottom lines. In a study of what financial analysts read, the Marsteller agency found that numbers are not necessarily grabbers.[19] Most analysts have access to tons of data from their own computer services, data they consider more reliable than the little charts that appear in ads. What they do want is interpretation of the numbers and the story behind the numbers.

Advocacy.   Advocacy, or issue, advertising is used when a company or organization wants to take a public stand on an issue. First Amendment tests have gone all the way to the Supreme Court on this issue, and the present thought is that companies have the right of free speech, too. In defending itself from consumer criticism, R. J. Reynolds, the beleagured tobacco company, has run an ad headlined, "We don't advertise to children." Machine tools company Warner & Swasey has run an ad that explains, "There is nothing gross about profit." Mobil has a long-running campaign defending the oil industry. One is headlined, "And now, the message the networks keep ignoring." On a less combative note Whirlpool asks, "Is the country in the autumn of its time?"

Advocacy advertising is used when an issue surfaces that is critical to the well-being of the company or organization. Usually, the institution has reason to believe that its side of the issue is not being covered adequately in the press and therefore it is necessary to buy space to guarantee that the company's position is presented (see Exhibit 15-7).

There are some built-in problems with issue advertising, particularly by corporations. The public automatically assumes bias and is less inclined to give the message a fair hearing. One way to overcome this problem is to try to make your message as unbiased and factual as possible. That means you need to present both sides of the issue. If you do that,

Memo To Those Who Write Memos:

Art Buchwald tells of the kid who visited his father's office. When asked what his father did, the kid said, "He sends pieces of paper to other people and other people send papers to him." When you draft a memo, remember other people love to "correct" drafts. The more textually taut you keep it, the less chance for others to pounce on it. The Lord's Prayer has 71 words. The Ten Commandments have 297. The Gettysburg Address has 271. The legal marriage vow has two. General McAuliffe at the Bulge made his point in one: "Nuts!" For practice, send your memo to yourself as a straight telegram at your own expense. Chances are, the less your telegram costs, the more effective your memo is—

Why Does Everyone Hate Meetings?

Three kinds of people attend meetings. Those who want progress, those who don't, and those who want to impress the chairman. 98% of the talk goes to 2% of the problem. Remember the story of the board of trustees who agreed unanimously to spend millions for an atomic reactor, then fell in wild dissension over the request by the freshman basketball coach for a new blackboard. Maybe the air is too soporific. Maybe the carafes of ice water tend to lubricate the long-winded. Maybe the chairs are too comfortable. (A fast food chain designed its chairs to be purposely uncomfortable so people wouldn't linger over their coffee.) At your next meeting, remove the chairs, empty the carafes, turn the thermostat down to 55. A stand-up meeting could be a stand-out.

Don't Be Afraid To Fail

You've failed many times, although you may not remember. You fell down the first time you tried to walk. You almost drowned the first time you tried to swim, didn't you? Did you hit the ball the first time you swung a bat? Heavy hitters, the ones who hit the most home runs, also strike out a lot. R. H. Macy failed seven times before his store in New York caught on. English novelist John Creasey got 753 rejection slips before he published 564 books. Babe Ruth struck out 1,330 times, but he also hit 714 home runs. Don't worry about failure. Worry about the chances you miss when you don't even try.

Let's Get Rid Of "The Girl"

Wouldn't 1979 be a great year to take one giant step forward for womankind and get rid of "the girl"? Your attorney says, "If I'm not here just leave it with the girl." The purchasing agent says, "Drop off your bid with the girl." A manager says, "My girl will get back to your girl." *What* girl? Do they mean Miss Rose? Do they mean Ms. Torres? Do they mean Mrs. McCullough? Do they mean Joy Jackson? "The girl" is certainly a woman when she's out of her teens. Like you, she has a name. Use it.

Exhibit 15-6: One of the most exciting corporate advertising campaigns has been a series of think pieces produced by United Technologies. (Courtesy of United Technologies Corporation)

there is less negative response when you state your view and support it with facts.

One of the favorable things about advocacy advertising is that there is a good chance it will be read. Starch research has found that the public sees well-presented issue ads as more interesting and it tends to read the copy more thoroughly than they read the copy in product advertising. The ads are seen as especially interesting if they follow an "op ed" think piece format.

Strategy *Objectives.* There are three primary objectives for institutional advertising: awareness, knowledge, and attitude change. Awareness is particularly important for new companies and for companies with fragmented images. Knowledge is the objective of advertising that attempts to tell people more about what the company is and what it does. Attitude change is the objective of issue or advocacy advertising, where an argument is being developed.

In addition, corporate advertising can improve employee morale and make it easier to recruit quality employees—who wants to work for a company that no one has heard of or that everyone has heard bad things about? It can also prepare the market by preselling the sales call.

Creativity. An example of classic image advertising in a difficult area is the E. F. Hutton campaign: "When E. F. Hutton talks, people listen." Ralph Nader, the consumer advocate, has described this campaign as "probably the deepest mental imprint image ad ever developed."[20] The campaign positioned E. F. Hutton as *the* most respected source for reliable investment information. What started out as a short-term advertising campaign has created a long-term image for the company.

Company slogans and logos are the two most obvious factors in the overall institutional image. Both are designed for long-term use, perhaps the life of the institution—although there are times when it is necessary to update a slogan or logo. Prudential has been through 14 versions of its Rock of Gibraltar symbol since 1938. Most recently it has been using an abstract one with simple black-and-white slanting lines. That version, however, is now being abandoned in favor of a clearly recognizable rock. Many companies are moving back to older, more recognizable symbols such as the star at Texaco, the peacock at NBC, and the stag at The Hartford.[21]

In an article in *Madison Avenue*, Herbert Krugman analyzed the history of General Electric's corporate slogans. In the early seventies, GE used "Progress is our most important product." In the late seventies, the company changed to "Progress for people." He observed that the new slogan was never able to register more than 21 to 23 percent Starch noted scores, while the old slogan continued registering 34 to 40 percent, even though it handn't been advertised for over 10 years. The average rating for a successful slogan, according to Krugman, is around 50 percent. "Progress for people" never reached that level, and it was replaced with "We bring good things to life." There was something magical about the "Good things" slogan. Krugman reported that "it generated a steeply rising slope of awareness and recognition never seen before in our history." The slogan achieved over 50 percent levels within 12 months. He says, "Good things" was successful because it was "not just a slogan, which implies just words, but also a melody, and also an accompanying set of pictures or visual images."[22] He says it was perfect for the multiple image of television advertising.

Style. Institutional copy often sounds like it is written with either concrete blocks or wallpaper; it either bludgeons you to death or bores you to death. That probably reflects the attitude of the writers, who may very well dislike this kind of assignment. It also tends to read like a tenth-

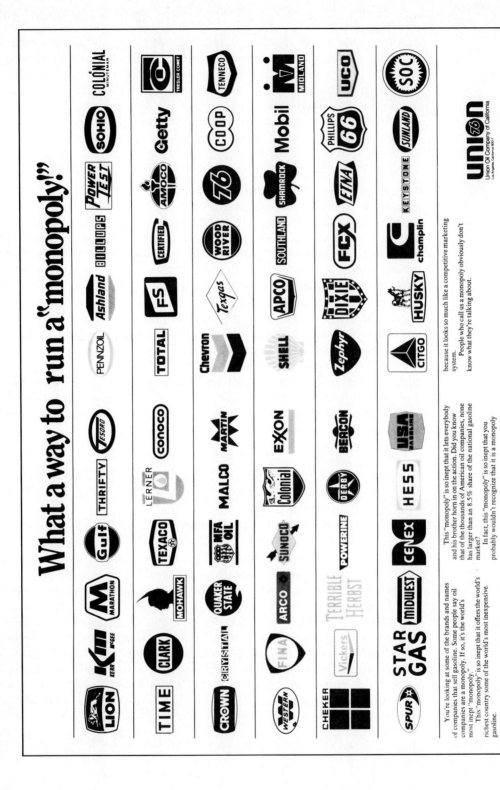

Exhibit 15-7: The "monopoly" advertisement by Union Oil is an example of an advocacy ad that states a corporate position on a controversial topic. (Courtesy of Union Oil Corp.)

grade essay and to be heavy with excess verbiage. Corporate stories should be just as interesting as product stories.

Ron Hoff criticizes the style of corporate ads that sound as if they were written in the "waiting room." Get inside the company, inside the offices, inside the factory and lines. He wants to see "hard hat copy" that makes the company come alive in whatever business it is in.[23] Hoff also suggests that you use emotion: "Companies marry, divorce, prosper, get sick and recover." There is high drama in corporate affairs, but it is rarely apparent in the company's ad copy.

Effectiveness   People are more likely to support a company about which they are knowledgeable. Opinion Research Corporation has found that "People who feel they know a company well are five times more likely to have a favorable opinion of the company than those who claim little familiarity."[24]

Yankelovich, Skelly, and White studied high corporate advertisers versus low corporate advertisers for 64 leading companies in 9 major industries by talking to 1,533 respondents in 25 major markets.[25] The study found there was a major difference in the public's evaluations of these companies depending upon their level of corporate advertising. For example, 48 percent were more familiar with the high advertisers, 30 percent had a more favorable attitude (on nine different factors), and 33 percent predicted they would be potentially more supportive of the company by buying the company's products, by buying stock, by recommending employment, and by being procompany in any disputes.

In a series of studies BBDO found that if people are familiar with a company and think the company's products represent good quality at a fair price, they are:

- Three times more willing to try a new product
- Three times more willing to pay a premium price
- Two and one-half times more likely to believe the company represents a good investment
- Two times as willing to believe management statements in labor disputes[26]

15.4 BUSINESS-TO-BUSINESS ADVERTISING

Business-to-business advertising is a category that includes a variety of different types of activities. The four basic categories included in business-to-business advertising include industrial advertising to manufacturers, trade advertising to the distribution channel, advertising to large-volume institutional purchasers, and advertising to professionals. The characteristic that holds all these different categories together is that the product or service being advertised is used somewhere in the professional area or in the design, manufacturing, or distribution processes. Furthermore, building awareness of business-to-business products can take years. It's a long-term equity-building program.

The various business categories all have different needs and respond to different appeals, but there is one thing that is common to all of the business advertising strategies: *an emphasis on information.* Business purchases are not made as a result of flowery language; they are based on strong reason-why messages.

Most purchases are made as a result of a personal sales call by a knowledgeable sales representative who can provide technical information and explain the intricacies of specifications. The role of advertising is to provide basic facts, to establish a reputation platform for the company, and to open the door for the salesperson. In an article in *Madison Avenue,* William Kinney makes the point that a product gets known, but not sold, through business advertising.[27]

However, the average cost of a sales call is increasing dramatically. According to the Laboratory of Advertising Performance (LAP), the cost of personal selling has exceeded advertising costs over the past 10 years, with ad costs rising 88 percent while personal selling costs increased 160 percent. In 1988 the LAP estimated the average cost of a sales call at $252.[28] Advertising has to work harder to make the sales call more effective.

Respondents to a survey by the Detroit chapter of the Business/ Professional Advertising Association found that advertising can't substitute for personal selling. Respondents say sales are maximized when advertising is used in conjunction with a personal sales call. Advertising does have a significant impact, however, as reported in the following chart from the survey[29]:

HOW SALESPEOPLE SEE B–to–B ADS			
	Very important	Somewhat important	Not important
New-product information	67%	30%	2%
Information about products	44	47	8
Source for forming opinions about products	26	52	20
Source for forming opinions about companies	33	47	19

Types of Business Advertising

Industrial. The heart of business advertising is the heart of the American economy—manufacturing. There are more than 250 business categories served by more than 2,600 industrial publications. Every manufactured product goes through an extensive process of design, production, and distribution. And at every step of the way there are products and services being used in the production.

Advertising to manufacturers focuses on how your product can help make their product better. They are interested in quality, durability, and design. Price is important because that is a factor in their gross profit margin. Specifications, of course, are critical. The product has to fit.

They are also interested in service and supply. If you are providing an instrument needed in their manufacturing process, how reliable is your service program? Likewise, if you are providing a component, they will want to know how reliable your supply is, particularly if this is an innovative product category where there are limited suppliers. For example, a computer manufacturer may have to shut down or go out of business if a critical microchip you supply is unavailable. Supply and service are not just code words in industrial advertising. If you let your manufacturers down, you can cost them millions of dollars.

Trade. Trade advertising in this discussion is advertising to all the various layers in the distribution channel. It is used to *push* a product through the channel as well as to sell products, services, and supplies to the various levels involved in distribution. Trade advertising goals are easy to summarize: *profitability and saleability.* Resellers want to know that your product will have a high turnover and not sit on the shelf gathering dust. They also want to know that they will make money selling it. Tell them how fast it will move and how much it will make. For example, an ad for kiwi fruit addressed grocers with the headline, "How to rid your store of these ugly little brown things." The copy suggested placing the kiwi fruit next to strawberries or melons.

Institutional. In another section, we discuss institutional advertising, which is image-oriented and seeks to sell the reputation of a company or an organization. In this chapter we are talking about advertising to institutions. By institutions we mean high-volume purchasers such as government, military, hospitals, schools, and restaurants. They consume huge amounts of supplies and services as they conduct their businesses, and they purchase these goods in a manner different from conventional consumers. For that reason, they have to be addressed differently in advertising messages.

Most high-volume purchasing is based on one factor: price. Many institutions purchase by bid, and many of them automatically give the contract to the low bidder. You move this market with special price deals and quantity discounts. There is only one other factor that is relevant to this market and that is quality. You can sometimes counter the price factor by using such arguments as durability and long life. If they get more for their money in the long run, then you may be able to override the low-bid decision rule. This is one area where a strong argument can affect the perception of the price-value relationship.

Professional. Advertising to professionals involves messages to people at work: architects, engineers, dentists, teachers, accountants, even advertising copywriters. All these people are served by professional publications, and the pages of these publications are filled with advertising for products that will help them do their job better.

There are two types of advertising messages directed to professionals. First, there are messages to them as *consumers.* In other words, they use things in their work such as drafting tables, calculators and computers, briefcases, and surgical tools. Second, they function as *influencers* and recommend things to buy in the corporate decision process. Purchasing agents, of course, are the primary professionals who buy things in behalf of the company, but all professionals are involved in some way. For example, an engineer may be the best source of information on what kind of gear is needed for a specific application. The supervisor or purchasing agent will seek this type of expert opinion and usually will get a recommendation on a supplier at the same time.

Professionals will be interested in your product if you can convince them it will help them do their work easier, faster, or with better quality. Appeals to convenience and time saving usually will be relevant to this audience. It is interested in anything that increases its professionalism. Sometimes an ego appeal may be appropriate. It may also appreciate any appeal that cuts costs and helps increase its personal profit.

Media Considerations

There are some distinctive characteristics of the media used in business-to-business advertising, and they affect how you develop the message. Primarily the media is print, in the form of journals, direct mail, or product literature. That means the messages can be designed as a "file filler" for long-term reference. Typically, such messages will be long on copy and provide more information than you may normally see in consumer advertising.

Business advertising tends to be sought after by its audience and used as a reference to product innovation within the industry. Typically, business publications are read as much for their ads as they are for their articles. Most business publications contain reader service cards, where you can mark an advertiser by the number of the ad and send off easily for additional product literature. That's how this "file filler" function works.

An article in *Advertising Age*'s special report on business-to-business advertising focused on new media. The article said that many of these are being used for sales presentations—such as the compact disc in its various forms, I (interactive) and V (video); corporate video networks on either cassette or satellite; and videotext. Even the fax machine is being used for direct response.[30]

Personal Expertise

Advertising copy is written for experts, and you will have to become a technical expert, too, if you expect to tell them anything they don't already know. Most agencies involved in business advertising specialize in certain areas and their staffs specialize even more. You can't write a pharmaceutical ad if you don't know anything about chemistry. You'll have a hard time writing agricultural ads if you've never been on a farm.

Creative Considerations

Approach. The emphasis is factual, but the tone is hard hitting in most successful business ads. Ads don't have to be dull to be effective. Business advertising is a very noisy environment, and people who specialize in that kind of advertising have to know how to break through the clutter. In a *Madison Avenue* interview, Peter Lubalin, creative director with Creamer Inc., says that their business advertising is designed to translate the product's strengths into "stopping power."[31]

In the same article William Foley, corporate services director for Marsteller, says their advertising philosophy is one of "confrontation." He explains, "We have determined that we need to land on the readers in the most surprising and/or intrusive way possible so that they will be compelled to pay attention."[32] Business advertising is strong, aggressive, and full of punch.

Business advertising is also image-conscious. A company's reputation is the most important thing it has to sell to another company. Part of the door-opening responsibility of business advertising is to establish the reputation platform of the company, to develop a receptive climate for the salesperson. Foley describes the Marsteller approach, which he says is "to grab *mind-share* before market share."

Design.   Most of the "stopping power" of an ad is created in the graphics. Business advertising is not afraid to use attention-getting, provocative visuals. Albert Molinaro, CEO for Klempner Advertising, a firm that specializes in business advertising, explained that "there is definite recognition in our specialized field on both the client's and agency's parts that the simpler and more dramatic presentation is more effective."[33]

Phil Burton includes a number of business ads in his book, *Which Ad Pulled Best*. A number of his "generalizations" derived from the analysis of research data deal with graphics. He concludes that higher-readership business ads tend to have *big illustrations*. He suggests using pictures of products in use rather than static tabletop shots, and he also recommends using people in the pictures to humanize the gears and machinery.[34]

Writing.   In his *Advertising Age* column, Sid Bernstein recommended three simple techniques for business-to-business advertising: news, case histories, and testimonials. He says these are always good, even if they don't rate high with high-level creative types.[35]

The most important thing to remember in business advertising is to use hard facts—no generalities, no flowery prose. *Prove* your point. Don't just state it. Phil Burton has found that industrial readers want details. You may even want to try graphic details like "call-outs," little pieces of copy around an illustration that point out significant details about the features. An ad for Magnetic Analysis Corporation asked, "Isn't it amazing what can go wrong with a simple screw?" A large picture of a screw was surrounded with call-outs that highlighted problems such as "wrong head diameter," "improper thread," "bad point," and "wrong shank diameter." Specifications are essential, but don't just run the list. Even in business advertising you have to sell, rather than just list, the features.

Burton warns that the headlines should be reader-oriented rather than advertiser-oriented. That's a fault he finds often in business advertising. He also suggests that headlines with all-encompassing claims do less well than specific claims. Burton suggests that general institutional copy is not as strong as case histories. He has also found that a disinterested third party is more believable proof for a claim than an obvious company claim. He notes that "brag and boast" copy is particularly repelling to business readers.[36]

Professionals and technical experts have very well developed "crap detectors" and low tolerance for patronizing comments. Don't try to tell them something they already know. They are the professionals, after all. Be informative, be friendly, but don't be preachy.

An example of interesting business-to-business copy is found in a campaign by Steelcase for its office furniture and modular systems. Using a "true confessions" format, the ads focus on very real problems that

Steelcase and its customers face—like a bad attitude about modular furniture, and the problems of keeping a shipment on schedule. For example, one ad features Fay Schroeder, staff designer in charge of interior planning at First Commerce Corporation's lead bank in New Orleans. According to the ad, "She needed a quality office system for the loan operations area but aesthetics were going head to head with economics." In her words, "We needed a comfortable and productive working environment. We certainly wanted it to look nice. But since it's a back office area, we didn't want to spend a lot of dollars on it." Her Steelcase rep suggested the Movable Walls system. She goes on to talk about how her opinion of movable wall systems changed after looking at the Steelcase system.

A second ad reads like an adventure thriller:

> Over at the Chair Plant in Grand Rapids they're still talking about Wayne Meuser, the night-shift foreman, and his assistant, Terry VandenAkker. Still shaking their heads and smiling.
>
> Just the other night, production crew got into a jam because their chrome vendor was having trouble getting a clean layer of chrome down on the T-line chair frames. Vendor tried everything, even sent over extras, trying to make schedule.
>
> But around 3:00 AM as they were welding and buffing out the last of the shipment and flecks of chrome started flying off, it got to be pretty clear that things weren't going to work out right.

The ad continues to tell how Wayne and Terry made sure the customer didn't come up two frames short by raiding Quality Control, where they took the masters to finish out the order. Terry explained how the plant superintendent took the news: "In the end he figured it would be a lot easier to replace the master frames than it would be to replace the customer." The ad ends with, "Steelcase has this motto: 'The schedule must be met at all costs!' All those boys did was take it literally."

15.5 PUBLIC SERVICE

Public service advertising is another aspect of social responsibility. The company, or a group of companies, will underwrite the advertising expenses of some good cause. One of the most successful national public service campaigns by a company is the Shell "Answer book" series developed by Ogilvy & Mather. This little "tip in" booklet gets consistently high magazine readership. Furthermore, the company has received more than 800,000 requests for copies.[37]

The Ad Council is an industrywide program administered by a foundation with representatives from throughout the advertising industry. The Ad Council takes on clients representing such causes as child abuse, forest fires, crime prevention, and Negro youth college education programs, and organizes donated creative and media buying services from its member agencies. Arrangements are made with the media to provide free space and air time and the campaign runs with totally donated services.

Drug-Free Campaign   One of the largest private sector, public service efforts is the Media-Advertising Partnership for a Drug-Free America, which operates in cooperation with the Ad Council. The idea for the Drug-Free America campaign came from a group of advertising executives who wondered if it would be possible to create a fundamental reshaping of social attitudes about drugs. They observed that many teenagers and young adults think that drugs are "cool." The campaign wants to turn that attitude around—to make young adults feel that it is not "cool" to do drugs, in other words, to "de-normalize" drugs (see Exhibit 15-8).

The Partnership was formed by eliciting extraordinary volunteer participation by advertising agencies, the media, the production industry, and the market research industry. The campaign was launched in March 1987, targeting preteens, teens, young adults, and influencers (peers, parents, healthcare professionals, teachers, and opinion leaders). Separate task forces and campaigns were developed for Black and Hispanic advertising.

In the first year 116 different executions were developed by more than 200 advertising agencies and production houses who donated their services to develop, produce, and distribute the ads to the media. The strategy for these ads was developed by a task force that included advertising and marketing research experts along with government and independent drug research experts.

Performer's unions such as SAG, SEG, and AFTRA allowed their members to work in the commercials and ads for free. Kodak donated all film and videotape necessary for production. Audiotape was donated by AGFA-Gevaert. Agencies paid for some of the other production costs; however, unprecedented involvement by the production industry resulted in tremendous cost savings.

Nine key media associations also supported the Partnership and its media plan calling for $500 million annually in donated media time and space. In the first year all three TV networks joined the effort, led by ABC, which contributed 216 commercials (half in prime time). Thirteen radio networks have been providing substantial play. More than 150 national magazines have agreed to participate, including *Reader's Digest*, *The New Yorker*, *Good Housekeeping*, *National Geographic*, *People*, *Time*, and *Sports Illustrated*. Six business publishers representing 422 publications have agreed to run the advertising. More than 1,200 full-page ads appeared the first year in newspapers such as the *Wall Street Journal* and the *Miami Herald*. *The New York Times* ran 37 full-page ads.

A major base research study, under the guidance of the Market Research Association, was conducted in 1987 and tracking research will measure changes in attitudes and usage among all target audiences over the three years of the advertising program. It's a formidable task and a phenomenal effort. Is it possible that the power of advertising can actually turn around America's attitude toward drugs?

A study released in March of 1989 by the National Institute on Drug Abuse found that crack use among America's high school students declined for the first time in 1988.[38] In addition, admitted use of cocaine and marijuana continued to decline. Dr. Lloyd Johnston, head of the University of Michigan's School of Social Research and director of the na-

Exhibit 15-8: This is one of the ads in the Drug-Free America campaign by the Media-Advertising Partnership.

tionwide survey of 16,000 high school seniors, said that the marked decline coincides with the Drug-Free America campaign. He found that the
ads have an extremely high recognition factor among adolescents and have
been well received. For example, the TV spots registered a 94 percent
recognition, with 74 percent saying the ads made them feel "less favorable" toward drug use.

15.6 PROMOTION

Since this book focuses on the creative side of advertising, we will discuss
various aspects of promotion, but from the viewpoint of what it can do
to support an advertising program.

Publicity Publicity is a very clear responsibility of the public relations staff. It involves getting media attention on behalf of your product in the form of
news coverage in the mass media and announcements and articles in the
trade press. The article is not paid for by the advertiser—in other words,
it is a form of "free" communication. Not only is it free, but information
that appears in the media as an article has more credibility than anything
you can buy in a display ad. Publicity, therefore, should be a highly valued
part of your promotional effort.

Most publicity efforts are oriented toward the total corporate or institutional communication program. Some publicity programs, however,
are specifically designed to support advertising and marketing efforts.
This is the type of publicity we will be concerned with in this chapter.

When the W. B. Doner agency hired the town of Hope, Indiana, to
boycott hamburgers in favor of Arby's roast beef sandwiches, it also created an unexpected media event. A lot of small towns vied for the honor,
and the day Hope was chosen the local newspaper had a huge headline,
"Hope Bans Burgers." An Indianapolis paper picked up the story and the
whole thing started to snowball with coverage on TV and in papers around
the country. In covering the event, *Adweek* commented, "The free ink
has raised Arby's profile and helped Arby's, which is outspent by
McDonald's 40-to-1, to stretch its budget."[39]

Many advertising campaigns need publicity support, either in the
mass media or in the trade press. Most campaigns are announced to the
trade with press releases. If there are special events, these are usually
considered newsworthy and may receive coverage from mass media as
well as trade media. Usually, coverage in the trade media is dependent
upon press releases that are provided to the publications.

Special events. As part of the publicity effort, you may want to
consider planning *special events*. These create excitement among consumers as well as among any dealers, sales staff, wholesalers, or other
resellers involved in merchandising your product. Special events such as
grand openings, ribbon cuttings, recognition programs, celebrity appear-
ances, and "stunts" of one kind or another demand a lot of planning—
for participants as well as for press coverage. The more unusual the special
event, the more likely it will be considered newsworthy and therefore
merit press coverage.

The success of special event promotions depends upon your ability to identify activities relevant to your target. Coors, for example, has gotten national and international publicity from its Rocky Mountain bicycle races; that's an activity that appeals to its young western market. A number of major national companies sponsor such competitions in everything from marathons, golf, and tennis to ultimate frisbee, one-on-one beach volleyball, and darts. The objective of such special events is to associate the product with a valued lifestyle.

Sales Promotion

Sales promotion is on the front line of product sales. It provides the last and most direct stimulus to move the goods. Sales promotion is also a dynamic growth area. Five years ago the average ratio between advertising and sales promotion (as a percent of the budget) was 60:40. Now it has turned around, and sales promotion is getting 60 percent of the marketer's budget, while advertising is getting only 40 percent. That reflects an industrywide shift from long-term brand building to short-term sales.[40]

The most direct sales promotion is to the consumer. This includes special price deals and incentives to get the consumer into the store to buy the product. This reflects a *pull* strategy, with consumer demand being used as a technique to pull the product through the distribution channel.

A second level of promotion is to the trade. Here the objective is to get the support of the relevant parts of the distribution chain such as wholesalers, brokers, dealers, sales representatives, even drivers. Finally there is the "reseller," the retailer who will be displaying your message in some form at the point of sale. Both types of promotion through the trade use a *push* strategy. We'll call these three categories consumer promotion, trade or channel promotion, and retailer promotion.

Consumer. The objective of consumer promotion is to create accelerated demand. While brand advertising is long-term and stimulates indirect action, sales promotion is short-term and stimulates direct action. It creates sudden bumps in the sales curve, and although the sales increase with the use of sales promotion, they tend to fall when the promotion is over.

To increase showroom traffic, Porsche, in one of the most targeted sales promotions ever, mailed 100,000 personalized posters showing a recent model with a vanity license plate bearing the recipient's name.

William Robinson, author of a column in *Advertising Age* on sales promotion as well as the definitive textbook on the subject, identifies 12 basic sales promotion techniques for consumer as well as trade promotion.[41] Typical forms of consumer promotions he identifies include sampling, coupons, price deals, free-in-the-mail premiums, self-liquidating premiums, contests, games, sweepstakes, refunds and rebates, bonus packs, stamps, and other continuity programs.

Coupons and sampling can be used to encourage *trial*. This is particularly important with new-product introduction, but it may also be important when you have a market where sales are low (see Exhibit 15-9). Mattel recently used a coupon program to boost Christmas sales of its toys. The coupons, which will be available in stores and on cereal boxes, encourage consumers to fill in their names and ages. This is especially important because they will generate a database of toy buyers.

Loyalty can also be triggered with a careful use of promotional techniques. What you want to stimulate is repeat buying. Premiums that ask for multiple proof-of-purchase stickers are aimed at continuity of purchase. Coupons on the package also encourage *repeat* purchases. Marketers are always looking for promotions that encourage repeat purchases rather than one-shot buys. Now retailers are beginning to sponsor Frequent Shoppers Clubs, which work like frequent flyers clubs, awarding merchandise in exchange for UPC codes off certain packages and brands.

A Brass Pelican direct mail piece has an interesting special promotion used by a paper division of Kimberly-Clark. It was sent to art directors and people in public relations and advertising who might specify paper. The piece was a contest to locate the final resting place of an old treasure ship, The Brass Pelican. Three clues were sent out along with old maps of the Bahamas. The winner got an island vacation.

Trade or channel.   Various products have different types of distribution channels. In some rare cases, the manufacturer may sell directly to the consumer or directly to the retailer. In other situations, the manufacturer sells to a wholesaler or a broker who then distributes the product to retailers. The first problem is informing the various links in the distribution chain about any special advertising or promotion campaigns that you may be planning. This kind of communication typically takes place through the trade press and direct mail.

The second problem is motivating key individuals to cooperate. Your campaign is not the most important thing on their minds. If you have to rely on the distribution chain for any help in your promotional effort, you must make it worth their while. You may motivate them with trade allowances and discounts. Or you may try gifts and contests. Incentive programs must not only relate to the advertising theme but also offer something of value to your target—in this case, the trade. When you plan incentive programs, you have to understand what turns these people on, and the best way to do this is to copytest your promotional ideas.

Retailer.   The last link in the distribution chain is the retailer, who is also the front line in sales. You need the support of the retailer whenever you undertake an advertising program that involves a special promotion. If you are producing point-of-purchase displays, counter racks, shelf talkers, and store banners, the success of your entire campaign depends upon the willingness of the retailer to use these materials. The problem is that he or she may be overwhelmed with such materials and that the majority of these merchandising materials may wind up unopened in the dumpster.

So how do you get cooperation? In a column on sales promotion in *Advertising Age*, Eugene Mahany identified some of the promotional goals that "turn on" grocers.[42] Primarily, "what turns on grocers is what turns their customers on." For example, he cites low prices and special price deals, anything that creates high-volume turnover, displays with built-in inventories, creative displays that capture impulse buyers, product tie-ins where the purchase of one leads to buying another, and anything that increases profit potential—such as trade allowances. In particular, they would like to know that there is substantial national advertising support that will create demand in their customers.

Campus Trial Pak™ introduces your product to students

Exhibit 15-9: College students are a very difficult group to reach, so advertisers use special promotions to reach them such as this "Campus Trial Pak," which is filled with product samples and coupons.

Creative Considerations

There are five primary considerations to keep in mind when planning sales promotions. First, this is a highly creative area. A sales promotion works best when it is novel and attention-getting. You won't win anyone's support with another handful of matchbooks and pens. Be *creative*.

Second, the sales promotion technique usually is utilized in support of some advertising program. It should be related thematically. If you are promoting a German beer, then it doesn't make sense to send sweepstakes winners to Hawaii. Give them a tour of the Black Forest. Build on the *creative concept*.

Third, make it *strategic*. Sales promotion is not just a bag of gimmicks. Every idea you propose should be used to accomplish some specific objective—preferably an objective that can't be reached with conventional advertising. These techniques work to solve very specific marketing problems, but you have to identify the problem before you can come up with a viable promotional idea.

Fourth, research has shown that multiple sales promotion techniques have high readership and really pull consumers. In other words, if you can combine a coupon, a sweepstakes, and a premium, then your promotion will pull more than any one technique by itself. There is a synergistic effect to promotional activity that really heats up the marketplace. *Multiply* your impact. For example, when *Dirty Dancing* was released as a video it carried a commercial for Nestle's White Alpine chocolate bar. In order to build interest and lengthen the peak rental period, Nestle sponsored a national sweepstakes and RCA Records sponsored a national dance contest.

Fifth, *tie in* with some other natural supporter to spread both the costs and the reach of the promotion. For example, hit movies spur tie-ins with toys, clothing, fast food restaurants, and retailers. For example, Frito-Lay used a Southwestern promotion for Doritos that tied in with Texas theme parks. Frito-Lay also has run tie-ins with sports teams such as the Cubs and the Bulls. Tie-ins give you a double-advertising whammy. Another example of a cross-promotion was the release of the new book *Power City.* The traditional book-signing party was held at a Wilshire Boulevard Maserati dealership; the author gave her major character a Maserati convertible in the hopes that the Italian carmaker would give the book some added promotion.

15.7 INTERNATIONAL ADVERTISING

Global advertising is the hot topic in the marketing and advertising industries. There are now some 40,000 companies in the United States that are engaged in international marketing, and that number is increasing every day. More foreign companies are moving into the lucrative United States market with its population of 240 million affluent consumers. Consequently, the United States marketplace is becoming a melting pot of products from diverse countries.

But the real action is elsewhere—in Europe, where the national boundaries are to be lowered by 1992, bringing 320 million consumers into a European single market, and in Japan and the other fast-developing countries along the Pacific Rim such as Korea, the Philippines, Malayasia, Singapore, and Hong Kong. Then there are the sleeping giants—Russia and China—who are only just beginning to get a taste of consumer culture. Regardless of where you work, you may find yourself working with foreign companies or handling foreign products as this international explosion touches every business—small as well as large.

The growth of large, successful marketers such as IBM, Ford, Sony, Procter & Gamble, Unilever, and Nestle, and the mergers and buyouts of the eighties have created a number of multinational companies and advertising agencies. There is a natural corporate evolution from one country, to regional blocks, to a global market. Along with this evolution comes a *global perspective.* These multinational corporations no longer think in terms of "home" markets and "foreign" products, suppliers, and consumers.

The Global Debate

global brand: one that is available throughout most of the world and uses the same name, design, and advertising strategy

A **global brand** is one that is available throughout the world. It has the same name and design and uses essentially the same creative strategy in advertising everywhere in the world. Coca-Cola, McDonald's and Marlboro are three widely recognized global brands.

Debate arises over the following question: How much can a brand be adapted for local tastes and culture and still be considered a global brand? In 1983 Harvard Professor Theodore Levitt raised the issue in a controversial article in which he said the time had come for global marketing, which he defined as selling the same products in the same manner everywhere. He argued that differences among nations are diminishing and that they should be ignored because people throughout the world are motivated by many of the same wants and needs.[43]

Similarities or differences? The huge London-based Saatchi & Saatchi advertising agency did adopt Levitt's philosophy and ran ads in 1984 in *The New York Times* and the *London Times* with the headline, "The opportunity for world brands." Saatchi's philosophy is that, while there are cultural differences, advertising strategies for most products can be based on universal needs. The agency advises its clients to recognize the similarities among people, rather than focusing on the differences.

One of Saatchi's largest clients is Procter & Gamble's Pampers. Saatchi makes the point that "Baby's bottoms are much the same the world over." What sells disposable diapers in one country sells disposable diapers in other countries as well. Pampers is sold everywhere with the same slogan, "Even when they're wet, they're dry," a slogan that appeals to mothers in Madrid, Maine, and the Middle East. An article in *Global Business* says, "In less than 30 years, the humble disposable diaper has done what generals couldn't do in hundreds of years. It has crossed national, cultural, and linguistic barriers to become accepted throughout the world."[44]

Consumer-Driven Targeting

Saatchi's revolutionary way of looking at targeting is consumer-driven rather than geography-driven. The focus is on cultural groups that transcend national boundaries, such as the youth market, technocrats and computer users, business travelers, mothers of infants, and people who worry about getting older.

A product's "culture" is based on groups of product users rather than on geography and national identity. This philosophy recognizes that real cultural differences are between generations and lifestyles, not between countries. A Japanese teenager would have more in common with a Swedish or American teenager than with a middle-aged Japanese business person.

The youth culture, in particular, is international. Likewise the women's market is similar around the world in the areas of beauty, fashion, and personal care. Products such as body sprays, perfumes, colognes, cosmetics, deodorants, and sanitary products have crossed national borders.

Adaptation and Standardization

The debate still continues as advertisers try to decide to what degree an advertising campaign can be standardized for worldwide presentation. Obviously the more standardized the campaign, the more cost-efficient it

KODACOLOR GOLD FILM

"OLYMPIC COLOR"   :30

ANNCR: (VO) Kodak presents the
Olympic Colors.

(MUSIC)

SINGERS: Red, white,

yellow, green,

white and blue...

Yellow (yellow), red,

white, blue,

blue, white

blue and yellow (yellow),

red, white (red, white),

yellow...color.

ANNCR: Kodak is Olympic Color.

Exhibit 15-10:   This is an example of a commercial that lends itself to global use. The Kodak ad "Olympic color" was created as a tie-in with the Olympics. It uses shots of athletes performing against various countries' flags. It works on the international level because of its dependence on dramatic visuals, strong music, and few words. (Copyright Eastman Kodak Company. Reprinted courtesy of Eastman Kodak Company)

is and the more advantageous it is to develop a tight brand image. Most experts feel that, while totally globalized campaigns may be possible, some adaptation is usually needed. In general, strategy is the most easily globalized and executions are more likely to need adaptation to local cultures.

Language. Almost all campaigns have to be adapted for language. A number of marketers that use global strategies shoot a master commercial and then dub a new audio track to accommodate the various languages. If there is a product shot, the package may need to be changed, also. This can be done by "gang shooting," with all the various countries' packages shot at the same time, or it can be done electronically using paintbox techniques to manipulate the image.

Executions. There are some significant differences between eastern and western cultures that may demand separate executions. While in English or German a word can be defined exactly, in Japanese a word can mean many things and is interpreted from the context.

Sales messages are different, too. In America, product differentiation and benefits are hammered out. The English are more prone to use wry humor and understatement to make their selling points. In Japan, the points of difference are illustrated by focusing on nuances and subtle interpretations—the different way people appear or behave in a commercial, for example. It's more indirect. Testimonials are not used in Japan because they are considered too hard-sell.

Advertising is also adapted to match settings and markets. Impulse, a cologne-based deodorant spray by Unilever, is sold in 70 countries and has been the brand leader in every European market it has entered. The concept of the advertising is standardized, but the executions vary. The concept is based on a romantic fantasy with a young woman being given flowers by a strange man. The phrase "Acting on Impulse" is used in all the advertisements. While the romantic appeal transcends national boundaries, the executions are done locally using local models and settings.

Universals   For those who elect to develop global campaigns, there are some universal languages that help transcend the problem of local language and culture. Visual communication using universally understood signs and symbols conveyed by satellite-based media systems is making an end run around language-based communication. The Federal Express ads (see Exhibit 11-1) as well as the Kodak ad (see Exhibit 15-10) use high-impact visuals to communicate nonverbally. And music has successfully crossed borders from the time of Bach and Beethoven to the current world tours of rock stars.

SUMMARY

This chapter has discussed direct response, retail, institutional, business-to-business, public service, promotional, and international advertising. You should know:

1. Direct response is the most selective, precise, personal, and accountable form of advertising.

2. Direct advertising is used in all media and is characterized by a response device.

3. Catalog copy is short and succinct and must convey the entire selling message.

4. Direct mail uses a personal letter format, long copy, and incentives to respond.

5. Retail advertising builds traffic, presents the store image, and emphasizes the price level of merchandise.

7. Institutional advertising focuses on corporate images, and it also establishes identity and capability, serves consumers and the community, speaks to the financial community, and addresses the public on issues and crisis situations.

8. Business-to-business advertising focuses on manufacturers, the distribution channel, institutions, and professionals.

9. Public service advertising is done by the industry for good causes.

10. Publicity in an advertising program uses news coverage on behalf of a product.

11. Sales promotion stimulates action by consumers, the trade or distribution channel, and retailers.

12. International advertising appeals to universal needs and uses simple copy, strong visuals, and music.

NOTES

1. Julie Liesse Erickson, "Burnett Pulls Clients into Direct-Response," *Advertising Age*, October 17, 1988, p. 10.

2. Bob Stone, "Twenty Questions Probe Top Concerns of Direct Marketers," *Advertising Age*, May 16, 1977, p. 77.

3. Stan Rapp and Tom Collins, *Maxi Marketing* (New York: McGraw-Hill, 1987), p. viii.

4. "Direct Mail Pieces Lack Creativity, Y & R President Claims," *Folio*, July 1978, p. 13.

5. Sid Bernstein, "Mail Order Is Burgeoning Giant," *Advertising Age*, March 26, 1979, p. 16.

6. David Ogilvy, *Confessions of an Advertising Man* (New York: Dell, 1964).

7. Judith Graham, "Shearson's New TV Spot Uses Direct-Response Pitch," *Advertising Age*, February 15, 1988, p. 65.

8. Richard M. Dubiel, "Advertising Copywriting and the Catalog: A Beginning Point," American Academy of Advertising Annual Conference, Chicago, April 1988.

9. Bob Stone, "Hail the Catalog Copywriter: The Good Ones Make Every Word Sell," *Advertising Age*, March 5, 1979, pp. 52–54.

10. Jim Powell, "The Lucrative Trade of Crafting Junk Mail," *New York Times*, June 20, 1982, p. F7.

11. Bob Stone, "Leading Direct Response Writer Shares His Copywriting Secrets," *Advertising Age*, June 13, 1977, p. 53.

12. Powell, op. cit.

13. Powell, op. cit.

14. Eliot DeY. Schein, "BW's Invitation," *Folio*, June 1978, pp. 40–41.

15. Ed Fitch, "Image Ads More Than Glad Tidings," *Advertising Age*, March 10, 1986, p. 42.

16. "Corporate Advertising," A special report by *Business Week*, 1984, p. 17.

17. Ibid.

18. Terry Haller, "Corporate Ads Doomed," *Advertising Age*, January 15, 1982, p. 47.

19. Ed Zotti, "An Expert Weighs the Prose and Yawns," *Advertising Age*, January 24, 1982, p. M11.

20. Ralph Nader, "Challenging the Corporate Ad," *Advertising Age*, January 24, 1983, p. M12.

21. "Company Symbols Look to the Past," *Wall Street Journal*, April 26, 1989, p. B1.

22. Herbert Krugman, "Tracking the Effects of Corporate Ads," *Madison Avenue*, April 1982, pp. 29–32.

23. "Ron Hoff Talks Corporate Advertising," *Wall Street Journal* house ad that ran in *Advertising Age*, June 27, 1977, pp. 16–17.

24. *Business Week*, op. cit., p. 5.

25. Ibid., p. 14.

26. Ibid., p. 15.

27. William Kinney, "Industrial's Hot New Creative," *Madison Avenue*, April 1982, pp. 72–76.

28. "Average Business-to-Business Sales Call Increases by 9.5%," *Marketing News*, September 12, 1988, p. 5.

29. "Business-to-Business Ads Impact Sales," *Inside Print*, April 1987, p. 12.

30. Neal Weinstock, "Businesses Embrace High-Tech Media," *Advertising Age*, June 20, 1988, p. S4.

31. Kinney, op. cit.

32. Ibid.

33. Verne Gay, "Special Report: Business-to-Business Advertising," *Marketing and Media Decisions*, May 1983, pp. 111–118.

34. Philip Ward Burton, *Which Ad Pulled Best*, 4th ed. (Chicago: Crain, 1981).

35. Sid Bernstein, "Hot to Fight Routine Ads," *Advertising Age*, June 20, 1988, p. 16.

36. Burton, op. cit.

37. Ogilvy & Mather house ad, "How to Create Corporate Advertising That Gets Results."

38. Kevin McCormack, "Research Says Ads Help Cut Drug Use," *Adweek*, March 13, 1989, p. 54.

39. Roy Furchgott, "Arby's Campaign Gets Media Boost as Burg Bans Burgers, for a Fee," *Adweek*, August 22, 1988, p. 2.

40. Graham H. Phillips, "Phillips: 'TV Ads Must Sell, as Well as Build Brands,'" *Adweek*, April 17, 1989, p. 30.

41. William A. Robinson, "12 Basic Promotion Techniques: Their Advantages—and Pitfalls," *Advertising Age*, January 10, 1977, pp. 50, 55.

42. Eugene Mahany, "Examine the 'Grocer Gestalt' to See What Turns Them On," *Advertising Age*, November 22, 1976, pp. 58–60.

43. Theodore Levitt, "The Globalization of Markets," *Harvard Business Review*, May–June 1983, pp. 92–102.

44. Sandra Harris, "Spreading the Global Message," *Global Business*, Summer 1988, pp. 10–15.

16

The Creative Side
of Campaigns

KEY POINTS

- A campaign is a series of ads connected by a central theme.
- Repetition of a central concept through a campaign has more impact than repetition of a one-shot ad which becomes monotonous.
- Variations on the theme maintain interest.
- Continuity is developed by repeating familiar elements.

16.1 NATURE OF CAMPAIGNS

campaign: a series of ads that are connected thematically

Many of the advertisements you have been studying and creating are "single-shot" ads. However, most advertising used by national advertisers is prepared as a **campaign**. An advertising campaign is a series of different ads in different media that are scheduled across a substantial time period. The different ads are all held together by a unifying campaign theme. A campaign may target one specific audience or it may address several different segments. It may focus on one specific product attribute or image, or it may cover all the attributes of the product.

A campaign is more than just a series of ads, however. It is a way of thinking, of planning. It involves a long and serious process of analyzing your situation, identifying possible alternatives, deciding the best approach, and testing your decisions. A campaign represents the ultimate in strategic thinking by marketing experts, copywriters, art directors, producers, promotion specialists, researchers, and media buyers. It is a team effort and it pulls the best ideas from different viewpoints and disciplines.

Objectives

Attention and involvement. One benefit of a campaign is increased attention power. People select "familiar" messages to attend to because they are comfortable and no risk. A campaign can give a message a familiar face. Bruce Stauderman, in an *Advertising/Marketing Review* column on campaigns, described the role of familiarity: "People recognize the pattern of the campaign."[1] Familiarity is also the foundation of closure. You can make familiar messages work for you by involving the audience in the completion of the message—but only if it has been exposed over a long period of time.

One shot versus repetition. Most national advertisers feel that a campaign works better than a one-shot ad. It takes more than one impression to make an impression. However, you can repeat the same ad only a few times before the audience realizes that this is the same old message and tunes it out. The secret is to repeat the concept but vary the details of the execution. That way you can continue to repeat the essential information without boring your audience. Stauderman pointed out, "The repetition of the sales message gets through to them; they're not bored with it because each time the manner of telling is pleasantly varied." He explained, "They instinctively appreciate the fact that you're not trying to jam the same ad down their throats with relentless monotony."[2]

At the same time you are also accruing interest. The more often the audience sees the message and its variations, the more likely it is to begin to develop some interest. A campaign can generate interest of its own more than an individual ad can. Of course, there are exceptions. There are boring campaigns that never catch fire and there are dynamic one-shot ads, like Wendy's "Where's the beef?" The Wendy's commercial took on a life of its own. The point is that, with a sustained campaign, the message itself becomes an event.

The primary purpose of repetition in advertising is memorability. Learning theory states that the more times people hear something, the more likely they are to remember it. Repetition is used to anchor a concept or an image in memory. Most advertisers say that a *minimum* of three repetitions is necessary to make any impression. Ads on television appear much more often than that. And jingles on radio may be repeated several times every hour.

So, how much repetition can an ad (or an audience) take? It's like fertilizer: A little bit is good, but if you put a lot on the plant, you're likely to burn it up. Media planners have elaborate formulas to predict the optimum level of repetition. Unfortunately, the critical factor in deciding on repetition is not media use but message strategy. Some messages can be repeated frequently; some can't.

Messages that can withstand lots of repetition are simple, usually brand image or product identification messages. More likely than not, they are jingles. Anything put to music can be repeated over and over. They are inoffensive and make few demands on the audience. In other words, they are easy to read, watch, or hear.

wear-out: consumers tire of a campaign and stop paying attention to it

Wear-out.   Some ads have an early point of diminishing returns. In other words, a lot of repetition builds **wear-out** rather than retention. Ads that are particularly susceptible to this burnout problem are heavily dramatic or emotional, slice of life, humorous, or novelty approaches. You don't have to see talking chipmunks too many times before you would rather not see them again. The more effective an ad is at getting attention, the less it can survive heavy repetition.

Forgetting.   Establishing the message in memory is an important objective, but there's another factor to be considered. How do you keep the message anchored there? Certain types of messages are easier to forget (or harder to remember) than others. They are lengthy or complex. The more involved the construction of the message, the harder it will be to anchor it. Simplify it as much as possible. Take the complex messages apart and express them in smaller chunks. And repeat them.

The point is that complex, hard-to-remember information needs to be "chunked" and simplified in order to be remembered. That is another objective of campaigns. They provide message structures that allow you to present complicated information in small pieces across a number of ads.

16.2 CAMPAIGN THEMES

Theme

campaign theme: a central idea around which variations are developed

The **campaign theme** in an advertising campaign must be a strong concept that can hold together diverse efforts. The theme is like the creative concept we discussed in the sections on creative strategy. It is the "big idea" that makes the campaign distinctive. You know that a campaign involves different ads for different audiences in different media at different times of the year. Now, what keeps those from being "one shots"? Only a strong theme can provide the necessary integration.

Mountain Dew has used the same campaign theme for years—teenagers having a wild time in rural river settings. But now Mountain Dew has decided its image needs changing so it's moving to more urban scenes.

When Pepsi moved to the classic "Pepsi generation" theme, an entirely new type of lifestyle advertising was created. That theme continues to be expressed in subsequent campaigns through the years even though the specific campaigns change.

Variations

A campaign is a series of ads built around one central theme. The various ads are designed to be different for very specific reasons. As you plan a campaign, think about the logic behind these variations on your theme and be prepared to justify the need for the various approaches.

Interest.   One reason for variation is simply to maintain interest. As has been mentioned, you can't repeat a message ad nauseam. Listening to a humorous commercial is like listening to a funny joke. The first time it catches all your attention; the second time you listen to it with fondness, remembering how funny it was. After that you get tired of hearing it. In order for humorous commercials to work, the producers develop a series of little sitcoms focusing on different product features. They use variation because humorous messages wear out in a hurry.

Media.   Another type of variation is by medium. Your review of the different media and their creative considerations should make it clear to you that the medium itself can affect the development and perception of the message. Each medium has its own peculiar strengths and weaknesses. You can't use exactly the same message in radio that you use on a billboard or in a brochure. Messages have to be designed specifically to take advantage of the media characteristics.

Schedule.   Calendar is another source of variation. If your campaign lasts an entire year, you are advertising across all seasons and through all holidays. Every season and every holiday is a peg for your message.

The campaign itself is planned against a calendar. There is a beginning, a middle, and an end to every campaign. Sometimes a campaign starts big and winds down to the end. Sometimes it starts small and builds up to a big climax. This schedule is part of the campaign strategy and should reflect what you know about the way the product is purchased and used. Special events may also affect the course of this calendar, and you may use a media blitz at a particular point to reinforce a special promotion. Opening ads tend to be different from sustaining ads and from special event announcements. Variations in your ads may develop in response to the campaign calendar.

Attributes.   The product itself may structure your variations. You may want to develop special ads to explain different attributes or features. An automotive campaign, for example, may include separate ads on mileage, engineering and durability, comfort, style, and price. Each ad is single-minded and focuses on that specific feature.

Target.   You may need different ads depending upon your targeted audience. You might have specified a business audience, for example, but within that market you may have engineers, accountants, and executives—all of whom are involved in the purchasing decision. That means you will need different ads for each target. Perhaps your campaign will need retail support, and in that case your dealers and distributors may be a separate audience whose interests are entirely different from those of the consumer groups.

Continuity

Slogan.   The number one continuity device in an advertising campaign is the slogan. Since "campaign planning" is a military metaphor, you might say that a slogan is the "battle cry." The troops rally round, and the memorable phrase is on everyone's lips. A good slogan generates its own excitement. Some campaign themes continue for years, such as Bell Telephone's "Reach out and touch someone." When it works, stay with it.

In an active market where the competition is intense, the campaign slogans are on the front line. Some of the memorable slogans used in the soft drink market include "Pepsi now," "Pepsi's got your taste for life," and "Catch the Pepsi spirit." Pepsi's chief competitor, the market leader, has kept the market alive with "Coke is it," "Have a Coke and a smile," "Look up America," and "It's the real thing." Other memorable soft drink slogans include "Be a Pepper" and "UnCola," which is a position as well as a slogan.

Another leader in its category is McDonald's. The McDonald's slogans have been particularly memorable. They include "Nobody can do it like McDonald's," "We do it all for you," "You, you're the one," and "You deserve a break today."

Obviously, the challenge in writing slogans is to come up with a phrase that sticks in the mind—something that hooks or sticks in the memory easily. It should reflect the character or personality of the product and the tone and atmosphere of the campaign. A slogan is designed to be repeated and remembered. Techniques used to increase this memorability factor include alliteration, rhyming cadence, and parallel construction.

See how many products you can identify from the following list of slogans. As you move through the list, analyze the slogan in terms of its ability to trigger the product category and brand name. Some of them are much more effective than others. Why?

1. You're going to like us
2. Taste as good as they crunch
3. A powerful part of your life
4. Carry the big fresh flavor
5. A breed apart
6. Lets the good times roll
7. We circle the world
8. It takes a licking and keeps on ticking
9. Always the leader
10. The closer you look, the better we look
11. A concern for the future
12. Gets the red out
13. Think what we can do for you
14. Strong enough for a man, but made for a woman
15. Ideas to build on
16. Gentle enough to use every day
17. America's storyteller
18. Today is the first day of the rest of your life
19. Doing what we do best
20. The spray that does it all
21. A household name, at work
22. I'll have a light
23. Getting people together
24. Stop babying yourself; eat hearty
25. We bring good things to life

a. Merrill Lynch
b. Wrigley Spearmint
c. Bud Light
d. TWA
e. General Electric
f. Westinghouse
g. PPG Industries
h. American Airlines
i. Boeing
j. Manville Corporation
k. Bank of America
l. Eastman Kodak
m. MasterCard
n. Scott Paper
o. Mack Trucks
p. Doritos
q. Visine
r. Total
s. Kawasaki
t. Lysol
u. Ford
v. Poli-Grip
w. Secret
x. Timex
y. Johnson's Baby Shampoo

(answers on page 407)

Characters and situations. In addition to slogans, characters may be used as a continuity device. Familiar characters from successful campaigns include the Keebler Elves, Charlie Chaplin and the *M*A*S*H* group for IBM personal computers, and Inspector 12 for Haines. All these characters starred in long-running campaigns.

Graphics. Johnnie Walker Red uses the color red as a visual theme. This long-running campaign, which is discussed in the chapter on color, has been built on all the warm, positive associations people have for this color. It includes pictures of sunsets, embers dying down in the fireplace, red flowers, and red Christmas cards. It is not only the use of the color that holds this campaign together; there is also continuity in the mood of the ads.

The theme, then, can be expressed in some dominant visual—through art or photo or the general "look" of the advertising. Continuity can be intensified by using a recognizable and distinctive layout. Type can even be a continuity device as in the antique, beat-up Cutty Sark typeface that is derived from the bottle.

Broadcast. Broadcast uses most of the same continuity devices—slogans, distinctive characters, colors, photos, artwork, animated effects, and type. Audio effects provide other continuity opportunities such as recognizable voices, music, or sound effects. Special visual effects in television sometimes are used as continuity devices.

Cross-media considerations. Continuity is enhanced by standardizing certain elements of the creative messages and repeating them from ad to ad. It is relatively easy to maintain continuity within print or within broadcast. The real challenge is when you have to make major leaps across media. How can you maintain continuity when you move from newspaper to television and then to billboards? If a print ad is tightly controlled and very formal, then the same feeling of enclosed space and formal movements should be retained in television. If the art is cartoon-style in print, then animation using the same drawing style should be used on television. If the format of your message strategy is a testimonial, then carry that across the media used in the campaign. If you use a slice of life in TV, then use it in print. Match the format across all the media.

The Heartbeat Campaign

The "Heartbeat of America" campaign for Chevrolet was developed at a time when, according to Sean Fitzpatrick, chief creative director at Campbell-Ewald, Chevrolet had not had one single campaign theme that had lasted longer than 6 months for the past 20 years. Furthermore Chevy research showed that there seemed to be a bias against Chevrolet on the part of young consumers.

In a speech to the American Advertising Federation, Fitzpatrick described the development of the campaign designed to solve that problem.[3] He said that everywhere the message was the same—young people had a clear idea of what Chevrolet was—and it wasn't good. They thought that Chevy used to be hot and no longer was. The objective was clear. Advertising had to reestablish a relationship between Chevrolet and young America, particularly because there were new products coming that young people would need to walk into a Chevy dealership to see.

Fitzpatrick said that a large majority of automotive advertising consisted of cars speeding down the road with a big piece of music and an

Exhibit 16-1: Chevrolet's "Heartbeat" campaign was reinforced through use of outdoor boards.

angry-sounding announcer; Chevrolet wanted to counter that trend with people-oriented advertising. Women should be shown as people who drive cars, not as objects that adorn them. He explained, "We committed ourselves to a focused emotional advertising campaign that featured the customer and would be designed to stand out in the category—to stir the imagination of the customer and build a new relationship between Chevrolet and the customer."

The breakthrough came when one of Campbell-Ewald's copywriters, who happens to be a poet in his spare time, developed the idea of a young boy living in a nineteenth-century town walking down a dusty road and seeing a brand new red Corvette convertible roaring by. Fitzpatrick said, "We all realized at that moment that we're selling not just cars but, rather, we were selling aspirations. The aspirations of a young boy or the aspirations of the smart consumer who wants the best value for the money." He observed, "Aspirations and being a part of the American life experience is what the 'Heartbeat of America' campaign is all about" (see Exhibits 16-1 through 16-4).

AMERICA'S HEARTBEAT

You're the rhythm on the road
You're a song on the street
A city, town, and country sound
America's heartbeat
Listen to the heartbeat

I can hear your heartbeat
Becoming strong and clear
At first it's just a whisper
The only thing I hear

Then somewhere down the road
There's a rhythm in my chest
A pounding, driving heartbeat
That will not let me rest

You know you keep me hummin'
Singing in the street
A city, town and country sound
America's heartbeat

America's heartbeat
That's today's Chevrolet

THE PULSE OF AMERICA

Listen . . .
Listen to the heartbeat
I can feel it deep inside
The beat is getting stronger
To come and take a ride

A different road to travel
A place I long to be
All across America,
Chevy's calling me.

It's America's heartbeat
Singing out to me.
It's America's Heartbeat
Chevy's rolling free.
It's America's Heartbeat
That's today's Chevrolet
It's America's Heartbeat
Going all the way!

IMAGINATION

A little magic
A little wonder
A touch of thunder under the
hood.

Just a bit more
Than you expected
You wonder how you got it so
good.

Imagination
Was the connection
Somebody finally did it your
way.

You're the heartbeat
of America
You're today's Chevrolet.

Exhibit 16-2: Lyrics to various jingles carrying the "Heartbeat" campaign theme.

Exhibit 16-3: A key visual from a television commercial for the Chevrolet "Heartbeat of America" campaign.

Campbell-Ewald decided to blitz America with the "Heartbeat" message on a nationwide radio buy four weeks before the campaign officially opened. The "Heatbeat" song was the focus, and the mission was to get America singing it. Fitzpatrick explains, "Radio was the perfect medium to allow the customer to half perceive and half create his own relationship with Chevrolet."

Then began a steady stream of television commercials featuring the various nameplates and fact-filled magazine and newspaper advertisements. As new models were launched, they, too, used commercials that tied in with the "Heartbeat" theme.

Fitzpatrick reported that after the first six months, the awareness of the campaign was absolutely phenomenal. A Bruskin research report showed that among young consumers an extraordinary 60 percent demonstrated unaided awareness of the "Heartbeat" theme. Another research company, ASI, reported that one of the television commercials broke every existing scoring record for a :30 automotive spot. McCollum Spielman ranks Chevy as the leading automotive company in breaking through clutter to cause awareness and consideration.

Exhibit 16-4: Two print ads showing different executions of Chevrolet's "Heartbeat" campaign.

Chevy's goal of appealing on a personal level seems to have worked. An industry analyst wrote, "The 'Heartbeat of America' is a gold mine because of the richness of ideas it embodies. It associates Chevrolet with the pulse of American life. . . . And it suggests that Chevrolet is in touch with the essence of who Americans *are* and what they *feel*."[4] Fitzpatrick concludes that "the 'Heartbeat' campaign has begun its job of reversing negative attitudes and providing a positive bias for Chevrolet."[5]

SUMMARY

This chapter has reviewed the creative side of campaign development. You should know:

1. Campaigns, rather than one-shot ads, are used to gain attention through familiarity, create memorability through repetition, assist learning, and delay forgetting.
2. Campaign variations are built on differences in media, schedule, product attributes, and targeted segments.
3. Continuity is developed through the use of a slogan, characters, consistent graphics, easily recognized music, and distinctive special effects.

NOTES

1. Bruce Stauderman, "The Case for Campaigns," *Advertising/Marketing Review*, September 1987, pp. 6–7.
2. Ibid.
3. "Where Does the Magic Come From?" a speech by Sean Kevin Fitzpatrick, American Advertising Federation annual convention, Orlando, Fla., June 9, 1987.
4. Ibid.
5. Ibid.

Answers to slogan quiz: 1-d, 2-p, 3-f, 4-b, 5-a, 6-s, 7-m, 8-x, 9-o, 10-u, 11-g, 12-q, 13-k, 14-w, 15-j, 16-y, 17-l, 18-r, 19-h, 20-t, 21-n, 22-c, 23-i, 24-v, 25-e

17

Copy Evaluation

KEY POINTS

- Every claim has to be provable, honest, and accurate.
- Advertising ideas are tested continuously as they are developed and after they are run.
- Professionals use guidelines and checklists to review an ad idea.
- Review boards are composed of senior executives who evaluate the work before it is shown to a client.
- Advertising is a guest in peoples' homes, so insulting or offending them will probably not create positive feelings about the brand or company.

John Wanamaker, a famous turn-of-the-century retailer, once quipped that he knew half his advertising didn't work, he just didn't know which half. Ninety years later a Chicago-based research company, Information Resources, has just reported that its research proves conclusively that TV advertising does indeed work—but only 50 percent of the time. About half the time, more TV advertising leads to increased sales of the product.[1] This wouldn't come as a big surprise to John Wanamaker.

The imprecision exists because advertising is an art that operates as much on intuition as science. And art—any art—depends more on intuition and the evaluation of experienced professionals than on scientific testing. In spite of that, the industry wants hard data. William Wells, head of research at DDB Needham, explains, "A great many clients are determined to find a way to get an objective measurement of advertising."[2]

Evaluation in advertising is a mixture of both judgment and scientific testing. Evaluation is employed, in one form or another, at every step in the process, both internally and externally. Internal evaluation includes everything from personal critiquing of one's own work to review boards and copytesting. External evaluation includes such non–client-directed research programs as Video Storyboard and Nielsen's "people meters" that evaluate home television watching. Regulatory agencies and consumer watchdog groups are also part of external evaluation.

17.1 EFFECTIVENESS

Ad evaluation is concerned with questions of effectiveness—Does it work? Does it do what needs to be done? What were the results?—as well as questions of good taste and good judgment—Is it fair and accurate? Does it mislead?

In his column in *Advertising/Marketing Review*, Bruce Stauderman laments the vacuum in which much advertising is produced. He says, "Ironically, those who need to know the most are told the least—the copywriter and art director, the very architects of the advertising." He recounts his experiences over the years of demanding to know from the account side or from the client, "What happened?"[3]

Another problem is the difficulty of measuring advertising effects. For package-goods giants like Procter & Gamble there are so many other marketing factors involved—the sales staff, promotions, competitive moves, pricing, etc.—that it is very difficult to isolate the effect of an advertisement.

Furthermore, there is little agreement on what should be measured. Most advertising is tested on the basis of communication effects—awareness and recall. Some feel, however, that those are inadequate, or at least low-level measures. For David Ogilvy, whose company has established the first advertising research and development think tank in the country (The Ogilvy Center for Research & Development), the important factor is *persuasion*—which means, primarily, attitude change. Other experts feel the test should be some kind of intent-to-buy measure.

Then there are those people such as Sid Bernstein, a respected *Advertising Age* columnist, who feel *sales* is the only real measure of advertising success. Bernstein says, "Its prime and only function is to sell something or help to sell something—a product, a service, an idea, even a religion."[4] Bernstein is joined by Leo Burnett's London-based researcher Simon Broadbent, who worked with the British Institute of Advertising Practitioners to develop an advertising effectiveness award program based on concrete measures of advertising performance. The goal of the award program is to move away from the low-level measures of awareness and recall and focus more closely on concrete behaviors such as sales and other forms of action.[5]

This chapter will look at the range of evaluation activities—both internal and external. We will start with the external, regulation, then move to the internal and discuss various types of copytesting as well as personal judgment.

17.2 REGULATION

This is not a section on advertising regulation. It's a quick discussion of what a copywriter needs to know about laws and regulatory groups. The important thing to remember is that every claim must be provable. Furthermore, the message—whether concept or execution—must not mislead or deceive the consumer. False advertising means the information is in some way untrue or inaccurate.

Substantiation

substantiate: to prove a claim, provide evidence

Every claim must be provable. In order to make a claim, particularly one that involves product or competitor's performance, the advertiser must be able to **substantiate** the claim with reliable and valid test results.

For example, several years ago when Chevrolet ran a campaign with the slogan "Nobody is bigger in small cars than Chevrolet," the agency had to have the data to back up such a statement. The agency and GM compiled enough substantiating production and sales records to fill a file cabinet.

The challenge often comes from a competitor. When d-Con tried to beef up its presence in the insecticide market, it made the claim that its new d-Stroy "killed roaches four times as fast as Combat," the leading roach bait. Combat immediately challenged the ad, alleging the claim was unsubstantiated.[6]

Campbell's Soup recently came in conflict with the Federal Trade Commission for ads that used the implied claim that "most of its soups make a positive contribution to a diet that reduces the risk of heart disease." The claim was not only unsubstantiated but also moved into the *misleading* category because it suggested that eating Campbell's Soup might help reduce the risk of heart disease.[7] In fact, Campbell's is high in sodium, which may be a contributor to heart problems; consequently, the ad is criticised for making an implied health claim and ignoring product characteristics that negate the claim.

Misleading and Deceptive

Misleading advertising means the ad says one thing but doesn't mean it or that it doesn't tell the whole truth or give the whole picture. The Campbell's Soup claim is a problem of omission. When Montgomery Ward switched to its "Lowest prices guaranteed" position, it was challenged by national regulatory boards who felt that the phrase was inaccurate and potentially misleading. It doesn't state the fact that the "lowest price" is charged only when customers present proof that a competitor offers the same item for less.[8]

Nestlé created the same kind of problems with advertising for Good Start, a new infant formula. It is promoted as "hypoallergenic," which means reduced in allergic potential but not nonallergenic. The Food and Drug Administration received complaints regarding a number of infants who had severe reactions to the product. FDA found that the formula actually is dangerous to some infants with severe milk allergies. Nestle had to provide scientific studies to support all the formula's health and nutrition claims, as well as studies relating to consumer perception of the term "hypoallergenic."[9]

The FTC and a judge have both found Kraft guilty of engaging in deceptive advertising by exaggerating the calcium content in its "Singles" processed cheese slices. Kraft advertising said that a Singles slice contains the same amount of calcium as five ounces of milk, when in reality each Kraft Singles slice is *made from* five ounces of milk. According to the FTC, one Singles slice contains only about 70 percent of the calcium found in five ounces of milk.[10]

False Advertising   Advertising that is false is simply wrong or not true. Mad River Traders, a New Jersey company, developed a new mineral water called "Vermont All Natural Soda." The only problem is that it was made with New Jersey tap water and bottled in Trenton. The Vermont attorney general convinced the start-up soda company to change its name and eliminate all other references to Vermont.[11]

In another case Bryan Foods, a Wisconsin-based maker of processed meats, antagonized Oscar Mayer when it ran a TV spot that noted that in New York, Oscar Mayer is the number one bologna but in New Orleans, Bryan is the top brand. The spot ended with the claim, "Bryan's. The #1 bologna from the south." While it is true that Bryan is the number one brand in a few individual southern markets, such as New Orleans, it is not number one overall in the region, as this claim implies.[12]

The aspirin industry got caught up in another problem with accuracy when a National Institute of Health study linked aspirin-taking to a reduction in heart attacks in healthy men. A number of aspirin makers placed ads announcing that an aspirin every other day has been shown to cut a man's chances of heart attack in half. These ads began appearing in the *New York Times*, as well as in local papers. In actuality the study reported a decrease in risk for men who had already had one attack. In other words, it is accurate to say that aspirin is beneficial for use against second heart attacks. Furthermore the study found that not all men tolerate aspirin well, and there was an increase in cerebral hemorrhages among some men. Both the FDA and FTC, along with the National Association of Attorney Generals, brought pressure on the companies to stop the advertising.[13]

Copyright/Trademark Protection   Original creative works, such as books, articles, and songs, are protected by copyright. To use such material you must get approval from the author or publisher. Trademarks are registered and can't be used by other products.

The Academy Awards ceremony was the setting for copyright infringement when Snow White in her blue-and-white shepherdess frock sang her way through a racy program. Disney executives were scandalized, along with most of the audience, and slapped the academy with a federal lawsuit charging copyright infringement. Disney is very vigilant about such things and files dozens of copyright suits every year to protect its characters.[14]

Licensing of real characters—their names, likenesses, and voices— is another hot issue. Bette Midler won a $10 million lawsuit against Ford

Motor Company and Young & Rubicam for using an imitation of Midler's singing voice in a TV spot for the Mercury Sable. Rodney Dangerfield is threatening to do the same for Park Inns International, which is using his sound-alike in commercials.[15] Even historical figures may become licensing issues. In the case of figures who have been dead for a long time, such as George Washington or Abraham Lincoln, the lack or absence of direct descendants usually allows marketers to use their names and likenesses freely. But for other historical figures, such as Charlie Chaplin, John Wayne, Ritchie Valens, Jimi Hendrix, Abbott and Costello, Babe Ruth, Elvis Presley, and Mark Twain, their heirs, estates, or management companies must be consulted.[16]

As part of its name protection, McDonald's has locked up the "Mc" prefix. When Quality Inns decided to open a new chain named "McSleep Inn," McDonald's filed suit and the judge ruled against Quality.[17] A number of companies have been persuaded not to use the "Mc" prefix by such action from McDonald's.

Other Practices

A number of retail practices have been challenged by regulatory action. "Reference pricing," advertising a price as if it were on sale when it has never been priced higher, is one type of problem. For example, Montgomery Ward was challenged by a state attorney general for advertising a swivel rocker as being on sale more than 65 percent of the time. Likewise, Sears was challenged for a "carpet cleaning sale" that never seemed to end.

Airline and rental car advertising is coming under more scrutiny because of activities by state attorney generals. The attorney generals want to see all the restrictions spelled out when airlines use price advertising. That requirement would effectively eliminate airline ads from television and radio. For rental cars they are demanding that all hidden costs be stated. Prescription drugs and other health products are also highly regulated. The FDA maintains stringent requirements spelling out all known side effects. All these demands for full and complete information make it difficult for advertisers in those categories to use television and radio.

Food is another highly controlled area. It has been the practice that food products are not allowed to make direct health claims. All-Bran startled the industry with ads in 1984 likening its cereal to a cancer prevention diet. Benefit, a new cereal by General Mills, claims that it reduces cholesterol; it comes very close to saying, "Eat this cereal and you're less likely to get heart disease." Undoubtedly this will prompt the FDA to scrutinize the entire area of food advertising and health claims.[18] The tobacco industry, of course, isn't allowed to advertise on television and, while beer can be seen on screen, it is against the law to show anyone actually drinking it.

Even special effects can incur the wrath of regulators. The CBS standards and practices department rejected a fast-action, quick-cut commercial for Maybelline's Shine Free mascara because the special effects in the spots could potentially trigger seizures in some epileptics. Strobe lights aren't allowed in commercials for the same reason.[19]

17.3 COPYTESTING

copytesting: scientific testing of the effectiveness of an advertisement

Ads are tested continuously throughout the creative process—either formally or informally. Formal testing of creative work is called **copytesting**.

Basically, there are two general categories of copytesting that concern the creatives: pre- and posttesting of the message. *Pretesting* is used in copy development; *posttesting* is used to evaluate the effectiveness of the ad after it has run. Pretesting often uses in-depth probing techniques aimed at small groups of prospects; posttesting uses carefully constructed random samples and simpler questions. The former is used to help in the development of the message; the latter is used to test its success.

Creative Strategy

The earliest type of official research involves testing and validating the strategy and translating the strategy decisions into creative ideas. In this early stage, tests are conducted to check the appeal, the promise, the benefit, and other strategic aspects of the approach. A lot of this testing uses 3 × 5 cards and convenience samples of the targeted audience—street corner surveys and mall intercepts, for example. The most common research technique used at this stage is the focus group, since this is primarily a probing effort looking at motivations and the reasons behind the responses.

Concept Testing

When the creative team has a handful of potential ideas, it is ready for concept testing. Alternative concepts can be evaluated with a card test containing a couple of sentences of verbal description of the idea. A reading is then possible without interference from execution details. For television commercials, a key visual might accompany the verbal description.

The result of this concept evaluation is a final decision on the best approach. You can also test the strength of the idea in terms of its attention-getting power and understandability. If you go back to your respondents a day or two later, you can also get a rough indication of memorability. If any one of the concepts appears to be outstanding, you can move on and start developing the executions. If none are outstanding, then it's time to start over again. It's easier to go back at this point and try for a new and stronger concept than it is to take a mediocre concept and try to make it great with dynamite execution. What separates great advertising from the rest (the other 99 percent) is the strength of the concept supported by dynamite execution. No amount of spit and polish will turn a tin concept into gold.

Executions

The next step in evaluation is execution testing. There are a thousand details in any execution, and every one of them could be handled in a dozen different ways. Artists rely on their professional judgment to sort out the best graphic treatment. Writers have an intuitive feel for the play of words.

Some of these decisions are more a function of audience response than of creative judgment, and in those situations execution testing may be appropriate. For example, the creative team can do excellent versions of the ad using either a straight spokesperson, a "common person" testimonial, or a celebrity. The decision may best be made by trying out the variations on the targeted audience in a focus group.

Likewise, you may want to know if there are any negative associations with a slogan, or if there is any problem with miscommunication of a headline. A quick set of intercept surveys can help answer those questions. Both concept testing and execution testing can be very helpful in the early development of the ad. Most of the testing at this point will use comprehensives or "roughs" for print and storyboards for television ideas.

Actual produced pieces are very expensive to develop for testing; however, they are produced and tested in those cases where an advertiser insists on research findings before committing the budget to a major media buy. A number of professional testing companies provide this service.

For these tests, the ads are prepared in as near to the final form as possible. Proofs and *mock-ups* of print ads and direct mail pieces are prepared. For magazines, the ads being tested may be in a portfolio with a number of other ads, or they may be "tipped in" to a magazine. Demo tapes are prepared for audio testing. Television commercials can be presented in several different ways. *Photomatics* are scenes shot from the storyboard and presented in a series of slides. An *animatic* is a videotape that has been shot from the storyboard with cuts, dissolves, zooms, and pans used to simulate action.

Evaluation at this stage compares alternative forms of an ad as well as how the ad compares to previous ads and the competition. The ads are also evaluated in terms of interest, miscommunication, associations, and product identification. Follow-up studies can be used to measure memorability.

Postevaluation

This is the province of the commercial research services that monitor advertising effectiveness, such as Starch, Burke, and Gallup and Robinson. There are more than 100 testing services, and they all have techniques that evaluate different aspects of an advertisement. For example, the Burke test evaluates television commercials in terms of "day after recall" (DAR). The Starch scores measure print ads for "noted," "seen/associated," and "read most" using aided recall techniques (see Exhibit 17-1).

Anheuser-Busch decided to drop separate advertising for Michelob Light after spending nearly $31.5 million in 1988 and building virtually no awareness. Rather than recalling the "Light up the night" theme, consumers were more likely to respond with regular Michelob's theme, "The night belongs to Michelob." Meanwhile Miller announced that its highly successful 15-year-old "Less filling, tastes great" campaign for Miller Lite is under review. Management explained, "It ain't broke and it's not tired, but clearly this campaign is 15 years old and nobody in the beer business has ever had a campaign for 15 years."[20] Backer Spielvogel Bates has been the agency behind the campaign.

DAR tests are primarily measures of attention and are criticized by many for both their validity as well as their reliability problems.[21] Affective responses created by emotional messages are ignored, and few of the services measure miscommunication, attitude change, or behavior/action. The direct response industry, of course, is very good at measuring such

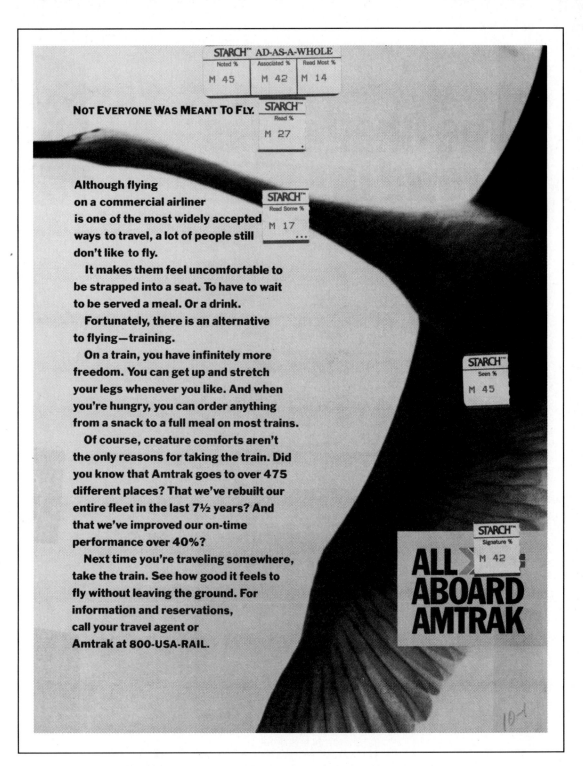

Exhibit 17-1: The Amtrak ''Meant to fly'' advertisement is an example of the kind of readership research available to magazine advertisers through the Starch service. (Courtesy of Amtrak and Starch INRA Hopper, Inc.)

factors as miscommunication, action, and attention, but that is the only area of the advertising industry that effectively tests a full range of communication effects.

Burke and Starch have evaluated thousands, perhaps even millions, of ads—and, because of this large comparative database, they have well-developed "norms" for the types of advertisements they test. These norms represent only the commercial performance on the limited types of effects measured by these services; however, these scores spell life and death for advertisements, as incomplete and imprecise as they may be.

A number of professionals, including David Ogilvy (and most every copywriter who has been burned by a low Burke score), will point out that readership or viewership is not the same as sales persuasion. An American Association of Advertising Agencies study was reported in a research source book by Jack Haskins used at the University of Tennessee.[22] This study listed the factors that advertising professionals would like to see evaluated. The percentages in the following list indicate the percentage of the professionals rating the particular dimension as having the "highest value" in evaluating an individual ad.

Comprehension	80%
Behavior	63
Attitude	63
Recall	63
Buying preference	53
Believability	38
Recognition	15
Persuasiveness	13
Ad-liking	13

The problem is that different advertisements do different things. It would be wonderful to be able to report an actual measure of effect on sales, yet this is the one effect that can't be measured reliably, except in retail advertising and direct response. In most national advertising, there are simply too many other variables affecting the sale to be able to measure the actual impact of the message. But there are effects that can be measured, and these should be clearly spelled out in the advertisement's objectives.

An article in *Adweek* by David Ogilvy and Joel Raphaelson illustrates this difference between viewership and persuasion.[23] Ogilvy and Raphaelson describe a rating service by the Mapes and Ross research firm that rates a commercial's ability to *change* brand preference. One of the interesting things their study found is that 21 percent fewer consumers reported a change in preference influenced by a celebrity in a commercial when compared with the average change for all commercials. However, the celebrity commercials had a 22 percent higher recall. Why would there be a −21 percent change in preference with a +22 percent recall?

Ogilvy and Raphaelson explain that messages such as these focus attention on the celebrity rather than on the product. This is a phenomenon known as "vampire creativity." You can achieve high information memorability that is only marginally related to the selling message while the product or brand gets lost. Good recall scores do not necessarily mean high persuasive effects.

Getting Good Scores An analysis of the Starch scores over hundreds of ads and a variety of product categories provides some clues on how to attain high Starch scores.[24] Some of the points are for the media buyers. For example, a double-page spread attracts 50 percent more readership. Second and third covers get about 30 percent more readership than a regular page. The back cover scores 60 percent higher. The following findings are more relevant to creative strategy:

- Color has 50 percent more readership than black and white.
- Wordiness is not significant; readership decreases only slightly with an increase in text.
- Photographs attract more interest than drawings.
- Ads with people have higher readership.
- Dogs, babies, and cute kids have high readership.
- Men tend to pay more attention to pictures of other men than to pictures of women.
- Women pay more attention to pictures of other women.
- Food ads with recipes are better read than those without.
- Food ads with appetite appeal are read more.
- Ads with coupons are read more.

Burke scores are used to evaluate television commercials, and there are specific ways to score high on this test. David Scott, creative director at Ogilvy & Mather, says it is easy to get a high Burke if you start off with something arresting. He calls it "the gorilla in a jock strap" technique.[25] Other commonly heard suggestions include:

- Use something irritating, exaggerated, or off the wall.
- Introduce the product in the first five seconds.
- Repeat the brand name five times.
- Use a strong benefit approach (promise them the moon).
- Depict your target audience in the commercial.
- Close with the name of the product and a visual that shows the name and package.

17.4 GUIDELINES

To make truly educated judgments, you have to be a longtime student of advertising. But you don't have to reinvent the wheel. Advertising professionals have been watching patterns and codifying them as checklists for years (see Exhibit 17-2). The Thompson-Luce formula was developed in the forties and included some 35 factors. The Townsend system began with 27 points for national print advertising and was later shortened to

CREATIVE CODE

American Association of Advertising Agencies

The members of the American Association of Advertising Agencies recognize:

1. That advertising bears a dual responsibility in the American economic system and way of life.

To the public it is a primary way of knowing about the goods and services which are the products of American free enterprise, goods and services which can be freely chosen to suit the desires and needs of the individual. The public is entitled to expect that advertising will be reliable in content and honest in presentation.

To the advertiser it is a primary way of persuading people to buy his goods or services, within the framework of a highly competitive economic system. He is entitled to regard advertising as a dynamic means of building his business and his profits.

2. That advertising enjoys a particularly intimate relationship to the American family. It enters the home as an integral part of television and radio programs, to speak to the individual and often to the entire family. It shares the pages of favorite newspapers and magazines. It presents itself to travelers and to readers of the daily mails. In all these forms, it bears a special responsibility to respect the tastes and self-interest of the public.

3. That advertising is directed to sizable groups or to the public at large, which is made up of many interests and many tastes. As is the case with all public enterprises, ranging from sports to education and even to religion, it is almost impossible to speak without finding someone in disagreement. Nonetheless, advertising people recognize their obligation to operate within the traditional American limitations: to serve the interests of the majority and to respect the rights of the minority.

Therefore we, the members of the American Association of Advertising Agencies, in addition to supporting and obeying the laws and legal regulations pertaining to advertising, undertake to extend and broaden the application of high ethical standards. Specifically, we will not knowingly produce advertising which contains:

a. False or misleading statements or exaggerations, visual or verbal.

b. Testimonials which do not reflect the real choice of a competent witness.

c. Price claims which are misleading.

d. Comparisons which unfairly disparage a competitive product or service.

e. Claims insufficiently supported, or which distort the true meaning or practicable application of statements made by professional or scientific authority.

f. Statements, suggestions or pictures offensive to public decency.

We recognize that there are areas which are subject to honestly different interpretations and judgment. Taste is subjective and may even vary from time to time as well as from individual to individual. Frequency of seeing or hearing advertising messages will necessarily vary greatly from person to person.

However, we agree not to recommend to an advertiser and to discourage the use of advertising which is in poor or questionable taste or which is deliberately irritating through content, presentation or excessive repetition.

Clear and willful violations of this Code shall be referred to the Board of Directors of the American Association of Advertising Agencies for appropriate action, including possible annulment of membership as provided in Article IV, Section 5, of the Constitution and By-Laws.

Conscientious adherence to the letter and the spirit of this Code will strengthen advertising and the free enterprise system of which it is part.   *Adopted April 26, 1962*

Exhibit 17-2: The Creative Code was developed to outline acceptable industry standards for advertising. (Courtesy of the American Association of Advertising Agencies)

9 critical points. David Ogilvy devised a scoring system for print advertising that highlighted 20 copy and layout factors. The purpose of a checklist is to provide a systematic way to review the ad to see if there are any glaring problems. With or without a checklist, all professionals go through a particular process every time they look at an ad idea.

The Ayer advertising agency has a little publication entitled *Evaluative Pre-Testing of Advertising*.[26] The booklet describes the functions of copytesting and also states the agency's criteria for a good ad:

- Produces the appropriate impression on the target audience
- Accurately communicates its intended message
- Does so intrusively
- Is perceived to be personally relevant—something the prospects can identify with
- Engages the emotions in some positive way
- Is believable and not overly irritating

John Kiel, senior vice president and creative director at Dancer, Fitzgerald, and Sample, wrote an article entitled "Can You Become a Creative Judge?"[27] In it, he developed eight rules to help the noninstinctively creative marketing person learn how to make creative judgments. His eight rules are as follows:

1. Make sure it adheres to strategy.
2. Make sure it is directed to the right target.
3. Make sure that it is single-minded.
4. Make sure you know what the creative people have in mind.
5. Make sure the advertising technique doesn't overpower the message ("vampire video").
6. Separate your personal prejudices from your judgment.
7. Make sure the advertising doesn't change the product image.
8. Have faith; let the creative people do their thing.

Kiel's points include both "things to look for" and "ways to look at" advertising. He is obviously very conscious of the role interactions between creatives and account management.

Charles Frazer, a University of Colorado professor, has developed another set of criteria for evaluating ads.[28] His criteria is a list of things to "look at." He has two major categories: *concept* and *execution*. Under concept, he suggests you consider the following:

1. Strategy
2. The central idea
3. Addressed to prospect
4. Distinctive
5. Tasteful
6. Teamwork of all elements

COPY CHASERS CRITERIA

I. THE SUCCESSFUL AD HAS A HIGH DEGREE OF VISUAL MAGNETISM

On average, only a small number of ads in an issue of a magazine will capture the attention of any one reader. Some ads will be passed by because the subject matter is of no concern. But others, even though they may have something to offer, fail the very first test of stopping the reader in his scanning of the pages.

Ads perish right at the start because, at one extreme, they just lie there on the page, flat and gray, and at the other extreme, they are cluttered and noisy and hard to read.

An ad should be constructed so that a single component dominates the area—a picture, the headline or the text— but not the company name or the logo.

Obviously, the more pertinent the picture, the more arresting the headline, the more informative the copy appears to be, the better.

II. THE SUCCESSFUL AD SELECTS THE RIGHT AUDIENCE

Often, an ad is the first meeting-place of two parties looking for each other.

So there should be something in the ad that at the reader's first glance will identify it as a source of information relating to *his* job interest—a problem he has or an opportunity he will welcome.

This is done by means either of a picture or a headline—preferably both—the ad should say to him, right away, "Hey, this is for you."

III. THE SUCCESSFUL AD INVITES THE READER INTO THE SCENE

Within the framework of the layout, the art director's job is to visualize, illuminate and dramatize the selling proposition.

And he must take into consideration the fact that the type of job a reader has dictates the selection of the illustrative material. Design engineers work with drawings. Construction engineers like to see products at work. Chemical engineers are comfortable with flow charts. Managers relate to pictures of people. And so on.

IV. THE SUCCESSFUL AD PROMISES A REWARD

An ad will survive the qualifying round only if the reader is given reason to expect that if he continues on, he will learn something of value. A brag-and-boast headline, a generalization, an advertising platitude will turn him off before he gets into the message.

The reward that the ad offers can be explicit or implicit, and can even be stated negatively, in the form of a warning of a possible loss.

The promise should be specific. The headline "Less maintenance cost" is not as effective as "You can cut maintenance costs 25%."

V. THE SUCCESSFUL AD BACKS UP THE PROMISE

To make the promise believable, the ad must provide hard evidence that the claim is valid.

Sometimes, a description of the product's design or operating characteristics will be enough to support the claim.

Comparisons with competition can be convincing. Case histories make the reward appear attainable. Best of all are testimonials; "They say" advertising carries more weight than "We say" advertising.

VI. THE SUCCESSFUL AD PRESENTS THE SELLING PROPOSITION IN LOGICAL SEQUENCE

The job of the art director is to organize the parts of an ad so that there is an unmistakable entry point (the single dominant component referred to earlier) and the reader is guided through the material in a sequence consistent with the logical development of the selling proposition.

A layout should not call attention to itself. It should be only a frame within which the various components are arranged.

VII. THE SUCCESSFUL AD TALKS "PERSON-TO-PERSON"

Much industrial advertising, unlike the advertising of consumer goods, is one company talking to another company—or even to an entire industry.

But copy is more persuasive when it speaks to the reader as an individual—as if it were one friend telling another friend about a good thing.

First, of course, the terms should be the terms of the reader's business, not the advertiser's business. But more than that, the writing style should be simple: short words, short sentences, short paragraphs, active rather than passive voice, no advertising cliches. Frequent use of the personal pronoun *you*.

A more friendly tone results when the copy refers to the advertiser in the first person: "we" rather than "the company name."

VIII. SUCCESSFUL ADVERTISING IS EASY TO READ

This is a principle that shouldn't need to be stated, but the fact is that typography is the least understood part of our business.

The business press is loaded with ads in which the most essential part of the advertiser's message—the copy—appears in type too small for easy reading or is squeezed into a corner or is printed over part of the illustration.

Text type should be no smaller than 9-point. It should appear black on white. It should stand clear of interference from any other part of the ad. Column width should not be more than half the width of the ad.

IX. SUCCESSFUL ADVERTISING EMPHASIZES THE SERVICE, NOT THE SOURCE

Many industrial advertisers insist that the company name or logo be the biggest thing in the ad, that the company name appear in the headline, that it be set in bold-face wherever it appears in the copy.

Too much.

An ad should make the reader want to buy—or at least consider buying—before telling him *where* to buy it.

Incidentally, many industrial ads are cluttered with lists of other products, factories and sales offices, name of parent company, names of subsidiaries or divisions, association memberships and other items, most of which are never looked at and which, if essential, could be set inside the copy area at the very end.

X. SUCCESSFUL ADVERTISING REFLECTS THE COMPANY'S CHARACTER

A company's advertising represents the best opportunity it has —better than the sales force—to portray the company's personality—the things that will make the company liked, respected, admired.

A messy ad tends to indicate a messy company. A brag-and-boast ad suggests the company is *maker*-oriented, not *user*-oriented. A dull-looking ad raises the possibility that the company has nothing to get excited about, is behind the times, is slowing down.

What we are talking about is a matter of subtleties, but the fact remains: like sex appeal (which is not easy to define), some companies have it, some don't. And whatever it is, it should be consistent over time and across the spectrum of corporate structure and product lines.

Of course, there has to be substance behind the picture. You can't—at least for very long—promise a silk purse and deliver a sow's ear.

Most successful companies have some sort of personality, and the advertising people should search for it and, finding it, transmit it to the people out there whom they want as friends.

Exhibit 17-3: The Copy Chasers criteria are used to evaluate copy in the business-to-business area. (Copyright 1985 by Crain Communications, Inc. Reprinted with permission)

Under execution, he lists the following areas:

1. Imaginative
2. Emphasize benefits
3. Aesthetically pleasing
4. Convincing argument
5. Simple and clear language
6. Strong opening and closing
7. Use medium to its fullest
8. Tie into theme

Both Kiel's and Frazer's lists are useful guides to objective evaluation of copy.

The "Copy Chasers" is a long-running column that appears in *Industrial Marketing* magazine.[29] In this column, a panel of well-respected professional copywriters who specialize in business-to-business advertising evaluate other ads currently running in the trade press. After decades of such an exercise, the Copy Chasers have developed a set of 10 "Judgments" that they use to guide their evaluations (see Exhibit 17-3).

A well-researched area in advertising is direct response, and a number of the greats in advertising have looked to this body of literature for their personal philosophy of ad evaluation. David Ogilvy and John Caples are two well-known names who built their philosophies on direct mail techniques. The Direct Mail Marketing Association has summarized the results of their many years of research and published it in association newsletters and seminars.[30] The following points have been gathered from DMMA materials and, while they relate specifically to direct response, they reflect basic and universal advertising techniques:

OPENING

- Develop a "hook"—something to mesmerize them during the first few dangerous seconds when they are trying to decide whether to read it or not.
- If you have an offer, lead with it.
- Use your most important benefit in the head—fire your biggest gun first.

BODY

- The lead's function is to massage the interest; do that by enlarging on the benefit.
- Copy should be benefit-oriented.
- Write "you" not "we" copy.
- Paint a word picture of your promise; dramatize it.
- Use conversational language; make it a letter to a friend.
- Use captions under all pictures.
- The closer you come to the tone of a personal letter, the higher the response.

- Make sure the product is clearly defined and explained.
- List and describe all special features.
- The body is written like a chain; all the facts are assembled link by link.
- Back every claim with proof.
- Tell a success story.
- Include testimonials and endorsements.

CLOSING

- Make it clear how to order or buy.
- Make a statement about the value to the purchaser—use comparison or metaphor to dramatize the value.
- Close with some push to act immediately—what will they lose if they don't act now?
- Rephrase the dominant benefit somewhere in the closing.
- In letters use a P.S. It can tie back to the headline, introduce another testimonial, or make an added inducement. Tremendously high readership.
- In direct response use no-obligation close (free trial), send no money, and money-back guarantee.

17.5 REVIEW BOARDS

review board: a group of senior agency executives who review campaign ideas before the final presentation to the client

Sometime after the creative team has made its decision on the best approach and the best execution, but before the final presentation to the client, a meeting with the upper management of the agency is held. Called a **review board**, this group serves as the agency's sounding board and quality control center. The idea is to make the account teams sell the approach to their peers and supervisors, admittedly the toughest critics of all. This serves as a practice presentation and a trial run on the explanation and justification techniques. Usually, review board members will ask tougher questions than the client, and that sharpens the team for the final client presentation. Review board presentations are also a way to keep upper management informed, and that's very important in large agencies.

17.6 PERSONAL JUDGMENT

Many people in advertising, managers as well as creatives, despise copytesting systems because they are so imprecise. Advertisers, however, want some assurance that an ad is a good one, and these numbers are considered better than nothing. In truth what is better than nothing, and better than a lot of copytesting services, is informed, educated *personal judgment.* Some researchers have even suggested that judgmental content analysis can predict DAR scores as effectively as the testing services.[31] Of course, even if that were possible, you might ask why it is desirable to predict the scores rather than other, more relevant dimensions of message effectiveness. But the point is that informed judgment may be just as reliable an indicator of advertising effectiveness as the simplistic scores.

Wally Olesen, director of Xerox Corporation, explained, "The right person to judge *anything* is the one who has earned the right to do so" by either having done it or having studied it.[32]

The "I Response"   The mark of a novice in advertising is someone who critiques an ad by saying: "I like it" or "I don't like it." For most advertising professionals, this "I response" is inappropriate. To be exact, it's irrelevant. No one cares if you like it or not. What matters is whether the ad works, and in order to evaluate that you have to consider the much more complicated questions of "What is ineffective and effective in advertising?" and, in particular, "What is good and bad for this ad in this situation?"

An Audience of One   It is true that novices may not have the experience to evaluate ads on the basis of "What I like," but this position changes as the professional develops maturity and experience in the field. Carl Walston, a copywriter for a number of agencies including Ogilvy & Mather and d'Arcy McManus & Masius, has developed a professional's approach which he calls "an audience of one."[33] Walston quotes advertising greats like Stan Freberg, Howard Gossage, and Hal Riney, all of whom wrote advertising that pleased themselves first of all. They were their own best audience.

Freberg explains, "You can't act like your tastes are one thing and the audience's tastes are another. If you don't like an ad, why should anybody else? And who are 'they?' We're all consumers." He concludes, "That's why I always create commercials for myself first of all." Freberg believes in creating "the genuinely enjoyable commercial" and is critical of most of the product pitches he sees because he thinks they are moronic and insipid. His most famous quote sums up his point of view: "People do not watch commercials. They do not read ads. They read or watch what interests them. Sometimes it happens to be advertising."[34]

Shirley Polykoff, a member of the Advertising Hall of Fame, also internalizes her experiences with the product. She advises, "It's only when you know yourself—when you can dig deep into your own motivations and recognize them—that you can understand what it is that other people want."[35]

With experience, when your own personal copy sense is developed, trust yourself to be your own first critic. But recognize that you also have the responsibility to be honest with yourself. If you ad is boring, tell yourself so. The "audience of one" concept works only for people who have judgment, objectivity, and tremendous integrity. And for some it doesn't work at all. David Ogilvy said, "I'm unable to judge the quality of my own work and I don't see how any copywriter can."[36]

17.7 DEVELOPING "COPY SENSE"

There are two fundamental dimensions to every critique: strategy and aesthetics. Both are equally important, and both need to be evaluated by people with expertise in the respective areas.

A strong, highly memorable, and evocative ad may be totally off target. No matter how much you "love it," it's not a "good" ad. Likewise, a perfectly targeted and well-positioned ad that reads like a marketing manager's memo will not be successful because it's dull as dishwater. No matter how many times it restates the position, it still must get attention and be remembered. A good ad is one that is both strategically effective and aesthetically pleasing. That's the art and the science of advertising.

Strategy

Strategy asks if the message is on target. Does it say the right things to the right person? Likewise, you must check to see that it solves the problems you originally identified and that it accomplished its objectives. If it doesn't work strategically, you may need to start over.

Aesthetics

The answer to the evaluation of the *creative concept* is usually yes or no. It either works (in terms of its audience) or it doesn't. And if it doesn't, start over. Rarely can you "fix" a problem with the creative concept by fiddling with it. If the creatives have done a successful job communicating, the problem lies with the idea. If the idea comes across, but fails in terms of attention and retention, then it's back to the boards.

The second area in aesthetic evaluation is the *execution*, the thousands of details involved in making the concept come to life. In contrast to critiquing the creative concept, evaluating the execution involves looking at the pieces. If the creative idea doesn't fly, everything is out the window. But if some of the execution details aren't right, it's still possible to "fix" the problem. It's important for people involved in critiquing to understand the difference between a fatal problem (the concept) and a fixable one (an execution detail).

It's also important to recognize the synergy of the details. An execution that works is one that works across all the details—the voices fit, the pacing is proper, the camera angles are precise—it all works together. And when it does work, don't fuss with it. Only pick at it if there is some element that seems to spoil the effect. Tinkering with the pieces can be terribly destructive, and if the tinkerer lacks aesthetic judgment to appreciate this integration, the magic can be killed by changing a single word.

The Key to Critiquing

Copy evaluation is complicated and problem-oriented rather than personal. A well-tuned critique is objective in a subjective area. The basic evaluation options can be summarized with a few simple statements.

A FEEDBACK FORMULA

1. It's great both strategically and aesthetically: **Let's run it.**
2. It's off strategically: **Better start over.**
3. It's off aesthetically:
   a. The creative concept doesn't work: **Better start over.**
   b. An execution detail doesn't work: **Let's fix it.**

If you're ever in a situation where you have to critique creative ideas, whether as a student or as a professional or manager, then you need to have a simple schema like this in mind. Knowing what it is you're evaluating depersonalizes the process. It's the structure that forces you to take an objective stance, to focus on the work rather than on the individual who did the work.

The procedure outline above guides the critique through a process and up to a point where someone has to say, "Yes, the strategy works" or "No, it doesn't." On that level, this critique becomes subjective. Evaluation of the strategy dimension is based on experience, good business sense, and, sometimes, research results. Copytesting may be important to the managers you have to work with who do not have a copy sense, but it shouldn't overpower business sense and experience.

Likewise, having sorted out the various types of aesthetic problems, someone at some point has to be able to say the creative concept does or doesn't work. Evaluation on this level now becomes a subjective one based on a well-developed sense of message needs and media aesthetics. Research can help a little, but the heart of this type of evaluation is creative intuition, aesthetic sensitivity, and experience.

17.8 A WORD ABOUT TASTE

Effective advertising is difficult to achieve, and consumers are becoming militant about ads they don't like, so it would seem that gambling on concepts of questionable taste would rarely pay off. Advertising that insults or offends people reflects poorly on the company or brand being advertised.

When you ask consumers what they like and remember about an ad, sometimes there are contradictions. Joe Isuzu, for example, consistently scores high on Video Storyboards' best remembered commercials. Many consumers find the parody of everything-we-love-to-hate-about-car salespeople to be funny. But in an *Advertising Age* survey of the "most hated" ads, Joe Isuzu was high on that list, too, particularly for women.[37]

Sometimes consumer dislike is category-related. The same *Advertising Age* study found that men rated feminine hygiene at the top of the list of ads they love to hate. Women, who rated feminine hygiene ads number two on their list, put beer and alcohol commercials at the top.

An article in *Adweek* described a Benson & Hedges print ad whose ambiguity apparently annoyed many consumers. It shows a bare-chested man, seemingly in pajamas, visiting (informally, of course) with a tableful of well-dressed people who are enjoying the end of a great dinner. Starch reports that it has never seen an ad generate such consumer hostility.[38]

Another cigarette company, Camel, is in trouble with its new "Old Joe" camel mascot campaign, which *Adweek* describes as "appealing to the caveman mentality." In its zest to reach a younger male audience, Camel takes "Old Joe" to the beach, giving him advice on how to woo women: "Run into the water, grab someone and drag her back to the shore, as if you'll save her from drowning. The more she kicks and screams, the better."[39]

Miller Beer had a similar problem with its 16-page insert for college students that coincided with spring break. The Miller insert depicted scantily clad women and portrayed students' priorities as being "beer, beach and babes." Several colleges refused to run the insert before Miller withdrew it and offered an apology.[40]

An angry secretary in Washington forced Pan American airlines to dump a radio commercial on the first day it ran, claiming that it was "totally sexist." In the commercial a female travel agent tells an executive that she has made a reservation for him and one for his secretary on Pan Am's new low-fare rate to London. Excited, he says, "I can't believe it." Then she says she also reserved a seat for his wife, and groaning, he says, "I can believe it." The angry secretary who heard the commercial called Pan Am officials as soon as she got to work. They quickly agreed to kill the commercial.[41]

If you were working on the account for Benson & Hedges, Camel, Miller, or Pan Am, how would you have evaluated these ideas as advertising concepts? Would you let them get by? How about this for a car headline—"Kick a little asphalt." And another print ad featuring a picture of a dog peeing on a boot to demonstrate the fact that the boots are waterproof? Or another ad for a tile company that shows a broken bottle of mustard on a tile floor with the headline, "At last, a tile you can poupon for years without leaving a stain." Sad to say, all three ran—the "Asphalt" ad, incidentally, was for the Volkswagen GTI. The copy on that particular ad ends,"After all, driving should be fun, not a pain in the asphalt." Cute, huh?

SUMMARY

1. In terms of regulation, creatives must consider claim substantiation, misleading and deceptive concepts and claims, false or inaccurate statements, and copyright and trademark infringement.
2. Pretesting provides help while the ad is being developed; posttesting evaluates the ad after it has run.
3. Pretesting occurs at three points: strategy, concept development, and execution.
4. The feedback formula is a framework for developing your personal judgment; it considers both strategy and aesthetics and helps you decide whether to run the ad, start over, or revise.

NOTES

1. Joanne Lipman, "Don't Blame Television, Irate Readers Say," *Wall Street Journal*, March 1, 1989, p. B6.
2. Jeffrey L. Seglin, "The New Era of Ad Measurement," *Adweek's Marketing Week*, January 23, 1989, pp. 22–25.
3. Bruce Stauderman, "Results," *Advertising/Marketing Review*, June 1987, pp. 6–7.
4. S. R. Bernstein, "Straying from the Path," *Advertising Age*, September 19, 1988, p. 53.

5. Simon Broadbent, ed., *Advertising Works 2* (London: Holt, Rinehart and Winston, 1983); Charles Channon, *Advertising Works 4* (London: Holt, Rinehart and Winston, 1987).

6. Laurie Freeman, "D-Con's Ad Claim Bugs Combat," *Advertising Age*, February 8, 1988, p. 46.

7. Guy Darst, "FTC Says Campbell's Soup Ads Were False," *Muncie Star*, January 27, 1989.

8. Janet Neiman, "Misleading Ads Casting Shadow Over Entire Industry," *Adweek*, September 26, 1988, pp. 32–34.

9. Alix M. Freedman, "Nestle Ad Claims for Baby Formula Probed in Three States," *Wall Street Journal*, March 2, 1989, p. B6.

10. Alix M. Freedman, "Charges by FTC Against Kraft Ad Upheld in Ruling," *Wall Street Journal*, April 7, 1989, p. B6.

11. Diane Tracy, "It's True That 'Cool Refreshment' Isn't What Trenton Brings to Mind," *Wall Street Journal*, April 17, 1989, p. B1.

12. Kelly Class, "No Baloney: Ad Tiff Leads to Lawsuit," *Adweek*, February 27, 1989, p. 3.

13. Patricia Winters and Steven W. Colford, "Rorer Joins Aspirin Fray," *Advertising Age*, February 8, 1988, p. 3; Jennifer Lawrence, "New Attacks on Aspirin Ads," *Advertising Age*, February 15, 1988, p. 1.

14. Richard Turner, "Well, Nobody Ever Claimed She Had a Sense of Humor," *Wall Street Journal*, April 3, 1989, p. 1.

15. Ruth Stroud, "Mimicked Mess: Midler Case May Curb 'Sound-Alikes,'" *Advertising Age*, July 11, 1988, p. 70; Nancy Bishop, "Sound-Alike Spot Gets No Respect," *Adweek*, September 26, 1988, p. G4.

16. Gary Levin, "Celebrity Licensing Gets Tougher," *Advertising Age*, February 1, 1988, p. 63.

17. Roy Furchgott, "Judge Takes 'Mc' Out of McSleep," *Adweek*, September 26, 1988, p. 3.

18. Dan Koeppel, "Will the FDA Swallow Big G's 'Benefit'?" *Adweek's Marketing Week*, April 17, 1989, p. 2.

19. Pat Sloan, "CBS Nixes Maybelline's SFX," *Advertising Age*, October 27, 1986, p. 41.

20. Ira Teinowitz, "A-B Switches Off Michelob Light Ads," *Advertising Age*, May 9, 1988, p. 24.

21. Lyman Ostlund, "Advertising Copy Testing: A Review of Current Practices, Problems and Prospects," *Current Issues and Research in Advertising*, University of Michigan Graduate School of Business, pp. 87–105.

22. William R. Swinyard and Charles H. Patti, "The Communications Hierarchy Framework for Evaluating Copytesting Techniques," *Journal of Advertising*, 8:3 (1979), pp. 29–36.

23. David Ogilvy and Joel Raphaelson, "Agency Boredom with Analysis Cripples Execution," *Adweek*, September 27, 1982, p. 72.

24. Edward Buxton, *Creative People at Work* (New York: Executive Communications, 1975), p. 143; Daniel Starch, *Measuring Product Sales Made by Advertising* (Mamaroneck, N.Y.: Starch, 1961); Philip Ward Burton, *Which Ad Pulled Best*, 4th ed. (Chicago: Crain, 1981).

25. Buxton, op. cit., p. 24.

26. *Ayer Research Perspective: Evaluative Pre-Testing of Advertising* (New York: Ayer Advertising, undated).

27. John Kiel, "Can You Become a Creative Judge?" *Journal of Advertising*, 4:1 (1975), pp. 29–31.

28. Charles Frazer, "Toward Some General Criteria for Evaluating Advertisements," American Academy of Advertising Conference, Minneapolis, 1977.

29. "Copy Chasers Seminar," *Ad Week*, sponsored by Crain Publishing Co., Chicago, August 1981.

30. Direct Mail Marketing Association. Collection of "Manual Releases" distributed annually at DMMA seminars.

31. Terry P. Haller, "Predicting Recall of TV Commercials," *Journal of Advertising Research*, 12:5 (October 1972), pp. 43–45.

32. Marybeth Lareau and Wally Olesen, "Is Your Thinking Big Enough to Recognize . . . The Big Idea?" *Madison Avenue*, November 1982, pp. 24–30.

33. Carl Walston, "An Audience of One," American Academy of Advertising, Orlando, Fla. 1990.

34. Stan Freberg, "Freewheeling Freberg," *Advertising Age*, September 12, 1988; Gregg Kilday, "Advertisements for Himself," *Northwest Portfolio*, March 1989, p. 21; Wayne Walley, "Freberg's Back on Target with Non-Advertising," *Advertising Age*, April 6, 1987.

35. Shirley Polykoff, "Will You or Won't You Take a Chance," *Advertising Age*, February 1, 1982, pp. 45–46.

36. Denis Higgins, *The Art of Writing Advertising: Conversations with . . .* (Chicago: Advertising Publications, 1965), p. 79.

37. Scott Hume, "'Most Hated' Ads: Feminine Hygiene," *Advertising Age*, July 18, 1988, p. 3.

38. Michael Hiestand, "Consumers Pan Benson & Hedges," *Adweek's Marketing Week*, April 10, 1989, p. 4.

39. Iris Cohen Selinger, "Does New Camel Ad Cross Boundary of Good Taste?" *Adweek*, April 17, 1989, p. 4.

40. Ira Teinowitz, "Miller Lite Hunts for New Creative," *Advertising Age*, July 25, 1988, p. 1.

41. Albert R. Karr, "How One Angry Secretary Eliminated 'Totally Sexist' Ad Aired for Pan Am," *Wall Street Journal*, April 14, 1989, p. B7.

INDEX